Commonwealth Small States
Issues and Prospects

Commonwealth Small States
Issues and Prospects

Edited by
Eliawony J Kisanga and Sarah Jane Danchie

Commonwealth Secretariat

Commonwealth Parliamentary
Association

Commonwealth Secretariat
Marlborough House
Pall Mall
London SW1Y 5HX
United Kingdom

Published by the Commonwealth Secretariat in association with the Commonwealth Parliamentary Association

Designed by SJI Services, New Delhi
Printed by Hobbs the Printers Ltd, Totton, Hampshire

Views and opinions expressed in this publication are the responsibility of the authors and should in no way be attributed to the institutions to which they are affiliated.

Wherever possible, the Commonwealth Secretariat uses paper sourced from sustainable forests or from sources that minimise a destructive impact on the environment.

Cover design by Tattersall, Hammarling and Silk

Copies of this publication may be obtained from

The Publications Section
Commonwealth Secretariat
Marlborough House
Pall Mall
London SW1Y 5HX
United Kingdom
Tel: +44 (0)20 7747 6342
Fax: +44 (0)20 7839 9081
E-mail: publications@commonwealth.int
Web: www.thecommonwealth.org/publications

ISBN: 978-0-85092-849-5

Contents

Figures and Tables

Tables

Figures

Acronyms

ACP — Africa, Caribbean and Pacific

ADB — Asian Development Bank

AGOA — African Growth and Opportunity Act

AOSIS — Alliance of Small Island States

APEC — Asia-Pacific Economic Co-operation Forum

ASCM — Agreement on Subsidies and Countervailing Measures

APQLI — Augmented Physical Quality of Life Index

ASEAN — Association of Southeast Asian Nations

BPOA — Barbados Programme of Action

CAP — Common Agricultural Policy

CAPAM — Commonwealth Association of Public Administration and Management

CARIBCAN — Caribbean – Canada

CARICOM — Caribbean Community and Common Market

CARIFTA — Caribbean Free Trade Area

CBFM — community-based fisheries management

CBI — Caribbean Basin Initiative

CCJ — Caribbean Court of Justice

CDP — Committee for Development Policy (UN) (pre-1998 was Committee for Development Planning)

CETs — Common External Tariffs

CHOGM — Commonwealth Heads of Government Meeting

CMGSS — Commonwealth Ministerial Group on Small States

COMSEC — Commonwealth Secretariat

CRP — Comprehensive Reform Programme (Vanuatu)

CSD — UN Commission on Sustainable Development

CSME — CARICOM Single Market and Economy

CTD — Committee on Trade and Development (WTO)

CVI	composite vulnerability index
DSU	dispute settlement understanding
EAF	ecosystem approach to fisheries
EBA	Everything But Arms (Agreement)
ECOSOC	UN's Economic and Social Council
EDI	economic diversification index
EEZ	exclusive economic zone
EIA	environmental impact assessment
ESW	special economic and sector work
EU	European Union
EVI	UN economic vulnerability index
FCCC	United Nations Framework Convention on Climate Change
FDI	foreign direct investment
FICs	Forum island countries (of the Pacific Community)
F-MAC	fisheries management advisory committees
FTAA	Free Trade Area of the Americas
GATS	General Agreement on Trade in Services
GATT	General Agreement on Tariffs and Trade
GDP	gross domestic product
GNI	gross national income
GNP	gross national product
GSP	Generalised System of Preferences
GSTP	Global System of Trade Preferences
HS	harmonised system
IBRD	International Bank for Reconstruction and Development
ICJ	International Court of Justice
IDA	International Development Association
IFC	International Finance Corporation
IMD	International Institute for Management Development
IMF	International Monetary Fund

LDC	least-developed country
MCA	Millennium Challenge Account
MDC	more-developed country
MFA	Multi-Fibre Agreement
MFN	most-favoured nation
MIGA	Multilateral Investment Guarantee Agency
MPA	marine protected areas
MSG	Melanesian Spearhead Group (Fiji, Papua New Guinea (PNG), Solomon Islands and Vanuatu)
MTSD	Management Training and Services Division (Commonwealth Secretariat)
NAFTA	North America Free Trade Agreement
NEAPS	national environmental action plans
NEPAD	New Partnership for Africa's Development
NGO	non-governmental organisation
NPM	new public management
OECD	Organisation for Economic Cooperation and Development
Ofsted	Office of Standards in Education (UK)
OPSR	Office for Public Sector Reform, Barbados
PACER	Pacific Agreement on Closer Economic Relations
PC	Pacific Community
PIASA	Pacific Islands Air Services Agreement
PICs	Pacific island countries
PICTA	Pacific Island Countries Trade Agreement
PPTF	Pacific Plan Task Force
PSC	Public Service Commission (Trinidad and Tobago)
PSMP	Public Service Modernisation Project (Jamaica)
PSRU	Public Sector Reform Unit (Barbados)
PTFA	preferential trading arrangements
RAMSI	Regional Assistance Mission to Solomon Islands
RDBs	regional development banks

RTA	regional trade agreement
S&D	special and differential
SACU	Southern African Customs Union
SDCs	small developing countries
SEWP	Small Economies Work Programme
SIDS	Small Island Developing States
SPARTECA	South Pacific Regional Trade and Economic Cooperation Agreement
SPC	Secretariat of the Pacific Community
SPS	sanitary and phytosanitary
SSMECI	small states manufactured export competitiveness index
SVEs	small vulnerable economies
TBT	technical barriers to trade
TMNP	temporary movement of natural persons
TRIMS	trade-related investment measures
TRIPS	trade-related aspects of intellectual property rights
UNCTAD	United Nations Conference on Trade and Development
UNIDO	United Nations Industrial Development Organisation
USP	University of the Pacific (Fiji)
VII	vulnerability impact index
VSO	Voluntary Service Overseas
WEF	World Economic Forum
WSSD	World Summit on Sustainable Development
WTO	World Trade Organisation

Foreword

This publication is the outcome of collaboration between the Commonwealth Secretariat and the Commonwealth Parliamentary Association. It arose as a result of a growing interest from the annual Commonwealth Parliamentary Association Small States Conference to discuss more in-depth issues of current concern to small jurisdictions. In the last decade, the Conference has concentrated on discussing the challenges that Small States face in overcoming their vulnerability and developing competitive economies in an increasingly liberal, global economy. The Commonwealth Secretariat has been invited to participate in these annual conferences by making presentations about its ongoing work on Small States.

Most chapters in the book examine the efforts and challenges of managing democracy and promoting economic development in small jurisdictions. The main message arising from the chapters is that although Small States remain vulnerable to a number of forces, there are nevertheless good prospects; that given good governance, effective macroeconomic policies, as well as support and recognition of their challenges from the global community, these countries can overcome these vulnerabilities. Small States also have the potential to develop viable and sustainable economies, exploiting the appropriate resources that exist in each of them. The book makes the case that for Small States to make this transition they would require effective support from the global community on a sustainable basis. The Commonwealth Secretariat has been for many years an advocate for the need for this sustained support.

I believe that the collection of papers in this book adds to that needed advocacy for Small States and will make a useful contribution to policymaking in Small States and the global community that supports them.

I would first like to thank Mr Raja Gomez, the former Director of Planning at the Commonwealth Parliamentary Association, who initiated the project with the Economic Affairs Division, Commonwealth Secretariat. I would also like to thank the authors of the chapters in this book as well as Mr Alan Smith who assisted in the organisation of the publication.

Indrajit Coomaraswamy
Director
Economic Affairs Division
Commonwealth Secretariat
Marlborough House
Pall Mall
London
SW1Y 5HX

Introduction

....

Eliawony J Kisanga and Sarah Jane Danchie

Small developing countries face special problems and challenges in an increasingly global economy.

Today 45 countries are classified as small states according to the World Bank/Commonwealth population threshold of below 1.5 million people.[1] The Commonwealth has 32 small states among its 53 members, so the Commonwealth Secretariat has made the needs of Small States one of its highest priority concerns. The seminal World Bank/Commonwealth Secretariat Joint Task Force Report on Small States, published in 2000, highlighted the vulnerability of Small States as a result of their susceptibility to natural disasters, limited institutional capacity, limited human resources, and lack of economic resources. The Secretariat has been a leading advocate for gaining international recognition that Small States are vulnerable and warrant special and differential treatment if they are going to succeed in effectively integrating into the global economy.

The Commonwealth Parliamentary Association (CPA) consists of the national, provincial, state and territorial Parliaments and legislatures of the Commonwealth. The Association's mission is to promote the advancement of parliamentary democracy by enhancing knowledge and understanding of democratic governance. It seeks to promote new policy debate among parliamentarians in the Commonwealth and to build an informed parliamentary community.

Since 1981 the CPA Small Countries Conference takes place alongside the Commonwealth Parliamentary Conference, in recognition that Small States of the Commonwealth have unique concerns. This session is dedicated to enabling members of parliament from small jurisdictions to discuss matters of common interest that cannot be sufficiently addressed during the main conference.

This book has been published jointly by the Commonwealth Secretariat and the Commonwealth Parliamentary Association and brings together issues of economic and political concern to Small States that are of interest to parliamentarians. It has been inspired by the discussions that have taken place in the Commonwealth Parliamentary Association's Small Countries Conference during the past few years. The book explores the global issues concerning the Environment, Trade, Economy, Regionalism, Governance, Education and Development. The chapters provide a detailed insight into how these issues **uniquely** impact upon small states. This publication also offers recommendations for actions that the global community needs to take to help small states to tackle volatility and vulnerability to attenuate their transition to the changing global world, to strengthen their capacity, and to exploit new opportunities and challenges arising from globalisation.

The first chapter in the book highlights the vulnerability of Small Island Developing States (SIDS) when faced with the effects of climatic change. Many Small States continue to be particularly vulnerable to natural disasters as many of them are low-lying islands and face submersion as the sea level rises. Experts predict that the incidence of extreme weather events such as cyclones, hurricanes, and tsunamis will increase in number and intensity and be associated with more frequent and intense impacts of global climatic change. These environmental risks threaten to seriously hamper the development efforts of small states.

This threat mobilised the Alliance of Small Island States (AOSIS) to ask the international community for support to help tackle the devastating impacts of global climate change. The AOSIS has been influential in shaping the agenda of the United Nations Framework Convention on Climate Change (UNFCCC) since its establishment in 1992. The author of the chapter, Gillespie, highlights how SIDS' ability to contribute to international climate negotiations through both the UNFCCC and the Kyoto Protocol has slowly disappeared. As a result, SIDS' urgent needs and concerns, which had strongly influenced the initiation of the FCCC process, have largely also disappeared.

The chapter highlights the necessity to redirect the international community's response to climate change from that of a reactive stance to a more preventative stance through mitigation measures. The author explores the possibility of moving the debate away from the FCCC process. However, Gillespie concludes that international environmental disputes can only be resolved within the FCCC process. He acknowledges that only the International Court of Justice (ICJ) can deal with the failure of sovereign governments who flout international environmental obligations and that the ICJ will only intervene if good faith is lacking. The chapter recognises, however, that lack of good faith is currently disguised by prolonging negotiations and not setting a deadline for an end to negotiations. It argues that the FCCC process must be reinvigorated and the near-gridlock in negotiations must be reversed to recognise the urgent needs of the SIDS. The catalyst could be an internal determination by key members or possibly an external examination by an independent body such as the ICJ. This catalyst will propel the necessary conclusion in accordance with good science, and back to the original FCCC goal, and thus the ultimate urgent needs of the SIDS.

As international trade liberalisation continues to progress, it is emerging that small states are facing particular difficulties from the fast pace of erosion of the trade preferences that they have enjoyed for decades.

In Chapter 2, Grynberg and Remy analyse the Small Economies Work Programme that sought to achieve recognition of the particular problems that confront small and vulnerable economies (SVEs) in the globalisation process. The authors argue that this much-needed work programme, which was finally agreed in the fourth session in Doha, was in fact a political compromise between SVEs and developed countries. The chapter highlights that an apparent contradiction in the wording of the relevant paragraph in the Doha Declaration is to the detriment of SVEs, as on the one hand it mandates Members to frame responses to trade concerns of SVEs, but on the other hand prohibits the creation of a sub-category of states. The paper argues that this definitional caveat insisted upon by developed countries impedes the special treatment needed by SVEs.

The authors seek to review the concerns and specificities of small states and highlight the peculiarities and natural disadvantages that inhibit their ability to at best thrive and at worse survive in the new multilateral trading pattern. They recognise the similarities between SVEs and least-developed countries (currently the only formally recognised group in the WTO to warrant special treatment). However they identify sufficient distinctions between SVEs and LDCs and believe that SVEs should be afforded special treatment. The chapter highlights the discomfort felt by some WTO members who oppose the creation of new categories, but emphasises the necessity of the categorisation and thus recognition of the special problems of smaller economies if the legitimate trade concerns of SVEs are to be addressed.

Horscroft also deals with trade issues in Chapter 3. She advances the counter argument to the assertion that the currently agreed and emerging international trade rules are beneficial for all states. Horscroft argues that the peculiar economic characteristics of small economies, namely size, vulnerability and governance capacity, constrain their potential to benefit from current international trade patterns. The author forecasts further exacerbation of the current situation of the marginalisation of small economies. She demonstrates the vital need for, among other things, the adjustment of multilateral trade rules in order to address the trade and development needs of small economies. Given the economic costs of their vulnerability to external shocks and natural disasters, they should be accorded special and differential treatment. The author recognises the formidable challenge facing small states in achieving the necessary response from the multilateral trade negotiating processes. She highlights the cost of being small undermining the bargaining power of small states in achieving beneficial outcomes from the interstate negotiating process that determines global trade rules. Horscroft's arguments are well supported by recent empirical evidence.

The third part of the book deals with issues concerning the performance of small states' economies and considers ways of evaluating performance.

In Chapter 4, Briguglio argues that the economic vulnerability index should include only inherent and permanent economic features which render a country exposed to forces outside its control. The paper also proposes that an index of resilience should be constructed to complement the vulnerability index, and to assess the degree to which economically vulnerable countries, individually or as a group, are moving ahead or otherwise in coping with or responding to economic vulnerability. A number of variables, which could be used to construct a composite resilience index, are proposed.

Redding and Venables, in Chapter 5, explore the economic implications of isolation and remoteness by reviewing the evidence on the impact of distance on trade costs and trade flows and the effects of remoteness on real incomes. The authors conclude that isolation and remoteness do have a negative impact on per capita income. They propose possible new technologies to overcome the spatial inequalities.

In Chapter 6, Joiner and Wignaraja seek to contribute to the process of new policy development in small states in the wake of globalisation. The authors focus on enabling small states to measure their industrial competitiveness in quantitative terms and benchmarking it against each other. They explore existing efforts to benchmark competitiveness and highlight a lack of inclusion of small economies and attempt to remedy this. The authors present the results of their small states manufactured export competitiveness index (SSMECI). The chapter then provides some explanations for the performance of small states. The authors recommend looking at detailed case studies of individual small states in order to truly understand the drivers of competitiveness.

The fourth part of the publication explores the issue of regionalism amongst small states. There has been increased interest amongst small states as they recognise the potential of regionalism for providing for small states' domestic needs. Due to their size, small state governments have difficulty in delivering all essential public services such as education, health, social welfare, etc. on their own. There is also a need for greater regional integration among small states in order to compete in the globalising world. The small states in southern Africa have successfully participated in a number of cooperative initiatives, such as a customs union (the Southern African Customs Union) and Common Monetary Area. The three chapters provided in Part 4 evaluate the progress of cooperative initiatives in the Caribbean and the Pacific.

In Chapter 7, Preville addresses the relevance of the work of Sir Arthur Lewis to the establishment of the CARICOM Single Market and Economy (CSME). Sir Arthur Lewis unfortunately died before the debate for the creation of the CSME became an issue. The author focuses on three themes; he discusses the background of the CSME, examines the work of Sir Arthur, who he believes is an 'integrationist', and concludes that given the present direction of CARICOM member states Sir Arthur's work is very relevant and has been pivotal and inspirational for CSME and in the broader sense of regionalism in the Caribbean. The CSME is the first step in the fulfilment of his prophecy.

Jayaraman, in Chapter 8, deals with the promotion of regional integration of the Pacific Island countries (PICs). The author reviews past efforts by PICs and assesses the weaknesses and strengths of these efforts for the purposes of building on these to avoid duplication of past errors of omission and commission. Measures for exploiting present opportunities are also explored. The author provides specific references to experiences in regional cooperation leading to ultimate integration from the Caribbean as that region shares many commonalities with the PICs. The author concludes with a discussion on future strategies.

Chapter 9 by Fa'asili, Fakahau, King and Vunisea makes a significant contribution to the management and development of fisheries in the South Pacific region, as it is the very first formal expression of having a regional mechanism for greater harmonisation of national policy regarding the management of coastal fisheries in PICs. The chapter draws on collaboration between the Commonwealth Secretariat and the Secretariat of the Pacific Community (SPC), the lead regional organisation on coastal fisheries management and development in the South Pacific. The main objective of the project was to work with fisheries agencies and other stakeholders to devise a strategic plan for the sustainable management and development of coastal fisheries.

Sutton has contributed two chapters covering governance issues. In Chapter 10 he examines democracy and good governance in small states by looking at general characteristics of politics in small states. He identifies processes that support and challenge democracy. This is followed by a record of democracy in small states. The author concludes that there is a necessity for the improvement and deepening of democracy and promotion of good governance for the future well-being and development of small states.

In Chapter 11, Sutton explores the experience of public sector reform in four Caribbean small states; Barbados, Jamaica, St. Lucia and Trinidad and Tobago. It sets out characteristics of public administration in small states and the shape of reform in the Caribbean. Professor Sutton raises some issues for further research and consideration.

Chapter 12 examines issues of migration and their impact on the education sector. Ochs explores the high incidence of teacher migration from small states and the long-term implications of this phenomenon. This report results from a series of efforts by members of the Commonwealth Secretariat, Commonwealth Ministers, and friends of the Commonwealth to develop international understanding of the teaching profession and the global challenge of teacher loss. Following the mandate from Jamaica to the Commonwealth Secretariat for assistance in addressing teacher loss in the Caribbean, representatives from eight countries in the region met in Barbados in July, 2002. Ministers of education from 32 small states signed the Savannah Accord. The chapter focuses on the areas of interest outlined in the Accord, such as the extent of teacher loss and its short- and long- term impact on the education systems of Commonwealth countries. This chapter contributes to gaining an insight into the global supply and demand of the teaching profession and thus informs the debate of Protocol A, included in the Protocol for the Recruitment of Commonwealth Teachers.

The final section of the book looks at the development of small states.

Chapter 13 examines the graduation issues for small vulnerable states that are least-developed countries (LDCs). It focuses on the process and experience. The paper indicates future policy direction for graduation, and identifies recommendations for a programme for their smooth transition.

In September, 2000 all Commonwealth member states of the United Nations adopted the Millennium Declaration consisting of a set of development goals with the aim of eradicating poverty and promoting human development throughout the world. The final chapter, Chapter 14, concentrates on the progress that Commonwealth small states have made towards achieving the Millennium Development Goals. The chapter shows that several countries are making good progress with many goals. However, Downes notes that small states in Africa and the Pacific have been confronted by serious challenges of resource and capacity constraints that have and will hamper their achievement of the goals by 2015. The chapter concludes with suggestions on the way forward for these small states and the role of the Commonwealth in assisting the small states to meet their development needs and goals.

This publication therefore covers a wide range of global issues, from environment to education. It is hoped that the book will contribute to building the knowledge and understanding of parliamentarians and policymakers in international organisations on how small states' special characteristics affect their development efforts in the new global economy, and thus help to identify opportunities for the international community to support small states to address the development challenges that they face.

Notes

1. This standard of size was agreed by the Commonwealth Advisory Group in producing its report, *A Future for Small States: Overcoming Vulnerability*, Commonwealth Advisory Group, 1997 and is used by the World Bank/Commonwealth Joint Task Force as a convenient yardstick for classifying all sovereign small states.

Part I
ENVIRONMENT

1. Small Island States in the Face of Climatic Change: The End of the Line in International Environmental Responsibility

Alexander Gillespie

1. Small island developing states in international law

Small island developing states (SIDS) are increasingly recognised as deserving of special consideration, both in international law generally and in international environmental law in particular. This special recognition has grown since the 1992 Earth Summit and was clearly reflected in the 1994 Programme of Action for the Sustainable Development of Small Island Developing States (to be revisited in 2004) and within the 2002 Plan of Implementation from the World Summit on Sustainable Development (WSSD, 2002a, Chapter VII). These documents all reflect the same consideration: that most SIDs face an uphill battle in meeting the challenges of sustainable development irrespective of climate change. They already need specific assistance to meet the economic, social and environmental problems that are already affecting them. Accordingly, as the Political Declaration of the 2002 World Summit on Sustainable Development concluded, the countries of the world would, among other things, 'continue to pay special attention to the developmental needs of Small Island Developing States' (WSSD, 2002b, Paragraph 24). Unfortunately for SIDs, however, the other dilemmas they face in achieving sustainable development are dwarfed by one environmental problem over all others: climatic change.

2. Climate change

'Climate change' refers to a change of climate which is attributed directly or indirectly to human activity that alters the composition of the global atmosphere and which is, in addition to natural climate variability, observed over comparable time periods (UNFCCC, 1992, Article 1. Definitions). Anthropogenic climate change is caused by 'greenhouse gases'. The primary greenhouse gases are carbon dioxide, methane, and nitrous dioxide. These gases are increasing in concentration in the atmosphere. The evidence for this may be seen in the oscillations of historical greenhouse gas concentrations through to more specific contemporary measurements. These measurements show concentrations of greenhouse gases not found in the atmosphere for thousands of years.

3. The sources of the pollutants

Modern industrial society is the primary culprit in terms of the creation of greenhouse gases. Since the industrial revolution industry, agriculture, and transport have all contributed vast amounts of emissions. Historically, the lion's share of these pollutants came from developed countries. This share may be seen in terms of sovereign output (i.e. the country's overall emissions) and per capita output (i.e. an individual's emissions from one country compared to an individual in another). Both types of output involve a different emphasis as well as a different political point of view IPCC (1996a, pp.7–8). For example, in the mid-1990s, the global average for per capita carbon dioxide emissions was 4,157kg, but the national figures ranged from 19,675kg for the United States through to 949kg for China, 652kg for India, all the way down to 2kg for Somalia (UNDP, UNEP, World Bank, WRI, 2000, p.282). Although there are some developing countries, such as Turkey, Korea and Mexico (Pearce, 1997), that are taking their per capita outputs to levels comparable to those of developed countries, the wide disparity in emissions on a per capita basis between the developed and developing world is expected to continue into the foreseeable future. Conversely, when viewed from a sovereign basis, with regard to developed countries (if viewed as a 100 per cent total of carbon dioxide emissions), the United States produces 36.1 per cent of total emissions, the Russian Federation 17.4 per cent, Japan 7.4 percent, Germany 7.4 per cent and the UK 4.3 per cent (Kyoto, 1997a, Annex). However, unlike the remaining differences between developed and developing countries with regard to greenhouse gas emissions on a per-capita basis, a clear change is occurring with regard to sovereign emissions. The key change is that the aggregate emissions from developing countries are growing at a much faster rate than those of developed countries (IEA, 2000, p.167). If such increases continue, it is expected that the developing world will be producing more carbon dioxide from the burning of fossil fuels by 2005 than all the industrialised countries were producing in 1988 (Pearce, 1988,). Between 2010–25, the developing world should be responsible for well over half of all global emissions (Pearce, 1997; MacKenzie, 1990, p.5; and Reddy, 1990, pp.63, 69). Certain key developing countries are expected to make exponential increases in their emissions. For example, by 2025 (if not earlier) China is expected to be the world's largest emitter, in overall terms, of greenhouse gases (Smil, 1994, pp.325–32).

4. Present changes and future predictions

The scientific evidence of global warming currently available is consistent with, but does not yet provide definitive proof of, the theories of climatic change (IPCC, 2001a, p.2). The current evidence consists of continual record breaking annual global temperatures (IPCC, 2001a), increased precipitation and storm activity, enhanced unusual weather patterns (IPCC, 2001a) over a number of (but not all) regions (IPCC, 2001a, n13.4), an increase in cloud cover over some regions (IPCC, 2001a), increased frequency and intensity of droughts in some regions (IPCC, 2001a, n13. 5), changes in species migration (Pearce, 2002a), shrinkage of glaciers, thawing of permafrost, later freezing and earlier break-up of ice on rivers and lakes, lengthening of mid- to high-latitude growing seasons, poleward and altitudinal shifts of plant and animal ranges, declines in some plant and animal populations, and earlier flowering of trees, emergence of insects, and egg-laying in birds. Associations between changes in regional temperatures and observed changes in physical and biological systems have been documented in many aquatic, terrestrial and marine environments (IPCC, 2001). There is also already evidence that sections of the ocean are becoming less saline and warmer (IPCC, 2001a).

Exactly where such trends will take us in the future, in terms of overall temperature changes, is a matter of debate. That is, the current estimates of what the temperature change will be by 2100 range between 1°C–5.8°C (IPCC, 2001a). The variance in this figure is due to unpredictable factors such as technology, demographic change, and economic development (IPCC, 2000, pp.1–15). This is an important point: the full effects of climate change are not unalterable and the choices that governments make in the present have the ability to influence any final outcome. Despite the fact that the climatic future is not set in concrete, it is likely that without radical changes to current emissions that humanity will witness temperature increases in the range of 0.1 to 0.2°C per decade over the short-term future (IPCC, 2001a, n13.13). Although these figures appear small, if they continue unabated they may come eventually to represent temperature changes that have not been seen for tens of thousands, if not hundreds of thousands, of years.

5. The impacts of climatic change upon SIDs

The adverse effects of climate change are those that alter the physical environment or biota, that in turn have significant deleterious effects on the composition, resilience, or productivity of natural and managed ecosystems, or on the operation of socio-economic systems, or on human health and welfare (FCCC, 1992, Article 1. Definitions). These adverse effects could result in significant impacts on many ecological systems and socio-economic sectors (COP, 1996). It is likely that these effects will be more pronounced on developing countries due to their restricted ability to adapt to quickly changing situations (IPCC, 1996a, p.10).

In terms of specific effects, climatic change will affect a vast number of ecologically related considerations. In terms of overall problems facing a large number of countries, it is expected that climatic change will, in certain areas, affect food production (output and location) (IPCC, 1996b, p.9 and IPCC, 1998, p.6), stress fresh water supplies (IPCC, 2001a, n20. 4, 8; and IPCC, 1998, p.5) increase the intensity of heat waves (IPCC, 2001a, n20, p.4; and WRI, UNDP & World Bank, 1999, pp.67–69), and, in conjunction with other factors, increase levels of certain diseases such as malaria and dengue fever IPCC, 1996b, p.12).

With particular regard to SIDs, a number of additional threats may be considered paramount. First, sea levels may slowly rise due to the thermal expansion of the oceans and the reactions of the icecaps [*they are reacting to the thermal expansion of the oceans? If not say 'to the rise in temperature' after 'icecaps'*] (IPCC, 2001a, n13.16). The time frame adopted for this scenario will affect the picture of the anticipated sea-level rise. As a rule, increases in the rise of sea levels are much greater the further the time frame is cast (IPCC, 2001a, n13.16). For example, in 500 years an eventual rise of 7 to 13 metres may be likely. However, the typical time frame is 100 years, and between 2000 and 2100 the global mean sea level is projected to rise by between 0.09 to 0.88 metres (IPCC, 2001a, n13.16).

Sea-level threats may have a detrimental effect on a number of industrialised and developing countries (IPCC, 1998, n30.7, 15–16). As bad as sea-level increases may be for these countries, however, it is the SIDs that are at the edge of extreme risk. This threat has been repeatedly recognised in the discussions of the United Nations Framework Convention on Climate Change (FCCC) (UNFCCC, 1992, Preamble. Paragraphs 12 & 19; see also Decision 1/CP. 7.3.), regional groupings such as the South Pacific Forum,[1] and the UN Global Conference for the Sustainable Development of Small Island Developing States, the latter of which noted:

> 'While small island developing states are among those that contribute least to global climate change and sea level rise, they are among those that would suffer most from the adverse effects of such phenomena and could in some cases become uninhabitable' (UN GCSDSIDS (1994).

This prognosis is possible given the fact that many SIDs rarely rise more than 3 to 4m above the present mean sea level (IPCC, 2003, p.34). A 1m rise could result in an 80 per cent land loss for the Majuro Atoll in the Marshall islands (IPCC, 1996a, n29.11). The Maldives consist of some 1,300 tiny islands, with an average size of only 1–2km^2 and an average height above sea level of only 1 to 1.5m (Wells, 1989). Tuvalu consists of five atolls and four separate reef islands and has a total land mass of only 23km^2, virtually all of which is less than 2m above sea level (*New Scientist*, 1989). Kiribati consists of 700km^2 on 33 islands, most of which are also less than 2m high (Pearce, 2000a). All of these SIDs are all directly at risk. Larger islands such as Tonga and Vanuatu are also threatened (New Scientist, 1992).

The overt threat to SIDs is due to the fact that the adaptive capacity of human and ecological systems is generally low in these areas, while their vulnerability is very high. The 2001 projected sea-level rise will probably cause enhanced coastal erosion, loss of land and property, the dislocation of people and the consequent threat of 'environmental refugees' (Beston, 2000; and Pearce, 1992), reduced resilience of coastal ecosystems, saltwater intrusion into freshwater resources, and high resource costs that will be necessary to respond to and adapt to these changes. Islands with very limited water supplies are also highly vulnerable to the impacts of climate change on the water balance. Tourism, an important source of income and foreign exchange for many islands, may face severe disruption from climate change and sea-level rise. Limited arable land and soil salinisation makes agriculture in SIDs, both for domestic food production and cash crop exports, highly vulnerable.

In addition to the problem of a rising sea-level, two further consequences of climate change may have a disproportionate affect upon SIDs. First, with regard to worsening weather patterns, the most commonly associated climatic phenomena linked to global warming are storms, tornadoes, and cyclones (Pearce, 2002d). The evidence, according to the insurance industry, is that weather-related damage has increased fourfold since 1960 (Pearce, 2002c).-Although this is an area of uncertainty (especially with regard to region-specific impacts), it is predicted that as the climate warms precipitation in certain areas will increase (IPCC, 2001a, n13.13), as will storm activity (IPCC, 2001a, n13.5, 16).

Second, climate change will have disruptive effects on specific ecosystems. Typically, the climatic change effects on ecosystems are linked to the ice caps and forests. However, there is an equally important body of work of direct relevance to SIDs relating to the effects upon oceans. Oceans sequest and store larger amounts of carbon than land-based reserves. In doing so, they retain heat storage and control thermal inertia. Accordingly, oceans are the 'flywheel' of the climate system (IPCC, 1996a, n29.14). Although the biological consequences of a changing climate upon the oceans are far from fully understood, it is believed that the change may bring about detrimental results by raising the temperatures of the oceans. This will probably change migratory patterns for a number of ocean species (Broecker, 1997), facilitate habitat destruction – especially in critical areas for dependent species (IPCC, 2001c, pp.2, 11), and may lead to drastic changes in ocean circulation, vertical mixing and overall climatic stability. Such effects could have strong implications in terms of nutrient availability, biological productivity and the structure and functions of the marine ecosystems most critically affected (Independent World Commission on the Oceans, 1998, p.45). For the species that are already endangered, the effects may be terminal. This is especially so where the species are endemic and have few migration options. Unfortunately, the biodiversity in and around SIDs often fits squarely within these criteria (IPCC, 2003, pp.31-4).

Coral reefs are key oceanic ecosystems and are often associated with SIDs. The prognosis for these ecosystems is typically one of advanced bleaching because of reduced calcification rates due to higher greenhouse gas levels. This may happen because coral reefs require highly stable environments, and temperature fluctuations of just one or two degrees above normal can have a devastating impact upon them (Pearce, 2002b). Episodes of coral bleaching over the past 20 years have been associated with several causes, including increased ocean temperatures. As of 2002, an estimated 16 per cent of the world's coral reefs have died from bleaching since 1998 (Pearce, 2002e). It is likely that future sea surface warming will increase stress on coral reefs and will result in the increased frequency of marine diseases (IPCC, 2001b, n30.12; and Dicks, 2003) In addition, mangrove, sea-grass beds, and other coastal ecosystems and their associated biodiversity may be adversely affected by rising temperatures and accelerated sea-level rise. Declines in coastal ecosystems will probably also have a negative impact upon reef fish and will threaten reef fisheries, as well as the livelihoods of those who rely upon such resources (IPCC, 2001b, n30.17).

In conclusion, the potential effects of climatic change upon SIDs are extreme. This is because not only will SIDs most likely experience the same effects of climatic change as other countries in terms of impacts on food, water, disease and heat waves, but they will also suffer a series of problems which will be uniquely detrimental to them. These are sea-level rise, increased erratic weather, and changing ecosystems. Each one of these effects will be difficult enough to manage. Cumulatively, the ultimate outcome may only be guessed at.

6. The international response to climate change

6.1 The accepted ecological limit and the scientific recommendations

The accepted ecological obligation to be regarded as the guide to international negotiations in this area is found in the FCCC. This guiding provision stipulates that the ultimate objective of the Convention is to achieve the:

> 'stabilisation of greenhouse gas concentrations in the atmosphere at a level that would prevent dangerous anthropogenic interference with the climate system. Such a level should be achieved within a time frame sufficient to allow ecosystems to adapt naturally to climate change, to ensure that food production is not threatened and to enable economic development to proceed in a sustainable manner' (UNFCCC, 1992, Article 2).

In hard numbers, the Intergovernmental Panel on Climate Change has suggested that to stabilise (not necessarily reduce) the build-up of greenhouse gases in the atmosphere to prevent a doubling of the pre-industrial concentrations of greenhouse gases will require emission reductions: 'to decline to a very small fraction of current emissions' (IPCC, 2001a, n13.12). The typical figure associated with this cut is an approximate reduction of 60 per cent in the current level of greenhouse gas emissions (for discussion see IPCC, 1995, p.11).

6.2 The international legal response

In spite of a long process of discussions, the 1992 FCCC failed to contain any hard goals on reducing greenhouse gas emissions. Rather, the soft obligation for developed countries was to reduce, by the end of the 1990s, their greenhouse emissions to 1990 levels (UNFCCC, 1992, Article 4(2)a). However, the soft target within the FCCC was soon recognised as inadequate and the signatories thereafter concluded the Kyoto Protocol. The final target adopted in the Kyoto Protocol obliged developed countries to reduce their greenhouse emissions by: 'at least 5 per cent below 1990 levels in the commitment period 2008 to 2012' (Kyoto Protocol, Article 3.(1). Note, the targets for developed countries are differentiated. Accordingly, not all countries have the same reduction target).

6.3 The difficulties between the ecological limits and the legal response

Despite the achievements of the Kyoto Protocol, there are three clear problems in this area which make the chasm between the scientific and legal responses very wide.

First, the overall targeted reduction period is remarkably limited. The defence against this is that it is hoped that the Kyoto Protocol targets will be increasingly revisited (ideally like those of the Montreal Protocol) as the scientific needs solidify – along with the will of the international community to confront the problem. Although this may be the desire, the first step of the Kyoto process (a 5 per cent reduction in the face of the necessary 60 per cent reduction) is comparatively small, when it is considered that the first step of the Montreal process was a 50 per cent cut in harmful emissions (Montreal Protocol, 1987, Article 2 & Annex A). This is not to demean the 5 per cent target, rather to point out that given the very slow rate of progress – based on both the size of the target and time within which it has to be achieved – if the international community continues at the same pace, it will, from the perspective of the SIDs, most probably be too late to make any meaningful difference.

The second difficulty is that although the 5 per cent reduction is comparatively small, it has already resulted in vast difficulties for one of the key greenhouse gas emitters – the United States – which has chosen to walk away from the Kyoto Protocol and refused to ratify it (Brown, P., 2001). This act not only diluted the overall effectiveness of the Protocol because of the absence of the world's largest emitter of greenhouse gases, but also threatened the existence of the overall Protocol, because 55 per cent of (developed) countries with reduction obligations have to ratify the Protocol before it comes into force (Kyoto Protocol, Article 25.1). The United States' refusal to ratify the Protocol meant that virtually every other industrialised country had to in order for it to enter into force.

The third problem is that the reductions envisaged by the Kyoto Protocol only apply to developed countries (Kyoto Protocol, Preamble, Paragraph 4). Moreover, any attempts to begin to place even the smallest of mandatory – as opposed to voluntary – limits upon the greenhouse gas emissions of developing countries have been forcefully resisted, despite the clear pressure from high-level fora such as the G8 (G8 Summit Communique, no date; G8 Environment Minister's Communique, no date). Although there may be strong political justifications for this point of view, from the perspective of those at the sharp end of the ecological effects of climate change, failure to include at least the primary developing countries – who will soon become the principal emitters of greenhouse gases – in any meaningful reductions of even stabilisation targets is very bad news.[2]

The result of these three points is that the Kyoto Protocol is a weak instrument in terms of its overall reduction goals, its failure to include the United States, and its failure to encompass developing countries.

7. SIDs within the climate change negotiations

7.1 Substantive influence

At the fourth formal meeting in the negotiations leading to the formation of the FCCC the Alliance of Small Island States (AOSIS) emerged as a group independent of both the industrialised and developing-country groupings. Their independent status developed because of their unique position in the climate change debate; of all countries, they are probably the most threatened by the effects of climatic change. As such, their desire to halt global warming is greater than any other countries (developed and developing) whose agendas may be complicated by any number of other objectives. This specific role has been evident since the late 1980s when gatherings such as the South Pacific Forum tried continually to focus world attention on the threats that they face from climate change. This problem, and the necessity to solve this problem, is, as the 1994 Global Conference on the Sustainable Development of Small Island Developing States noted, of 'utmost importance to small island developing states' (Report of the Global Conference on the Sustainable Development of Small Island Developing States, 1994, Annex I, Section III, Paragraph 19. The particularly vulnerable status of SIDs was reconfirmed at the 2002 World Summit on Sustainable Development (WSSD, 2002, Paragraph 36).

Such needs and vulnerabilities have resulted in the SIDs receiving special recognition within the FCCC (UNFCCC, 1992, Article 4(8)a), and being given advanced speaking rights there. They made notable use of their special status in the mid-1990s by trying to achieve meaningful reduction targets, such as that proposed by AOSIS for a 20 per cent reduction in greenhouse gases by industrialised countries in 1995. Unfortunately, this proposal met with little success (Report of the COP, 1995, Part One, Proceedings, Paragraph 57 & 58). Thereafter, their advanced speaking rights failed to make any noticeable impact on the international diplomatic landscape.

Despite this omission at the FCCC level, the SIDs continue to reiterate their 'deep concerns' about climate change in a number of other fora that are easier for SIDs to control. For example, in the South Pacific Forum, the members continue to call for: 'urgent action to reduce greenhouse emissions and for further commitments in the future by all major emitters' (Thirty Third Pacific Island Forum, 2002, PIFS (02) 8. Paragraph 24 & 25). Within the South Pacific context, such demands have become a clear source of tension with some of the SIDs' more reticent neighbours, such as Australia, who have refused to ratify the Kyoto Protocol (Thirty Third Pacific Island Forum, 2002, PIFS (02) 8. Paragraph 26). The overall disappointment with both the United States and Australia with regard to this matter cannot be understated. This is probably best displayed by the serious consideration given in the region by some of the SIDs to attempt to sue both Australia and the United States over their failure to ratify the Protocol (Christie, 2002).

7.2 Special considerations for SIDs within the FCCC

In addition to their special status within the workings of the FCCC, the SIDs are also unique in their link to climate-related financial assistance to meet the adverse effects of climate change. In this regard they are at the front of the queue in terms of financial assistance for both capacity building and general assistance to meet their reporting and public education goals. Likewise, with regard to financial assistance for adaptation to climate change the SIDs are at the front of this staggered process (UNFCCC). Finally, a dedicated fund exists to help the most vulnerable countries (UNFCCC, Article 3(2) & 4.(4)) of which the SIDs (along with the least developed countries) are, once more, at the forefront (UNFCCC, 1992, Article 4. 8. Decision 6/CP.7. Additional guidance to an operating entity of the financial mechanism). The Fund for helping the most vulnerable countries focuses largely on the initial stages of adaptation by making sure that national adaptation plans[3] are adequate and that the capacity-building process of these countries is well supported by suitable experts.

8. Moving outside of the conventional debate

When the overt risks posed to SIDs are juxtaposed against the limited and precarious nature of the Kyoto Protocol, the question needs to be asked: what can be done to improve the situation? A number of suggestions have been advanced and fall into the categories of broadening the leverage via human rights considerations and/or realigning the debate in terms of broad obligations regarding sustainable development, as enshrined in international law.

8.1 Human rights vs inter-sovereign negotiations

Given the dire nature of the current international legal situation, some commentators have suggested that there may be merit in pursuing actions in other international or political arenas, with a view to enhancing the legal status of the citizens of SIDs in the face of climate change. Such ideas typically include conventional or/and evolving human rights theories. The traditional human rights claims, when viewed from a SIDs perspective, may invoke key articles from the Universal Declaration of Human Rights, such as article 15 which provides that no-one shall be denied their nationality (see the Universal Declaration of Human Rights (1948) reprinted in Evans, 2003, pp.36, 41). More liberal approaches argue that there is (or should be) a human right to a clean and secure environment which should be enforced. The genesis of this claim comes from the 1972 Stockholm Declaration on the Human Environment which stated as its first principle:

> 'Man has the fundamental right to freedom, equality and adequate conditions of life, in an environment of a quality that permits a life of dignity and well-being, and he bears a solemn responsibility to protect and improve the environment for present and future generations.'

The last two words of this principle, pertaining to the so-called rights of 'future generations', add an extra layer of depth to these arguments. This is especially so given the near endless manner in which the language of the 'rights and interests of future generations' has become entwined in the documents of international law and international judgments (see Gillespie, 1997, Chapter 5). For example, the International Court of Justice (ICJ) in its Advisory Opinion on the Legality of the Threat or Use of Nuclear Weapons (ICJ Reports, 1996, para. 29) clearly stated:

> 'the environment is not an abstraction but represents the living space, the quality of life and the very health of human beings, including generations unborn'.

Given the fact that many of the forecasted detrimental effects of climate change will happen in the future and ultimately effect the generations yet unborn, this ideal has a particularly strong resonance.

Despite the philosophical allure of such ideas revolving around human rights discourses, it needs to be clearly recognised that these will not solve the problem of adequately confronting climatic change. There are three reasons for this. Firstly, the appeal of the rights of future generations is only an idea. Moreover, as an idea, it is philosophically lacking in terms of both theory and possible application (Gillespie, 1997, n94). Beyond acting as a moral compass, the future generations argument has no legal standing in international law. Likewise, so-called human rights based upon environmental considerations have no standing in international law. The international community has already backed away from the strength of Principle 1 of the Stockholm Declaration. This retreat can clearly be seen with the first principle of the Rio Declaration in 1992 ('Human beings are at the centre of concerns for sustainable development. They are entitled to a healthy and productive life in harmony with nature.') which represented a clear watering down of the Stockholm Declaration on this idea. The 2002 World Summit on Sustainable Development followed suit and presented an even thinner version than both of its predecessors on this point. It is also significant that no treaty refers explicitly to the right to a decent environment in such terms. This failure is not hard to understand when the slow progress of the rights discourse development is recognised. Even more widely accepted ideas, such as those relating to the rights of indigenous people, that exist now (let alone in the future) are currently struggling to be recognised (see Gillespie, 2001a; and 2000).

The final problem is one of substance based upon the current international system (Birnie and Boyle, 2002, p.256). The difficulty is that climate change, as with all major international environmental problems, has to be dealt with on a state-to-state basis. To argue otherwise is to confuse apples and oranges. The solution to this problem will come from agreements between sovereign states. This means that the rights that individuals may or may not possess will not, in this context, provide the leverage necessary to achieve the desired goals within in the Westphalian system that the global community currently inhabits. For example, when New Zealand and Australian citizens were concerned about the detrimental health and environmental effects of French atmospheric (ICJ, 1974b) and underground (ICJ, 1995) nuclear testing in the South Pacific, they did not posit their cases upon the rights of individual citizens. Accordingly, the ICJ resolved the dispute through obligations owed between countries and not to individuals within them. Likewise, when countries were concerned that their water supply from neighbouring countries was being detrimentally affected, their claim was not based on the effects on the individual but on the obligations owed between states in this area (ICJ, 1997). Finally, when citizens of countries were threatened with complete and utter destruction by the possible use of nuclear weapons that other countries possess, the case was not presented on the basis of human rights (as clearly nuclear war must run contrary to every possible human right) but on the basis of state relations as traversed through a number of international state-to-state documents and obligations (ICJ, 1996). This is not to suggest that human rights approaches do not have merit. Nothing could be further from the truth. Rather, this is to point out that human rights approaches will not provide the platform necessary to achieve change in this arena.

8.2 Sustainable development

Given the limitations of the rights approach, as well as the current difficulties with the Kyoto Protocol, some commentators have suggested that attempts should be made to achieve leverage by arguing that the actions of many countries with regard to greenhouse gas emissions are blatantly unsustainable from a SIDs perspective. Given the mantra-like quality of 'sustainable development' emanating from the 1972, 1992, and 2002 international conferences where, in the last one at least, the signatories pledged their 'Commitment to Sustainable Development' (WSSD, 2002c), this would appear a very strong argument due to its universal acceptance. In addition, when juxtaposed against the extremity of the climate change and SIDs debate it should be very easy to apply. Indeed, if sustainable development is to mean anything, at its base it would have to encompass a states' basic right not to be obliterated by the acts of other states that have a negative environmental impact.

Although this claim has an intuitive appeal to it, it too is doomed to failure. In an ideal world, the phrase 'sustainable development' could be aired and all would agree and know what was meant by it. However, we do not live in an ideal world and the term 'sustainable development' has become increasingly lost in a labyrinth of political (Gillespie, 2001b) and philosophical (Gillespie, 1997) considerations.

Such fundamental differences, which are inherent in the term 'sustainable development', have a direct bearing on the question of whether sustainable development can, in any sense, be considered to be an enforceable legal principle as opposed to a moral goal. Indeed, it is possible to identify the main elements of the concept of sustainable development, such as the moral consideration of future generations. However, their specific normative implications are far from certain in relation to the manner is which they relate to each other in terms of international environmental concerns, let alone with regard to human rights law or international economic law (see Birnie and Boyle, 2002, p.85). One only has to examine the potpourri of ideas that accompanied the declarations in 1972, 1992 and 2002 to realise that although such declarations may contain many lofty ideals, when these are properly thought through, they may, in fact, be at loggerheads with each other. Accordingly, a consensus on the meaning of sustainable development or on how to implement it in individual cases is clearly lacking in the international arena (Birnie and Boyle, 2002, p.95). This failure is obvious in practice where bodies such as the ICJ have steered away not only from the broader debates about the principles of what is or is not sustainable development, but also from the labyrinth of weighing social, political, philosophical, and economic values in the sustainable development debate. As such, it is much easier for the ICJ to slip into an examination of justiciable questions which focus on procedurally related issues in the sustainable development debate (such as the adequacy of environmental impact assessments, etc.). Thus, it is only when the ideals of sustainable development can actually be run through some existing and agreed standards or principles that the adequacy of the goals and processes can be meaningfully evaluated.

9. Understanding the international court of justice: The climate negotiations as the only game in town

Between 1994 and 1996, the ICJ struggled with the question pertaining to the legality of nuclear weapons. Although it eventually came to the conclusion that to use nuclear weapons in self defence as a last resort was not illegal, it did, however, set out a number of caveats along the way. Of particular note for this discussion was the idea that the question of the legality of nuclear weapons could ultimately be decided outside of an ongoing international process. That is, the states that possess nuclear weapons were already engaged in the Non Proliferation Treaty with its promise to: 'pursue negotiations in good faith on effective measures relating to cessation of the nuclear arms race at an early date and to nuclear disarmament, and on a treaty on general and complete disarmament under strict and effective international control' (Non-Proliferation Treaty, 1968, Article IV). It was because of this ongoing process within an existing, specific, international framework which was/is designed to conclude the substance of the question before the ICJ, that the ICJ decided that the possession of such weapons could not be illegal. This was because – somewhat obviously – if they already had such weapons and were trying to negotiate a way to rid themselves of them, until the negotiations were concluded, the weapons could not, ipso facto, be considered illicit. The same conclusion would exist for the climate change context.

This treaty provided what the ICJ called the 'broader context' (ICJ, 1996) in which to pursue and conclude such negotiations in good faith. This obligation of good faith in international negotiations is repeated in numerous other international instruments[4] and in other ICJ cases such as those relating to Nuclear Testing (ICJ, 1974a) and the Gabcikovo-Nagymaros Project (ICJ, 1997, para 142). In the latter instance, the Parties were directed back to the negotiating table to: 'look afresh at the affects on the environment ... [and find] ...a satisfactory solution' (ICJ, 1997, para 140). Moreover, this obligation to return to the bargaining table was not to be taken lightly because:

'The Court is mindful that, in the field of environmental protection, vigilance and prevention are required on account of the often irreversible character of damage to the environment and of the limitations inherent in the very mechanism of reparation of this type of damage' (ICJ, 1997, para 140).

The conclusion of the Gabcikovo–Nagymaros judgment, like that on the Legality of Nuclear Weapons, is particularly telling. That is, beyond the obligations to negotiate in good faith:

> 'It is not for the Court to determine what shall be the final result of these negotiations to be conducted by the Parties. It is for the Parties themselves to find an agreed solution that takes account of the objectives of the Treaty, which must be pursued in a joint and integrated way, as well as the norms of international environmental law...' (ICJ, 1997, para 141).

10. Conclusion

SIDs are already vulnerable to globalisation in conventional economic, social and environmental terms. They are, however, particularly vulnerable to one environmental problem above all others, climate change. Climate change has the propensity to change radically the ecology of SIDs at multiple levels and, in certain instances, it may threaten their very existence. Even for those SIDs that can survive sea-level rises, they will still have to contend with climatic changes which will most likely affect everything from the species that they harvest through to their status as a tourist destination.

The good news is that the international community has agreed to a treaty and protocol which have the agreed underlying objective of stabilising greenhouse gas concentrations in the atmosphere at a level that would prevent dangerous anthropogenic interference with the climate system. The bad news is that the Kyoto Protocol is nowhere near achieving this goal given the meagreness of the target, the failure of the United States to accept it, as well as the failure to include developing countries. Accordingly, given the way the negotiations are currently heading, it is likely that the international community will fail in the goal it has set itself.

This failure is already being reflected in the climate negotiations themselves, where the SIDs have slowly disappeared from making the substantive suggestions and actions akin to their original privileged role in the FCCC forum. Currently, the SIDs' influence appears to be one of being trapped within the financial mechanisms of the regime which are closer to adapting to climate change, rather than trying to stop the problem at source. In other words, the battle is already lost and the best approach for SIDs is to prepare for the inevitable rather than taking the lead at forcing mitigation. This retreat is regrettable as the climate future is open for capture.

Given this scenario, the question must be asked: Where to from here? Are there other ways to secure the rights and interests of the SIDs? Within this realm, suggestions have ranged from using human rights claims through to re-orientating the debate to one of wide-ranging discussions about what is, or is not, sustainable development. Both of these approaches are doomed to failure if the objective is to solve the problem at hand by stopping the encroaching problem, rather than allowing it to occur.

If the objective is to solve the problem and protect the interests of those who are most at risk, it is essential that the climate negotiations are reinvigorated. Moreover, the International Court of Justice is clear on this point: when negotiations are ongoing in a distinctive forum, it will not interfere with those discussions unless they are being conducted in bad faith or are clearly diverting from either established principles or the goals of the Convention they are operating under. Here is the nub: given the accepted goal of the FCCC and the current dismal position of the Kyoto Protocol, it is possible that a failure of good faith is occurring, especially when viewed from the perspective of the SIDs given the limited time frame in which climate change must be confronted. As such, if the objective is to protect the interests of the citizens of the SIDs, two options need active consideration. First, the influence of SIDs needs to be reactivated and strongly enhanced within the FCCC negotiations. Second, there may be merit in seeking an ICJ advisory opinion in this area – to see if good faith is being met in the context – as the consequences of climate change and the current international failure to meet the FCCC goals are both spectacular failures that future generations in the SIDs will have to inherit.

Notes

1. For example: 'global warming and sea level rise were among the most serious threats to the Pacific region and the survival of some island states.' South Pacific Forum Communique. Paragraph 29. Available from www.forumsec.org.fj/docs/fc93.htm.

2. This is not to suggest that reduction targets for developing countries should be simply forced upon them. Clearly, developed countries have to take the lead in this process, due to their clear historical legacy for the cumulative build-up of greenhouse gases in the atmosphere. Moreover, despite the fact that the developing countries emissions will eventually eclipse those of the industrialised countries, the continuing disproportionate per-capita emissions, in line with the technological and economic ability to successfully confront climate change should actually make the burden fall more on the developed world. However, the bold point remains that the developing countries are not obliged to make any greenhouse reductions (irrespective of the linkages for why this is, or ought to be another way).

3. UNFCCC, 1992, Decision 28/CP.7. Guidelines for the Preparation of National Adaptation Programmes of Action (NAPAs). These were clearly going well, as in 2002 the COP decided they did not need to be reviewed. See Decision 9/CP.8. Review of the guidelines for the preparation of national adaptation programmes of action.

4. This basic principle is set forth in Article 2, paragraph 2 of the Charter. It was reflected in the Declaration on Friendly Relations between States (resolution 2625 (XXV) of 24 October, 1970) and in the Final Act of the Helsinki Conference of 1 August, 1975. It is also embodied in Article 26 of the Vienna Convention on the Law of Treaties of 23 May, 1969, according to which '[e]very treaty in force is binding upon the parties to it and must be performed by them in good faith'.

References

YBIEL 2 (1991) *Yearbook of International Environmental Law 2*. Oxford University Press, Oxford. p.112.

YBIEL 8 (1997) *Yearbook of International Environmental Law 8*. Oxford University Press, Oxford. pp.184–5.

Adler, R. (1999) 'Fresher Waters', *New Scientist*, July 31, p.22.

Adler, R. (2001) 'Here Comes the Rain', *New Scientist*, December 22, p.11.

New Scientist (2000) 'All Change', *New Scientist*, November 4, p.13.

AOSIS Protocol. (1994) Noted in *YBIEL 5*. Oxford University Press, Oxford. p.164.

Beston, A. (2000) 'Climate Refugees', *NZ Herald*, Feb 15, A5.

Birnie, P. and Boyle, A. (2002) *International Law and the Environment*. Oxford University Press, Oxford, 2nd edn.

Broecker, W. (1997) 'Thermohaline Circulation: The Achilles Heel of our Climate System?', *Science*, 278, pp.1582-8.

Brown, L. (2001) *Vital Signs: 2000-2001*. Earthscan, London.

Brown, P. (2001) 'US Isolated By Treat to Arrest Climate Change', *Guardian Weekly*, July 26, p.1.

Christie (2002) 'Lawsuits may be next weapon in climate change fight.' March 6, Reuters. Available from: www.enn.com/news/wire-stories/2002/03/03062002/reu_46587.asp

Cocker, M. (1999) 'Coral Reefs Don't Like It Hot', *Guardian Weekly*, Dec 19, p.32.

COP, 1996 The Geneva Ministerial Declaration. Report of the Second Session of the COP, Geneva. 1996. FCCC/CP/1996/15/Add.1. 29 Oct. 1996. Annex. Para 2.

Depledge, J. (1999) 'Coming Of Age At Buenos Aires', *Environment*, 41(7), pp.15, 18.

Desai, B. (1999) 'Institutionalising the Kyoto Accord', *Environmental Policy and the Law*, 29(4), p.159.

Dicks, L. (2003) 'Worm Brings Death to Coral', *New Scientist*, Apr 12, p.16.

Ecologist (1999) 'The World's Coral Reefs In Hot Water', *Ecologist*, 29(3), p.1.

Edwards, R. (1999) 'Freezing Future', *New Scientist*, Nov 27, p.6.

Edwards, R. (2003) 'The Mother of All El-Nino's Revealed', *New Scientist*, Jan 18, p.4.

Epstein, P. (2000) 'Is Global Warming Harmful To Health?', Scientific American, August, pp. 36-43.

Evans, M. (2003) Universal Declaration of Human Rights, 1948. Reprinted in *Blackstones's International Law Documents*, M. Evans (ed). Blackwells London, pp.36, 41.

G8 Environment Minister's Communique. Available From www.g7.utoronto.ca/g7/environment/2001trieste/communique.html, Paragraph 8.

G8 Summit Communique. Available from www.g7.utoronto.ca/g7/summit/1998birmingham/finalcom.htm

Gillespie, A. (1997) *International Environmental Law, Policy & Ethics*. Oxford University Press, Oxford..

Gillespie, A. (2000) 'Biodiversity, Indigenous Peoples & Equity in International Law', *New Zealand Journal of Environmental Law*, 4, pp.1-49.

Gillespie, A. (2001a) 'Aboriginal Subsistence Whaling: A Critique of the Inter-Relationship Between International Law and the International Whaling Commission.' *Colorado Journal of International Environmental Law and Policy*, 21(1), pp.79-139.

Gillespie, A. (2001b) *The Illusion of Progress: Unsustainable Development in International Law and Policy*. Earthscan, London.

ICJ (1974a) Nuclear Tests (Australia v. France), Judgment of 20 December 1974, *ICJ Reports 1974*, p.268, para. 46.

ICJ (1974b) Nuclear Tests Case (NZ v France). ICJ 1974. December 20. General List Number 59.

ICJ (1995) Request for an Examination of the Situation in Accordance with Paragraph 63 of the 1974 ICJ Judgment of NZ v. France. ICJ 1995. September 22. General List No. 97.

ICJ (1996) Legality Of The Threat Or Use Of Nuclear Weapons. 8 July General List No. 95. para 98.

ICJ (1997) Case Concerning The Gabcíkovo-Nagymaros Project. 25 September (Hungary/ Slovakia) ICJ 1997. 25 September. General List No. 92

ICJ (1996) Legality of the Threat or Use of Nuclear Weapons. 8. July General List No.95, para. 29.

IEA (2000a) Decision 11/CP.4. National communications from Parties included in Annex I to the Convention. COP 4 (1998). Buenos Aires. FCCC/CP/1998/16/Add.1. 20 January 1999. 47. Paragraph 10 (b).

IEA (2000b) International Energy Outlook 2000. IEA, Washington.

Independent World Commission on the Oceans (1998) The Ocean: Our Future. Cambridge University Press, Cambridge.

IPCC (1995) Climate Change 1994: Radiative Forcing of Climate Change. Cambridge University Press, Cambridge.

IPCC (1996a) Climate Change 1995: Economic and Social Dimensions. Cambridge University Press, Cambridge.

IPCC (1996b) Climate Change 1995: Impacts, Adaptations and Mitigation. Cambridge University Press, Cambridge.

IPCC (1998) The Regional Impacts of Climate Change: An Assessment of Vulnerability. Cambridge University Press, Cambridge.

IPCC (2000) Emission Scenarios. Cambridge University Press, Cambridge.

IPCC (2001a) Climate Change 2001: The Scientific Basis. Cambridge University Press, Cambridge.

IPCC (2001b) Climate Change 2001: Impacts, Adaptation and Vulnerability. Cambridge University Press, Cambridge.

IPCC (2001c) Third Assessment Report: Summary for Policy Makers. Geneva, IPCC.

IPCC (2003) Climate Change and Biodiversity. IPCC Technical Paper V, Geneva.

MacKenzie, D. (1990) 'Communication Gaps Undermine Reports on Global Warming', New Scientist, June 23, p.5.

MacKenzie, D. (1994) 'No Advance In Sight On Greenhouse Treaty', New Scientist, September 10, p.6.

Montreal Protocol on substances that deplete the ozone layer. 19 International Legal Materials (1987) p.111. Article 2 & Annex A.

New Scientist (1990) 'Growing Greenhouse', New Scientist, March 3, p.10.

New Scientist (1989) 'Toodleloo Tuvalu', New Scientist, March 25, p.22.

New Scientist (1992) 'Don't Let Us Drown, Islanders Tell Bush', New Scientist, June 13, p.6.

New Scientist (1995) 'Hot Air In Berlin', New Scientist, March 25, p.3.

New Scientist (2001) 'Sea For Yourself', New Scientist, Apr 21, p.23.

New Scientist (2002a) 'Hotting Up', New Scientist, March 30, p.15.

New Scientist (2002b) 'Heat Seeking Fish Holiday in Cornwall', New Scientist, May 18, p.25.

The Non-Proliferation Treaty on Weapons of Mass Destruction (1968). Article IV.

Oberthur, S. (1995) 'The First Conference of the Parties', *Environmental Policy and the Law*. 25(4), p.144.

Pearce, F. (1988) 'Time For Politicians To Act', *New Scientist*, Oct 15, p.21.

Pearce, F. (1992) 'Yields Tumble In Greenhouse World', *New Scientist*, Apr. 18, p.4.

Pearce, F. (1997) 'Countdown to Chaos,' *New Scientist*. Nov 29. p.22.

Pearce, F. (1999a) 'All Bets Are Off', *New Scientist*, Sep 18, p.5.

Pearce, F. (1999b) 'US Gives Kyoto The Cold Shoulder', *New Scientist*, Nov 13, p.12.

Pearce, F. (2000a) 'Turning Back the Tide', *New Scientist*, Feb 12, pp.44-6.

Pearce, F. (2000b) 'Washed Off the Map', *New Scientist*, Nov 25, p.5.

Pearce, F. (2002a) 'Its Started', *New Scientist*, March 30, p.11.

Pearce, F. (2002b) 'Grief on the Reef', *New Scientist*, Apr 20, p.11.

Pearce, F. (2002c) 'Insurers Count the Cost', *New Scientist*, July 27, p.7.

Pearce, F. (2002d) 'Europe's Wake Up Call', *New Scientist*, Aug 24, p.4.

Pearce, F. (2002e) 'Its Started', *New Scientist*, March 30, p.11.

Reddy, A. (1990) 'Energy For the Developing World', Scientific American, September, pp.63, 69.

Report of the Conference Of the Parties, UNFCCC, Berlin, 1995. FCCC/CP/1995/7. 24 May 1995. Part One, Proceedings. Paragraph 57 & 58.

UN, Report of the Global Conference on the Sustainable Development of Small Island Developing States. A/CONF.167/9. October, 1994. Annex I, Section III.

Schrope, M. (2000) 'Corals Face Catastrophe', *New Scientist*, May 27, p.8.

Schrope, M. (2002) 'Global Warming, Global Fever', *New Scientist*, June 29, p.22.

Simon, P. (1992) 'Why Global Warming Could Take Britain By Storm', *New Scientist*, Nov 7, pp.35-7.

Smil, V. (1994) 'China's Greenhouse Gas Emissions', *Global Environmental Change*, 4(5), pp. 325-32.

South Pacific Forum (1988) Fiji Communique. Ministry of Foreign Affairs, Wellington, New Zealand Paragraph 32.

South Pacific Forum (1989) Kiribati. Communique. Ministry of Foreign Affairs, Wellington, New Zealand Paragraph 20.

South Pacific Forum (1990) Vanuatu. Communique. Ministry of Foreign Affairs, Wellington, New Zealand Paragraph 6 & 7.

Stockholm Declaration on the Human Environment (1972)

Tangen, K. (1999) 'The Climate Change Negotiations: Buenos Aires and Beyond', *Global Environmental Change*, 9, pp.175-8.

Thirty Third Pacific Island Forum (2002) (Fiji, August 2002). PIFS (02) 8. Paragraph 24 & 25. South Pacific Regional Environment Programme (SPREP), Samoa.

UN GCSDSIDS (1994) Report of the Global Conference on the Sustainable Development of Small Island Developing States. A/CONF.167/9. October, 1994. Annex I, Section III

UNDP, UNEP, World Bank, WRI (2000) *World Resources 2000-2001*. Oxford University Press, Oxford.

UNFCCC COP (1992) United Nations Framework Convention on Climate Change. United Nations Conference on Environment and Development A/AC.237/18. May 15. 1982

Wells, S. (1989) 'Gone With The Waves', *New Scientist*, Nov 11, p.29.

WRI, UNDP and World Bank (1999) *World Resources 1998-1999*. Oxford University Press, Oxford.

WSSD (2002a) Plan of Implementation for the 2002 World Summit on Sustainable Development. Johannesburg.

WSSD (2002b) *The Johannesburg Declaration on Sustainable Development*. 2002. A/CONF 199/20.WSSD/ September 4 2002.

Part 2
TRADE

2. Small Vulnerable Economy Issues and the WTO

Roman Grynberg and Jan Yves Remy

I. Introduction

Since the second Ministerial Conference of the WTO[1] held in Geneva in 1998 there has been an attempt by small vulnerable economies (SVEs)[2] to achieve some measure of recognition of the particular problems that confront them in the process of globalisation. At the failed Seattle Ministerial Conference the establishment of a work programme for small economies was agreed to by members,[3] but as the draft text was not accepted it was left until the fourth session in Doha before a Small Economies Work Programme (SEWP) was agreed.[4]

This chapter addresses several issues pertaining to the apparent contradiction in the wording of the work programme agreed to at Doha, which on the one hand mandates Members to frame responses to trade concerns of small, vulnerable economies, but on the other prohibits the creation of a sub-category of states. The relevant paragraph of the Ministerial Declaration was a political compromise between the small economy proponents of the WTO work programme and the developed countries which insisted on the definitional caveat. It has created a conundrum of sorts for negotiators, as it seems impossible to target responses to the concerns of a group that is yet to be defined or recognised because WTO Members have consistently refused to recognise SVEs as a distinct category. While the creation of a WTO sub-category of members is explicitly prohibited in the work programme this does not nullify the right of any WTO member or group of members to make a proposal during negotiations that includes such a group of countries.

This chapter seeks to review the concerns and specificities of small states, thereby highlighting the peculiarities and natural disadvantages that inhibit the ability of SVEs to thrive, and at times survive, in the multilateral trading context. It then considers the implicit definitions and other sub-categorisations relating to smallness that already exist in various WTO agreements, as well as in its administrative practice. We argue that small states have many characteristics that are similar to, but sufficiently distinct from, that of least-developed countries (the only formally recognised group in the WTO) which warrants special treatment of them in the WTO.[5] This chapter argues, however, that such special treatment can begin only with a definition, which it goes some way in advancing. Lastly, we briefly examine the discussions currently taking place in WTO sessions pursuant to the work programme, which underscores the intense discomfort that some WTO members may feel with the creation of new categories. Irrespective of this stated uneasiness, however, this chapter argues that they have already done so during the Uruguay Round and must do so implicitly or explicitly if they are to address the legitimate trade concerns of small vulnerable states.

2. Small states, globalisation and the WTO

Prior to any discussion of definitions, the first question that must be answered is why SVEs require particular attention in the WTO. SVEs comprise small states and small island states which in particular suffer from a combination of inherited and inherent characteristics that impede their ability to integrate into the global economy. These characteristics include smallness, physical isolation from markets, dispersion of small pockets of populations, and a small and highly specialised human and physical resource base. Together these characteristics raise the operating cost structure of small economies and render market adjustment more difficult. The high cost structure that has traditionally been associated with these economies has meant that many have predicated their export trade upon products or services where the export price includes either market or institutionalised quasi-rents, as few other activities have proven viable for these very small producers. These market based quasi-rents have been based on either short temporary booms that have facilitated resource extraction activities and created transitory rents or short-term niche markets. The institutional sources of quasi-rent have stemmed from trade preferences, tax concessions, or sovereignty-based activities.

Historically, SVEs have become dependent upon these forms of export-oriented activities primarily because few other exports ever developed. Merchandise exports in particular have been based on high rates of trade preference resulting from high most-favoured nation (MFN) tariffs, or preference donors have created quota-based systems such as the Sugar and Banana Protocols. It is these particularly distortive trade measures that are most beneficial to SVEs because they offer guaranteed access under quota for what are often small volumes that would otherwise not be traded. In so doing these measures have addressed the marketing constraints faced by SVEs.

Since the creation of the WTO in 1995 these high rates of trade preference, along with the tariff quotas, have been diminished by a series of disputes and on-going negotiations that have shaken the foundations of SVE economies. These include:

(a) The Banana Dispute, which has not only caused a major restructuring in the Caribbean and parts of Africa, but is forcing a complete realignment of trade regimes throughout the ACP regions and necessitating reciprocity in the ACP–EU trade relationship.

(b) The Sugar Dispute between Brazil/Australia/Thailand and the EU over subsidies in the EU sugar regime will force similar adjustment in at least twelve small ACP states that have been substantial beneficiaries of the Sugar Protocol of the Cotonou Agreement.

(c) The Thailand–Philippines/EU mediation over margins of preference for canned tuna has further eroded the competitive position of a number of small states including Mauritius, Papua New Guinea, Fiji and Seychelles.

(d) The Fisheries Subsidies negotiations threaten to undermine the revenue of small coastal developing states that are highly dependent upon fisheries access arrangements.

(e) The full implementation of the provisions of the ASCM (Agreement on Subsidies and Countervailing Measures) will, by 2008, undermine the ability of many small developing countries to use their current range of export incentives in the Export Processing Zones.

Nonetheless, the economic adjustments and loss of quasi-rents in export-oriented activities brought about by these changes in the WTO are not the only cause for concern. In addition, the OECD's Harmful Tax Initiative has undermined the development of off-shore finance centres located predominantly in small states which have used this sector to diversify away from the high trade-preference-dependent activities. Thus the international trade policy shift that has occurred in recent years has thoroughly undermined the export sector of small states.

In fact, no other group of developing countries, including least-developed countries (LDCs), has been obliged to undertake such wide-ranging adjustments necessitated by the last decade of globalisation. This is the reason for the particular problems of small states which, in the WTO context, include:

(a) loss of trade preferences stemming from MFN liberalisation and WTO disputes;

(b) application of rules, including ASCMs, in a manner that does not recognise the inherent economic characteristics of small states; and

(c) implementation of complex and burdensome WTO obligations that are beyond the capabilities of small states with very small administrations.

3. WTO precedents on sub-categorisation of members, including small economies

WTO provisions have created a number of sub-categories of Members, and in the process have set precedents that may be useful for present purposes. These precedents usually constitute provisions on special and differential treatment for small Members or small suppliers, although it is noteworthy that preferential treatment is not true in all cases. For instance, small Members pay proportionately higher contributions to the WTO budget than larger Members. This has been justified from the earliest days of the GATT 1947 by the cost to the Organisation of providing services to Members.

MFN Treatment and Non-Discrimination among its Members are among the most basic principles of the WTO. However, there is an increasing amount of trade being carried out on the basis of exceptions to these basic rules and which allow for differentiation among Members. For instance, there are provisions permitting free-trade areas and customs unions or preferences for developing countries and LDCs. Tulloch has also drawn attention to the fact that special characteristics, interests and concerns of various groups of countries, other than developing countries or least-developed countries, are recognised and accommodated in some of the WTO Agreements (Tulloch, 2001, p.258).

LDCs constitute the only sub-category of WTO Members that is clearly agreed and defined. The WTO has agreed that LDCs are those countries designated as such by the United Nations, and who are Members of the WTO. As this grouping is clearly defined, LDCs are specifically referred to and granted special and differential treatment in many WTO Agreements, including the Decision on Measures in Favour of Least-Developed Countries appended to the Final Act of the Uruguay Round.

Apart from these references to LDCs, the WTO also recognises other sub-groupings within the broader category of developing countries. This has often been done either explicitly or implicitly through the creation of *de minimis* thresholds that in effect distinguish small states and often entitle them to special and or preferential treatment. This is reflected in the following WTO Agreements and practices:

(a) The Agreement on Agriculture and its related Decision contain special provisions for net food-importing developing countries (Article 16). Article 6:2 also contains special provisions for low-income or resource-poor producers in developing countries, which are aimed at encouraging diversification from growing illicit narcotic crops (Article 6.2).

(b) The ASCM also grants developing countries with a per capita GNP below US$1,000 the same treatment as least-developed countries in respect of export subsidies (Article 3 and Annex VII). Other developing countries are granted a transitional period to phase out their export subsidies on non-agricultural products, unless they have reached export competitiveness in particular products. Furthermore, the ASCM defines export competitiveness to exist if a developing country Member's exports of the product in question have reached a share of at least 3.25 per cent in world trade in the relevant period (Article 27.6). The agreement also provides for the termination of any countervailing duty investigations as soon as the authorities determine that the volume of subsidised imports represents less than 4 per cent of the total imports of the like product in the importing Member concerned (Article 27.10). Significantly, at the Doha Ministerial Conference, while explicitly rejecting the creation of a new category of small states, another *de minimis* threshold was established for defining the conditions under which developing country members may obtain an extension of the right to use prohibited export subsidies.[6]

(c) The Agreement on Implementation of Article VI of GATT 1994 provides that the volume of dumped imports shall normally be regarded as negligible if the volume of dumped imports from a particular country is found to account for less than 3 per cent of imports of the like product in the importing Member, unless the countries which individually account for less than 3 per cent of the imports of the like product in the importing Member collectively account for more than 7 per cent of imports of the like product in the importing Member (Article 5:8). The Agreement also provides that due account shall be taken of any difficulties experienced by interested parties, in particular small companies, in supplying information (Article 6).

(d) The Agreement on Safeguards lays down that safeguard measures shall not be applied against a product originating in a developing country Member as long as its share of imports of the product concerned in the importing Member does not exceed 3 per cent, provided that the developing country Members with less than 3 per cent import share collectively account for no more than 9 per cent of the total imports of the product concerned (Article 9, Agreement on Safeguards).

(e) The Agreement on Textiles and Clothing lays down that meaningful improvement in access for exports of Members that are subject to restriction and account for 1.2 per cent or less of the total volume of restrictions applied by the importing Member concerned (Agreement on Textiles and Clothing, Article 2). Special and differential treatment provisions under the agreement provide that Members whose total volume of textile and clothing exports is small in comparison with the total volume of exports of other Members and who account for a small percentage of total imports of that product into the importing Members (Article 6:6(a)). Furthermore special consideration to be given to wool products from wool-producing country Members whose economy and textiles and clothing trade are dependent on the wool sector, whose total textile and clothing exports consist almost exclusively of wool products, and whose volume of textile and clothing trade is comparatively small in the markets of the importing Member (Article 6:6(b)).

(f) In the Doha Declaration dealing with Technical Cooperation and Capacity Building, Ministers agreed that priority shall be accorded to small, vulnerable, and transitional economies, as well as Members and Observers without representation in Geneva (Ministerial Declaration WT/MIN(01)/DEC/1, 20 November 2001, Paragraph 38). Members with a relatively small share of world trade are subject to less frequent review of their trade regime under the Trade Policy Review Mechanism (GATT (1994) Annex 3 Trade Policy Review Mechanism, para. C(ii)).

(g) The rules setting contributions to the WTO budget, drawn up under Article VII of the Agreement establishing the Organisation, provide that each Member's contribution is a function of its share of world trade. However, these rules provide that Members with less than 0.015 per cent of world trade pay a minimum contribution of 0.015 per cent of the budget (this figure has been modified on a number of occasions in the past and was reduced from 0.03 per cent from the budget year 2000).

4. A small matter of definition

While WTO members have been emphatic in their opposition to the creation of a separate category of SVEs and have frequently restated their support for the principles of non-discrimination, they have nonetheless systematically created at least seven *de minimis* thresholds in various agreements and administrative arrangements, which reveals a preference for rules dependent upon the size of the particular member. As mentioned above in the Introduction, the difficulty arises because the mandate undertaken by WTO members is to '…frame responses to the trade-related issues identified for the fuller integration of small, vulnerable economies into the multilateral trading system…'. Clearly such responses, if they are to involve any derogation from, or alteration of, existing WTO rules, will by definition require WTO Members to differentiate between those members to whom the derogation or alteration of obligations applies and those outside that group. However, because WTO members went on to say that they would not create a new sub-category of WTO Members, the Doha mandate creates an impossible conundrum for policymakers and negotiators.

In fact, should WTO Members desire it, the task of defining SVEs is far from impossible. Quite inadvertently, WTO Members may in fact have created a defined, albeit imperfect, category of 'vulnerable' states. The ECOSOC definition of an LDC, the only category of WTO members officially recognised, is defined by three criteria, one of which is the UN Economic Vulnerability Index (EVI). If a country's rating on the EVI is greater than 31 then it is deemed to be vulnerable. If it is greater than 36 then a country is deemed to be highly vulnerable. In order to be an LDC, a country must rank above 36. Unfortunately only 128 UN Members have been classified on the EVI. The first 96 countries on the list in Annex 3 of this chapter would qualify as 'vulnerable' using this criterion. However, one limitation of the list is that while EVIs have been calculated for 128 countries, they do not include all WTO Members and acceding countries, notably transition economies.

For expository purposes, one could use a trade criterion of 0.05 per cent of world trade for measuring 'smallness'. This threshold would categorise some 86 WTO Members as small. In total these 86 states account for 1.5 per cent of world trade, and if the trade of least-developed countries is subtracted then the total amount of world trade potentially affected by the WTO recognising small economies, as a group, is a mere 1.1 per cent (see Annex 2).

Unfortunately, if individual thresholds are chosen there are some anomalies that would be created. This is because at least five countries, namely Cyprus, Malta, Iceland, Singapore and Lichtenstein, are either small or vulnerable economies. This could be resolved, however, if EU members are excluded on the basis that any criteria would be restricted to developing countries. In this way, Cyprus, Malta and Lichtenstein would be excluded. In addition, if one uses both filters – that is, 'small' and 'vulnerable' – Iceland and Singapore would also be excluded.[7] Notably, the Doha Ministerial mandate uses both these terms in its language.

This raises the question of the choice of thresholds for the definition of small. There is little doubt that the threshold chosen for expository purposes is *ad hoc* in nature. There is and can be no legitimate theoretical explanation for the choice of 0.05 per cent as a threshold except for the purely practical consideration that it excludes the most egregious anomalies, something that would be necessary in order to satisfy WTO members that a trade advantage was not being offered to high-income developed countries. In defence of such an *ad hoc* approach to the definition of small, one need look no further than WTO practice itself, as WTO Members in the past have never provided a justification for the particular choice of *de minimis* thresholds in any of the WTO Agreements.

For the moment, this definitional debate could be largely academic because, as will be seen below, the demands currently being made by SVEs in WTO negotiations may not as yet require a formal definition *per se*. However, the emerging situation and debate suggests that it may soon be necessary for proponents of a definition to develop at least the contours of a working definition in order to address more specifically the economic and trade concerns of Members. Significantly, given the precedence above, there are a host of possible definitions and approaches to the issue that could be employed depending upon the circumstances.

5. Small economy issues in the dedicated sessions of the WTO

Discussions concerning small economies in the WTO have taken place in four dedicated sessions of the Committee on Trade and Development (CTD). This Committee was entrusted with the task of ensuring compliance with, and completion of, the Doha mandate regarding small economies.[8]

The dedicated sessions have shown the small economies representatives to be the agenda-setters, as they have taken the lead in initiating and steering discussions thus far. In particular, a grouping of SVEs[9] has submitted papers and tabled various proposals specific to their circumstances. In their first paper, the SVEs underscore the characteristics that make them vulnerable, and the implications that these characteristics have on their trade and development (see WT/COMTD/SE//Rev 1*, 3 May 2002). In sessions of the CTD, SVE representatives have also recounted their day-to-day hardships in trying to operate in a multilateral trading context. Although the developed countries have been generally supportive of these papers and have encouraged the sharing of individual experiences, they have at times raised the definitional issue, with the wearying precaution that the mandate clearly restricts sub-categorisation of the kind that appear to interest SVEs (see in this regard, minutes of the Dedicated Sessions, available at WT/COMTD/SE/M/1,2,3 and 4).

The actual proposals tabled by SVEs thus far address concerns of smaller economies generally, and are relatively modest in scope.[10] They are expressly intended to complement others submitted in specific negotiating groups. Their coverage is both procedural and substantive in nature, and is aimed generally at improving administrative procedures for SVEs, as well as towards refashioning current rules to better suit and accommodate their needs. Developed countries have in general been amenable to the former, but as regards the rule-based proposals, they have indicated discomfort with the idea of changing rules to address the need of a sub-category of WTO Members.[11] Many SVEs have, however, indicated their intention to present, and to have their proposals accepted as a packaged and all-inclusive deal.

Not surprisingly, one of the proposals made seeks to retain the margins of preferences for small economy exports. However, this has led to some contention within the small economies camp, and in particular concern from the likes of some Latin American countries, who self-define as small economies, and who would want existing preferences extended to all small economies. However, a number of the proponents of the proposal feel that such a blanket application to all self-professed small economies would have the effect of diluting any advantage or benefit to SVEs. This would be an area where a definition could be helpful.

Less contentious were proposals on Article XXIV and Regional Trading Arrangements which seek to ensure non-reciprocity in regional trade agreements between developed and small economies. Small economies have proposed that sufficient space for policy development specific to their needs be retained in the WTO, and that developed countries do not require concessions in negotiations that are inconsistent with the development, financial and trade needs of smaller economies.

Most proposals are aimed at improving how the rules of various WTO Agreements work and affect small economies. One such proposal regarding the ASCM seeks to ensure that small economies are not made subject to the provisions of paragraph 1(a) of Article 3 of the ASCM, requiring the phasing out of fiscal incentives. The proposal further provides that the rules and procedures of the Agreement be modified for small economies. However, developed countries have generally not seen the need for such special treatment of smaller economies, arguing that current procedures are working well, and that any special consideration would encourage sub-categorisation of the kind prohibited under the mandate. Other more administrative proposals that call for the explicit recognition of the right of small economies to designate regional bodies as their 'competent authorities' for the purposes of that Agreement, have been more generally supported by developed countries, with some instances of voluntary pledges for the provision of technical assistance. A similar proposal in the context of the Sanitary and Phytosanitary (SPS) and Technical Barriers to Trade (TBT) Agreements has likewise been welcomed, and developed countries have been generally supportive of any requests for technical assistance in the establishment of joint and shared missions for current non-resident Members.

Proposals for the revision of some rules in the Safeguard Agreement for small economies, including those relating to the definition of domestic industry; serious injury; investigations; reporting requirements; causation and non-attribution principle; and the right of compensation and/or retaliation; were not embraced by developed countries who drew attention to the fact that Article XIX of the Agreement already catered to developing countries. The proponents have, however, responded that the rules of the Safeguards Agreement entail cumbersome administrative procedures which would need to be simplified for smaller economies.

There have also been proposals for developed countries to assist small economies in complying with their obligations under the SPS and TBT Agreements through (a) the use of the former's technology and technical facilities on preferential and non-commercial terms, preferably free of costs; and (b) appropriate flexibility for small economies in dealing with timeframes and notifications requirements. Again, developed countries reacted to these proposals negatively by suggesting that technical regulation was also a problem for them, and that smaller economies could focus instead on the notification requirements of these Agreements. Some developed countries have even suggested the increased use of electronic technology to access such notifications. According to smaller economies however, the plight of the developed countries was not comparable to that of smaller developing ones, and flexibility needed to be incorporated into the timeframe and notification requirements.

Proposals on the dispute settlement body were met with comments from developing countries that many of the issues raised were already being discussed in the context of special and differential S&D treatment in dispute settlement understanding DSU negotiations. The proponents expressed their awareness and intention to participate concurrently in these discussions as well. On issues of graduation and accession of small economies from LDC status, there is general agreement that these issues would have to be considered to develop acceptable guidelines and procedures for small economies.

The proponents of all of these proposals attempted to make them the basis of recommendations to the General Council (this request is contained in the Communication found at WT/COMTD/SE/W/8), as required under the mandate. However, lack of consensus, particularly by developed countries, on the suitability and workability of some proposals, and on the issue of how to prevent the creation of a two-tier system of rights and obligations within the WTO, prevented the forwarding of these proposals.

6. Conclusion

The present discussions in the WTO underscore the discomfort among developed countries with the idea of explicitly recognising a sub-category of smaller economies, and further SVEs. However, it is hard to surmise how execution of the mandate in paragraph 35, requiring the framing of trade-related responses to problems of smaller vulnerable economies, can occur without the logical first step of defining and clarifying what is a small vulnerable economy. The existence of clear precedents in the text and practice of the WTO exposes the possibility and indeed desirability of doing so, once the requisite political will exists. In order for small states within the WTO to gain any measure of success in current trade negotiations, they must first and foremost achieve recognition as a separate sub-grouping within the Membership of the WTO.

Notes

1. Ministerial Declaration, Second Session, Ministerial Conference of the World Trade Organization WT/MIN(98)/DEC/1, 25 May 1998, (98-2149), Geneva, 18 and 20 May 1998, adopted on 20 May, 1998, para 6:

   'We remain deeply concerned over the marginalization of least-developed countries and certain small economies, and recognize the urgent need to address this issue which has been compounded by the chronic foreign debt problem facing many of them.'

2. The authors are keenly aware that there is a substantial difference between small states and small economies. Small economies include the self-selected group of WTO members that includes countries as large as Sri Lanka, Cuba and Bolivia, who are not necessarily small states. Small economies often do not face the constraints imposed by very small administrative capacity to implement WTO agreements. Employing the World Bank/Commonwealth criteria of a population of 1.5 million would have excluded these larger countries. The WTO mandates and nomenclature refer to small economies but the problems addressed in this paper refer to the problems of small states, which are usually more vulnerable and have vastly different problems, both economically and administratively, to some of the larger 'small economies' that are members of the small economies group at the WTO. For the purposes of this paper, reference to small states, as distinct from small economies, will be to small vulnerable economies.

3. The later versions of the draft text of the Seattle Ministerial Declaration contained no square brackets in the section pertaining to small economies but the draft ministerial declaration was not endorsed by WTO members.

4. Ministerial Declaration, Fourth Session, Ministerial Conference of the World Trade Organization, WT/MIN(01)/DEC/1, 20 November, 2001, (01-5859), Doha, 9–14 November, 2001, adopted on 14 November, 2001, para 35.

   'We agree to a work program, under the auspices of the General Council, to examine issues relating to the trade of small economies. The objective of this work is to frame responses to the trade-related issues identified for the fuller integration of small, vulnerable economies into the multilateral trading system, and not to create a sub-category of WTO members. The General Council shall review the work program and make recommendations for action to the Fifth Session of the Ministerial Conference.'

5. The category of least-developed country is defined by the UN's Economic and Social Commission and is external to the WTO. The category of developing country is determined in the WTO by self-election, which has meant that until very recently high-income countries such as South Korea, Israel and Singapore have chosen to define themselves as developing countries.

6. Procedures for extensions under Article 27.4 for certain developing country members G/SCM/39, 20 November, 2001. The provisions state:

   Programs eligible for extension pursuant to these procedures, and for which members shall therefore grant extensions for calendar year 2003 as referred to in 1(c), are export subsidy programs (i) in the form of full or partial exemptions from import duties and internal taxes, (ii) which were in existence not later than 1 September, 2001, and (iii) which are provided by developing country members (iv) whose share of world merchandise export trade was not greater than 0.10 per cent, (v) whose total Gross National Income (GNI) for the year 2000 as published by the World Bank was at or below US$20 billion, (vi) and who are otherwise eligible to request an extension pursuant to Article 27.4, and (vii) in respect of which these procedures are followed.

7. It should be noted that the UN has not classified Iceland on the vulnerability index, and if it were included, given its dependence on a very narrow range of exports, it may also have an EVI classification above 31.

8. See the Framework and Procedures of the Work Program given to the CTD on 1 March by the General Council, at WT/L/447. This requires the CTD to, among other things, conduct these discussions in scheduled Dedicated Sessions; to report regularly to the General Council, which has overall responsibility for ensuring that responses to the trade related concerns identified in these Dedicated Sessions are arrived at; and where necessary to work with the other relevant subsidiary bodies of the WTO. The WTO Secretariat is also instructed to provide relevant information and factual analysis to inform discussions taking place in these Dedicated Sessions.

9. These include Barbados, Belize, Bolivia, Cuba, Dominican Republic, El Salvador, Fiji Islands, Guatemala, Haiti, Honduras, Jamaica, Mauritius, Nicaragua, Papua New Guinea, Paraguay, Saint Lucia, Solomon Islands, Sri Lanka, and Trinidad and Tobago.

10. The proponents of this submission were Barbados, Belize, Bolivia, Dominican Republic, Guatemala, Honduras, Mauritius and Sri Lanka. See WT/COMTD/SE/W/3 for entire exposition of these proposals, and the backgrounds informing them.

11. The general response to these proposals has been encouraging and supportive, with a few pointed questions being asked, in particular by the developing countries in dedicated sessions. Notably, the US has tendered a written questionnaire to the proposal's proponents, in which they have sought clarification and further information on the proposals. The full version of the questions posed by the United States, and the responses received from the proponents of the proposal, are available at WT/COMTD/SE/W/7.

References

Tulloch, Peter (2001) 'Small Economies in the WTO' in David Peretz, Rumman Faruqui and Eliawony J. Kisanga (eds) *Small States in the Global Economy*. Commonwealth Secretariat and World Bank, London and Washington.

Annex I

Table of Other Negotiating Proposals Made or to be Made in Favour of Small Developing States in the WTO

Subject area/relevant WTO agreement	Background	Content of proposal
Fisheries Subsidies (ASCM, including Article XVI GATT GATT 1994: GATT Agreement on Subsidies and Countervailing Measures Article 1, Article 3.1, Article 27, Article 6, Annex VII)	SVEs have relatively high dependence on domestic and export fisheries. Large exporting countries seeking to negotiate fish eries subsidies on the basis that subsidies have a harmful effect on sustainable fish catches. SVEs fisheries' interests extend to the following mian areas: revenue generation from access fees: domestic and foreign fishers operating for export in the Exclusive Economic Zone (EEZ) and territorial sea, artisan fisheries within their territorial sea.	Ensure that Article 1 of the ASCM is clarified to explicitly exclude certain types of assistance from definition of subsidy: (including access fees and development assistance, fiscal incentives to domestication and fisheries development, artisanal fisheries)
TRIPs (Article 67)	Due to limited capacity many SVEs are unable to implement complex rules and procedures in Trade-Related Aspects of Intellectual Property Rights (TRIPs). Article 67 of TRIPs makes provision for developed countries to assist with such implementation, upon request. However, SVES often have problems even identifying their needs to make such requests, and they are not able to implement this agreement.	Explicit recognition that SVEs may designate regional body as competent authority for implementation of the TRIPs Agreement. This should be assisted by developed countries through the provision of technical and financial assistance.
Regional Trade Arrangements (RTAs) (in particular, Article XXIV and Enabling		Provisions in Article XXIV to be interpreted to incorporate incomplete reciprocity for SVEs as contained in Enabling Clause.

Subject area/relevant WTO agreement	Background	Content of proposal
Clause, para.3 Understanding on the Interpretation of Article XXIV GATT 1994)		In particular, to incorporate notion of **flexibility** in 'substantially all trade' in Article XXIV:8 to accommodate asymmetric liberalisation between developing countries with less than average of 0.05% of world merchandise export (in last five years) and developed countries, suitable to the circumstances of SVEs.

Flexibility to entail:

1) Asymmentry in timetabling of tariff reduction and elimination during transitional periods.

2) Any FTAs involving SVEs and developed countries (as referred to above) should be 'exceptional' cases and 'reasonable length of time' to be 25 years. |
| Trade Preferences | SVEs are particularly trade-preference dependent. | |
| - Part IV of GA TT 1994 and Enabling Clause | The erosion of trade preferences jeopardises the future of small vulnerable economies in critical areas such as agriculture and manufacturing.

Current WTO negotiations and rules threaten these arrangements. | 'Grand fathering' of existing margins of trade preferences for products and small economies accounting for less than 3.25% of world trade. |
| Agreement on Subsidies and Countervailing Measures (ASCM): | SVEs suffer from the combined effect of diseconomies of scale caused by their small size and physical isolation, which together necessitate | SVEs **shall be granted** a **permanent** exemption from the provisions of paragraph 1 (a) of Article 3, (ASCM). |
| Article XVI GATT 1994, ASCM Article 27, Annex VII, | compensatory measure to offset these inherent cost disadvantages. Moreover without these | SVEs should be allowed subsidies to reduce the cost of marketing exports of non-agricultural |

Subject area/relevant WTO agreement	Background	Content of proposal
Doha Ministerial Declaration (c)	compensatory measures SVEs will be unable to attract investment. WTO provisions 'recognise that subsidies may play an important role in economic development programmes of developing country members' and provide flexibility for certain developing countries in the application of subsidies. The agreement does not grant the necessary flexibility to small vulnerable economies. Moreover, existing fiscal incentives are required to be phased out under current WTO rules.	products (including export promotion and advisory services) including handling, upgrading and other processing costs of international transport and freight. SVEs should be allowed to provide internal transport and freight charges on export shipment, provided or mandated by governments on terms more favourable than for domestic shipments for non-agricultural products.
Agreement on Agriculture (Article 9)	SVEs suffer from the combined effect of diseconomies of scale caused by their small size and physical isolation, which together necessitate compensatory measures to offset these inherent cost disadvantages. Moreover without these compensatory measures SVEs will be unable to attract investment. WTO provisions 'recognise that subsidies may play an important role in economic development programmes of developing country members' and flexibility for certain developing countries in the application of subsidies. The agreement does not grant the necessary flexibility to small vulnerable economies. Existing fiscal incentives are required to be phased out under current WTO rules.	

Annex 2

Total Trade in Goods and Services
Sorted by average percentage share 1998–2000

	Total trade in goods and services (million US$)	1998	1999	2000	average 1998–2000 share (%)	average 1998–2000 share (%)	2000
1	United States	1,995,459	2,140,380	2,472,460	2,202,766.33	15.42	15.9397
2	Germany	1,218,840	1,234,558	1,254,113	1,235,837.33	8.65	8.0851
3	Japan	798,199	858,549	986,299	881,015.50	6.17	6.3586
4	United Kingdom	768,695	785,237	825,536	793,155.93	5.55	5.3221
5	France	731,704	727,349	732,608	730,553.77	5.11	4.7230
6	Italy	579,021	562,534	582,028	574,527.63	4.02	3.7523
7	Canada	495,867	542,234	611,711	549,937.23	3.85	3.9436
8	Netherlands	470,123	478,530	498,210	482,287.47	3.38	3.2119
9	Hong Kong, China	421,225	414,030	480,701	438,651.93	3.07	3.0990
10	China	370,790	410,582	529,792	437,054.73	3.06	3.4155
11	Belgium	348,938	350,891	369,704	356,511.06	2.50	2.3834
12	Spain	320,745	338,836	351,379	336,986.63	2.36	2.2653
13	Korea, Republic of	271,556	314,496	397,768	327,940.23	2.30	2.5644
14	Mexico	266,941	304,037	371,196	314,058.00	2.20	2.3931
15	Taipei, Chinese	249,946	267,659	326,699	281,434.67	1.97	2.1062
16	Singapore	242,905	262,601	314,723	273,409.57	1.91	2.0290
17	Switzerland	227,374	224,514	227,770	226,552.40	1.59	1.4684
18	Sweden	192,021	201,625	203,029	198,891.60	1.39	1.3089
19	Austria	186,779	192,644	192,737	190,719.97	1.34	1.2426

Total trade in goods and services (million US$)	1998	1999	2000	average 1998–2000 share (%)	average 1998–2000 share (%)	2000
20 Malaysia	150,633	171,972	206,268	176,291.13	1.23	1.3298
21 Ireland	177,698	154,761	166,780	166,412.80	1.16	1.0752
22 Russian Federation	161,701	137,624	178,007	159,110.67	1.11	1.1476
23 Australia	149,809	156,840	168,397	158,348.67	1.11	1.0856
24 Denmark	122,920	132,072	141,222	132,071.20	0.92	0.9104
25 Thailand	114,216	127,543	153,201	131,653.27	0.92	0.9877
26 Brazil	131,701	117,513	135,585	128,266.33	0.90	0.8741
27 India	104,162	113,484	135,728	117,791.47	0.82	0.8750
28 Norway	107,252	109,576	124,058	113,628.80	0.80	0.7998
29 Indonesia	98,397	97,629	125,587	107,204.33	0.75	0.8096
30 Turkey	109,261	93,734	112,557	105,184.00	0.74	0.7256
31 Saudi Arabia	79,745	91,292	121,052	97,363.37	0.68	0.7804
32 Poland	95,059	90,360	103,368	96,262.33	0.67	0.6664
33 Finland	88,571	86,083	92,189	88,947.67	0.62	0.5943
34 Portugal	78,805	79,802	79,092	79,233.00	0.55	0.5099
35 Israel	67,768	76,919	91,433	78,706.37	0.55	0.5895
36 Philippines	76,572	75,732	77,673	76,658.87	0.54	0.5007
37 United Arab Emirates	67,950	70,100	79,701	72,583.77	0.51	0.5138
38 Czech Republic	67,449	66,978	73,113	69,179.83	0.48	0.4714
39 South Africa	66,972	63,614	69,247	66,610.93	0.47	0.4464
40 Argentina	69,339	60,067	63,246	64,217.40	0.45	0.4077
41 Hungary	53,811	55,677	63,849	57,778.93	0.40	0.4116

Total trade in goods and services (million US$)	1998	1999	2000	average 1998–2000 share (%)	average 1998–2000 share (%)	2000
42 Greece	41,026	60,336	70,741	57,367.60	0.40	0.4561
43 Luxembourg	43,203	48,099	52,062	47,787.95	0.33	0.3356
44 Venezuela	38,898	38,720	53,649	43,755.67	0.31	0.3459
45 Chile	40,285	37,228	43,059	40,190.67	0.28	0.2776
46 Egypt	32,738	35,636	39,291	35,888.33	0.25	0.2533
47 *Ukraine*	36,449	32,295	37,055	35,266.33	0.25	0.2389
48 New Zealand	31,701	34,354	35,050	33,702.00	0.24	0.2260
49 Colombia	30,648	27,180	29,941	29,256.17	0.20	0.1930
50 Vietnam	25,473	27,641	34,475	29,196.33	0.20	0.2223
51 Nigeria	23,120	25,754	37,125	28,666.10	0.20	0.2393
52 Slovak Republic	28,338	25,210	28,685	27,410.77	0.19	0.1849
53 Algeria	22,114	24,781	34,119	27,004.43	0.19	0.2200
54 Kuwait	23,071	24,148	31,619	26,279.33	0.18	0.2038
55 Romania	22,259	21,197	26,132	23,196.00	0.16	0.1685
56 Slovenia	22,516	21,906	22,071	22,164.27	0.16	0.1423
57 Morocco	20,646	21,806	22,438	21,629.77	0.15	0.1447
58 Pakistan	21,031	20,351	22,030	21,137.33	0.15	0.1420
59 Croatia	19,210	17,909	18,262	18,460.07	0.13	0.1177
60 Dominican Republic	16,298	17,169	19,697	17,721.50	0.12	0.1270
61 Tunisia	17,327	17,763	17,624	17,571.50	0.12	0.1136
62 Peru	17,949	16,477	18,048	17,491.33	0.12	0.1164
63 *Kazakhstan*	14,601	13,670	19,259	15,843.43	0.11	0.1242

Total trade in goods and services (million US$)	1998	1999	2000	average 1998–2000 share (%)	average 1998–2000 share (%)	2000
64 Panama	16,947	14,785	15,767	15,832.93	0.11	0.1016
65 Bangladesh	13,273	14,578	16,259	14,703.23	0.10	0.1048
66 Costa Rica	13,903	15,342	14,732	14,659.10	0.10	0.0950
67 *Belarus*	15,203	13,039	15,721	14,654.10	0.10	0.1013
68 Oman	12,645	13,273	17,696	14,538.07	0.10	0.1141
69 Sri Lanka	12,341	12,290	14,430	13,020.10	0.09	0.0930
70 Bulgaria	11,932	12,321	14,614	12,955.50	0.09	0.0942
71 *Libyan Arab Jamahiriya*	13,137	11,624	13,607	12,789.10	0.09	0.0877
72 Qatar	8,823	10,360	13,687	10,956.77	0.08	0.0882
73 Angola	8,141	10,614	13,652	10,802.10	0.08	0.0880
74 Ecuador	11,624	9,441	10,885	10,649.97	0.07	0.0702
75 Lithuania	11,354	9,528	10,912	10,598.03	0.07	0.0703
76 *Syrian Arab Republic*	9,183	10,227	11,818	10,409.33	0.07	0.0762
77 Cuba	8,982	9,589	10,495	9,688.67	0.07	0.0677
78 Bahrain	7,946	9,005	11,587	9,512.27	0.07	0.0747
79 Estonia	8,786	8,098	9,735	8,872.87	0.06	0.0628
80 Côte d'Ivoire	9,434	9,293	7,649	8,791.87	0.06	0.0493
81 Guatemala	8,442	8,419	9,361	8,740.87	0.06	0.0603
82 Jordan	8,605	8,298	9,037	8,646.33	0.06	0.0583
83 Macau, China	7,995	8,158	9,453	8,535.37	0.06	0.0609
84 *Lebanon*	8,946	8,119	8,369	8,478.00	0.06	0.0540
85 Cyprus	8,323	8,333	8,575	8,410.37	0.06	0.0553
86 El Salvador	7,524	7,822	9,242	8,195.80	0.06	0.0596

Total trade in goods and services (million US$)	1998	1999	2000	average 1998–2000 share (%)	average 1998–2000 share (%)	2000
87 Uruguay	8,571	7,472	7,877	7,973.07	0.06	0.0508
88 Jamaica	7,358	7,420	7,851	7,543.13	0.05	0.0506
89 Paraguay	8,645	6,732	6,241	7,205.97	0.05	0.0402
90 *Uzbekistan*	6,817	6,347	7,594	6,919.10	0.05	0.0490
91 Latvia	6,973	6,454	7,077	6,834.67	0.05	0.0456
92 Malta	6,165	6,611	7,507	6,760.77	0.05	0.0484
93 Trinidad and Tobago	6,066	6,414	7,506	6,661.73	0.05	0.0484
94 Iceland	5,993	6,174	6,368	6,178.40	0.04	0.0411
95 Zimbabwe	5,679	5,896	6,644	6,073.07	0.04	0.0428
96 Kenya	6,309	5,706	6,184	6,066.20	0.04	0.0399
97 Ghana	5,963	6,264	5,657	5,961.17	0.04	0.0365
98 Yemen	4,574	5,411	7,510	5,831.80	0.04	0.0484
99 Honduras	5,187	5,227	5,714	5,376.13	0.04	0.0368
100 Mauritius	5,219	5,446	5,312	5,325.63	0.04	0.0342
101 Brunei Darussalam	4,748	5,383	5,740	5,290.57	0.04	0.0370
102 *Bosnia and Herzegovina*	4,979	5,467	5,412	5,285.87	0.04	0.0349
103 Botswana	4,801	5,525	5,435	5,253.37	0.04	0.0350
104 *Bahamas*	4,556	4,881	5,613	5,016.50	0.04	0.0362
105 Gabon	4,245	4,511	5,066	4,607.20	0.03	0.0327
106 Cameroon	4,154	4,727	4,889	4,589.97	0.03	0.0315
107 Myanmar	4,477	4,206	4,762	4,481.87	0.03	0.0307
108 Papua New Guinea	3,963	3,975	4,669	4,202.50	0.03	0.0301
109 Namibia	3,493	3,625	4,087	3,735.00	0.03	0.0263

Total trade in goods and services (million US$)	1998	1999	2000	average 1998–2000 share (%)	average 1998–2000 share (%)	2000
110 Azerbaijan	3,414	3,171	4,107	3,564.03	0.02	0.0265
111 Congo	2,656	3,384	4,576	3,538.60	0.02	0.0295
112 TFYR Macedonia	3,433	3,337	3,824	3,531.33	0.02	0.0247
113 Bolivia	3,522	3,269	3,498	3,429.53	0.02	0.0226
114 Tanzania, United Republic of	3,373	3,298	3,290	3,320.53	0.02	0.0212
115 Senegal	3,047	3,171	2,982	3,066.60	0.02	0.0192
116 Sudan	2,542	2,387	3,829	2,919.47	0.02	0.0247
117 Nicaragua	2,447	2,819	2,888	2,718.13	0.02	0.0186
118 Barbados	2,595	2,695	2,832	2,707.17	0.02	0.0183
119 Nepal	2,343	2,763	2,967	2,690.87	0.02	0.0191
120 Cambodia	2,243	2,511	3,248	2,667.20	0.02	0.0209
121 Uganda	2,581	2,524	2,574	2,559.67	0.02	0.0166
122 Congo, Democratic Republic of	2,609	2,176	2,053	2,279.33	0.02	0.0132
123 Swaziland	2,387	2,197	1,973	2,185.93	0.02	0.0127
124 Zambia	2,173	2,046	2,177	2,132.03	0.01	0.0140
125 Fiji	1,846	2,060	2,405	2,103.83	0.01	0.0155
126 Madagascar	1,821	1,953	2,530	2,101.40	0.01	0.0163
127 Mozambique	1,663	2,061	2,174	1,965.73	0.01	0.0140
128 Georgia	1,983	1,634	1,852	1,823.13	0.01	0.0119
129 Albania	1,222	1,618	2,168	1,669.20	0.01	0.0140
130 Moldova, Republic of	2,013	1,383	1,602	1,666.10	0.01	0.0103
131 Haiti	1,488	1,650	1,692	1,609.93	0.01	0.0109
132 Guinea	1,605	1,533	1,568	1,568.80	0.01	0.0101

Total trade in goods and services (million US$)	1998	1999	2000	average 1998–2000	average 1998–2000 share (%)	2000
133 Tajikistan	1,392	1,429	1,879	1,566.90	0.01	0.0121
134 Mali	1,512	1,630	1,546	1,562.93	0.01	0.0100
135 Guyana	1,485	1,414	1,471	1,456.80	0.01	0.0095
136 Armenia	1,344	1,281	1,484	1,369.67	0.01	0.0096
137 Kyrgyz Republic	1,521	1,222	1,215	1,319.33	0.01	0.0078
138 Benin	1,305	1,425	1,215	1,314.90	0.01	0.0078
139 Mongolia	1,204	1,178	1,410	1,264.13	0.01	0.0091
140 Togo	1,188	1,065	1,361	1,204.77	0.01	0.0088
141 Malawi	1,238	1,267	1,083	1,195.87	0.01	0.0070
142 Lao People's Democratic Republic	1,057	1,016	1,217	1,096.63	0.01	0.0078
143 Lesotho	1,156	1,035	1,016	1,069.00	0.01	0.0065
144 Burkina Faso	1,150	1,009	883	1,014.07	0.01	0.0057
145 Antigua and Barbuda	952	997	947	965.47	0.01	0.0061
146 Seychelles	880	977	994	950.00	0.01	0.0064
147 Suriname	968	849	907	907.97	0.01	0.0058
148 Maldives	833	892	904	876.40	0.01	0.0058
149 St. Lucia	799	821	782	800.43	0.01	0.0050
150 Belize	693	791	882	788.53	0.01	0.0057
151 Mauritania	831	748	781	786.77	0.01	0.0050
152 Chad	800	752	765	772.17	0.01	0.0049
153 Niger	768	656	639	687.80	0.00	0.0041
154 Gambia	558	524	550	544.13	0.00	0.0035
155 Grenada	409	478	530	471.90	0.00	0.0034

Total trade in goods and services (million US$)	1998	1999	2000	average 1998–2000 share (%)	average 1998–2000 share (%)	2000
156 Djibouti	434	464	495	464.10	0.00	0.0032
157 Cape Verde	411	469	447	442.30	0.00	0.0029
158 Rwanda	430	455	434	440.03	0.00	0.0028
159 Central African Republic	443	398	411	417.23	0.00	0.0026
160 St. Vincent and the Grenadines	400	412	375	395.63	0.00	0.0024
161 Bhutan	332	371	436	379.50	0.00	0.0028
162 Solomon Islands	407	411	273	363.97	0.00	0.0018
163 St.-Kitts and Nevis	336	358	391	361.70	0.00	0.0025
164 Dominica	300	326	312	312.93	0.00	0.0020
165 Vanuatu	261	255	294	270.30	0.00	0.0019
166 Burundi	230	178	193	200.40	0.00	0.0012
167 Samoa	204	200	187	196.83	0.00	0.0012
168 Sierra Leone	166	150	238	184.70	0.00	0.0015
169 Guinea-Bissau	92	135	171	132.83	0.00	0.0011
170 Tonga	123	124	145	130.73	0.00	0.0009
171 *Federal Republic of Yugoslavia*	..	..	..	–	–	–
172 *Andorra*	..	..	..	–	–	–
173 *Liechtenstein*	..	..	..	–	–	–
TOTAL	13,441,042	13,905,731	15,511,380	14,286,051.25	100.0000	100.0000

Source: World Trade Organization, Statistics used for calculation of budget contributions.
Note: Countries that are underlined have observer status with the WTO by 2000

Commonwealth Small States

Annex 3

United Nations Economic Vulnerability Index
Sorted by Vulnerability

S.No.	Country name	EVI
1	Kiribati	74.32
2	Tuvalu	73.68
3	Chad	64.41
4	Liberia	63.62
5	Gambia	61.83
6	Cambodia	61.00
7	Saudi Arabia	60.01
8	Sao Tome and Principe	59.07
9	Niger	58.98
10	Benin	58.68
11	Tonga	58.63
12	Nigeria	58.41
13	Somalia	58.04
14	Seychelles	57.02
15	Saint Lucia	56.99
16	Cape Verde	56.98
17	Uganda	56.52
18	Dominica	56.05
19	Guinea-Bissau	55.91
20	Rwanda	55.85
21	Qatar	55.84
22	Equatorial Guinea	55.81
23	United Arab Emirates	55.55
24	Comoros	55.36
25	Angola	55.19
26	Libyan Arab Jamahiriya	54.01
27	Solomon Islands	53.93
28	Lesotho	53.11
29	Samoa	52.45
30	Democratic Republic of the Congo	51.89
31	Zambia	51.82
32	Saint Vincent & the Grenadines	51.65

| --- | --- | --- |
33	Burundi	51.55
34	Guyana	51.41
35	Brunei Darussalam	51.07
36	Syrian Arab Republic	51.04
37	Saint Kitts and Nevis	50.26
38	Iran (Islamic Republic of)	50.00
39	Gabon	49.96
40	Myanmar	49.82
41	Mongolia	49.73
42	Yemen	49.54
43	Oman	49.05
44	Mali	48.41
45	Bahrain	48.15
46	Congo (Republic of)	46.90
47	Djibouti	46.60
48	Sierra Leone	46.30
49	Guinea	45.77
50	Laos	45.65
51	Haiti	45.61
52	Dominican Republic	45.54
53	Bahamas	45.37
54	Togo	45.30
55	Afghanistan	44.89
56	Burkina Faso	44.58
57	Ethiopia	44.58
58	Sudan	44.45
59	Suriname	44.28
60	Grenada	43.67
61	Nicaragua	43.16
62	Ghana	43.13
63	Paraguay	43.05
64	Central African Republic	42.43
65	Bhutan	42.27
66	Lebanon	41.90
67	Malawi	41.57
68	Cuba	41.50
69	Mauritania	41.42

S.No.	Country name	EVI
70	Papua New Guinea	41.40
71	Vanuatu	41.31
72	Algeria	41.30
73	Antigua and Barbuda	41.20
74	Tunisia	41.08
75	Zimbabwe	40.94
76	Senegal	40.86
77	Belize	40.47
78	Trinidad and Tobago	39.03
79	Malta	38.98
80	Fiji Islands	37.39
81	Mozambique	37.36
82	Barbados	36.54
83	Nepal	36.37
84	Tanzania (United Republic of)	36.23
85	Honduras	35.73
86	Mauritius	35.21
87	Swaziland	35.02
88	Morocco	33.82
89	Venezuela	33.79
90	Côte d'Ivoire	32.81
91	Democratic People's Republic of Korea	32.31
92	Maldives	32.18
93	Cameroon	31.59
94	Jamaica	31.18
95	Singapore	31.02
96	Viet Nam	31.02
97	Cyprus	29.87
98	Ecuador	29.40
99	Panama	28.89
100	El Salvador	28.36
101	Kenya	27.75
102	Jordan	27.70
103	Bolivia	27.24
104	Eritrea	27.06
105	Madagascar	26.75
106	Sri Lanka	26.18

S.No.	Country name	EVI
107	Peru	26.13
108	Guatemala	25.99
109	Chile	25.09
110	Philippines	25.00
111	Egypt	24.85
112	Colombia	24.28
113	Uruguay	24.09
114	Costa Rica	23.99
115	Bangladesh	23.77
116	Israel	23.35
117	South Africa	22.43
118	Pakistan	22.21
119	Turkey	19.33
120	Thailand	17.92
121	Indonesia	17.38
122	Malaysia	16.55
123	Korea (Republic of)	16.09
124	Mexico	15.47
125	Argentina	15.22
126	Brazil	15.20
127	India	12.20
128	China	4.18

Source: United Nations, Economic and Social Council

3. Small Economies and Special and Differential Treatment: Strengthening the Evidence, Countering the Fallacies

Virginia Horscroft

1. Introduction

Small economies present a particular challenge to the multilateral trade regime: will it adjust to arrest their increasing marginalisation in world trade, a marginalisation that is undermining their development prospects significantly? This challenge questions whether emerging international trade rules are damaging the trade and development interests of small economies and, if so, whether derogations from those rules can avert such damage. An answer that more favourable treatment offers small economies the potential for a beneficial means of insertion into world markets is incomplete, however, without considering the negotiating context from which trade rules emerge. Whether or not favourable treatment is likely to result from the interstate bargaining process, determining the rules is the more problematic aspect of the challenge that small economies pose to the multilateral trading system.

This chapter argues that the peculiar economic characteristics of small economies combine to constrain their potential to benefit from the globalisation of markets under currently agreed trade rules. Though supported by recent empirical evidence, these arguments are contentious (see Briguglio, 1995, pp.1615–20; Encontre, 1999, p.265; WTO, 1999; UNCTAD, 2004a; and Grynberg, 2001a, p.289–91 for sympathetic reviews of small economies' special concerns, and Srinivasan, 1986; Streeten, 1993; Easterly and Kraay, 2001; and Page and Kleen, 2004, p.82 for opposing reviews) and require engaging with contrary views refuting that small size undermines trade competitiveness, that vulnerability to external economic shocks and natural disasters has real economic costs, and that small economies' characteristics are peculiar and worthy of specific responses. The chapter goes on to argue that, as the implications of emerging trade rules are realised, the marginalisation of small economies will be exacerbated. Whilst modifying multilateral trade rules is not the only initiative required to address the specific trade and development needs of small economies, it is argued to be vital. The likely economic decline of these states in the absence of favourable treatment will undermine the legitimacy of the multilateral trade regime, particularly its assumption that trade liberalisation on the basis of agreed rules is mutually advantageous. The more significant difficulty, this chapter suggests, is not demonstrating this predicament convincingly but achieving the necessary response as an outcome of trade negotiating processes. Here, the special characteristics of small economies undermine their bargaining power and likelihood of achieving beneficial outcomes from the interstate negotiating processes that determine global trade rules. The chapter concludes that it is not necessarily the case that agreed and emerging international trade rules are beneficial for all states: small economies can make a development case for more favourable treatment.

The economies considered 'small' for the purposes of this chapter are listed in Table 3.1, alongside their key economic indicators.[1]

2. The costs of being small

When trading internationally in a real world characterised by cross-border transaction costs, size **does** matter. Indeed being small, economically, is a meaningful concept only where transaction costs make national economies distinct entities. Thus, being small is integrally related to remoteness and insularity (Salmon, 2003, p.133): a small nation perfectly integrated into a larger contiguous market may not be small economically (Winters and Martins, 2004a, p.148), but a remote or insular nation facing significant transport costs may be. Once the size of its domestic market matters, the trade predicament of a small economy will be compounded by the importance of economies of scale in production (Winters and Martins, 2004a, p.8). Where transaction costs impede trade, small economies will have limited opportunities to benefit from globalising markets.

To understand the logic of the predicament facing small developing economies, consider a state with a small domestic market that faces significant trade transaction costs. Its small domestic market arises from its small population and associated low total GDP. Being small contributes to high transport costs via low and infrequent volumes – costs exacerbated by remoteness or insularity (see Briguglio, 1995, p.1617). Simple economic models can demonstrate that transport costs can stop trade from being feasible in such scenarios (Winters and Martins, 2004a, pp.3–8; see also Srinivasan, 1986, p.211). If limited trade continues, imports of production inputs will bear an excess cost from transport and, where transaction costs prohibit such imports, inputs will be produced domestically at high per unit costs given the small domestic market and consequent inability to exploit economies of scale. Similarly, non-tradable goods like roads and the protection of property rights will be produced domestically at high per unit costs. Wherever higher production and export costs outweigh small states' differential advantages over competitors, even in areas of comparative advantage, their exports will require premium prices in world markets to sell at all (Winters and Martins, 2004a, p.1).

Table 3.1 Small economies and key economic indicators

Small Economy	Population 2003 ('000s)	Land Area (km²)	Total GDP 2003 ($US millions)	World Trade Share 2000 (%)	UN EVI[a] 2000 (ranking)	Cmwlth CVI[b] 2000 (ranking)	Per Capita GNI 2003 ($US)	LDC	SIDS	WTO
Antigua and Barbuda	79	442	757	0.0061	73	8	9,160		☑	☑
Barbados	271	430	2,628	0.0183	82	37	9,270		☑	☑
Belize	259	22,696	928	0.0057	77	22	3,190			☑
Bhutan	874	47,000	645	0.0028	65	20	660	☑		obs
Botswana	1,722	581,730	7,388	0.0350	16	29	3,430	LLDC	☑	☑
Cape Verde	470	4,033	831	0.0029	16	23	1,490	☑	☑	obs
Comoros	600	2,235	323		24	16	450	☑	☑	
Djibouti	705	23,200	625	0.0032	47	15	910	☑		☑
Dominica	71	751	255	0.0020	18	6	3,360		☑	☑
Equatorial Guinea	494	28,051	2,894		22	7	930	☑	obs	
Fiji	835	18,274	2,251	0.0155	80	25	2,360		☑	☑
Gabon	1,344	267,668	5,605	0.0327	39	54	3,580			☑
Gambia	1,421	11,295	386	0.0035	5	10	310	☑		☑
Grenada	105	344	439	0.0034	60	11	3,790		☑	☑
Guinea-Bissau	1,489	36,125	236	0.0011	19		140	☑	☑	☑
Guyana	769	214,969	742	0.0095	34	17	900			☑
Jamaica	2,640	10,990	7,817	0.0506	94	53	2,760		☑	☑
Kiribati	96	726	58		1	4	880	☑	☑	
Lesotho	1,793	30,355	1,135	0.0065	28	31	590	☑	☑	☑
Maldives	293	298	696	0.0058	92	9	2,300	☑	☑	☑
Marshall Islands	53	181	106				2,710		☑	☑

Small Economy	Population 2003 ('000s)	Land Area (km²)	Total GDP 2003 ($US millions)	World Trade Share 2000 (%)	UN EVI[a] 2000 (ranking)	Cmwlth CVI[b] 2000 (ranking)	Per Capita GNI 2003 ($US)	LDC	SIDS	WTO
Mauritius	1,225	2,040	5,225	0.0342	86	47	4,090		☑	☑
Federated States of Micronesia	125	702	241				2,090		☑	
Namibia	2,015	824,292	4,658	0.0263		46	1,870			☑
Nauru	13	21							☑	
Palau	20	459	132				7,500		☑	
Papua New Guinea	5,502	462,840	3,395	0.0301	70	55	510		☑	☑
St. Kitts and Nevis	47	261	370	0.0025	37	13	6,880		☑	☑
St. Lucia	161	539	693	0.0050	15	18	4,050		☑	☑
St. Vincent and the Grenadines	109	388	371	0.0024	32	14	3,300		☑	☑
Samoa	178	2,831	323	0.0012	29	5	1,600	☑	☑	obs
São Tomé and Principe	157	964	54		8	1	320	☑	☑	obs
Seychelles	84	455	720	0.0064	14	21	7,480		☑	obs
Solomon Islands	457	28,896	257	0.0018	27	12	600	☑	☑	☑
Suriname	438	163,265	952	0.0058	59	24	1,990		☑	☑
Swaziland	1,106	17,364	1,845	0.0127	87	19	1,350	LLDC	☑	☑
Timor-Leste	810	14,874	314				430	☑	☑	
Tonga	102	650	163	0.0009	11	3	1,490		☑	obs
Trinidad and Tobago	1,313	5,130	10,201	0.0408	78	62	7,260		☑	☑
Tuvalu	10	26			2			☑	☑	
Vanuatu	210	12,189	283	0.0019	71	2	1,180	☑	☑	obs

Small Economy	Population 2003 ('000s)	Land Area (km²)	Total GDP 2003 ($US millions)	World Trade Share 2000 (%)	UN EVI[a] 2000 (ranking)	Cmwlth CVI[b] 2000 (ranking)	Per Capita GNI 2003 ($US)	LDC	SIDS	WTO
Averages-										
Small economies	743	69,268	1,716	0.3766 (Sum)			2,748			
All least-developed countries	14,348	411,629	4,736				310			
All middle-income countries	32,151	740,280	64,468				1,920			
High-income OECD countries	38,068	1,265,457	1,177,779				29,310			
World	30,152	626,436	174,790				5,500			

LLDC - recognised by the UN as a landlocked developing country, but not as a least developed country (LDC) obs - country has 'Observer' status in the WTO

[a] United Nations 'Economic Vulnerability 'Index'

[b] Commonwealth Secretariat 'Commonwealth Vulnerability Index'

Source: World Bank (2004), Commonwealth Secretariat (2003), Atkins et al (2000), WTO (2004a), UNCTAD (2003c) and UNCTAD (2004c)

Comprehensive data have now been compiled substantiating this trade predicament of small economies. Analysis by Winters and Martins (2004a) provides strong evidence that businesses in small states face large and significant cost inflation factors relative to firms in the median state, sufficient to undermine their potential for competitiveness even in areas of comparative advantage (Winters and Martins (2004a, pp.130-47), using various indicators of policy quality, find no evidence that economic policy is worse is small states than in large, and thus reject the hypothesis that the revealed inefficiencies are self-inflicted.). Summary results, presented in Table 3.2, indicate that cost inflation factors in micro states exceed 50 per cent in six of 11 key production inputs, and for small states exceed 30 per cent in five of the inputs, relative to the median state. These detrimental competitiveness implications are captured in the cost inflation factors calculated for representative electronics, garments and tourism businesses (Table 3.3): garments manufacturing costs in micro states are estimated to exceed those in the median state by 36.3 per cent, whilst tourism services costs in small states are estimated to exceed those in the median state by 28.5 per cent. Winters and Martins (2004a, pp.118-24) illustrate the damaging implications of their findings by calculating the resultant returns to factors of production in the likely scenario that small states are price-takers in world markets, taking import costs as given and receiving the world price for their exports. Using the example of electronics assembly in a micro state, if infrastructure services costs are also fixed (Winters and Martins (2004a, p.120) argue that this assumption is reasonable, given that the costs recorded in the dataset approximate general equilibrium results.), exports could not be competitive

Table 3.2. Production cost inflation in micro and small economies

Area of cost[a]	Micro[b]	Small[c]
Airfreight average	31.8	4.1
Seafreight average	219.6	70.5
Unskilled wages average	60.1	31.6
Semi-skilled wages average	22.4	12.1
Skilled wages average	38.0	20.3
Telephone marginal costs	98.5	47.2
Electricity marginal costs	93.1	47.0
Water marginal costs	0.0	0.0
Fuel average	53.8	28.3
Personal air travel average	115.7	56.8
Land rent average	-3.5	-17.2

[a] All figures show the percentage deviation of costs from those in the median economy
[b] 'Micro' economy estimates are based on Anguilla (population approximately 12,000)
[c] 'Small' economy estimates are based on Vanuatu (population approximately 200,000)
[source uses 'Very Small' for Vanuatu estimates, and 'Small' for economies the size of Singapore (population approximately 4 million), which well exceeds 'small' in this paper]
Source: Winters and Martins (2004a: 102-3)

Commonwealth Small States

Table 3.3 Cost inflation factors in micro and small economies

Industry[a]	Micro[b]	Small[c]
Electronic Assembly	36.4	14.3
Clothing	36.3	14.3
Hotels and Tourism	57.5	28.5

[a, b, c] See Table 3.2
Source: Winters and Martins (2004a: 119)

Table 3.4 Penalties to value-added in micro and small economies

Factor of Production Bearing Penalty[a]	Electronics		Clothing		Tourism	
	Micro[b]	Small[c]	Micro[b]	Small[c]	Micro[b]	Small[c]
All Domestic Supplies	-38.8	-11.6	-40.1	-12.0	-36.2	-17.4
Value Added	-88.0	-29.2	-86.0	-28.6	-71.9	-34.0
Capital	-245.1	-91.8	-263.9	-99.9	-202.1	-98.4
Labour	-175.5	-62.5	-161.0	-57.3	-116.5	-56.6

[a, b, c] See Table 3.2
Source: Winters and Martins (2004a: 119)

unless capital made losses larger than its profits in the median state or, if capital were remunerated, would not be competitive even if labour earned zero wages. Even in small states, if capital is the residual factor, it must earn near-zero returns if exports in any of the three example industries are to be competitive at world prices (see Table 3.4). Winters and Martins (2004a, p.119) describe their findings as 'devastating'.

These data make concrete the substantial economic costs of being small and remote (Winters and Martins, 2004a, p.102), challenging the argument that being small is not a disadvantage in a globalising world (see Page and Kleen, 2004, p.82; and Read, 2004, p.368). They also challenge ubiquitous assertions that services are less affected by transport and scale costs in small economies (see World Bank, 2002a, p.16; and Page and Kleen, 2004, pp.81-83), offering evidence that services exports can be subject to even higher cost inflation factors than goods exports (Winters and Martins, 2004a, pp.113-6). The findings demonstrate the insufficiency of policy recommendations for small states to specialise in their areas of comparative advantage and trade their way to higher welfare levels. Indeed, argue Winters and Martins (2004b, p.4), comparative advantage need not be enough. Small states, like all states, have comparative advantages; what sets them apart is that even if they specialise in these, trade transaction costs and the inherent inefficiencies of small size may prevent trade from being remunerative. Without remunerative returns to capital, small states will be unable to attract investment; without remunerative returns to labour, human development will be impeded (Winters and Martins, 2004a, pp.119-20). Rather than being 'extreme' (Page and Kleen, 2004, p.79), this analysis simply uses new empirical evidence to verify an existing possibility within conventional economic theory. Small states do have comparative advantages, but these need not be 'operational' (Winters and Martins, 2004a, p.1).

These findings also clarify the types of economic opportunities small states can exploit. Where small economies face world market prices for their exports they are unlikely to be competitive, ruling out the export of generic goods and services. Their export potential is in markets where forms of rent exist or can be created for exploitation. Argues Grynberg (2001a, p.292), '...while in other economies these quasi-rents constitute a basis for high profits, in small states they are often a precondition for productive commercial activity as rents are necessary to cover inherently high operating costs'. Examples include scarcity rents in commodity markets, for example Solomon Islands' timber (Grynberg (2001a, pp.291-3) and Encontre (1999, p.267) provide overviews of small economies' rent-based exports), niche market rents from location-specific factors like tropical beaches for tourism in the Caribbean and time zones for data processing in Fiji, and niche market rents from branding as in the cases of Jamaican Rum and Fiji Water (competitiveness in most other exports from small states relies on institutions like trade preferences and tax concessions, discussed below). Rents, however, can be transient (Armstrong and Read, 2002, pp.2-3; and Grynberg, 2001a, pp.293-5). Encontre (1999, p.261) appraises small economies' experience with niche markets as being typically unsuccessful, characterised by commercial ventures with very short life-spans. Thus, whilst small economies certainly have opportunities to benefit from globalisation, competitiveness requires their productive activities to be limited to those serving specialist markets where shifting rents can be created and exploited, so they are far from having stable foundations for their economic development.

At the same time, small economies have the most to gain from international trade (Streeten, 1993, p.198; and Read, 1999, p.9). Their small domestic markets, narrow resource endowments and inability to exploit economies of scale mean that the welfare they can attain under autarky is very low indeed (see, for example, Read, 2004, p.365; Encontre, 1999, pp.268-9; and Burki, 2001, p.10). International trade should offer these states the opportunity to overcome their small size and increase their welfare, but this section has argued that nothing in economic theory guarantees that they will be able to operationalise this potential in the presence of significant transaction costs (Winters and Martins, 2004a, pp.3-8). Their possible marginalisation in the face of globalisation is a pressing concern, particularly because it is they that are most dependent on international trade to improve their economic welfare (Winters and Martins, 2004a, pp.1-2). Small economies have both limited opportunities to benefit from globalising markets and the most to lose from such marginalisation (see Grynberg and Razzaque, 2003, p.30).

3. The costs of vulnerability

Small economies are particularly vulnerable to external shocks from world markets and natural disasters (Atkins et al., 2001, p.63), because of the severe constraints they face in diversifying their production and trade (Briguglio, 1995, p.1616; and Jansen,

2004, p.14; Grynberg and Razzaque, 2003, p.53; Read, 1999, p.7; and Briguglio, 1995, p.1616 argue that small economies' typically limited resource endowments exacerbate this lack of diversification). Thus Atkins et al. (2000, p.1) state, 'There is growing international recognition that high economic exposure, remoteness and isolation, and proneness to natural disasters have a debilitating effect on small economies, despite the fact that some of them exhibit relatively high per capita incomes'. Indeed, their vulnerability index ranks 27 small economies among the 30 most vulnerable developing countries (Atkins et al., 2000, pp.25–33). This section will explore the adverse economic impact of vulnerability on small economies.

3.1 Vulnerability to external economic shocks

A number of small economies' characteristics make them both highly exposed to external economic shocks and extremely vulnerable to consequent adverse effects. First, the limited production possibilities of their domestic economies make small states highly dependent on trade (Briguglio, 1995, p.1616), with trade accounts typically very open (see Figure 3.1) (see also World Bank, 2002b, p.18). Secondly, their production activities and more so their exports are highly concentrated in a very small number of products (see Figure 3.2), with Jansen (2004, p.14) arguing that small economies' export concentrations are very similar to those in least-developed countries (LDCs). Thirdly, small economies' exports are directed to a very limited number of markets (Dehn, 2000c, pp.10, 22; World Bank, 2002b, p.18; UNCTAD, 2003a, p.7; and Jansen, 2004, pp.1, 6). Fourthly, generally the products in which small economies' exports are concentrated are commodities (Jansen, 2004, p.12). UNCTAD (2003a: 5), finds that for the subset of small island only do they face significant challenges in diversifying their

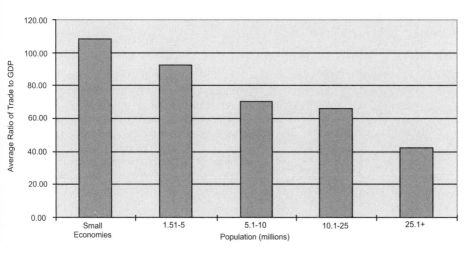

Figure 3.1. Openness to trade in small economies.

Note: The 'small economies' category refers to those countries listed in Table 3.1 for which data were available; the number of observations in each category is 38, 41, 30, 32 and 34 respectively

Source: Jansen (2004) and author's own calculations

economic activity and export bases (Jansen, 2004, pp.6-7, 14), the World Bank (2002b, pp.18-9) argues that small economies have '…a smaller pool of human and institutional resources to draw on to help predict, mitigate, and manage the effects of shocks'. Their small financial systems, with little liquidity and constrained access to international capital, also make it difficult for small states to implement macroeconomic policies to smooth the impact of shocks (see World Bank, 2001).

This exposure and vulnerability has a destabilising impact on small economies (Auffret, 2003a, pp.4, 7; Jansen, 2004, p.1; and World Bank, 2002b, p.21). Atkins et al. (2000, pp.5-9) find the income volatility of small states to be the highest in the developing world. Empirical evidence also demonstrates that small states' openness to trade increases the volatility of their output levels and growth rates (Easterly and Kraay, 2001, p.104; World Bank, 2002b, p.18; and Jansen, 2004, pp.1, 6). Their high export concentrations are found to play a major role in exacerbating the income volatility of small states, through terms-of-trade volatility (Jansen, 2004, pp.9-12). Also, extreme concentrations in commodity exports are shown to exacerbate volatility (Dehn, 2000c, p.10). It is widely recognised that such volatility of income and consumption aggregates *does* matter for economic growth and welfare (see Jansen (2004, p.1), who cites the relevant evidence from the literature, as well as Auffret (2003a, pp.4, 7); Collier and Dehn (2001, p.2); Atkins et al. (2000, p.7); and Easterly and Kraay (2001, pp.104-5). On terms of trade shocks, see Dehn (2000a, p.23). On uncertainty and private investment, see the different findings of Dehn (2000b, p.3) and Jansen (2004, pp.3-4). Whether or not other characteristics of small economies work to counteract the negative growth impact of volatility[2] makes it no less true that high volatility in key macroeconomic aggregates like income and consumption affects growth negatively (Read, 2004, p.369). And as Read (2004, p.372) argues, small states' vulnerability to external economic

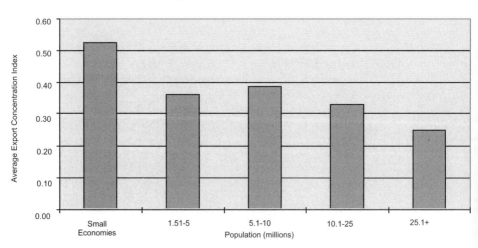

Figure 3.2. Export concentration in small economies.

Note: The 'small economies' category refers to those countries listed in Table 3.1 for which data were available; the number of observations in each category is 27, 33, 24, 30 and 31 respectively

Source: Jansen (2004) and author's own calculations

shocks will only *increase* with globalisation and small states' greater integration into world markets.

3.2 Vulnerability to natural disasters

The development prospects of small economies are also constrained by the 'multifaceted' welfare effects of natural disasters (Charveriat, 2000, p.10), to which they are both highly exposed and peculiarly vulnerable. Small states' exposure is geographic, from their typical location within hurricane and cyclone belts, and sometimes seismic activity zones (Charveriat, 2000, pp.47-56; Freeman et al., 2003, p.8; Rasmussen, 2004, p.5; Atkins et al., 2000, p.3; and Auffret, 2003a, p.13). Small states' vulnerability is socioeconomic, arising from the interaction of a number of their characteristics. First, frequently small size means that natural disasters devastate entire countries, hence aggregate effects are marked relative to large states where these are mitigated by regional variations in the impact on economic activity (Charveriat, 2000, pp.21, 39). Secondly, dependence on agriculture for output and exports increases the economic damage of natural disasters, particularly weather events (Charveriat, 2000, p.21). Thirdly, small economies' narrow resource bases and undiversified economic activities and exports concentrate risk (Freeman et al., 2003, p.9). Fourthly, their relatively low incomes impede household and state expenditure capacities on preventative measures. Fifthly, inefficient, incomplete or entirely absent insurance markets reduce scope for managing risk (Rasmussen, 2004, p.4; World Bank, 2001, p.12; and Gurenko and Lester, 2004, p.3).

The exposure and vulnerability of small developing states is evident from the data on natural disasters summarised in Table 3.5. Small states are widely recognised as being the most vulnerable to natural disasters because of their exposure, having the highest frequency of natural disasters in the world relative to population or land area (Rasmussen, 2004, p.3; Encontre, 1999, p.262; International Workshop, 2004, p.2; Atkins et al., 2000, p.30; World Bank, 2002b, p.18; and IMF, 2003, p.7). As these states develop, the economic cost of their natural disasters will rise 'exponentially' (Benson and Clay, 2003, p.76). That prospect, combined with predicted increases in the frequency and intensity of damaging weather events, leaves SIDS estimated to be facing annual losses from natural disasters exceeding 10 per cent of their GDP by 2050 (Freeman et al., 2003, p.8).

Empirical evidence on the economic impacts of natural disasters in small economies shows the significant challenge to trade and development that these pose (for evidence summarised in this paragraph, see Rasmussen (2004, pp.5-11); Freeman et al. (2003, p.11); Charveriat (2000, pp.15-21, 36-9); Benson et al. (2001, pp.12-7); ECLAC and IDB (2000, pp.7-12); World Bank (2002b, pp.25-7); and IMF (2003, pp.10-11). Typically, disasters are associated with immediate sharp contractions in output and GDP growth, contractions exacerbated by the share of agriculture in economic activity. External trade balances worsen substantially, both from the shocks to exports arising from output shocks and damage to trade infrastructure, and from surges in imports

Table 3.5. The extreme vulnerability of small economies to natural disasters 1970-2003

Country grouping^a	Incidence of natural disasters			Population impact of natural disasters	
	Number of events^b	Events/population (index)	Events/land area (index)	Number of events with record of affected persons	Total affected persons (percentage of 2003 population)
Small economies	432	1,229	290	303	67.8
of which:Africa	177	1,051	174	117	93.2
Caribbean/Latin America	96	1,384	697	67	53.2
Pacific	149	1,652	500	110	47.9
SIDS	285	1,495	882	204	46.6
Other least-developed countries	1,446	175	126	1,130	109.5
Other developing countries	4,126	74	93	3,130	101.1
Developed countries	1,450	140	84	748	5.4
World	7,454	100	100	5,311	88.6

a Only countries with at least one natural disaster during 1970-2003 are included, yielding: 37 small economies of which 13 are in Africa, 11 are in the Caribbean or Latin America, 10 are in the Pacific, and 26 are SIDS; 34 other LDCs; 89 other developing (or transition) countries; and 23 developed countries. Data for country groupings reflect weighted averages of the data for the individual countries therein, calculated on the basis of aggregate group data, rather than reflecting simple averages of individual country data.

b Only natural disasters involving at least 10 people being killed, at least 100 people being affected, a call for international assistance, or the declaration of a state of emergency are recorded in EM-DAT; 2004 data are excluded because they are preliminary as yet.

Source:EM-DAT (2005), World Bank (2004) and UNCTAD (2004c); author's own calculations

occurring to underpin reconstruction. Current account deficits worsen, sometimes to 'staggering' dimensions (see, in particular, Rasmussen, 2004, p.8). Public finances worsen also, from higher expenditure requirements and a reduced revenue base. Generally, increased foreign aid and official assistance are insufficient to offset these fiscal impacts. (Freeman et al. (2003, p.14) cite Inter-American Development Bank evidence that an average of 8.6 per cent, and at most 25 per cent, of direct disaster costs are covered by international assistance. Dependence on overseas assistance is itself a form of risk exposure, increasingly unwise as real official development assistance declines, according to Charveriat, 2000, p.1). As a result of foreign borrowing to fund fiscal and current account deficits, typically external debt to GDP ratios increase. Frequently inflation also becomes a concern. Although the proprortion of the population affected by natural disasters in small states is relatively low, it is a significant real cost to the labour force nonetheless. These severe macroeconomic consequences are, of course, in addition to the psychological and social effects of human suffering (see especially Charveriat, 2000, pp.10–12), the impact of which typically is most acute for the poor (see, in particular, Freeman et al., 2003, p.10; and Charveriat, 2000, p.26).

Furthermore, natural disasters can have significant economic effects on small states beyond the short term. Incomplete reconstruction of damaged capital will necessarily reduce future growth, a growth effect that can emerge from a shortfall or delay in reconstruction financing (Auffret, 2003a, p.17; ECLAC and IDB, 2000, pp.13–14; IMF, 2003, p.9; and Charveriat, 2000, pp.13, 22–4). Reconstruction may not even be possible, where factor endowments such as coral reefs are destroyed (Charveriat, 2000, p.23; and ECLAC and IDB, 2000, p.15). The redirection of capital from planned projects to reconstruction imposes an opportunity cost on productive capacity and growth, in the likely event that the marginal improvement of reconstructed over pre-disaster capital is less than would have been the rate of return from the planned projects forgone (Charveriat, 2000, p.23). Moreover, risk reassessments and disaster-induced solvency problems may reduce the investment attractiveness and capacity of vulnerable regions (Auffret, 2003a, p.28; Freeman et al., 2003, p.13; and Charveriat, 2000, pp.23–5). Damage to education and health infrastructure, together with household-level effects reducing access to these services, reduce human capital formation – a foundation for future economic growth (Freeman et al., 2003, p.13; Charveriat, 2000, p.23; and Encontre, 1999, p.262). Vulnerability to natural disasters is also strongly correlated with income and consumption volatility, with consequent welfare effects (Rasmussen, 2004, p.11; Auffret, 2003a, pp.4, 7, 15; and World Bank, 2002b, p.45). In addition, detrimental long-term effects arise from the increases in poverty typically associated with natural disasters ECLAC and IDC, 2000, p.16; and Charveriat, 2000, p.26). There is also evidence that worsening public finances go beyond short-term fiscal deficits, to significant reallocations of public resources away from capital expenditure and social sector programmes (Benson and Clay, 2003, pp.77, 83. See also ECLAC and IDB, 2000, p.15; Charveriat, 2000, p.23; Gurenko and Lester, 2004, p.3; IMF, 2003, p.4; Freeman et al., 2003, p.13; and evidence of the mirroring of this behaviour by donors in Benson and Clay, 2003, p.76). Finally, higher external debt increases the future risk exposure of small states, expanding the debt servicing drain on public finances and possibly increasing the risk premiums that financiers demand (Charveriat, 2000, pp.13, 24; Freeman et al. 2003, p.11-13; and ECLAC and IDB, 2000, p.15).

These considerations make the argument that natural disasters do not affect long-term economic growth highly improbable.[3] If there has been little empirical evidence of long-term lower economic growth in disaster-prone states, not only is it now emerging,[4] but this is largely the result of there being little empirical work at all on the long-term impacts of natural disasters (Rasmussen, 2004, p.11).

Critics contend also that vulnerability to natural disasters is endogenous, implying that policy remedies are readily available to small states at reasonable cost (see Page and Kleen, 2004, p.79). However, small economies face significant impediments in reducing their vulnerability to natural disasters. The constrained governance capacities of state institutions make problematic the formulation and enforcement of vulnerability-reducing regulations (on these prescriptions, see Rasmussen, 2004, p.14; and IMF, 2003, p.13). Continuously shifting vulnerabilities, arising from altered exposure due to climatic changes and from altered vulnerability due to socioeconomic change, exacerbate governance problems by requiring frequent re-evaluations of risks and appropriate preventative measures (see IPCC (2001) on climate change, in particular for SIDS; and Benson and Clay (2003, pp.78-80) and Benson et al. (2001, p.88) on changing socioeconomic vulnerabilities). Moreover, the costs of preventative measures can be 'inordinately' expensive (Freeman et al., 2003, p.16). Market inefficiencies ensure that disaster insurance, if available at all, is highly volatile and typically requires prohibitively high premiums in small states (Rasmussen, 2004, pp.12-13; Freeman et al., 2003, p.17; World Bank, 2001, pp.9-10; and Auffret, 2003b, p.13. See also Benson and Clay, 2003, p.78; and Gurenko and Lester, 2004, p.2). Standard policy prescriptions for economic diversification into areas of comparative advantage (see Rasmussen, 2004, p.14; IMF, 2003, p.8; and Freeman et al., 2003, p.15). are of little utility where small size constrains diversification (Charveriat, 2000, p.22), comparative advantages are held in activities – like agriculture and tourism – particularly vulnerable to natural disasters, and more disaster-resistant activities like manufacturing are uncompetitive. As with external economic shocks, therefore, small economies face substantial obstacles in attempting to reduce their vulnerability to natural disasters.

4. The costs of governance

A very important scale economy that small states cannot exploit is governance (see Schahczenski, 1990; and Braun et al., 2002; see Srinivasan, 1986, p.211 for an opposing view). Whilst poor governance, in terms of democracy, stability and the rule of law, is not a pressing issue for small states (see Table 3.6) (see also Winters and Martins, 2004a, pp.130-47; and Collier and Dollar, 2001, p.16. On the relationship between good governance and economic success see Burnside and Dollar, 1997), policy capacity and the costs of best practice are. The substantial capacity requirements and costs of implementing international trade agreements (see Finger and Schuler, 2002, p.501; Michalopoulos, 2002, p.69; and Armstrong and Read, 2002, p.16) are a severe concern for small developing countries, whose human and financial resources are dwarfed by the complex array of international trade disciplines with which they must work (on implementation costs, see Finger and Schuler, 2002, p.501). This section will focus on a further relationship between costly governance and trade capacity critical in small states: the way in which state institutions augment the trade capacity of the private sector.

Economies of scale in governance arise from the population-invariant minimum set of responsibilities a state has towards its citizens and with respect to other states, government functions typically exhibiting high fixed and low marginal costs (Briguglio, 1995, p.1617; Farrugia, 1993, p.221; Encontre, 1999, p.265; and Armstrong and Read, 2002, p.2). Governance in small states is thus generally more costly per capita than in large states (see Hausmann (2004) for evidence of the poor performance of independent states in the Caribbean relative to their dependent neighbours, and Bertram (2004, pp.345-50) for similar findings in the Pacific). Both Murray (1981, pp.245-7) and Armstrong and Read (2002, p.2-3) argue that conventional policy and economic models assume, without making explicit, a minimum state size and administrative resource base which small states fall below. Frequently, these prohibitive costs of adequate governance are mitigated by understaffing among professionals and a reduction in the scope of state responsibilities (Farrugia, 1993, p.222; and Gay, 2004, p.4). Small populations, especially those experiencing skilled labour emigration, present a significant challenge to the recruitment of qualified and experienced officials for public institutions (Briguglio, 1995, p.1617; Murray, 1981, pp.250-4; and Gay, 2004, p.15). The result is 'problematic governance capacity': state officials are severely overstretched relative to their responsibilities, and sometimes relative to their skills and experience, whilst even these limited state responsibilities may be inadequate to the needs of the population in the current global context.

Small states' governance constraints affect the trade capacity of their private sectors, especially given the latter's inexperience in international trade and lack of required

Table 3.6. 2002 governance indicators for small economies

Governance indicator[a]	Observations[b]	Average[c]
Voice and accountability	40	0.28
Political stability	29	0.32
Government effectiveness	37	-0.17
Regulatory quality	38	-0.22
Rule of law	38	-0.06
Control of corruption	38	-0.09

[a] Estimates range from -2.5 to +2.5, with estimates for the full sample averaging zero
[b] Number of observations varies with missing data
[c] Simple average of estimated scores, none of which are significantly different from zero even at the 10% level
Source: World Bank Institute (2002) and author's own calculations

entrepreneurial skills (see World Bank, 2002a, p.29 on the entrepreneurial skills base in Pacific Islands). For example, if a small state's facilitation of trade is ineffective, consumers and exporters will bear costs arising from inefficient customs, standards and quarantine regulations. States may be unable to facilitate the extremely costly certification systems vital for niche marketing (see Vossenaar (2004, pp.74-82) on barriers to entry in niche markets; and Saqib (2003, pp.270-1) on costly certification). Government responsibilities may not feasibly extend to the provision of access to overseas market information - including regulatory information - to their private sectors (English and de Wulf, 2002, pp.160-2; Wilson, 2002, p.428; and Grynberg, 2001a, p.294). That information is a non-rival good that is otherwise extremely costly to individual entrepreneurs, yet is vital for access to transitory niches. Small states may also underachieve in negotiating the product - especially commodity - pathways that are the means by which their private sectors can realise market access abroad (see Wilson (2002, pp.431-2) on technical barriers to trade, and Malua (2003, pp.185, 187) and Vossenaar (2004, p.79) for case studies).

Their problematic governance capacities make it difficult for small states to reduce trade transaction costs through trade facilitation and to negotiate product pathways for their exports - state activities that are vital to the trade capacities of their private sectors.

5. Characteristics in combination

Thus far, this chapter has presented arguments and evidence regarding the significant economic costs imposed on small states by their size, vulnerability to external economic shocks and natural disasters, and problematic governance capacities. In each case, it is through a **combination** of many characteristics of small states that these costs are generated (see also Salmon (2002, p.4) on this point). The small size of an economy, for example, is important only in the context of trade transaction costs such as those arising from remoteness and insularity. Small economies are highly vulnerable to external economic shocks where they are open to trade and have undiversified exports. Similarly, their vulnerability to substantial economic damage from natural disasters results from small economies' exposure to such disasters combined with small land areas, large agricultural shares of production, and incomplete insurance markets. Finally, small economies' governance capacities are problematic for trade in cases where indivisibilities exist in trade facilitation and skilled human capital is scarce.

It follows that cross-country econometric analyses regressing economic growth on any one characteristic - distances to major markets, population sizes, numbers of natural disasters, and so forth - may not yield significant results. Large contiguous states with great distances between capitals will offset the detrimental effects of distance for small insular states. Small states integrated into and contiguous with regional markets will offset the detrimental effects of small domestic markets for small remote states. Large developed states experiencing many natural disasters will offset the detrimental growth impacts of natural disasters on developing countries with small land areas. Because it is combinations of characteristics that engender disadvantages, it is erroneous to treat these characteristics as being separable for analytical purposes (for an example of such an approach, see Page and Kleen, 2004, p.80). For the same reason, it is mistaken to argue as Srinivasan (1986, p.217) does that small economies do not face a special predicament because, 'Many of the problems allegedly faced by small economies are...not peculiar to them', a position echoed by Page and Kleen (2004, p.80). Instead, since it is the combination of many characteristics of small economies that yields the significant economic costs that undermine their trade prospects, states exhibiting those multiple characteristics have a strong case for special consideration. The interaction of characteristics deriving from small size, vulnerability, and governance capacity impedes the potential of small economies to integrate into globalising markets on a competitive basis, and thereby mitigate the constraints on their development posed by size.

6. The limits of regionalism

The standard recommendation for small states to mitigate the deleterious effects of their small size, vulnerability, and governance capacities, is regionalism (see Streeten, 1993, p.197). Thus, for example, the integration of small economies into regional markets is argued to overcome the limits of small domestic markets and the constraints on their exploiting economies of scale (Hausmann, 2004; and Streeten, 1993, pp.197–8). Regional cooperation is meant to mitigate small states' vulnerability to natural disasters, particularly regarding the costs of preventative actions and the capacity to absorb damage. Regional government is proffered as a solution to indivisibilities in governance via the exploitation of scale economies and the regional provision of public goods and infrastructure (Streeten, 1993, p.197; and Schiff and Andriamananjara, 1998, pp.2–3). As Murray (1981, p.247) argues, small states are to be 'scaled up' to suit existing 'doctrines of effective administration'. In the extreme, small states are recommended to cease to be states (see Srinivasan, 1986, p.211). Consequently, the existence of the opportunity for regional integration is argued to make persistent small size an endogenous characteristic, a policy choice for which small states should bear the costs.

It is beyond contention that regionalism has much to offer small economies. It is also readily apparent that small states have recognised these advantages and forged various regional groupings incorporating, to different degrees, integrated markets, natural disaster cooperation, and elements of regional governance (see, for example, South Pacific Forum Secretariat, 2001). However, there are strict limitations on the extent to which regionalism can **solve** the trade predicaments of small economies.

First, full market integration among a region of small economies will not necessarily make those states better off, or more able to compete in global markets. The most obvious reason is trade diversion, with economic models demonstrating that the integration of a group of small economies may reduce their aggregate welfare (Schiff, 1996, pp.11, 32; Read, 1999, p.15; and World Bank, 2002a, pp.10–11). Empirical analysis also calls into question the degree to which geographical regions of small states can be assumed to be regions in economic terms. Bertram (2004, pp.345, 352), for example, provides evidence that the small economies of the Pacific do not form an economic region, and cites similar evidence for geographic regions elsewhere (see also Encontre, 1999, p.265). Eliminating trade barriers, even achieving regulatory harmonisation, will not necessarily eliminate trade transaction costs and forge a large single market in any of the main geographic regions where small economies are concentrated. Substantial transaction costs will persist from remoteness and insularity; aggregating populations yields numbers not only still small in global terms, but also misleadingly implies a single domestic market. On this basis, the World Bank (2002a, pp.7–8) criticises regional integration among Pacific Islands because it will yield a still small 'aggregate' market dispersed over hundreds of islands with extremely high intra-regional transport costs, and virtually identical patterns of economic activity and comparative advantage.

Secondly, regional cooperation is unlikely to alleviate fully the economic costs of vulnerability to natural disasters. Small states are already cooperating to enhance their capacity to provide public goods such as early warning systems, cooperation which could increase to encompass risk pooling (World Bank, 2001, p.13). The degree of risk covariance within regions, however, together with their relatively low income levels throughout, must constrain the potential of regionalism to enhance coping strategies. Moreover, the extremely similar patterns of economic activity and exports within regions of small states suggest that mitigating vulnerability through diversification at a regional level will be problematic. Additionally, the most significant limitations on disaster insurance appear to arise not from inadequate regional cooperation but from weaknesses in global reinsurance markets (see Freeman et al., 2003, p.17; Rasmussen, 2004, p.10; and World Bank, 2001, p.10).

Thirdly, regional government is not a complete solution for governance problems in small states. It offers, and is being used to produce substantial economies of scale in policy development and in negotiations with states outside the region (Winters and Martins, 2004a, p.148; Schiff and Andriamananjara, 1998, pp.2, 29; and South Pacific Forum Secretariat, 2001, pp.507–9). However, the dispersion of regional populations among remote insular land areas inhibits the potential for the efficient regional provision of public goods and infrastructure. Additionally, the recruitment problems posed by small populations and skilled labour emigration are mitigated – not eliminated – at the regional level.

This section contends not that regionalism does not offer opportunities for small states to mitigate the costs imposed by their economic size, vulnerability, and governance capacities, but that these opportunities are limited. Small economies' predicaments cannot be eliminated entirely by regional integration, and it is thus mistaken to attribute this predicament to the policy choices of those states.

With the advantages of regionalism qualified, policy prescriptions shift to global integration for small states (World Bank, 2002a, p.10; and Schiff, 2002, p.18), implying that small states' disadvantages arise from their lack of integration into the global economy (see Page and Kleen, 2004, p.43). By any measure of trade exposure, the degree of global integration of small economies is not deficient nor – as the next sections will demonstrate – will more integration necessarily benefit small states facing inherent challenges to their competitiveness. Instead, what small economies require is a more beneficial means of insertion into international markets than they currently experience.

7. Being ill-equipped to benefit from globalisation

The foregoing sections have explored small economies' peculiar disadvantages in their potential to exploit opportunities arising from globalisation. These constraints on their global competitiveness are persistent, to varying degrees, and condition an expectation of small economies' increasing marginalisation in world trade and declining development prospects. This expectation is not radical, with Winters and Martins (2004a, p.2) arguing that, in the absence of mitigating policies by the international community, small economies will become worse off as the world economy globalises. Encontre (1999, p.269) adds that most SIDS are likely to gain 'little benefit' from the process of multilateral trade liberalisation,[5] with UNCTAD's Officer-in-Charge (2004a, p.v) arguing that SIDS' intrinsic disadvantages means they will be 'unable to seize these [globalisation] opportunities unless certain special measures to compensate their disadvantages are granted to them by their development partners'. Grynberg and Razzaque (2003, pp.52–3) demonstrate that small economies are already being marginalised in world trade flows, while Braun et al. (2002) provide evidence of the declining relative economic performance of newly independent states, such as small economies, largely as a result of the associated decline in the size of their secure market access which the existence of sovereignty – even with open trade policies – necessarily implies (see also Hausmann, 2004. Additionally, World Bank (2002b, pp.2–3) data indicate the declining average growth rate of GDP in Pacific Islands since the 1970s, to a point of virtual stagnation.). Bertram (2004, p.344) finds similar evidence for small independent states in the Pacific, as well as for the whole group of SIDS.

This argument is not about the past growth performance of small economies, and their ensuing current levels of per capita income. Nothing in the argument is invalidated by evidence that small economies are not currently the world's lowest per capita income group, or have not suffered the world's lowest growth rates in recent years (see Easterly and Kraay, 2001, pp.97–8 and Page and Kleen, 2004, pp.80–2 in particular, but also Read, 2004, p.368). As the data in Table 3.7 indicate, the recent historical growth performance of small economies has exceeded that of LDCs. Beyond the averages, it is important to recognise that the relatively better performance of some small economies masks the poor growth record and current low per capita income levels of others. In particular, 16 of the 41 small economies considered in this chapter are LDCs (representing one third of LDCs) (note also that of these, UNCTAD (2004b, p.5) regards seven as 'regressing' economies, and a further four as 'slow-growth' economies), and a further two are land-locked developing countries. Briguglio (1995, p.1615) cautions that per capita income data conceal the reality of small economies' threatened economic viability, and Read (2004, p.365) argues that, 'Globalization represents a particularly significant threat to the continued survival of many successful small island states as

Table 3.7. Average annual GDP growth 1990–2000

Country grouping[a]	GDP growth rate (%)	Per capita GDP growth rate (%)
Small economies[b]	3.6	1.9
All least-developed countries	3.6	1.1
All developing countries	4.8	3.0
Developed market economies	2.4	1.7

[a] The definition of country groupings is given in UNCTAD (2003c: x)
[b] Simple average, excluding Nauru, Palau and Timor-Leste due to missing data
Source: UNCTAD (2003c) and author's own calculations

independent entities given the greater susceptibility of their economies to changes in the international system'. However, relatively good past economic performance has led some analysts to argue that it is difficult for small economies to 'make a development case' for special and differential treatment (Page and Kleen, 2004, p.82). As Winters and Martins (2004a, p.1) argue, that reasoning is invalid because it is based on historical data only:

> ...ignoring the question of [whether] small countries are likely to be able to respond to the changes brought about by globalisation and the ability of small countries to respond to present and future changes in the global trading system. For small states the policy issue is not past performance but rather whether they are well positioned, given the globalisation of trade, to capitalise and achieve growth rates similar to those achieved in the past.

The validity of a future expectation cannot not be judged on the basis of historical data.

This historical economic performance of small economies occurred in the context of their particular mode of insertion into specific market structures in the global economy in that period. By contrast, expectations about future economic performance must account for recent and imminent changes in the global economy and multilateral trading system, altering both that mode of insertion and the structures of particular markets of interest to small economies. A relevant global economic change, for example, is the declining real value of aid and declining share of it accruing to small economies typically heavily reliant on it. A relevant change within the multilateral trading system would exist if, for example, the selection of markets being liberalised and distortions dismantled were detrimental to the export competitiveness of small economies. Analysts have typically assumed that there must exist advantages of small size – asserting greater social cohesion, bureaucratic flexibility, less popular resistance to change, greater solidarity, fewer vested interests, a disproportionately strong international voice, and freedom from interference by major powers (Streeten, 1993, pp.199–200; Srinivasan, 1986, pp.211, 214; WTO, 2002, p.11; and Armstrong and Read, 2002, p.8) – sufficient to offset small economies' lack of international competitiveness. These advantages, if they exist, need have had no such strong offsetting effects on competitiveness if, instead, the relatively good average growth performance of small economies has arisen from their historically favourable means of insertion in the global economy.

8. Being vulnerable to harm from globalisation

Thus far, this chapter has explored why small economies are poorly positioned to exploit the opportunities emerging from globalisation. Equally critical is the threat that further globalisation of markets according to currently agreed multilateral trade rules will damage the economic welfare of small economies. Underpinning this threat is the dependence of most small states on trade preferences for the feasibility of their key exports to major markets in developed countries (Grynberg, 2001a, pp.274-9). Tariff preferences are already eroding as a consequence of multilateral trade liberalisation and the proliferation of free trade agreements (Schiff, 2002, p.14). In compliance with WTO dispute rulings, small economies also face the imminent modification or dismantling of especially favourable subsidy preference schemes for their commodities.[6] This section will show how preferential access to markets in developed countries has been vital to the economic performance of small states, how vulnerable these states are to preference erosion, and the gravity of the economic consequences of their loss of preferences.

Small economies enjoy a considerable degree of preferential access to the markets of their former colonial and major regional powers, particularly for the tropical commodities that colonial rule structured as their comparative advantages. Small economies' access to preferential arrangements is summarised in Table 3.8.[7] The value of these preferences to small economies has been substantial, flowing through terms-of-trade gains, greater export values and volumes, higher GDP, greater employment (especially in rural areas), a degree of stability in 'farm gate' prices, higher household incomes, and increased government revenue.[8] Reviewing the literature on the impact of preferences, Alexandraki and Lankes (2004, pp.6–7) argue that preferences have enhanced market access relative to the counter-factual of no preferences, encouraged export-driven economic development, and provided valuable transfers to small economies. UNCTAD (2003a, p.7) argues that preferential margins have been sufficient to compensate for the inherent lack of competitiveness of the exports of small – in particular island – economies. Alexandraki and Lankes (2004, p.24) calculate that, among non-LDC developing countries, 11 of the 12 states receiving the highest total preference margins for their exports are small economies (note also that small economies are among the LDCs facing the highest losses from preference erosion, according to Subramanian, 2003, p.12; see also Tangermann, 2000, p.16). These data dispel assumptions that middle-income status alone is sufficient to avert the problems of adjusting to liberalising markets. The findings, reproduced in Table 3.9, indicate clearly the size and importance of trade preferences, with preference margins adding a quarter or more to the value of exports for the top six of these small economies. For sugar, for example, small economies account for nearly 93 per cent of the total ACP sugar quota volume in the EU market, and hold another tenth of that volume again from US sugar quotas (author's own calculations based on data in Mitchell, 2004, pp.31, 39).

Table 3.8 The major preferential trade arrangements of small economies

Small economy by region	EU		US			Canada		Japan	Australia & New Zealand
	Cotonou	EBA	CBI	AGOA	GSP-LDC	CARIBCAN	GSP LDC	GSP LDC	SPARTECA
Africa									
Botswana	☑			☑					
Cape Verde	☑	☑		☑	☑		☑	☑	
Comoros	☑	☑			☑		☑		
Djibouti	☑	☑		☑	☑		☑		
Equatorial Guinea	☑	☑			☑		☑	☑	
Gabon	☑			☑					
Gambia	☑	☑		☑	☑		☑	☑	
Guinea-Bissau	☑	☑		☑	☑		☑	☑	
Lesotho	☑	☑		☑	☑		☑	☑	
Mauritius	☑			☑					
Namibia	☑			☑					
São Tomé and Príncipe	☑	☑		☑	☑		☑	☑	
Seychelles	☑			☑					
Swaziland	☑			☑					
Asia									
Bhutan		☑			☑		☑	☑	
Maldives		☑					☑	☑	
Timor-Leste									
Caribbean and Latin America									
Antigua and Barbuda	☑		☑			☑			
Barbados	☑		☑			☑			
Belize	☑		☑			☑			
Dominica	☑		☑			☑			
Grenada	☑		☑			☑			

Small economy by region	EU		US			Canada		Japan	Australia & New Zealand
	Cotonou	EBA	CBI	AGOA	GSP-LDC	CARIBCAN	GSP LDC	GSP LDC	SPARTECA
Guyana	☑		☑			☑			
Jamaica	☑		☑			☑			
St. Kitts and Nevis	☑		☑			☑			
St. Lucia	☑		☑			☑			
St. Vincent and the Grenadines	☑					☑			
Suriname	☑								
Trinidad and Tobago	☑		☑			☑			
Pacific									
Fiji	☑								☑
Kiribati	☑	☑			☑		☑	☑	☑
Marshall Islands	☑								☑
Federated States of Micronesia	☑								☑
Nauru	☑								☑
Palau	☑								
Papua New Guinea	☑								☑
Samoa	☑	☑			☑		☑	☑	☑
Solomon Islands	☑	☑					☑	☑	☑
Tonga	☑								☑
Tuvalu	☑	☑			☑		☑	☑	☑
Vanuatu	☑	☑			☑		☑	☑	☑

Source: EC (2004a), EC (2004b), USTR (2004a), USTR (2004b), USTR (2004c), Trade Point (2005), Government of Canada (2002), Ministry of Foreign Affairs (2004) and Pacific Islands Forum Secretariat (1998)

Small economies' extreme vulnerability to significant economic damage from the loss of preferences arises from the highly preference-dependent structure of their exports and production. This dependence is characterised by the concentration of their exports in a very small number of commodities, the directing of those commodities to a limited range of markets, costs of production that market – rather than preferential – prices would not cover, and a lack of competitiveness in entering alternative productive activities and export markets (UNCTAD (2003a, p.7) argues that these trade patterns for SIDS are similar to those of LDCs). Thus Alexandraki and Lankes (2004, pp.5-6, 11) conclude that preference erosion is a significant source of vulnerability for countries with deep preferential access to major developed-country markets, an undiversified export base concentrated in commodities enjoying preferential access, and high export concentration in those markets where preferences are set to decline. Exemplifying export concentrations, preferential beef exports account for 98 per cent of Botswana's agricultural exports to the EU, with equivalent figures of 97 per cent for bananas from St. Vincent and the Grenadines and 83 per cent for sugar from Mauritius (data from Tangermann (2000, p.10); see also Mitchell (2004, p.19) for data on sugar export concentration).

The economic damage that will ensue for small economies that lose their historically vital preferential access to major markets is estimated to be substantial. Alexandraki

Table 3.9. Preference margins by product for most vulnerable middle-income countries

Country	Total preference margin	Percentage of preference margin accounted for by preferences for:			
		Sugar	Bananas	Garments[a]	Other
Mauritius	39.9	84	0	13	3
St. Lucia	32.9	0	94	2	4
Belize	29.3	47	23	0	30
St. Kitts and Nevis	28.7	94	0	0	6
Guyana	24.2	95	0	1	4
Fiji	24.1	96	0	1	2[b]
Dominica	15.9	0	97	0	3
Seychelles	12.2	0	0	0	100
Jamaica	9.7	67	8	7	18
St. Vincent and the Grenadines	9.4	0	89	0	11
Albania	8.9	0	0	48	52
Swaziland	8.2	97	0	1	2
Middle-income countries[c]	4.9	42	19	12	27

[a] Garments includes textiles and clothing
[b] Discrepancy in original source
[c] Average for 76 middle-income developing countries, weighted by margin
Source: Alexandraki and Lankes (2004, p.24)

and Lankes (2004, p.25) estimate that 11 of the 12 worst affected middle-income developing countries will be small economies, with estimated losses shown in Table 10. Sugar and banana preferences are the main source of vulnerability.[9] For a 40 per cent reduction in preference margins, losses of a fifth to nearly a quarter of total exports are estimated for the most vulnerable small economies, as depicted in Figure 3.3 (assuming a supply elasticity of 1.5). Even with a zero supply elasticity, the losses from a 40 per cent reduction in preference margins as a share of exports, GDP and government revenue, are substantial for these small economies (see Table 3.10).[10] Guyana stands to lose the equivalent of over 5 per cent of GDP, Mauritius nearly 25 per cent of government revenue. Overall Alexandraki and Lankes (2004, pp.8, 26) argue that preference erosion is most acute for SIDS, and that aggregate losses are several times larger for middle-income developing countries than for LDCs. Among LDCs, Subramanian (2003, pp.9–10, 13–4) makes similar findings: small economies are among those with the highest preference dependence, poised to lose most from preference erosion.

In light of the above, it is clear that multilateral trade liberalisation in agriculture will not necessarily make small economies better off. They are significant beneficiaries of current market distortions, will suffer absolute welfare losses when these distortions are dismantled, and have little potential to diversify into economic activities in which

Table 3.10. Macroeconomic losses from preference erosion in most vulnerable middle-income countries.

Country	Loss as a % of Goods Exports			Losses Assuming Zero Supply Elasticity (e=0)			
	e=1.5	e=1.0	e=1.0	Absolute ($US millions)	% of Goods & Services Exports	% of GDP	% of Government Revenue
Mauritius	−23.7	−19.6	−11.5	−201	−7.2	−4.4	−24.4
St. Lucia	−20.9	−17.2	−9.8	−4	−1.1	−−0.6	−1.9
Belize	−19.6	−16.1	−9.1	−18	−4.1	−2.1	−8.0
St. Kitts and Nevis	−19.3	−15.9	−8.9	−3	−1.8	−0.8	−1.9
Guyana	−17.3	−14.2	−7.9	−41	−6.2	−5.8	−17.7
Fiji	−17.2	−14.0	−7.8	−41	−3.8	−2.2	−9.1
Dominica	−12.6	−10.2	−5.5	−2	−1.9	−0.9	−2.3
Seychelles	−9.5	−7.7	−4.2	−10	−1.9	−1.6	−3.7
Jamaica	−8.4	−6.8	−3.5	−46	−1.4	−0.6	−2.2
St. Vincent and the Grenadines	−8.2	−6.6	−3.4	−5	−2.7	−1.3	−4.3
Albania	−7.7	−6.3	−3.3	−10	−1.2	−0.2	−1.0
Swaziland	−7.2	−5.8	−3.0	−21	−1.8	−16.	−5.8

Source: Alexandraki and Lankes (2004: 25-6)

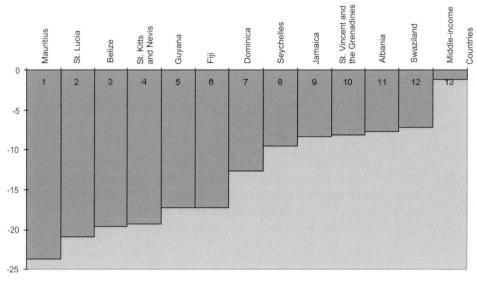

Figure 3.3. Losses from preference erosion as a percentage of merchandise exports
Source: Alexandraki and Lankes (2004, p.25)

their exports will be competitive (see Grynberg and Razzaque (2003, p.52) on the absolute welfare loss to preference dependent states caused by the Uruguay Round; and Mattoo and Subramanian (2004, p.3) for a discussion of the ambivalence of small states to further trade liberalisation). UNCTAD (2003a, pp.16–18, 32) demonstrates that under all feasible scenarios for agricultural liberalisation in the Doha Round, SIDS will suffer absolute welfare losses. Of these, Mauritius, Jamaica and Fiji will suffer the largest losses. Only if general agricultural liberalisation is augmented by providing SIDS with tariff-free access for *all* of their commodity exports to *all* major developed-country markets will they be better off.

The foregoing does not preclude the validity of findings that preference schemes, particularly interventions in EU and US commodity markets related to subsidy preferences, are grossly market distorting and enormously wasteful to operate (see Mitchell, 2004, p.18; Borrell, 1999, p.8; and Oxfam, 2004, p.1). For recipients, such schemes may impose a significant administrative burden (see Panagariya, 2002, pp.1429–30; and Keck and Low, 2004, pp.11–12), impede the efficient allocation of productive resources (Subramanian, 2003, p.2; Page and Kleen, 2004, p.26; and Levantis et al., 2003, p.1), and act as a disincentive to trade liberalisation, including through recipients' reluctance to participate in reciprocal trade negotiations (see Ozden and Reinhardt, 2003, pp.20–21; Panagariya, 2002, p.1416; Keck and Low, 2004, pp.13–14; Alexandraki and Lankes, 2004, p.5; Kennes, 2000, p.99; and Brock and McGee, 2004, p.15). Their persistence may well be driven more by the vested interests of producers, processors and distributors in developed countries, than by the trade interests of declared recipients (see Watkins, 2004, pp.20–5; Subramanian, 2003, p.2; Borrell, 1999, pp.13, 19; Ozden and Sharma, 2004, p.12; and Anderson, 2004, p.6). Furthermore, preferences

Commonwealth Small States

may have benefited their donors by reducing developing country pressure to free markets in their export interests (see Watkins, 2004, p.41; Panagariya, 2002, p.1430; Page and Kleen, 2004, p.41; Levantis et al., 2003, p.1; and Subramanian, 2003, p.2). That their existence is lamented does not mean that removing preferential schemes will be any less damaging to small economies, however (Levantis et al. (2003, p.2) make a similar argument). Simply because preference dependent states are few and would lose only a fraction of what global welfare would gain from liberalisation (see Mitchell, 2004, pp.26-7; and Panagariya, 2002, p.1426) does not make that loss any less detrimental to the development prospects of small economies.

For preference-dependent states, the alternative policy to pursuing extended preferences is 'adjustment', a term implying that there exists an alternative sustainable development path. Yet, for the reasons outlined earlier, small economies may lack both the potential for competitiveness in exports historically benefiting from preferences and the robust macroeconomic situations to absorb the impact of collapsing industries (see Alexandraki and Lankes (2004, p.5) on factors affecting states' capacities to manage preference losses). Small economies also face significant competitiveness constraints in entering new economic activities and non-preferential markets, arising from combinations of characteristics associated with their small size, vulnerability to external economic shocks and natural disasters, and governance capacity (UNCTAD (2003b, p.20), for example, demonstrates this predicament with respect to the Windward Islands). Certainly, preferences have encouraged small economies to maintain industries which are inefficient by best-practice standards, thus inhibiting their incentives to shift to patterns of production and trade that are sustainable in the absence of preferences (Page and Kleen, 2004, p.28). This chapter argues that, at least in the near future, the feasibility of alternative employments for these production resources should not be assumed automatically.

Salmon (2002, p.11) offers a necessary caution against the kind of reasoning that consists in affirming after the fact that providing preferences was not legitimate for small economies since they have performed well, when their good performance has arisen precisely from those preferences. Small economies have benefited substantially from preferential access to subsidised markets in the developed world, yet their economies are now precariously positioned as these market-distorting subsidies are reduced and non-LDC small economies are set to lose preferential access (Grynberg, 2001a, p.279). Transfers, equivalent to previous preference rents,[11] need not have equivalent effects if channelled through donors' aid administrations according to their development priorities (Page and Kleen (2004, p.65, 91). For an example of this intention, see EC (2005, p.6). Even direct financial transfers (Alexandraki and Lankes (2004, p.27) argue that targeting such transfers would be straightforward) would not necessarily engender the same macroeconomic outcomes (see, for example, the modelling of different compensation scenarios in Levantis et al., 2003, pp.6-8): what small economies lose with preferences is the feasibility of engaging in productive export activities at remunerative prices, with concomitant gains in foreign exchange, employment, and stability of trade and transport patterns. Adequate compensation would therefore involve funding the economic transition to equivalently remunerative export industries, including possibly persistent subsidies to make comparative advantages operational in the near future. A more palatable alternative to donors, discussed earlier, might be the extension of tariff-free access for all exports from all small economies into all developed-country markets. Otherwise, globalisation along the lines of currently agreed multilateral trade rules will make small economies worse off, making a strong development case for more favourable treatment for small economies.

9. Small economies' predicament as a trade concern

At the core of the present economic predicament of small economies is trade: small economies rely on trade to enhance their development prospects beyond the constraints of small size, yet face severe limitations on their potential for competitiveness in world markets. Moreover, their predicament is a relevant concern for trade negotiations; a failure to address it is a threat to the legitimacy of the multilateral trade regime (Grynberg, 2001a, p.305; and Keck and Low, 2004, p.8; Grynberg, 2001a, p.305; and Keck and Low, 2004, p.8). This is not to say that appropriate modifications of trade agreements will be sufficient to alleviate small economies' development problems, nor that other international forums and organisations will not prove vital to this effort (Page and Kleen, 2004, p.70; and Grynberg, 2001b, p.339). The UNCTAD, World Bank, IMF and Commonwealth Secretariat, as well as bilateral and NGO donors, can, and in many cases already are, playing critical roles (see, for example, UNCTAD, 2004a; World Bank, 2003; IMF, 2003; and Commonwealth Secretariat, 2003). But this does not make multilateral, regional and bilateral trade negotiations any less relevant to the predicament of small economies.[12]

Four specific avenues through which current trade negotiations affect the development prospects of small economies are noteworthy here. First, agreed and impending multilateral trade rules threaten to erode or dismantle the preferential access on the basis of which small economies have participated successfully in world markets in the past. Secondly, the selective liberalisation of global markets under multilateral rules omits markets of particular relevance to small economies, notably semi- and un-skilled labour services. Thirdly, elements of agreed multilateral trade rules constrain the policy space available to small states – or the international community – to improve their development prospects. Examples include proscriptions preventing small states – whether from their own resources or international assistance – from offering investment incentives to export industries (see English and de Wulf, 2002, pp.164-9; and Grynberg, 2001a, pp.272, 298) or subsidising transport services. Fourthly, small states are especially disadvantaged in their capacity to challenge the abuse of trade rules by other states; accommodating this weakness in the redesign of rules and the allocation of technical assistance could prove valuable.[13]

Given the importance of trade regimes to the development prospects of small economies, it is often asserted that small economies should embrace multilateral trade rules with greater vigour (see Burki, 2001, pp.9-10; Kennes, 2000, p.9; and World Bank,

2002a, p.3). Such arguments conflate free trade with currently agreed multilateral trade rules. The integration of small economies into an idealised global free market is very different from the insertion of small economies into world markets on the terms of currently agreed trade rules. Emerging from a process of interstate negotiation and bargaining, trade rules are widely recognised as being biased in favour of the economic interests of major powers (see Finger and Winters (2002, pp.53-5) on exclusion of the interests of the weak; Ozden and Reinhardt (2003, p.5) and Oyejide (2002, pp.505-6) on the structural biases in GSP schemes, and Freund (2003, pp.5, 23) on biases in trade agreements between unequal powers). Negotiated rules come with no guarantee of being beneficial to the welfare of any one participant. When small economies 'integrate into the global economy' by becoming subject to multilateral trade rules, the markets of export interest to them and into which they are inserted are not necessarily those that are free, nor will their participation in negotiations necessarily change that (see Ozden and Reinhardt (2003, p.3) for the opposite assumption of effective bargaining power). Thus, for example, small economies are bound by intellectual property rules defined by developed countries in the WTO (see Subramanian, 2003, pp.169-72), but their semi- and un-skilled labour cannot move freely into industrialised markets (Chanda, 2002, p.307). In a later section, this chapter will address the suggestion that the value to small economies of multilateral rules *per se* overrides whatever terms those rules might contain (Page and Kleen, 2004, p.82. See also Armstrong and Read (2002, p.11) for a discussion of small states and trade rules as public goods).

10. The feasibility of favourable treatment for small economies

This chapter has brought together evidence that small economies face substantial challenges to competitive participation in world markets, in support of the contention that the trade of small economies requires more favourable treatment if they are to avoid the imminent prospect of marginalisation (Grynberg and Razzaque, 2003, p.1). This section will argue that such favourable treatment is feasible, and furthermore that it would impose a negligible financial cost on the international community. The only significant cost would be ideological; as Winters and Martins (2004a, p.149) argue, attaining the favourable treatment that small economies require would necessitate '...conscious policy-shifts in the major capitals'.

If small economies were to be accorded duty- and quota-free access for all of their exports in major markets (see Hoekman et al., 2003, pp.10, 19) for equity arguments in support of this inclusion; see also Mattoo and Subramanian, 2004), derogations from WTO rules would be required. It is the current WTO-incompatibility of this necessary discrimination among developing countries that has enabled larger or more competitive developing countries to challenge successfully the existing preferences accorded to small economies. (Successful challenges that some developed countries are using as levers to direct small states into reciprocal trade agreements in order to preserve something of their current preferential access.) The life of tariff preferences is of course finite, their value eroding with multilateral liberalisation, but even finite preferences would provide small economies with a necessary reprieve. WTO rules could also be adjusted to benefit small economies in areas such as the feasibility of their access to and retaliatory measures under dispute settlement (Delich, 2002, pp.76-8), the extent of their benefits from technical assistance programmes (Mattoo and Subramanian, 2004, 6), and the achievement of a degree of rule-ordering of their accession processes (on accession, see Grynberg, 2001a, p.307; Grynberg, 2001b, pp.333-4; and Langhammer, 2000).

In addition to tariff-free access for their exports, small economies would benefit from amendments to specific WTO agreements that are unduly prejudicial to their interests (for a broader framework within which these specific suggestions could fit, see ICTSD (2003) or Keck and Low (2004). Exemptions from subsidies disciplines, for example, are necessary to allow state interventions to overcome market failures that are undermining particular trade opportunities for small economies (Davenport, 2001, p.10). Whilst it is not feasible for small economies to use domestic resources to subsidise their way out of their pervasive cost disadvantages, exemptions from subsidies disciplines would also avert the WTO-incompatibility of subsidies for the trade of small economies that are sourced internationally. Alongside free market access for their exports, Winters and Martins (2004a, p.149) argue that such international subsidisation of small economies' trade is one of the few possible policy responses that could sustain small economies' participation in world markets. A second example is that small economies require long transition periods for the implementation of WTO disciplines, the extreme costs and complexity of which are beyond the current resources, capacity and development interests of small states (Hoekman et al. (2003, pp.5, 16) and Finger and Schuler (2002, pp.493, 501); see also Rodrik (2002, p.8-9) and Page and Kleen (2004, p.56). In place of a fixed transition period, compliance could be required only once state institutions and resources – including any forthcoming technical assistance – are sufficient for implementation to be effective. A final example is provided by current fisheries negotiations. It is vital to the interests of small coastal states that derogations prevent new rules from reducing their revenue from fisheries access fees and associated development assistance, impeding their efforts to domesticate their fisheries industries, and disallowing their support to artisanal fisheries activities (for the details of how fisheries negotiations affect small states, see Grynberg (2003, pp.69-72) and also Vossenaar (2004, p.67).

Incorporating specific derogations from particular rules to target the needs of certain categories of states has extensive precedent in the WTO (see Davenport (2001, pp.4-5) and Grynberg (2001a) for examples of such derogations). Without overarching recognition of the special circumstances of small economies such as that provided by the Doha Declaration and Small Economies Work Program (SEWP) (see WTO, 2001, p.7-8; and also Tulloch, 2001), however, it will prove harder for small states to leverage such derogations in specific negotiating groups. And without overarching tariff preferences or international subsidisation of small economies' trade as the foundation of the international response to the trade predicament of small economies, rule derogations will amount to little more than piecemeal concessions lacking the potential to tackle that predicament effectively.

In pursuing the recognition of their interests in multilateral trade negotiations, small economies encounter opposition even at a conceptual level. Non-discrimination and reciprocity are described as the 'pillars' of the WTO (Freund (2003, p.2), which rule derogations for some states are accused of undermining (Ozden and Reinhardt, 2003, p.4).[1] Yet, as Keck and Low (2004, p.3) state, 'The battle to establish the principle that a set of uniform multilateral rights and obligations among a deeply diverse set of nations could not serve the best interests of all parties was won a long time ago'. What appears to be particularly threatening to proponents of the doctrine that trade liberalisation necessarily advantages all, is the prospect of rule derogations for small economies based on the argument that small states otherwise would not benefit from globalisation (see Page and Kleen, 2004, pp.79-80). Apart from conflating current multilateral rules with free trade, this attitude also supposes faith in free trade to be hopelessly fragile if favourable treatment for small economies, explicable and justifiable *within* economic models of comparative advantage, can undermine it. Still, critics argue that special and differential treatment can only be temporary, if 'equal treatment' is to remain a core principle of the WTO (Page and Kleen, 2004, pp. 46, 77), supposedly invalidating the claims of small economies because their small size, remoteness and exposure to natural disasters are permanent. But, favourable treatment of small economies' trade is not expected to alter fixed features like small size, large distances to markets, and frequent natural disasters (for the contrary position, see Page and Kleen, 2004, pp.15, 46, 80). Such features merely act as identifiers of likely candidates for assistance. Instead, more favourable treatment is intended to alleviate the *effects* that combinations of the characteristics of small economies have on their trade competitiveness. These effects are persistent, but aspects of them may reduce in intensity in the medium term in specific cases, for example if transport costs decline significantly, or if complete and competitive disaster insurance markets develop.

It has been suggested that special and differential treatment, in as far as it detracts from the systemic value of consistent rules, injures the interests of weak participants like small states in the multilateral trade regime (see Page and Kleen, 2004, pp.7-8, 81). However, one cannot extrapolate from the idea that international rules are a public good the argument that small administrations can gain particular benefit from implementing them, without accounting for the cost that complex and often inappropriate disciplines impose. The systemic value of the trade regime to all members could reasonably be expected to be sufficient to absorb the negligible cost of rule derogations for a group of states accounting in aggregate for only a fraction of 1 per cent of world trade (see Grynberg and Razzaque, 2003, p.11). If the rules are inappropriate for small economies, negotiating derogations within the framework of the trade regime supports their interests. The marginal nature of small economies in the world trading system makes incredible claims that more favourable treatment of them would impose significant financial costs on others (see Breckenridge, 2002, p.11). UNCTAD (2003a, p.19) demonstrates for agriculture that free access for the exports of SIDS would have virtually no effect on the welfare of other developing countries; Winters and Martins (2004a, p.150) argue that the costs to the international community of subsidising all exports from small states would be 'perfectly manageable' (see also Davenport, 2001, pp.1, 17-8; and

Stevens, 2002, pp.25-6). The cost to the legitimacy of the international trade regime if it does not adjust to accommodate the trade predicament of small economies may be more substantial, however (Stevens, 2002, p.1; and Drahos, 2004, pp.9-10). The further marginalisation of small economies in world trade will expose the insincerity of the rhetoric of mutually advantageous negotiated trade liberalisation.

11. Small states, negotiating weaknesses

Possessing a good case for favourable treatment in trade negotiations is important, but the value of a good argument arises not of itself but from its contribution to the bargaining power of the states concerned. What weakens small states' prospects of attaining special and differential treatment in multilateral negotiations are their substantial disadvantages in other aspects of bargaining power. Most critically, small economies lack market power, and thus the potential to make credible threats impelling others to negotiate with them (on elements of bargaining power see Drahos, 2004, pp.6-8; and also Mattoo and Subramanian, 2004, p.3). Their intelligence networks, gathering and analysing information about their trade performance and economic interests, also are weak from the extremely constrained research capacities of their bureaucracies and also of the relatively small firms implied by their small market sizes. If market power and intelligence networks are the most important elements of bargaining power, the prospects of small states attaining more favourable trade treatment as a negotiated outcome are bleak.

In an attempt to mitigate this weakness, small states have used their enrolment power to form coalitions among the collection of states that share small, vulnerable or island characteristics. The coalition does not benefit from greater bargaining power through market size, since the aggregated market of members is still insignificant in global terms. But this coalition has used the support of international organisations well, its intelligence networks have been strengthened by the pooling of state and regional administrative resources, and its cohesiveness has strengthened the voice of these states in multilateral negotiations. Cohesion and voice, however, have depended crucially on the inclusion in the coalition of states whose larger populations or economic success lead opponents to question the deservedness of special treatment (Davenport, 2001, p.1; and Hein, 2004, pp.6-7 discuss this point). But these inclusions are vital to the negotiating power of the group. Cohesion depends on including all states perceiving themselves and perceived by the group as small; splitting traditional regions of small states by excluding Papua New Guinea or Jamaica on the basis of population, or Barbados or Trinidad and Tobago on the basis of per capita income, would be extremely costly to group cohesion (see Narlikar, 2003, pp.2, 27-9, 183; including the critical statement: 'Stability of allies is a crucial asset for the weak'). Voice depends on including strong states to lead the group; excluding Mauritius, Jamaica or Barbados on grounds of size or success would cost the group historical leaders, links to information networks in other coalitions, and states with strong economic interests in the Small Economies Work Programme (SEWP) (see Narlikar, 2003, pp.16, 183). If membership were fixed exactly by small population or lower/middle income thresholds, the bargaining power of the coalition would dissipate: critics could be satisfied that no anomalies remained, but equally would no longer have to engage with the group's demands (see Encontre (2004, pp.92, 98) and (Hein, 2004, pp.12–13, 20) for emphasis on the need to strictly define group membership).

This discussion of the negotiating process from which multilateral trade rules emerge should temper suggestions that the continued presence – rather than exit – of small states in the WTO indicates that they must derive a net benefit from its agreements (Page and Kleen, 2004, pp.43, 82). WTO negotiations involve an unrolling of 'consensus', starting with the most powerful economies and progressively incorporating other major players and coalitions until it reaches the periphery – populated by small states – by which time the 'consensus' is a foregone conclusion (see Narlikar, 2003, p.37; Drahos, 2004, pp.11,17; and Brock and McGee, 2004, p.9). Furthermore, the governance capabilities of small states are so constrained that they have little capacity even to assess the implications for their development prospects of the many alternative proposals coming forward. Thus, for small states in multilateral negotiations, concepts like informed choice and cost-benefit analysis are somewhat irrelevant (on this point see Drahos, 2004, pp.4–10; and also Finger and Winters, 2002, p.55). To a limited extent, it is appropriate to characterise international trade rules – for example, liberalisation commitments – as public goods negotiated with the resources of major powers and upon which small states can free ride (Armstrong and Read, 2002, pp.15–6; see also Page and Kleen, 2004, p.82; and Narlikar, 2003, p.37). It is equally feasible, however, that rules determined in the absence of input from small states will prove adverse to their interests, with an alternative characterisation of the process being of small states getting damaged in the cross-fire of negotiations between major powers (Grynberg, 2001b, p.334; Grynberg, 2003, p.70; and Watkins, 2004, pp.16–17).

12. Conclusion

This chapter has presented evidence that the globalisation of markets under existing and emerging multilateral trade rules will damage the trade and development interests of small economies. Arresting their further marginalisation in world trade is not a simple matter of domestic economic 'adjustment' towards productive activities and trade patterns that are sustainable in globalised markets. Instead, characteristics of small economies, centring around their size, vulnerability and governance capacity, combine to yield significant cost disadvantages large enough to undermine substantially these states' capacities to participate in trade on a remunerative basis, even in areas of comparative advantage. Where small economies cannot obtain premium prices for their products abroad, their exports will struggle to be feasible. Any diminished trading success will only compound the deleterious effects of small size on their economic welfare, with increasing marginalisation in world trade being the last thing that small economies can afford.

This chapter has also shown that preferential access to major developed country markets has contributed to the relatively good historical income and growth performances of small economies, preferences that are now being eroded or dismantled. As Armstrong and Read (2002, p.19) conclude, 'Strict adherence to axiomatic multilateralism and the creation of a level playing-field for international trade is therefore likely to deprive small states of many niche opportunities by removing marginal but critically important sources of protection which contribute to their growth success'. At the same time, the significant challenges to their competitiveness posed by their small size, vulnerability and constrained governance make it extremely difficult for small economies to take advantage of new opportunities emerging from the globalisation of markets.

At the current juncture of international trade negotiations, small economies are precariously positioned: certain to lose from the greater liberalisation of markets for their key exports, they lack the bargaining power to achieve more favourable treatment and greater trade-related assistance that might forestall otherwise disquieting economic prospects in the near future. Among the necessary international responses, multilateral trade rules can be adjusted to accommodate the concerns of small economies, but whether major powers will be willing to negotiate this adjustment, and thereby support the legitimacy of the international trade regime, is less certain.

Notes

1. This chapter does not aim to address the appropriate delineation of small economies; such discussions can be found in Davenport (2001, pp.1–2), Atkins et al. (2000, p.4), Hein (2004), Read (1999, pp.2–5) and Encontre (2004). The list in Table 3.1 is of independent developing states with populations under the standard threshold of 1.5 million, excluding those with GNI per capita above US$9,386 ('high income' in World Bank terminology), but including those above the population threshold identified by the Commonwealth Secretariat as exhibiting similar 'small' characteristics (Botswana, Jamaica, Lesotho, Namibia and Papua New Guinea).

2. Easterly and Kraay (2001: 102-8) argue that the negative effect of volatility on growth in small states is offset by the positive effect of their openness to trade on growth, which appears to lead Page and Kleen (2004: 81) to infer that volatility itself does not matter.

3. See Page and Kleen (2004, p.79), whose argument to that effect appears to be based on Encontre (1999, pp.263-4). The latter compares average growth rates with natural disaster incidences in SIDS over two decades, without engaging in statistical analysis to hold other factors constant, to observe only that both high- and low-growth performers experience both high and low disaster incidences.

4. See Freeman et al. (2003, p.11), Charveriat (2000, p.1), ECLAC and IDB (2000, pp.12-6), Benson et al. (2001, p.92) and Auffret (2003, p.28). Benson and Clay (2003, p.76) state, 'Disasters, especially when these reoccur frequently, appear to have longer-term consequences for economic growth, development, and poverty reduction'. Similarly Freeman (2003, p.11) argues, 'The macroeconomic and developmental implications of natural disaster[s] can be both large and long lasting'.

5. The other exception he notes is any SIDS that are able to enhance the global competitiveness of their merchandise exports, which the earlier cited evidence regarding business costs in small economies would appear to make unlikely.

6. See Oxfam (2004, pp.2–3) on WTO disputes and the EU sugar regime, Mitchell (2004, pp.34, 38) on catalysts for change in the US sugar regime, and Laurent (forthcoming, pp.2–9) on WTO disputes and the EU banana regime. Note this chapter will use 'tariff preferences' to refer to preference schemes based on simple tariff concessions, and 'subsidy preferences' to refer to preference schemes based on tariff-free quota access to subsidised markets abroad.

7. See Panagariya (2002, pp.1419–21) on ACP–EU schemes, and Ozden and Sharma (2004, pp.5–6) for an overview of the CBI. Note that in the absence of specific preferential schemes, non-LDC small economies must rely on Generalised System of Preferences (GSP) schemes. The smaller preferential margins available under GSP than under ACP–EU arrangements, for example, is suggested by Tangermann (2000, p.21). See also Grynberg (2001a, p.279).

8. See UNCTAD (2003a, p.18) on the substantial benefits; Ozden and Sharma (2004, p.12) on accruing preference rents; Subramanian (2003, p.2) on terms-of-trade and export gains; Armstrong and Read (2002, p.8) on export multiplier effects; Choraria (2004, p.13–14) for value-chain analyses, Laurent (forthcoming, p.13) and Melville (2003, p.105) on rural multiplier and development effects; and Romalis (2003, pp.10–12) for discussion of the large, significant growth benefits of preferential access.

9. To what extent this vulnerability might be mitigated in the short term by Economic Partnership Agreements, if these preserve aspects of current preferential arrangements (Schiff (2002, pp.15–17), is yet to be seen; but preferential prices will anyway fall as EU reforms to the relevant parts of the Common Agricultural Policy (CAP) commence.

10. Note also that these findings exclude the effects of preference erosion in minor ACP–EU schemes (beef, veal and rum), and in markets outside Canada, the EU, Japan and the US. Thus, the results miss the impact of eroding Australian and New Zealand preferences on Pacific Islands, and the impact of the withdrawal of Multi-Fibre Agreement (MFA) quotas on small economies (Alexandraki and Lankes (2004, pp.6, 10, 18)). Ozden and Sharma (2004, p.3), for example, find that the withdrawal of MFA quotas would be the equivalent of virtually eliminating the benefits of the CBI to garments industries in the Caribbean.

11. These are advocated because they make explicit the aid transfer to recipients previously occurring through preferences, without imposing the global welfare losses of the market interventions underpinning those preferences. See Mitchell (2004, p.27), Borrell (1999, pp.8, 17), Page and Kleen (2004, pp.11, 14, 16, 63), Fowler and Fokker (2004, pp.34–5) and Kennes (2000, p.103).

12. It is, for example, mistaken to argue as Page and Kleen (2004, p.43) do that because trade does not necessarily lead to development, the readjustment of trade rules is not necessarily relevant to the promotion of development.

13. See Wilson (2002, pp.428–31) on non-tariff barriers to trade; and Davenport (2001, p.10) on the importance of protecting small states from anti-dumping and countervailing measures. Protecting small economies from parallel trade-related abuses is also important: see, for example, the OECD's 'Harmful Tax Initiative' which incorporates a protectionist intent in its 'unfair' tax competition provisions, threatening the viability of financial services industries with demonstrated probity in small economies (see Grynberg et al. (2003, pp.2–6, 10–12, 19–23), Armstrong and Read (2002, p.21) and Read (2004, p.371)).

References

Alexandraki, K. and H.P. Lankes (2004) *The Impact of Preference Erosion on Middle-Income Developiong Countries, IMF Working Paper 169*. International Monetary Fund, Washington, DC.

Anderson, K. (2004) *The Challenge of Reducing Subsidies and Trade Barriers, World Bank Policy Research Working Paper 3415*. World Bank, Washington, DC.

Armstrong, H.W. and R. Read (2002) *The Importance of Being Unimportant: The Political Economy of Trade and Growth in Small States*. University of Lancaster, Lancaster.

Atkins, J.P., S. Mazzi and C.D. Easter (2000) *A Commonwealth Vulnerability Index for Developing Countries: The Position of Small States*. Commonwealth Secretariat, London.

Atkins, J.P., S. Mazzi and C.D. Easter (2001) 'Small States: A Composite Vulnerability Index', in *Small States in the Global Economy*, D. Peretz, R. Faruqi, and E. J. Kisanga (eds). Commonwealth Secretariat, London, pp.53-92.

Auffret, P. (2003a) *Catastrophe Insurance Market in the Caribbean Region: Market Failures and Recommendations for Public Sector Interventions, World Bank Policy Research Working Paper 2963*. World Bank, Washington, DC.

Auffret, P. (2003b) *High Consumption Volatility: The Impact of Natural Disasters?, World Bank Policy Research Working Paper 2962*. World Bank, Washington, DC.

Benson, C. and E. Clay (2003) 'Economic and Financial Impacts of Natural Disasters: An Assessment of Their Effects and Options for Mitigation: Synthesis Report'. Overseas Development Institute, London.

Benson, C., E. Clay, F.V. Michael and A.W. Robertson (2001) *Dominica: Natural Disasters and Economic Development in a Small Island State, Disaster Risk Management Working Paper 2*. World Bank, Washington, DC.

Bernal, R.L. (2001) 'Globalisation and Small Developing Economies: Challenges and Opportunities,' in *Small States in the Global Economy*, D. Peretz, R. Faruqi, and E. J. Kisanga (eds). Commonwealth Secretariat, London, pp.39-51.

Bertram, G. (2004) 'On the Convergence of Small Island Economies with Their Metropolitan Patrons', *World Development*, 32, pp.343-64.

Borrell, B. (1999) *Bananas: Straightening out Bent Ideas on Trade as Aid*. Centre for International Economics, Canberra and Sydney.

Braun, M., R. Hausmann, and L. Pritchett (2002) *The Proliferation of Sovereigns: Are There Lessons for Integration?* Harvard University, Kennedy School of Government at Harvard University and Kennedy School of Government at Harvard University/Center for Global Development.

Breckenridge, A. (2002) 'Developing an Issues-Based Approach to Special and Differential Treatment'. Paper presented to the Trade and Integration Network, Third Meeting, 19-20 March 2002. Inter-American Development Bank, Washington, DC.

Briguglio, L. (1995) 'Small Island Developing States and Their Economic Vulnerabilities', *World Development* 23, pp.1615-32.

Brock, K. and R. Mcgee (2004) *Mapping Trade Policy: Understanding the Challenges of Civil Society Participation. IDS Working Paper 225*. Institute of Development Studies, Brighton.

Burki, S.J. (2001) 'Integrating Small States in a Fast-Changing Global Economy,' in *Small States in the Global Economy*, D. Peretz, R. Faruqi, and E. J. Kisanga (eds) Commonwealth Secretariat, London, pp.7-10.

Burnside, C. and D. Dollar (1997) *Aid, Policies, and Growth. World Bank Policy Research Working Paper 1777*. World Bank, Washington, DC.

Chanda, R. (2002) 'Movement of Natural Persons and the GATS: Major Trade Policy Impediments,' in *Development, Trade, and the WTO: A Handbook*, B. Hoekman, A. Mattoo, and P. English (eds). World Bank, Washington, DC, pp.304-14.

Charveriat, C. (2000) *Natural Disasters in Latin Amercia and the Caribbean: An Overview of Risk. Research Department, Working Paper 434*. Inter-American Development Bank, Washington, DC.

Choraria, J. (2004) *A Note on Commodity Value Chains Compression: Coffee, Cocoa and Sugar*. Commonwealth Secretariat, London.

Collier, P. and J. Dehn (2001) *Aid, Shocks, and Growth. World Bank Policy Research Working Paper 2688*. World Bank, Washington, DC.

Collier, P. and D. Dollar (2001) 'Aid, Risk and the Special Concerns of Small States,' in *Small States in the Global Economy*, D. Peretz, R. Faruqi, and E. J. Kisanga (eds). Commonwealth Secretariat, London, pp.11-38.

Commonwealth Secretariat (2003) *Small States: Economic Review and Basic Statistics*. Commonwealth Secretariat, London.

Davenport, M. (2001) *A Study of Alternative Special and Differential Arrangements for Small Economies*. Commonwealth Secretariat, London.

Dehn, J. (2000a) *Commodity Price Uncertainty and Shocks: Implications for Economic Growth. Working Paper 10*. Centre for the Study of African Economies, Oxford.

Dehn, J. (2000b) *Commodity Price Uncertainty in Developing Countries. Working Paper 11*. Centre for the Study of African Economies, Oxford.

Dehn, J. (2000c) *Private Investment in Developing Countries: The Effects of Commodity Shocks and Uncertainty. Working Paper 12*. Centre for the Study of African Economies, Oxford.

Delich, V. (2002) 'Developing Countries and the WTO Dispute Settlement Mechanism,' in *Development, Trade, and the WTO: A Handbook*, B. Hoekman, A. Mattoo, and P. English (eds). World Bank, Washington, DC, pp.71-80.

Drahos, P. (2004) *When the Weak Bargain with the Strong: Negotiations in the WTO*. Australian National University, Canberra.

Easterly, W. and A. Kraay (2001) 'Small States, Small Problems? Income, Growth and Volatility in Small States,' in *Small States in the Global Economy*, D. Peretz, R. Faruqi, and E. J. Kisanga (eds). Commonwealth Secretariat, London, pp.93-116.

EC (2004a) 'ACP-EU Agreement'. European Commission, 18 February, 2005, Brussels. http://europa.eu.int/comm/development/body/cotonou/index_en.htm.

EC (2004b) 'Generalised System of Preferences'. European Commission, 18 February, 2005, Brussels. http://europa.eu.int/comm/trade/issues/global/gsp/eba/ug.htm.

EC (2005) 'Action Plan on Accompanying Measures for Sugar Protocol Countries Affected by the Reform of the EU Sugar Regime'. Commission Staff Working Paper SEC(2005)61. European Commission, Brussels.

ECLAC and IDB (2000) A Matter of Developent: How to Reduce Vulnerability in the Face of Natural Disasters. Economic Commission for Latin America and the Caribbean / Inter-American Development Bank, Mexico and Washington, DC.

EM-DAT (2004) EM-DAT: The OFDA/CRED International Disaster Database. Université Catholique de Louvain, Brussels. 18 February, 2005, www.em-dat.net.

Encontre, P. (1999) 'The Vulnerability and Resilience of Small Island Developing States in the Context of Globalization', Natural Resources Forum, 23, pp.261-70.

Encontre, P. (2004) 'SIDS as a Category: Adopting Criteria Would Enhance Credibility', in Is a Special Treatment of Small Island Developing States Possible?, UNCTAD (ed.). UNCTAD/LDC/2004/1.United Nations Conference on Trade and Development, New York and Geneva, pp.91-102.

English, P. and L. De Wulf (2002) 'Export Development Policies and Institutions,' in Development, Trade, and the WTO: A Handbook, B. Hoekman, A. Mattoo, and P. English (eds). World Bank, Washington, DC, pp.160-70.

Farrugia, C. (1993) 'The Special Working Environment of Senior Adminstrators in Small States', World Development, 21, pp.221-26.

FBS (2004) 'Major Domestic Exports'. Fiji Bureau of Statistics, Suva. 2 February, 2005, http://www.spc.int/prism/country/FJ/stats/Key%20Stats/Foreign%20Trade/8.5_Major%20Domestic%20Exports.xls.

Finger, J.M. and P. Schuler (2002) 'Implementation of WTO Commitments: The Development Challenge', in Development, Trade, and the WTO: A Handbook, B. Hoekman, A. Mattoo, and P. English (eds). World Bank, Washington, DC, pp.493-503.

Finger, J.M. and L.A. Winters (2002) 'Reciprocity in the WTO', in Development, Trade, and the WTO: A Handbook, B. Hoekman, A. Mattoo, and P. English (eds). World Bank, Washington, DC, pp.50-60.

Fowler, P. and R. Fokker (2004) A Sweet Future? The Potential for EU Sugar Reform to Contribute to Poverty Reduction in Southern Africa. Oxfam International, Washington, DC.

Freeman, P.K., M. Keen and M. Mani (2003) Dealing with Increased Risk of Natural Disasters: Challenges and Options. IMF Working Paper 197. International Monetary Fund, Washington, DC.

Freund, C. (2003) Reciprocity in Free Trade Agreements. World Bank Policy Research Working Paper 3061. World Bank, Washington, DC.

Gay, D. (2004) 'How Economies Participate in the WTO: Vanuatu's Suspended WTO Accession'. Paper prepared for the Institute for International Business, Economics & Law. University of Adelaide, Adelaide.

Government of Canada (2002) Improving Access for the Products of the Least Developed Countries (LDCs) to the Canadian Market. Government of Canada, Ottawa. 18 February, 2005, http://www.dfait-maeci.gc.ca/tna-nac/2ldc-dis02-en.asp.

Grynberg, R. (2001a) 'Trade Policy Implications for Small Vulnerable States of the Global Trade Regime Shift', in Small States in the Global Economy, D. Peretz, R. Faruqi, and E. J. Kisanga (eds). Commonwealth Secretariat, London, pp.267-328.

Grynberg, R. (2001b) 'The Pacific Island States and the WTO: Towards a Post-Seattle Agenda for Small Vulnerable States', in Small States in the Global Economy, D. Peretz, R. Faruqi, and E. J. Kisanga (eds). Commonwealth Secretariat, London, pp.329-42.

Grynberg, R. (2003) 'WTO Fisheries Subsidies Negotiations: Implications for Fisheries Access Arrangements and Sustainable Management', in *Fisheries Issues in WTO and ACP-EU Trade Negotiations*, R. Grynberg (ed.). Commonwealth Secretariat, London, pp.59-82.

Grynberg, R. and M.A. Razzaque (2003) *The Trade Performance of Small States*. Commonwealth Secretariat, London.

Grynberg, R., S. Silva, and J.Y. Remy (2003) *Plurilateral Financial Standards and Their Regulation: The Experience of Small Developing States*. Commonwealth Secretariat, London.

Gurenko, E. and R. Lester (2004) *Rapid Onset Natural Disasters: The Role of Financing in Effective Risk Management*. World Bank Policy Research Working Paper 3278. World Bank, Washington, DC.

Hausmann, R. (2004) 'Sovereignty and Prosperity: The Challenges of Small States'. Paper presented to the World Bank Small States Forum, October 3, 2004. World Bank, Washington, DC.

Hein, P. (2004) 'Small Island Developing States: Origin of the Category and Definition Issues,' in *Is a Special Treatment of Small Island Developing States Possible?*, UNCTAD (ed.). UNCTAD/LDC/2004/1. United Nations Conference on Trade and Development, New York and Geneva, pp.1-22.

Hoekman, B. (2002) 'The WTO: Functions and Basic Principles', in *Development, Trade, and the WTO: A Handbook*, B. Hoekman, A. Mattoo, and P. English (eds). World Bank, Washington, DC, pp.41-9.

Hoekman, B., C. Michalopoulos and L.A. Winters (2003) *More Favorable and Differential Treatment of Developing Countries: Towards a New Approach in the WTO*. World Bank Policy Research Working Paper 3107. World Bank, Washington, DC.

ICTSD (2003) 'Spaces for Development Policy: Revisiting Special and Differential Treatment'. Paper prepared for the joint ICTSD-GP International Dialogue 'Making Special and Differential Treatment More Effective and Responsive to Development Needs', 6-7 May, 2003. International Centre for Trade and Sustainable Development, Geneva.

ICTSD and IISD (2004) 'Special and Differential Treatment'. *Doha Round Briefing Series: Developments Since the Cancun Ministerial Conference*, Volume 3(13). International Centre for Trade and Sustainable Development and International Institute for Sustainable Development, Geneva and Winnipeg.

IMF (2003) *Fund Assistance for Countries Facing Exogenous Shocks*. International Monetary Fund, Washington, DC.

INAMA, S. (2004) 'Preferential Market Access and Erosion of Preferences: What Prospects for SIDS?,' in *Is a Special Treatment of Small Island Developing States Possible?*, UNCTAD (ed.). UNCTAD/LDC/2004/1. United Nations Conference on Trade and Development, New York and Geneva, pp.23-55.

International Workshop (2004) 'Report on the International Workshop on Economic Vulnerability and Resilience of Small States,' 1-3 March 2004. Commonwealth Secretariat, Economics Department of the University of Malta, Islands and Small States Institute at the Foundation for International Studies of the University of Malta, Malta.

IPCC (2001) *Climate Change 2001: The Scientific Basis and Climate Change: Impacts, Adaptation, and Vulnerability: Summary for Policymakers*.Intergovernmental Panel on Climate Change, Geneva. 2 February, 2005, www.ipcc.ch.

Jansen, M. (2004) *Income Volatility in Small and Developing Economies: Export Concentration Matters. WTO Discussion Paper 3.* World Trade Organization, Geneva.

Keck, A. and P. Low (2004) *Special and Differential Treatment in the WTO: Why, When and How? WTO Staff Working Paper [ERSD-2004-03].* World Trade Organization, Geneva.

Kennes, W. (2000) *Small Developing Countries and Global Markets: Competing in the Big League.* Macmillan Press, Basingstoke.

Langhammer, R.J. and M. Lücke (2000) *WTO Negotiations and Accession Issues for Vulnerable Economies. Kiel Working Paper 990.* Kiel Institute of World Economics, Kiel.

Laurent, E. (forthcoming) 'Small States in the Banana Dispute: And the Environment for Bananas from the Eastern Caribbean Countries, Following the Implementation of the Reforms of the European Union's Banana Market'. Commonwealth Secretariat, London.

Levantis, T., F. Jotzo and V. Tulpule (2003) *Ending of EU Sugar Trade Preferences: Potential Consequences for Fiji. ABARE Current Issues 03.2.* Australian Bureau of Agricultural and Resource Economics, Canberra.

Malua, M.B. (2003) 'Case Study: The Pacific Islands,' in *Turning Losses into Gains: SIDS and Multilateral Trade Liberalisation in Agriculture.* UNCTAD, Canberra. UNCTAD/DITC/ TNCD/2003/1. United Nations Conference on Trade and Development, New York and Geneva, pp.171–204.

Mattoo, A. and A. Subramanian (2004) *The WTO and the Poorest Countries: The Stark Reality. IMF Working Paper 81.* International Monetary Fund, Washington, DC.

Melville, G. (2003) 'Case Study: The Windward Islands', in *Turning Losses into Gains: SIDS and Multilateral Trade Liberalisation in Agriculture,* UNCTAD (ed). UNCTAD/DITC/ TNCD/ 2003/1. United Nations Conference on Trade and Development, New York and Geneva, pp.97–126.

Michalopoulos, C. (2002) 'WTO Accession', in *Development, Trade, and the WTO: A Handbook,* B. Hoekman, A. Mattoo, and P. English (eds). World Bank, Washington, DC, pp.61–70.

Mitchell, D. (2004) *Sugar Policies: Opportunities for Change. World Bank Policy Research Working Paper 3222.* World Bank, Washington, DC.

MoFA (2004) *Beneficiaries of Japan's GSP.* Ministry of Foreign Affairs of Japan, Tokyo. 18 February, 2005: http://www.mofa.go.jp/policy/economy/gsp/benef.html.

Murray, D.J. (1981) 'Microstates: Public Administration for the Small and Beautiful', *Public Administration and Development,* 1, pp.245–56.

Narlikar, A. (2003) *International Trade and Developing Countries: Bargaining Coalitions in the GATT & WTO.* Routledge, London.

OXFAM (2004) An End to EU Sugar Dumping? Implications of the Interim WTO Panel Ruling in the Dispute against EU Sugar Policies Brought by Brazil, Thailand, and Australia. Oxfam International, Washington, DC.

Oyejide, T.A. (2002) 'Special and Differential Treatment,' in *Development, Trade, and the WTO: A Handbook,* B. Hoekman, A. Mattoo, and P. English (eds). World Bank, Washington, DC, pp.504–8.

Ozden, C. and Reinhardt, E. (2003) *The Perversity of Preferences: GSP and Developing Country Trade Policies, 1976-2000. World Bank Policy Research Working Paper 2955.* World Bank, Washington, DC.

Ozden, C. and Sharma, G. (2004) *Price Effects of Preferential Market Access: The Caribbean Basic Initiative and the Apparel Sector. World Bank Policy Research Working Paper 3244.* World Bank, Washington, DC.

Page, S. and Kleen, P. (2004) *Special and Differential Treatment of Developing Countries in the World Trade Organization.* Overseas Development Institute, London.

Panagariya, A. (2002) 'EU Preferential Trade Arrangements and Developing Countries', *The World Economy*, 25, pp.1415-32.

PIFS (1998) 'SPARTECA: What Is SPARTECA?'. Pacific Islands Forum Secretariat, Suva. 18 February, 2005. http://www.forumsec.org.fj/docs/SPARTECA/Sec1.htm.

Rasmussen, T.N. (2004) *Macroeconomic Implications of Natural Disasters in the Caribbean. IMF Working Paper 224.* International Monetary Fund, Washington, DC.

Read, R. (1999) *The Case for Special and Differential Treatment of Small Island Developing States (SIDS) under the WTO.* University of Lancaster, Lancaster.

Read, R. (2004) 'The Implications of Increasing Globalization and Regionalism for the Economic Growth of Small Island States', *World Development*, 32, pp.365-78.

Rodrik, D. (2002) 'Trade Policy Reform as Institutional Reform', in *Development, Trade, and the WTO: A Handbook*, B. Hoekman, A. Mattoo, and P. English (eds). World Bank, Washington, DC, pp.3-10.

Romalis, J. (2003) *Would Rich Country Trade Preferences Help Poor Countries Grow? Evidence from the Generalized System of Preferences.* University of Chicago, Chicago.

Salmon, J.M. (2002) *The Treatment of Small and Vulnerable Island Economies in the EPA Negotiations.* Université des Antilles et de la Guyane.

Salmon, J.M. (2003) 'Case Study: The Indian Ocean Islands,' in *Turning Losses into Gains: SIDS and Multilateral Trade Liberalisation in Agriculture*, UNCTAD (ed.). UNCTAD/DITC/TNCD/2003/1. United Nations Conference on Trade and Development, New York and Geneva, pp.127-69.

Saqib, M. (2003) 'Technical Barriers to Trade and the Role of Indian Standard-Setting Institutions,' in *India and the WTO*, A. Mattoo and R.M. Stern (eds). World Bank and Oxford University Press, Washington, DC, pp.269-98.

Schahczenski, J.J. (1990) 'Development Administration in the Small Developing State: A Review', *Public Administration and Development*, 10, pp.69-80.

Schiff, M. (1996) *Small Is Beautiful: Preferential Trade Agreements and the Impact of Country Size, Market Share, Efficiency, and Trade Policy. World Bank Policy Research Working Paper 1668.* World Bank, Washington, DC.

Schiff, M. (2002) *Regional Integration and Development in Small States. World Bank Policy Research Working Paper 2797.* World Bank, Washington, DC.

Schiff, M. and S. Andriamananjara (1998) *Regional Groupings among Microstates. World Bank Policy Research Working Paper 1922.* World Bank, Washington, DC.

South Pacific Forum Secretariat (2001) 'Sharing Capacity: The Pacific Experience with Regional Co-Operation and Integration', in *Small States in the Global Economy*, D. Peretz, R. Faruqi, and E. J. Kisanga (eds). Commonwealth Secretariat, London, pp.507-31.

Srinivasan, T.N. (1986) 'The Costs and Benefits of Being a Small, Remote, Island, Landlocked, or Ministrate Economy', *World Bank Research Observer*, 1, pp.205-18.

Stevens, C. (2002) *The Future of Special and Differential Treatment (SDT) for Developing Countries in the WTO. IDS Working Paper 163*. Institute of Development Studies, Brighton.

Streeten, P. (1993) 'The Special Problems of Small Countries', *World Development*, 21, pp.197–202.

Subramanian, A. (2003) 'Financing of Losses from Preference Erosion'. WT/TF/COH/14 Communication from the IMF, 14 February. World Trade Organisation, Geneva.

Subramanian, A. (2003) 'India as User and Creator of Intellectual Property: The Challenges Post-Doha,' in *India and the WTO*, A. Mattoo and R.M. Stern (eds). World Bank and Oxford University Press, Washington, DC and Oxford, pp.169-95.

Tangermann, S. (2000) 'The Cotonou Agreement and the Value of Preferences in Agricultural Markets for the African ACP'. Paper prepared for UNCTAD. Institute of Agricultural Economics, Gottingen.

Tortora, M. (2002) 'Annotated Agenda on the Acp Parallel Trade Negotiations at the WTO and with the EC: The Critical Path and the Work to Be Done'. WEB/CDP/REPT/5. United Nations Conference on Trade and Development, New York and Geneva.

Trade Point (2005) 'Trade Agreements: Caribcan'. Trade Point, Port of Spain. 18 February, 2005. http://www.tradetnt.com/caribcan.shtml.

Treebhoohun, N. (2001) 'The Mauritian Experience,' in *Small States in the Global Economy*, D. Peretz, R. Faruqi, and E.J. Kisanga (eds). Commonwealth Secretariat, London, pp.457-79.

Tulloch, P. (2001) 'Small Economies in the WTO', in *Small States in the Global Economy*, D. Peretz, R. Faruqi, and E.J. Kisanga (eds). Commonwealth Secretariat, London, pp.257-66.

Tussie, D. and M.F. Lengyel (2002) 'Developing Countries: Turning Participation into Influence', in *Development, Trade, and the WTO: A Handbook*, B. Hoekman, A. Mattoo, and P. English (eds). World Bank, Washington, DC, pp.485-92.

UNCTAD (2003a) *Turning Losses into Gains: SIDS and Multilateral Trade Liberalisation in Agriculture*. UNCTAD/DITC/TNCD/2003/1. United Nations Conference on Trade and Development, New York and Geneva.

UNCTAD (2003b) *Major Developments and Recent Trends in International Banana Marketing Structures*. UNCTAD/DTIC/COM/2003/1. United Nations Conference on Trade and Development, New York and Geneva.

UNCTAD (2003c) *UNCTAD Handbook of Statistics*. TD/STAT.28. United Nations Conference on Trade and Development, New York and Geneva.

UNCTAD (2004a) *Is a Special Treatment of Small Island Developing States Possible?* UNCTAD/LDC/2004/1. United Nations Conference on Trade and Development, New York and Geneva.

UNCTAD (2004b) *The Least Developed Countries Report 2004*. UNCTAD/LDC/2004. United Nations Conference on Trade and Development, New York and Geneva.

UNCTAD (2004c) *Development and Globalization: Facts and Figures*. UNCTAD/GDS/CSIR/2004/1. United Nations Conference on Trade and Development, New York and Geneva.

USTR (2004a) 'Caribbean Basin Initiative'. Office of the United States Trade Representative, Washington, DC. 18 February, 2005. http://www.ustr.gov/Trade_Development/Preference _Programs/CBI/Section_Index.html

USTR (2004b) *2004 Comprehensive Report on U.S. Trade and Investment Policy toward Sub-Saharan Africa and Implementation of the African Growth and Opportunity Act*. Office of the United States Trade Representative, Washington, DC.

USTR (2004c) 'Addendum (to U.S. Generalized System of Preferences Guidebook)'. Office of the United States Trade Representative, Washington, DC. 18 February, 2005: http://www.ustr. gov/assets/Trade_Development/Preference_Programs/GSP/asset_upload_file90_5432.pdf

Vossenaar, R. (2004) 'Trade and the Environment: An Important Relationship for SIDS', in *Is a Special Treatment of Small Island Developing States Possible?*, UNCTAD (ed.). UNCTAD/LDC/2004/1. United Nations Conference on Trade and Development, New York and Geneva, pp.57–90.

Watkins, K. (2004) *Dumping on the World: How EU Sugar Policies Hurt Poor Countries*. Oxfam International, Washington, DC.

Wilson, J.S. (2002) 'Standards, Regulation, and Trade: WTO Rules and Developing Country Concerns', in *Development, Trade, and the WTO: A Handbook*, B. Hoekman, A. Mattoo, and P. English (eds). World Bank, Washington, DC, pp.428–38.

Winters, L.A. and P.M.G. Martins (2004a) *Beautiful but Costly: Business Costs in Small Remote Economies*. Commonwealth Secretariat, London.

Winters, L.A. and P.M.G. Martins (2004b) *When Comparative Advantage Doesn't Matter: Business Costs in Small Economies*. Commonwealth Secretariat, London.

World Bank (2001) *Catastrophe Risk Management: Using Alternative Risk Financing and Insurance Pooling Mechanisms*. World Bank, Washington, DC.

World Bank (2002a) *Pacific Islands Regional Economic Report: Embarking on a Global Voyage: Trade Liberalization and Complementary Reforms in the Pacific*. World Bank, Washington, DC.

World Bank (2002b) *Caribbean Economic Overview 2002: Macroeconomic Volatility, Household Vulnerability, and Institutional and Policy Reponses*. World Bank, Washington, DC.

World Bank (2003) 'World Bank and IMF Announce Plans to Support Developing Countries with Trade-Related Adjustment Needs in the WTO Round', News Release 2004/62/S. World Bank, Washington, DC. 20 January, 2005. http://web.worldbank.org/WBSITE/EXTERNAL/ NEWS/ 0,,contentMDK:20124989~menuPK:34463~pagePK:64003015~piPK:64003012~theSitePK:4607,00.html.

World Bank (2004) 'World Development Indicators Database', World Bank, Washington, DC. 31 January, 2005. http://www.esds.ac.uk.

World Bank Institute (2002) 'Governance Research Indicators Dataset', World Bank, Washington, DC. 2 February, 2005. http://www.worldbank.org/wbi/governance/govdata2002/index.html.

WTO (1999) *Proposals for Addressing Concerns on Marginalization of Certain Small Economies*. WT/GC/W/361, 12 October, 1999. World Trade Organization, Geneva.

WTO (2001) Ministerial Declaration: Adopted on 14 November 2001. WT/MIN(01)/DEC/1, 20 November 2001. World Trade Organization, Geneva.

WTO (2002) *Small Economies: A Literature Review: Note by the Secretariat*. WT/COMTD/SE/W/4, 23 July 2002. World Trade Organization, Geneva.

WTO (2004a) *Members and Observers*. World Trade Organization, Geneva. 1 February, 2005. http://www.wto.org/english/thewto_e/whatis_e/tif_e/org6_e.htm.

WTO (2004b) Doha Work Programme: Decision Adopted by the General Council on 1 August 2004. WT/L/579, 2 August 2004. World Trade Organization, Geneva.

1 Ozden and Reinhardt (2003: 4).

1 Based on data in UNCTAD (2003c); see also Grynberg (2001b: 330) and Briguglio (1995: 1622), and Collier and Dollar (2001: 23) on higher per capita aid receipts in small states than in large.

Part 3
ECONOMIC PERFORMANCE

4. Economic Vulnerability and Resilience: Concepts and Measurements

Lino Briuglio

I. Background

Chapter 17 of Agenda 21, emanating from the 1992 UN Conference on Environment and Development, asserts that small island developing states are a special case for both environment and development, and that they face special challenges in planning and implementing sustainable development. The Programme of Action for the Sustainable Development of Small Island Developing States (SIDS Programme of Action), approved during the 1994 UN Global Conference held in Barbados, identified the priority areas for action to address the special challenges faced by SIDS. During the Barbados Global Conference and in many subsequent international fora on the sustainable development of SIDS, it was established that small island developing states merit special consideration in view of a number of factors, including economic vulnerability.

The Barbados Programme of Actions (BPoA) for the sustainable development of SIDS was endorsed by the General Assembly in 1994 in its resolution 49/122 of 19 December 1994, with Paragraphs 113 and 114 calling for the development of a vulnerability index (indices) for small island developing States (SIDS) as follows:

'Small island developing States, in cooperation with national, regional and international organizations and research centres, should continue work on the development of vulnerability indices and other indicators that reflect the status of small island developing States and integrate ecological fragility and economic vulnerability. Consideration should be given to how such an index, as well as relevant studies undertaken on small island developing States by other international institutions, might be used in addition to other statistical measures as quantitative indicators of fragility.'

In 1996 the Commission on Sustainable Development called on 'the relevant bodies of the United Nations system to accord priority to the development of the index'. Subsequently the Department of Economic and Social Affairs 1997, engaged two consultants, Professor Lino Briuglio of the University of Malta and Dr Dennis Pantin of the University of the West Indies, one to develop an economic vulnerability index, and the other to develop an ecological vulnerability index. The Department also convened an ad hoc expert group to review the technical work of the consultants and to make appropriate recommendations. The meeting, held at UN headquarters in December 1997, concluded that 'Judging from the results of a number of studies using a diversity of approaches, in particular, two reports of the Commonwealth Secretariat, the report of UNCTAD and the reports of consultants that were submitted to the meeting, the group concluded that .... as a group small island developing States are more vulnerable than other groups of developing countries.' (A/53/65 - E/1998/5) (see www.un.org/documents/ecosoc/docs/1998/e1998-5.htm).

One outcome of this meeting was the development of the economic vulnerability index by the Committee for Development Policy (of the UN ECOSOC), which it uses as one of the criteria to identify the least-developed countries and to decide which countries are to be graduated from the list of LDCs (UN CDP, 2005; Encontre, 2004).

Other international fora, including the 1999 UN General Assembly special session and the International Meeting on the 10-year review of the BPoA held in Mauritius in January 2005,[1] as well as various meetings of experts convened by the Commonwealth Secretariat between 1996 and 2000, gave prominence to the economic vulnerability of SIDS.

At the Commonwealth Heads of Government Meeting (CHOGM) held in Malta 25–27 November, 2005, the issue of economic vulnerability was again on the agenda, and member states issued a statement titled the 'Gozo Statement on Vulnerable Small States' which highlighted the high degree of economic vulnerability of these states.[2]

Original studies and recent updates of the economic vulnerability index carried out by the University of Malta (Briguglio 1992, 1993, 1995, 1997), Briguglio and Galea (2003) and Farrugia (2004) again confirm this tendency.

More recent meetings organised by the Commonwealth Secretariat and the University of Malta, in March 2004, March 2005 and April 2006, led to the construction of a resilience index, which when juxtaposed against the vulnerability index assessed the risk of being harmed by external shocks (see http://events.um.edu.mt/resilience2007).

2. What makes countries economically vulnerable?

Economic vulnerability stems from a number of **inherent** and **permanent**[3] economic features, including:

- a high degree of economic openness, rendering these states particularly susceptible to economic conditions in the rest of the world;

- dependence on a narrow range of exports, giving rise to risks associated with lack of diversification;

- dependence on strategic imports, in particular energy and industrial supplies, exacerbated by limited import substitution possibilities; and

- insularity, peripherality and remoteness, leading to high transport costs and marginalisation from the main commercial centres.

SIDS tend to be particularly vulnerable because of their small size and insularity. Small size forces SIDS to resort to international trade more than other group of countries. They need to find export markets due to their small domestic market, and they need to import heavily, due to their lack of natural resources. At the same size, the small size of their market limits the possibilities for diversification.

Small size leads to additional constraints, since it limits SIDS's ability to reap the benefits of economies of scale, leads to high infrastructural, administrative and other overhead costs, and poses additional constraints, such as limited attraction for foreign direct investment (FDI).

Small size also leads to the prevalence of natural monopolies and oligoplistic structures, leading to high consumer costs. Transforming a government monopoly into a private business may even make matters worse, due to fact that a private monopoly is often less accountable to consumers than the public sector.

3. The Economic Vulnerability Index

3.1 The University of Malta and Commonwealth Secretariat Indices

The economic vulnerability indices as developed by Briguglio, the Commonwealth Secretariat and Crowards, generally include a relatively small number of variables, often limited to three to five. One reason for this is that many economic variables are correlated, and one variable can be used to represent others.

The most frequent variables used as components of economic vulnerability indices relate to:

- economic openness;

- export concentration;

- dependence on strategic imports, such as fuel and food; and

- peripherality.

3.1.1 Economic openness

Economic openness captures the degree to which a state is susceptible to economic conditions in the rest of the world. It is often measured by expressing exports or imports, or an average of both, as a percentage of GDP.[4]

Dependence on a narrow range of exports

The range of exports captures the extent to which a country lacks export diversification, a condition that exacerbates the degree of economic openness. This is usually measured by the export concentration index devised by UNCTAD, which only covers merchandise. Briguglio (1997) argued that export concentration can also be observed in the trade in services, especially in tourism and financial services, and he devised a concentration index with services and exports included.

Peripherality

Peripherality is associated with insularity and remoteness, leading to high transport costs and marginalisation. The problem with remoteness and insularity is that these variables cannot be measured directly by taking the number of kilometres from a main commercial centre, the nearest island or the nearest continent. In the case of certain islands, a relatively large proportion of international trade is directed to and from their ex-colonising powers, even though other centres of commercial activity could be more proximate. In other words, measuring remoteness by taking distance in kilometres may convey the wrong sort of information regarding insularity and remoteness, for economic purposes. Two variables which may reflect the effects of remoteness are (a) the ratio of FOB/CIF factors and (b) the ratio of transport and freight costs to imports. The second has been considered to be more meaningful in studies that utilise the 'peripherality' variable.

Dependence on strategic imports

This variable is intended to measure the extent to which a country's livelihood depends on imports. There are obvious vulnerability connotations, when a country depends heavily on imported energy and industrial supplies for production and on imported food for consumption. Various indices have been used for this purpose. Briguglio (1997) and Atkins et al (2001) suggested that this variable can be measured as average imports of commercial energy as a percentage of domestic energy production.

These variables are suitably standardised, and combined together in a composite index. In some studies, the summing procedure involved weighting.[5]

A recent study conducted by Briguglio and Galea (2003) updated the vulnerability index using these variables and reconfirmed that SIDS tend to:

- be more exposed to international trade;

- have higher concentration indices;

- be more dependent on strategic imports; and

- have higher transport costs than other groups of countries.

As a result SIDS tends to have higher economic vulnerability scores.

3.2 The CDP Vulnerability Index

An alternative formulation of the vulnerability index is that proposed by the by the Committee for Development Policy (CDP) of the UN ECOSOC. According to the CDP, the Economic Vulnerability Index developed by the Committee reflects the risk posed to a country's development by exogenous shocks, the impact of which depends on the magnitude of the shocks, and on structural characteristics that determine the extent to which the country would be affected by such shocks.

Originally, the variables used in the CDP index were (1) population size; (2) share of manufacturing and modern services in GDP; (3) merchandise export concentration; (4) instability of agricultural production; and (5) instability of exports of goods and services. A number of modifications were proposed by the Committee at its seventh session (UN CDP, 2005), and the index now consists of seven indicators, namely: (1) population size; (2) remoteness; (3) merchandise export concentration; (4) share of agriculture, forestry and fisheries in gross domestic product; (5) homelessness owing to natural disasters; (6) instability of agricultural production; and (7) instability of exports of goods and services.

The CDP uses this index as one of the criteria for the identification of least-developed countries (LDCs) and for deciding which countries are to be graduated from the list of LDCs. The CDP Vulnerability Index assigns importance to instability, which implies that countries with relatively unstable export growth or agriculture production will register higher vulnerability scores. The variables 'share of agriculture, forestry and fisheries' and 'merchandise export concentration' are intended to capture the extent to which a country is structurally exposed to shocks. The index is also assumed to capture the structural handicaps that explain the high exposure of the economy, namely economic smallness, (measured with a population variable[6]) and remoteness.

4. Vulnerability and resilience

Resilience can be defined in many ways, but here it is defined as the ability to recover from or adjust to change. This definition is associated with the coping ability of an economically vulnerable country.

Resilience may be inherent or nurtured. The inherent aspect of resilience may be considered as the **obverse of vulnerability**, in the sense that inherently resilient countries should register low vulnerability scores.

Nurtured resilience is that which is developed and managed, often as a result of some deliberate policy. In this sense, a country can adopt policies which enable it to withstand its inherent vulnerability, thereby nurturing its resilience. This is of course what is meant by resilience building. On the other hand, a country can adopt polices which exacerbate its inherent vulnerability.

	Countries that adopt policies to withstand vulnerability	Countries that adopt polices that exacerbate vulnerability
Inherently vulnerable countries	The 'self-made' scenario	Worst-case scenario
Inherently resilient countries	Best-case scenario	The 'prodigal son' scenario

Four possible scenarios

We can therefore consider four possible country scenarios with regard to vulnerability and resilience as follows:

This method of defining vulnerability in terms of inherent features and resilience in terms of policy measures has a number of advantages, including:

(a) The vulnerability measurement would refer to features on which a state has little or no control and therefore cannot be attributed to bad governance. In other words, a country with a high inherent vulnerability score cannot be described as having self-inflicted vulnerability.

(b) The resilience component would refer to what a country can do in perms of policy. In this regard, the international donor community can be a source of support to enable vulnerable countries to build up their resilience.

Usefulness of considering resilience building

The issue of resilience building in small states is important because it carries the message that these states should not be complacent regarding their development possibilities, even if inherently economically vulnerable. In other words, they should adopt measures to build economic, environmental and social resilience (see Briguglio et al., 2006).

In addition, the discussion on resilience sheds light on why a number of vulnerable small states have managed to do well economically in spite of (and not because of) their inherent economic vulnerability. Briguglio (2002) has referred to this reality as the 'Singapore Paradox'.[7]

5. Measuring resilience

Briguglio et at (2006) have constructed a resilience index, to complement the vulnerability index, and to assess the degree to which economically vulnerable countries, individually or as a group, are moving ahead or otherwise, in coping with or withstanding economic vulnerability.

The variables selected for this purpose were:

(a) good governance, which consisted of five components, namely (i) judicial independence; (ii) impartiality of courts; (iii) the protection of intellectual property rights; (iv) military interference in the rule of law; and (v) political system and the integrity of the legal system; the data was derived from: Gwartney and Lawson, 2005);

(b) macroeconomic stability which was measured by made up of the simple average of the following three variables: (i) the fiscal deficit to GDP ratio; (ii) the sum of the unemployment and inflation rates; and (iii) the external debt to GDP ratio; the major data sources was the International Monetary Fund;

(c) market reform which was derived from the Economic Freedom of the World and is intended to measure the extent to which regulatory restraints and bureaucratic procedures limit competition and the operation of financial, labour and product markets; daa was derived from the Gwartney Lawson (2005).

(d) social development which was measured by the education and health indices of the Human Development Index for the years 2000 to 2002 (UNDP, 2002; 2003; 2004).

6. Concluding considerations

A number of considerations emerge from this write-up:

(a) The Economic Vulnerability Indices produced so far indicate clearly that small states, particularly SIDS, tend to be more economically vulnerable than other groups of countries.

(b) Many small states have managed to register high GDP scores in the past in spite of their inherent economic vulnerability. This suggests that these states have adopted policies to withstand or cope with their vulnerability.

(c) SIDS with a relatively low GDP per capita are vulnerable and poor, and therefore merit special attention and support by the donor community, to enable them to strengthen their resilience

(d) Building economic resilience to cope with and withstand economic vulnerability should take centre stage in the sustainable development strategy of such states. The international donor community should assist small states that do not have the resources or the capacity to strengthen their resilience

(e) It would be useful to construct a resilience index, to complement the vulnerability index, and to assess the degree to which economically vulnerable countries, individually or as a group, are moving ahead or otherwise, in coping with or withstanding economic vulnerability.

Notes

1. There were three regional meetings in the run-up to the Mauritius meeting, respectively held in Samoa (October 2003) for the Pacific region, Cape Verde (September 2004) for the AIMS region, and Trinidad and Tobago (October 2003) for the Caribbean region. The interregional meeting was held at The Bahamas in January 2004. In all these meetings, the vulnerability of SIDS was extensively discussed.

2. The document is available at: www.thecommonwealth.org/document/147536/gozo_statement_on_vulnerable_small_states.htm

3. There are human-induced measures (possibly as a result of bad policies or lack of awareness) which exacerbate the inherent vulnerability of SIDS. In this paper these are considered to be man-made actions leading to the weakening of resilience against vulnerability.

4. During the December 1997 UN meeting on the Vulnerability Index, it was argued that this variable should not form part of the vulnerability index because high dependence on foreign trade is not a disadvantage but a strength of SIDS. As a result, the Committee for Development Policy (UN ECOSOC) excluded this variable from its Vulnerability Index.

5. The Commonwealth Vulnerability index uses Least Squares Method to derive the weights. Briguglio and Crowards use equal weights, although they have also experimented with variable weights.

6. The population size indicator is very problematic, if the index is to be used in the context of SIDS, since it will bias the index in favour of small states, thereby begging the question. It would therefore not be proper to use this sub-index to show that small states are more vulnerable than larger ones.

7. It is sometimes argued that many small states have managed to register high GDP scores in the past, partly as a result of the preferential trade arrangements that they enjoyed, and the incentive package they were allowed to put in place to attract FDI. However, the success of the likes of Singapore, Cyprus, Malta, Barbados and other small states cannot be attributed simply to trade preferences.

8. This could happen if, for example, two or more variables reflect the same underlying changes, in which case they would be measuring the same thing and, if included in a composite index, would implicitly increase the weight of that underlying change.

References

Atkins, J., S. Mazzi and C. Easter (2001) 'Small States: A Composite Vulnerability Index' in D. Peretz, R. Faruqi and J. Eliawony (eds) *Small States in the Global Economy*. Commonwealth Secretariat, London.

Atkins, J., S. Mazzi and C. Ramlogan (1998) *A Study on the Vulnerability of Developing and Island States: A Composite Index*. Commonwealth Secretariat, London.

Briguglio, L. (1992) *Preliminary Study on the Construction of an Index for Ranking Countries According to their Economic Vulnerability*. UNCTAD/LDC/Misc.4 1992.

Briguglio, L. (1993) *The Economic Vulnerabilities of Small Island Developing States*. Study commissioned by CARICOM for the Regional Technical Meeting of the Global Conference on the Sustainable Development of Small Island Developing States, Port of Spain, Trinidad and Tobago, July 1993.

Briguglio, L. (1995) 'Small Island States and their Economic Vulnerabilities', *World Development* Vol.23(9), pp.1615–32.

Briguglio, L. (1997) *Alternative Economic Vulnerability Indices for Developing Countries.* Report prepared for the Expert Group on Vulnerability Index, United Nations Department of Economic and Social Affairs-UN(DESA), December 1997.

Briguglio, L. and W. Galea (2003) 'Updating the Economic Vulneability Index', *Occasional Papers on Islands and Small States, No. 2003–4.*Islands and Small States Institute, Malta.

Briguglio, L., G. Farrugia Cordina and S. Vella (2006) 'Conceptualising and Measuring Economic Resilience', in L. Briguglio, G. Cordina and E. Kisanga (eds) *Building the Economic Resilience of Small States.* Commonwealth Secretariat and the University of Malta, Malta, pp.265–88.

Chander, R. (1996) 'Measurement of the Vulnerability of Small States'. Report prepared for the Commonwealth Secretariat, April 1996.

Crowards, T. (1999) *An Economic Vulnerability Index, with Special Reference to the Caribbean: Alternative Methodologies and Provisional Results.* Caribbean Development Bank, Barbados.

Crowards, T and W. Coultier (1998) *Economic Vulnerability in the Developing World with Special Reference to the Caribbean.* Caribbean Development Bank, Barbados.

Easter, Christopher D. (1998) *Small States and Development: A Composite Index of Vulnerability.* Small States: Economic Review and Basic Statistics, Commonwealth Secretariat, London, December 1998.

Encontre, P. (2004) 'Economic Vulnerability of Small island Developing States', in L. Briguglio and E. Kisanga (eds) *Economic Vulnerability and Resilience of Small States.* Commonwealth Secretariat and the University of Malta, pp.72–103.

Farrugia, N. (2004) 'Economic Vulnerability: Developing a New Conceptual Framework and Empirically Assessing Its Relationship with Economic Growth', unpublished Masters dissertation, Economics Department, University of Malta.

Gwartney, J. and R. Lawson (2005) *Economic Freedom of the World 2005.* Fraser Institute, Vancouver.

UN Committee for Development Policy (2005) *The Report on the seventh session (14-18 March 2005) of the CDP.* United Nations Publications, New York..

UNDP (2002, 2003, 2004) *Human Development Report.* Oxford University Press, New York.

5. The Economics of Isolation and Distance

Stephen J Redding and Anthony J Venables

I. Introduction

This chapter explores the economic implications of isolation and remoteness. Evidence of the impact of distance on trade costs and trade flows is reviewed, and the effects of remoteness on real incomes are investigated. Empirical work confirms the predictions of theory, that distance from markets and sources of supply can have a significant negative impact on per capita income. The possible implications of new technologies for these spatial inequalities are discussed.

A recent programme of research at the Centre for Economic Performance at the London School of Economics evaluated the effects of geography in determining trade flows, the location of economic activity, and the extent of income differentials between countries.[1] Although not directed especially at the problems faced by small or isolated economies, the central issues researched are the interactions between scale and proximity. There are benefits to be derived from being large and from being close to centres of economic activity, and the research seeks to understand these benefits, assess their magnitude, and evaluate the rate at which they fall off with distance from the centre. The purpose of this chapter is to draw out some of the implications of this research for small and isolated economies that are deprived of these benefits.

The point of departure is to ask 'Why do isolation and distance matter for economic performance?'. There are several main considerations. The first is simply that having good access to markets is valuable for firms. The access can derive from two sources: one is proximity to other countries with good export markets, and the other is domestic scale, i.e. the extent to which the home market can provide an alternative to exports. Countries that are both remote and small forego both these sources of market access. The second consideration is access to suppliers of intermediate and capital goods. Again, the supply of these goods can be from imports or domestic supply, and remoteness and smallness will have the effect of impeding the supply and raising the prices of these goods. A further penalty may arise if the flow of ideas and technologies is curtailed with distance. Although the determinants of these flows are not well understood, there is a good deal of evidence that proximity to centres of technology matters in both the development and application of R&D.

These forces can give rise to spatial clustering of economic activity, showing up both at the level of a single industry (e.g. electronics in Silicon Valley or financial services in London) and at a more aggregate level (the formation of cities and industrial districts). There is evidence – derived from studies of sub-national data in both the US and the EU – that productivity levels are higher where economic activity is dense, with causality running from density to productivity (Ciccone and Hall (1996) for the US, Ciccone (2002) for the EU). This effect can be a source of benefit for small and densely populated city states – a Singapore or Hong Kong effect. However, many more countries lack the scale to develop their own clusters of activity, and suffer the cost of remoteness from existing centres.

Although this is not an exhaustive list of the costs of smallness, the remainder of this chapter will focus on drawing out some of the facts that have been established concerning these forces. (Other factors that are important are economies of scale in public sector activities and the commodity concentration of small countries' exports, with the associated high levels of variability of export earnings.) We look first (Section 2) at the direct effects of distance on economic interactions, particularly the costs of making trades across space. We then turn (Section 3) to their implications for per capita income levels. Finally, (Section 4), we present a few ideas on the possible effects of new technologies on these relationships.

2. The direct costs of distance

2.1 Distance and economic interactions

However much we hear about globalisation, a startling feature of economic life is how local most economic interactions are, and how sharply they decline with distance. Trade economists have explored this relationship with 'gravity models' in which bilateral trade flows are explained by the economic mass (for example GDP) of the exporter and importer countries, and 'between-country' variables such as distance, and perhaps also by whether they share a common border, language, or membership of a regional integration agreement. Extensive data permits the gravity trade model to be estimated on the bilateral trade flows of one hundred or more countries, and studies find that the elasticity of trade flows with respect to distance is around -0.9 to -1.5. This implies that volumes of trade decline very steeply with distance. Table 1 expresses trade volumes at different distances relative to their value at 1,000km: with a representative value of this elasticity -1.25, doubling distance more than halves trade flows; by 4,000km volumes are down by 82 per cent and by 8,000km down by 93 per cent.

Similar methodologies have been used to study other sorts of economic interactions and are also reported in Table 5.1. Portes and Rey (1999) study cross-border equity transactions (using data for 14 countries accounting for around 87 per cent of global equity market capitalisation, 1989-96). Their main measure of a country's mass is

Table 5.1. Economic interactions and distance (Flows relative to their magnitude at 1,000km)

	Trade (0= -1.25)	Equity flows (0= -0.85)	FDI (0= -0.42)	Technology
1,000 km	1	1	1	1
2,000 km	0.42	0.55	0.75	0.65
4,000 km	0.18	0.31	0.56	0.28
8,000 km	0.07	0.17	0.42	0.05

Sources: see text.

stock market capitalisation, and their baseline specification gives an elasticity of trans-actions with respect to distance of -0.85. This indicates again how – controlling for the characteristics of the countries – distance matters. Other authors have studied foreign direct investment flows. Data limitations mean that the set of countries is quite small, and the estimated gravity coefficient is smaller, although still highly significant; for example, Di Mauro (2000) finds an elasticity of FDI flows with respect to distance of -0.42. The effect of distance on technology flows has been studied by Keller (2001) who looks at the dependence of total factor productivity (TFP) on R&D stocks (i.e. cumu-lated R&D expenditures) for 12 industries in the G7 countries, 1971–95. The R&D stocks include both the own-country stock, and foreign-country stocks weighted by distance using an estimated parameter. Both own- and foreign-country stocks are sig-nificant determinants of each country's TFP and so too is the distance effect, with R&D stocks in distant economies having much weaker effects on TFP than do R&D stocks in closer economies. The final column in Table 5.1 illustrates Keller's results by computing the spillover effects of R&D in country's more distant economies relative to an economy 1,000km away; the attenuation due to distance is once again dramatic.[2]

In addition, we also know that borders have a major effect in reducing economic interactions. Evidence from Canada–US trade suggests that even that most innocuous of borders has a huge impact. On average, the exports of Canadian provinces to other Canadian provinces are some twenty times larger than their exports to equivalently situated US states (Helliwell, 1997), and evidence from urban price movements sug-gests that the border imposes barriers to arbitrage comparable to 1,700 miles of physi-cal space (Engel and Rogers, 1996). Overall then, these facts tell us that geography still matters greatly for economic interaction.

2.2 The magnitude of shipping costs

Underlying the rate of decline of these interactions are a variety of costs. The easiest to measure and observe are freight charges, although other costs of time in transit and information costs are quite possibly more important.

Shipping costs on short or heavily used routes are typically quite low. For the US freight expenditure incurred on imports was only 3.8 per cent of the value of imports;

equivalent numbers for Brazil and Paraguay, for example, are 7.3 and 13.3 per cent (Hummels, 1999a, from customs data). However, these values incorporate the fact that most trade is with countries that are close, and in goods that have relatively low transport costs. Looking at transport costs unweighted by trade volumes gives much higher numbers. Thus if we take all possible bilateral trade flows for which data is available (some 20,000 combinations of importer and exporter countries), the median cif/fob ratio is 1.28, implying transport and insurance costs amounting to 28 per cent of the value of goods shipped. Looking across commodities, an unweighted average of freight rates is typically two to three times higher than the trade weighted average rate.

2.3 Determinations of shipping costs

Estimates of the determinants of transport costs are given in Hummels (1999b) and Limao and Venables (2001). These studies typically find elasticities of transport costs with respect to distance of between 0.2 and 0.3, meaning that a doubling of the distance over which goods are shipped increases freight costs by around 20 per cent. Sharing a common border substantially reduces transport costs and overland distance is around seven times more expensive than sea distance.

In addition to the effects of distance and mode transport, shipping costs are highly route specific, reflecting densities of traffic flow and monopoly power. For example, the cost of shipping a standard container 13,000km from Baltimore to Durban is US$2,500; shipping it 1,600km further to Lusaka costs an additional $2,500, while the 347km from Durban to Maseru (Lesotho) costs an additional $7,500. (Quotes from the shipping company used by the World Bank, cited in Limao and Venables 2001). Fink, Mattoo and Neagu (2000) study the impact of anti-competitive practices in the shipping industry, and estimate that these raise prices by more than 25 per cent: the break-up of private carrier agreements would, they estimate, save transport costs of $2 billion per year on imports to the US alone.

2.4 Landlocked countries

Landlocked countries face severe cost penalties. Research by Limao and Venables (2001) indicates that a representative landlocked country has transport costs approximately 50 per cent greater than does a representative coastal economy. Infrastructure quality (as measured by a composite of index of transport and communications networks) is also important. While this matters for all countries, it is particularly important for landlocked countries, as being dependent on both their own and their transit countries' infrastructure (at the 75th percentile of the distribution) makes landlocked countries' transport costs a full 75 per cent higher than those of a representative coastal economy.

These higher transport costs have a large impact on trade flows. The median landlocked economy (controlling for other factors) has trade flows 60 per cent lower than the median coastal economy. If, in addition, there is poor own infrastructure and transit-country infrastructure, then trade is 75 per cent lower than for the median costal economy.

2.5 The costs of time in transit

Direct shipping costs are only part of the costs of distance. Also important are search costs, that is finding and identifying trading partners and co-ordinating trades. Time in transit is important, and perhaps increasingly important as firms seek to apply 'just-in-time' management methods. Recent work by Hummels (2000) provides interesting evidence on the magnitude of time costs. He analyses data on some 25 million observations of shipments into the US, some by air and some by sea (imports classified at the 10-digit commodity level, by exporter country, and by district of entry to US for 25 years). Given data on the costs of each mode and the shipping times from different countries he is able to estimate the implicit value of time saved by using air transport. The numbers are quite large. The cost of an extra day's travel is (from estimates on imports as a whole) around 0.3 per cent of the value shipped. For manufacturing sectors, the number goes up to 0.5 per cent, costs that are around 30 times larger than the interest charge on the value of the goods. One implication of these is that freight costs alone (and the cif/fob ratio) grossly understate the costs of distance. Another is that transport costs have fallen much more through time than suggested by looking at freight charges alone. The share of US imports going by air freight rose from zero to 30 per cent between 1950 and 1998, and containerisation approximately doubled the speed of ocean shipping. Together these give a reduction in shipping time of 26 days, equivalent to a shipping cost reduction worth 12–13 per cent of the value of goods traded.

2.6 Remoteness and real income

The previous section made the point that distance matters greatly for economic interactions. How does this feed into the distribution of income across countries? A number of mechanisms might be at work, including the effects of investment flows and technology transfers. Here, to illustrate effects, we concentrate just on the way in which trade flows can generate international income gradients between central and peripheral countries.

The effect of distance on factor prices is easily seen through a simple example. Suppose that half of a firm's costs are intermediate goods, and one third labour, the remaining being returns to capital. How does the wage that a firm can afford to pay (while just breaking even) depend on the costs it has to bear on shipping its output to final consumers and importing its intermediate inputs? It turns out that a firm that faces 20 per cent transport costs can only afford to pay labour approximately 20 per cent as much as can a firm that faces zero transport costs. As transport costs rise to 30 per cent the wage the firm can afford to pay drops to 10 per cent, and at 40 per cent transport costs the firm can survive only if it pays its workers nothing. These numbers are based on an example where the cost of capital is the same in the remote country as in the centre. If this cost is higher, then wages in remote countries are depressed even further.

The point of this example is that in remote locations value added gets squeezed in two ways – the firm receives less for its output and pays more for imported equipment and intermediate goods. This means that even quite modest transport costs can have quite a dramatic effect on the wage that firms can afford to pay, and suggests that there will be quite steep 'wage gradients' from central to peripheral locations.

Redding and Venables (2001) measure these wage gradients for a sample of 101 countries.[3] Trade data are used to calculate economically correct measures of 'foreign market access' (FMA). This, like a measure of market potential, aggregates expenditure in different countries, with weights inversely proportional to distance and also depending on whether countries share a common border, are islands, or are landlocked. (The relative importance of these factors is found from econometric estimation of some specifications of a gravity model, see Redding and Venables (2001) for details). Thus, countries close to large foreign export markets have a high value FMA, while remote countries have low value FMAs.

Figure 5.1 presents the scatter plot of the relationship between this variable and per capita income (both measured in logs, country codes given in Annex 1), illustrating a strong positive relationship between the variables. For example, looking just within Europe, there is evidence of a wage gradient from Belgium/Luxembourg (countries with the best foreign market access) through France, Britain, to Spain, Portugal and Greece. Several other points stand out. One is that a number of countries are able to escape the consequence of remoteness from export markets – for example Australia, New Zealand, Japan, and the US. However, looking at the bottom right-hand area of the figure, good foreign market access provides a safety net against very low incomes – despite the relatively poor performance of former communist countries.

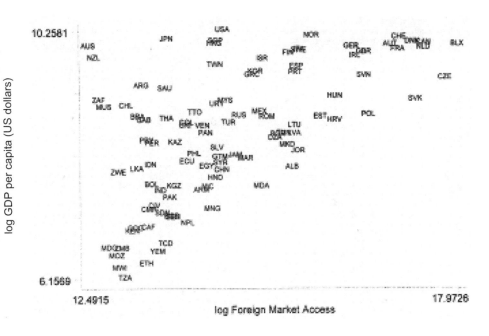

Figure 5.1. GDP per capita and FMA

As noted in the introduction, market access is derived both from proximity to export markets and from access to a large domestic market. Both proximity and scale matter. The scale effect was absent from Figure 5.1, but is included in Figure 5.2, where the horizontal axis is the sum of foreign market access (FMA) and 'domestic market access' (DMA) – a measure of domestic market size adjusted for the area of the country. Combining these effects provides very strong evidence of a wage gradient, indicating the importance of both proximity and scale in determining income levels.

Figures 5.1 and 5.2 just give market access (the penalty of being remote from markets), but 'supplier access' also matters. One of the mechanisms by which geographical remoteness depresses wages is the high price of imported equipment and intermediate goods in remote locations. Figure 5.3 presents some direct empirical evidence on the relationship between access to sources of supply and the relative price of these goods. The horizontal axis gives the proper measure of access to foreign suppliers of manufactures (FSA), again derived from trade data, and the vertical axis gives the relative price of machinery and equipment in countries for which data is available. We see a statistically significant negative relationship, confirming that remote countries have to pay higher prices for these goods, which contributes to the squeeze on wages that firms in these countries can afford to pay.

2.7 Quantifying the effects

Per capita incomes depend on additional factors, not just market and supplier access, and Redding and Venables undertake econometric analysis incorporating a set of other

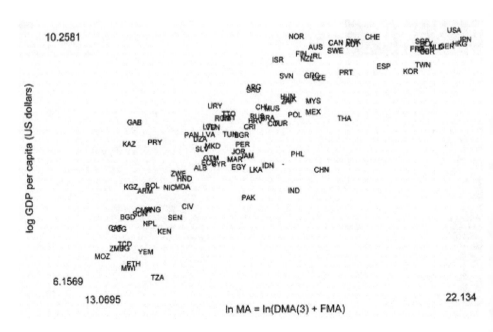

Figure 5.2. GDP per capita and MA = DMA(3) + FMA

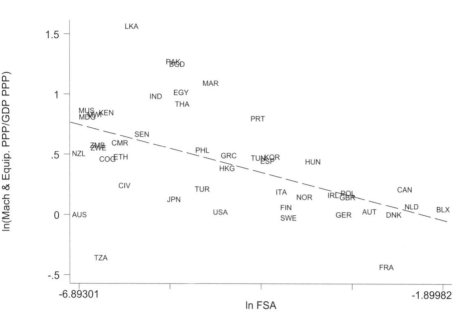

Figure 5.3. Relative price of machinery & equipment and FSA

variables. These include measure of endowments and of the quality of institutions, which are important determinants of per capita incomes levels. However, the geographical variables remain highly significant determinants of per capita income levels even once these further variables have been added in.

One way of illustrating the quantitative importance of geography is to undertake a set of hypothetical experiments of the form: suppose we move country A to the location of country B then, holding other things equal, what would happen to country A's income? Tables 5.2 and 5.3 report the results of a few experiments of this type. Being landlocked and being an island both have a negative effect on real income, and the first column indicates that the penalty from being landlocked is substantial – removing it would raise income by 25 per cent. (The model specification means that the same proportional effect is experienced by all countries.) The cost of island status is smaller, costing around 7 per cent of GDP (Column 2), while Column 3 reports a trade policy experiment: changing countries' trade openness (as measured by the Sachs-Warner (1995) openness index) from the 1994 value to the most open possible. This too yields extremely large income gains, of around 25 per cent for countries that were, in 1994, quite economically closed.

Column 4 reports the experiment of moving a country from its present location to that of Hungary, on the edge of the EU. The dramatic increase in FMA brought about by this change means that, for some of the most remote economies in the sample, income increases by nearly 80 per cent.

Table 5.2. Percentage change in real income from openness

Country	(1) Access to cost status	(2) Loss of island	(3) Become open	(2) Distance (Central Europe)
		Variable		
Australia		7.3%		
Sri Lanka		7.3%	20.79%	67.4%
Zimbabwe	24.0%		27.7%	
Paraguay	24.0%		25.3%	79.7%
Hungary	24.0%		26.5%	58.3%

Notes: Actual values for the Sachs and Warner (1995) openness index are 1 in Australia, 0.2321 in Sri Lanka, 0.038 in Hungary, 0.077 in Paraguay, and 0 in Zimbabwe.
Source: Redding and Venables (2000)

Common borders are also important for facilitating trade and improving market access, and Table 5.3 quantifies their importance by the hypothetical experiments of closing borders. The effects reported show that smaller countries gain very substantially from access to a large neighbour, as illustrated for Mexico and the Czech Republic. However two small neighbours, the two African economies, neither of which has a large market or a supply of manufactured products to offer, only experience extremely small border effects. An implication of this is that South–South regional integration schemes yield very limited benefits compared to fuller integration into the world economy as a whole.

3. New technologies: The death of distance?

Technical progress has lead to substantial reductions in trade costs in the last 40 years. Shipping and airfreight rates have both fallen, although the decline in these rates ended in the 1960s and 1980s respectively. We have already commented on the cost reductions associated with the speeding up of shipping.

Table 5.3. Percentage change in real income from border effects

Removal of common border	Effect on per capita income	
Germany – Czech Republic	Germany	Czech Republic
	-0.1%	-25.7%
US – Mexico	US	Mexico
	-0.5%	- 27.2%
Zimbabwe– Zambia	Zimbabwe	Zambia
	- 0.05%	- 0.11%

Source: Redding and Venables (2000)

In addition to these changes the development of information and communications technologies (ICT) has made the transmission of digital information virtually free. These technologies bring great benefits to isolated and distant economies, allowing faster and cheaper exchange of information and ideas. However, it is not clear that they overturn all the economic disadvantages of isolation or lead to the 'death of distance' as suggested by some authors (Cairncross, 2001). In this section we offer a few remarks about the likely implications of these new technologies for isolated and distant economies.

3.1 Weightless inputs and outputs

In some activities inputs and outputs can be digitalised - made 'weightless' - and shipped virtually free of charge. These activities can be related to lower wage economies, as recent experience indicates. The highly successful Indian software and IT-enabled services sectors had output in 2000 of $8 billion with exports of $4 billion. IT enabled services - call centres ('customer interaction centres'), medical transcriptions, finance and accounting services - had exports to the US of $0.26 billion, predicted to grow to $4 billion by 2005 (*The Economist*, 5 May, 2001). These are substantial-sized activities, compared to total Indian exports of $45 billion in 2000, but are less than 1 per cent of total US imports of around $950 billion. (For further discussion of the concept of weightlessness and the implications of new information and communication technologies for economic growth, see Quah, 1997 and 2001).

Development of these activities may prove extremely valuable to isolated and distant economies, although a couple of provisos need to be made. First, as activities are codified and digitised, so not only can they be moved costlessly through space, but also they are typically subject to very large productivity increases and price reductions. Thus, the effect of ICTs on, say, airline ticketing, has been primarily to replace labour by computer equipment, and only secondarily to allow remaining workers to be employed in India rather than the US or Europe. There is continuing technical progress in these activities so, for example, technology that can capture voice or handwriting will soon make Indian medical transcription obsolete. This suggests that even if more activities become weightless the share of world expenditure and employment attributable to these activities will remain small - perhaps as little as a few per cent of world GDP.

The second point is that small economies will face intense competition in attracting these activities, as the experience of India already suggests. There is a sense in which 'weightless' activities are the natural comparative advantage of remote economies, since these economies have a comparative disadvantage in transport intensive goods (Venables and Limao, 2002). However, success will require both the telecommunications infrastructure and the skill base to attract investments.

3.2 ICT and the costs of remote management

Recent years have seen the growth of both outsourcing and foreign direct investment (FDI), with the associated development of production networks or production chains.

FDI has grown faster than either income or trade. The growth of production networks has been studied by a number of researchers. One way to measure its growth is by looking at trade in components, and Yeats (1998) estimates that 30 per cent of world trade in manufactures is now trade in components rather than final products. Hummels, Ishii and Yi (2001) chart trade flows that cross borders multiple times, such as when a country imports a component and then re-exports it embodied in some downstream product. They find that for 10 OECD countries the share of imported value added in exports rose by one third between 1970 and 1990, reaching 21 per cent of export value.

Both FDI and outsourcing involve, in somewhat different ways, a fragmentation of the structure of the firm, as production is split into geographically and/or organisationally different units. From the international perspective this fragmentation offers the benefits of being able to move particular stages of the production process to the lowest cost locations – labour-intensive parts to low-wage economies, and so on. However, as well as involving potentially costly shipping of parts and components, it also creates formidable management challenges. Product specification and other information have to be transferred, and production schedules and quality standards have to be monitored. Do new technologies reduce the costs of doing this?

To the extent that pertinent information is 'codifiable' the answer is likely to be yes. The use of ICT for business-to-business trade is well documented, although it is reported to often reduce the number of suppliers a firm uses, rather than increase the number. In mass production of standardised products designs can be relatively easily codified; where the production process is routine, daily or hourly production runs can be reported and quality data can be monitored.

However, in many activities the pertinent information cannot be codified so easily. There are two sorts of reasons for this. One is the inherent complexity of the activity. For example, frequent design changes and a process of ongoing product design and improvement (involving both marketing and production engineering) may require a level of interaction that – at present – can only be achieved by face-to-face contact. The second reason is to do with the fact that contracts are incomplete, and people on either side of the contract (or in different positions within a single firm) have their own objectives. It is typically expensive or impossible to ensure that their incentives can be shaped to be compatible with meeting the objectives of the firm. While new technologies may reduce the costs of monitoring, it seems unlikely that these problems of incomplete contracts are amenable to a technological fix.

What evidence is there? On the one hand, there is the fact that in recent years there has been a dramatic increase in the outsourcing of activities to specialist suppliers, suggesting that difficulties in writing contracts and monitoring performance have been reduced. On the other hand, a number of empirical studies point to the continuing importance, despite new technologies, of regular face-to-face contact. Thus, Gaspar and Glaeser (1998) argue that telephones are likely to be complements, not substitutes, for face-to-face contact, as they increase the overall amount of business interaction. They suggest that, as a consequence, telephones have historically promoted the development of cities. The evidence on business travel suggests that as electronic communications have increased so too has travel, again indicating the importance of face-to-face contact. Leamer and Stoper (2000) draw the distinction between 'conversational' transactions – that can be done at a distance by ICT – and 'handshake' transactions that require face-to-face contact. New technologies allow a dispersion of activities that only require 'conversational' transactions, but might also increase the complexity of the production and design process, and hence increase the proportion of activities that require 'hand-shake' communication.

Overall then, it seems that there are some relatively straightforward activities where knowledge can be codified, new technologies will make management from a distance easier, and relocation of the activity to lower wage regions might be expected. But monitoring, control, and information exchange in more complex activities still requires a degree of contact that involves proximity and face-to-face meetings. Perhaps nowhere is this more evident than in the design and development of the new technologies themselves.

3.3 The speeding up of production

New technologies provide radical opportunities for speeding up parts of the overall supply process. There are several ways this can occur. One is simply that basic information – product specifications, orders and invoices – can be transmitted and processed more rapidly. Another is that information about uncertain aspects of the supply process can be discovered and transmitted sooner. For example, retailers' electronic stock control can provide manufacturers with real time information about sales and hence about changes in fashion and overall expenditure levels. For intermediate goods, improved stock controls and lean production techniques allow manufacturers to detect and identify defects in supplies more rapidly. These changes pose the interesting question: if some elements of the supply process become quicker, what does this do to the marginal value of time saved (or marginal cost of the delay) in other parts of the process? In particular, if one part of the process that takes time is the physical shipment of goods, then will time-saving technical changes encourage firms to move production closer to markets, or allow them to move further away?

There are some reasons to think that the effect might encourage firms to move production closer to markets. The new opportunities created for rapid response can be exploited only if all stages of production are fast. The highly successful Spanish clothing chain, Zara (*The Economist*, 19 May, 2001) provides an example. It uses real-time sales data, can make a new product line in three weeks (compared to the industry average of nine months), and only commits 15 per cent of production at the start of the season (industry average 60 per cent). It also does almost all its manufacturing (starting with basic fabric dyeing and continuing through the full manufacturing process) in-house in Spain, with most of the sewing done by 400 local co-operatives (compared to the extensive outsourcing of other firms in the industry). (For a formal analysis of the idea that new technologies may encourage firms to move production closer to markets, see Evans and Harrigan (2001).)

Just-in-time production techniques provide a further example. New technologies have allowed much improved stock control and ordering, and a consequent movement of suppliers towards their customers. In a study of the location of suppliers to the US automobile industry Klier (1999) finds that 70–80 per cent of suppliers are located within one day's drive of the assembly plant, although even closer location is limited by the fact that many suppliers serve several assembly plants. He also finds that the concentration of supplier plants around assembly plants has increased since 1980, a timing that he points out is consistent with the introduction of just-in-time production methods. The leader in the application of just-in-time techniques is Toyota, whose independent suppliers are on average only 59 miles away from its assembly plants, to which they make eight deliveries a day. By contrast, General Motor's suppliers in North America are an average of 427 miles away from the plants they serve, and make fewer than two deliveries a day. As a result, Toyota and its suppliers maintain inventories that are a quarter of General Motor's, when measured as a percentage of sales (*Fortune*, 8 December, 1997).

These examples suggest that, at least in some activities, remote economies may become more marginalised as a consequence of new technologies.

3.4 Clustering still matters

The arguments above suggest that new technologies will facilitate the relocation of some activities to lower wage locations. Other activities may become increasingly locked in to established centres. However, for activities that can relocate, clustering is likely to be important. Foreign direct investment projects will tend to go to locations where investors can see that other investors are doing well. Firms will want to move to locations where there is a deep pool of skilled labour and a network of local suppliers. These factors may militate against relocation of these activities to small countries.

Overall then, while it is clear that new technologies will bring many benefits, allowing isolated and remote countries closer contact with the outside world, the 'death of distance' view is misplaced. It is far from clear that new technologies will provide a straight-forward development strategy for these countries.

4. Conclusions

The review of research in this paper is partial in its coverage. For example, we have not discussed the implications of smallness for export concentration and for vulnerability, instead we concentrated on the costs of isolation and distance. These factors choke off economic interactions, mean that potential investors can only pay low wages, and reduce real income. New technologies bring benefits, but need further study. Some activities will become more entrenched in existing centres, others will relocate, and the relocation will likely lead to the formation of new clusters.

What are the policy implications of the preceding analysis? We offer just a few points. The first is that improvements in infrastructure are important. Changes that reduce isolation will affect prices in the economy, having non-marginal effects that need to be properly evaluated by social cost–benefit analysis. These changes do not necessarily require physical investments. Our discussion of the costs of time in transit points to the importance of port, customs, and other frontier delays in deterring investments. The example of Intel's investment in Costa Rica is instructive: Intel went ahead with a $300 million chip facility only after the government of Costa Rica had guaranteed rapid customs clearance of imports, free of bureaucratic and administrative blockages. Similarly, the discussion of shipping costs pointed to the barriers created by ocean shipping cartels. Competition policy at the international level is needed to break up these cartels.

Second, development strategies need to look carefully at what the comparative advantages of small, distant, and isolated economies really are. Traditional analysis points almost exclusively to factor endowments and factor prices, but additional factors need to be taken into account. In addition to looking to their factor endowments and the factor intensity of industries, remote economies should look to the 'transport intensity' of industries. Small economies should look to the importance of scale in different sectors, and not just scale within the individual firm, but scale defined to include the size of viable clusters of firms and pools of skilled labour.

Finally, while geography matters, so too do many other factors, including trade policy, institutions, and factor endowments. Restrictive trade policy has the effect, like distance, of making a country more economically remote from the rest of the world. Spatial analysis suggests that clustering is important for many activities, indicating that small initial advantages can translate into large differences in outcomes, as 'cumulative causation' drives the growth of the cluster. This highlights the importance of good initial conditions in the business environment.

Notes

1. The main analytical work is summarised in Fujita, Krugman and Venables (1999), see also Limao and Venables (2002). Empirical work is summarised in Overman, Redding and Venables (2001), and see also Redding and Venables (2001). This paper is based partly on Venables (2002). The Centre for Economic Performance is funded by the UK Economic and Social Research Council.

2. To try and identify the channels through which technical knowledge is transmitted Keller investigates not just distance between countries, but also the volume of trade between them, their bilateral FDI holdings, and their language skills (the share of the population in country I that speaks language J). Adding these variables renders simple geographical distance insignificant; around two-thirds of the difference in bilateral technology diffusion is accounted for by trade patterns, and one-sixth each through FDI and language. However, all these variables are themselves declining with distance.

3. Wage gradients can be estimated within as well as between countries. Thus for the United States, Hanson (1998) provides evidence that variation in wages across counties is linked to differential access to markets, even after controlling for a variety of other considerations such as levels of human capital and amenities. For Mexico, Hanson (1996, 1997) finds a regional wage gradient centred on Mexico City prior to trade liberalisation and the partial break-

down of this regional wage gradient after liberalisation as production re-orientated towards the United States.

References

Cairncross, F. (2001), 'The death of distance 2.0; how the communications revolution will change our lives', Harvard Business School Press, Cambridge.

Ciccone, A. (2002), 'Agglomeration effects in Europe', 46, 213-227 European Economic Review.

Ciccone, A and R. Hall (1996) 'Productivity and the Density of Economic Activity', American Economic Review, 86(1), 54-70.

Di Mauro, F., (2000) 'The impact of economic integration on FDI and exports; a gravity approach', CEPS working document no 156, Brussels.

Dickens, P. (1998) 'Global shift; transforming the world economy' Chapmans, London.

Economist, (May 5 2001), 'Outsourcing to India'.

Economist, (May 19 2001), 'Floating on air'.

Engel C. and J.H. Rogers, (1996), 'How wide is the border', American Economic Review, 86(5), 1112-25.

Evans, C and Harrigan, J (2001) "Distance, Time, and Specialization", paper presented at CEPR Erwit Conference, London School of Economics.

Feenstra, R.C (1998) 'Integration of trade and disintegration of production in the global economy', Journal of Economic Perspectives, 12, 31-50.

Fink, C., Mattoo, A., and Neagu, I.C. (2000). "Trade in International Maritime Service: How Much does Policy Matter? " mimeo, World Bank, http://www1.worldbank.org/wbiep/trade/papers_2000/maritime.pdf

Fortune, (Dec 8th, 1997) 'How Toyota defies gravity'.

Fujita, M., P. Krugman and A.J. Venables, (1999) 'The spatial economy; cities, regions and international trade', MIT press Cambridge MA.

Gallup, J.L. and J. Sachs (with A.D. Mellinger), (1999) 'Geography and economic development', in B. Pleskovic and J.E. Stiglitz (eds), Annual World Bank Conference on Development Economics, 1998, World Bank, Washington DC.

Hanson, G (1996) 'Localization Economies, Vertical Organization, and Trade', American Economic Review, 86(5), 1266-78.

Hanson G (1997) 'Increasing Returns, Trade, and the Regional Structure of Wages', Economic Journal, 107, 113-133.

Hanson G (1998) 'Market Potential, Increasing Returns, and Geographic Concentration', NBER Working Paper, 6429.

Helliwell, J. (1997) 'National Borders, Trade and Migration', National Bureau of Economic Research working paper ;no 6027, Cambridge MA.

Hummels, D. (2000), 'Time as a trade barrier', mimeo Purdue University.

Hummels, D., J. Ishii and K-M Yi (2001) 'The Nature and Growth of Vertical Specialization in World Trade' Journal of International Economics, 75-96.

Keller, W. (2001), 'The geography and channels of diffusion at the world's technology frontier', processed University of Texas.

Klier, T.H. (1999) 'Agglomeration in the US auto supply industry' Economic Perspectives, Federal Reserve Bank of Chicago, 1999.1, 18-34. http://www.chicagofed.org/publications/economicperspectives/1999/ep1Q99_2.pdf

Leamer, E. and M. Storper, (2000) 'The economic geography of the internet age', processed UCLA

Limao N. and A.J. Venables (2001), 'Infrastructure, geographical disadvantage, transport costs and trade', World Bank Economic Review, 15, 451-479.

OECD (1999), 'The software sector; a statistical profile for selected OECD countries', OECD Paris

Overman, H.G., S.J. Redding and A.J. Venables 2003) "The economic geography of trade, production, and income: a survey of empirics", Handbook of International Trade, ed J. Harrigan, Basil Blackwell.

Portes, R and H. Rey, (1999), 'The determinants of cross-border equity flows', CEPR Discussion Paper, 2225.

Quah, D (1997) "Increasingly weightless economies", Bank of England Quarterly Bulletin, vol. 37 no. 1, pp. 49-56.

Quah, D (2001) "The weightless economy in economic development", Ch. 4 in Information Technology, Productivity, and Economic Growth: International Evidence, ed. Matti Pohjola, Oxford University Press, 2001, 72-96

Redding, S. and A.J. Venables, (2004) "Economic Geography and International Inequality", Journal of International Economics, 62(1), 53-82.

Sachs, J and Warner, A (1995) 'Economic Reform and the Process of Global Integration', Brookings Papers on Economic Activity, 0(1), 1-95.

Venables, A.J. (2002) 'Geography and international inequalities: the impact of new technologies', Annual World Bank Conference on Development Economics 2001, eds B. Pleskovic and N.H. Stern.

Venables, A.J. and N. Limao (2002), Geographical disadvantage: a Heckscher-Ohlin-von Thunen model of international specialisation', Journal of International Economics

Yeats, A. (1998) 'Just how big is global production sharing' World Bank Policy Research Working Paper no. 1871.

Annex I

Table A1: Countries in Figure 5.2 and Table 5.2.

1. Albania (ALB)	28. Estonia (EST)	55. Morocco (MAR)		82. Singapore (SGP)
2. Argentina (ARG)	29. Ethiopia (ETH)	56. Moldova (MDA)		83. El Salvador (SLV)
3. Armenia (ARM)	30. Finland (FIN)	57. Madagascar (MDG)	84. Slovak Rep. (SVK)	
4. Australia (AUS)	31. France (FRA)	58. Mexico (MEX)		85. Slovenia (SVN)
5. Austria (AUT)	32. Gabon (GAB)	59. Macedonia (MKD)	86. Sweden (SWE).	
6. Bangladesh (BGD)	33. UK (GBR)	60. Mongolia (MNG)		87. Syria (SYR)
7. Bulgaria (BGR)	34. Greece (GRC)	61. Mozambique. (MOZ)	88. Chad (TCD)	
8. Belg./Lux (BLX)	35. Guatemala (GTM)	62. Mauritius (MUS)	89. Thailand (THA)	
9. Bolivia (BOL)	36. Hong Kong(HKG)	63. Malawi (MWI)	90. Trinidad IT. (TTO)	
10. Brazil (BRA)	37. Honduras (HND)		64. Malaysia (MYS)	91. Tunisia (TUN)
11. C Afr. Rep. (CAF)	38. Croatia (HRV)	65. Nicaragua (NIC)	92. Turkey (TUR)	
12. Canada (CAN)	39. Hungary (HUN)	66. Netherlands (NLD)	93. Taiwan (TWN)	
13. Switzerland (CHE),	40. Indonesia (IDN)	67. Norway (NOR)	94. Tanzania (TZA)	
14. Chile (CHL)		41. India (IND)	68. Nepal (NPL)	95.Uruguay (URY)
15. China (CHN)		42. Ireland (IRL)	69. New Zeal. (NZL)	96. USA (USA)
16. Cote d'Ivoire (CIV)	43. Israel (ISR)	70. Pakistan (PAK)	97. Venezuela (VEN)	
17. Cameroon (CMR)	44. Italy (ITA)	71. Panama (PAN)	98. Yemen (YEM)	
18. Congo Rep. (COG)	45. Jamaica OAM)	72. Peru (PER) 99.	South Mr. (ZAP)	
19. Colombia (COL)		46. Jordan OOR)	73. Philippines (PHL)	
20. Costa Rica (CRI)	47. Japan OPN)	74.Poland (POL)		
21. Czech Rep. (CZE)	48. Kazakhstan (KAZ)	75. Portugal (PRT)		
22. Germany (DEU)	49. Kenya (KEN)	76. Paraguay (PRY)		100. Zambia (ZMB)
23. Denmark (DNK)	50. Kyrgyz Rep. (KGZ)	77. Romania (ROM)		101. Zimbabwe (ZWE)
24. Algeria (DZA)	51. Korea, Rep. (KOR)	78. Russia (RUS)		
25. Ecuador (ECU)	52. Sri Lanka (LKA)	79. Saudi Arab. (SAU)		
26. Egypt (EGY)		53. Lithuania (LTU)	80. Sudan (SDN)	
27. Spain (ESP)		54. Latvia (LVA)	81. Senegal (SEN)	

6. Measuring Competitiveness in Small States: Introducing the SSMECI

Ganeshan Wignaraja and David Joiner

1. Introduction

Policymakers in small states are increasingly focusing on economic competitiveness in the wake of globalisation. The process of world economic integration – associated with falling trade barriers, increasing technological progress, inflows of foreign direct investment and demanding international markets – poses unprecedented adjustment challenges for small states and enterprises within them (see Commonwealth Secretariat, 1997; Wignaraja, 1997; Peretz, Faruqi and Kisanga, 2001; and Gounder and Xayavong, 2001). Policymakers are deeply concerned about the prospect of declining domestic enterprises and even industrial marginalisation in an open, integrated world economy. They also want to reap the positive aspects of globalisation, notably access to new markets and new technologies, for enterprise development. These issues have fuelled a search for appropriate policy responses to globalisation in small states.

This chapter seeks to contribute to the process of new policy development in small states by measuring their industrial competitiveness record, in quantitative terms, and benchmarking them against each other. Benchmarking exercises of this type allow governments in small states to assess their country's performance in relation to:

- countries at a similar level of development, or of similar characteristics, which they would like to outperform; and

- countries at a higher level of development, whose performance they wish to emulate, and whose policy strategies they could learn from in order to achieve it.

Section 2 explores other efforts to benchmark competitiveness and highlights the lack of coverage of small economies in these exercises. Section 3 attempts to remedy this gap by constructing a small states manufactured export competitiveness index (SSMECI) and presents the results. Section 4 provides some explanations for the competitiveness record in small states, and Section 5 concludes.

2. Current benchmarking initiatives and their appropriateness for small states

Benchmarking of the type being undertaken here on competitiveness performance across countries has been the focus of increasing interest in recent years. Current benchmarking initiatives include the following:

- The World Economic Forum's (WEF) Global Competitiveness Report;

- The International Institute for Management Development's (IMD) World Competitiveness Yearbook;

- The United Nations Industrial Development Organisation's (UNIDO) World Industrial Development Report; and

- Wignaraja and Taylor (2003).

Table 6.1 summarises the key features of these four initiatives.

The work of the WEF and the IMD, both based in Switzerland, has largely dominated the global competitiveness benchmarking industry. Annual rankings of competitiveness in developed and developing countries have been produced for 24 years by the WEF's *Global Competitiveness Report* and for 13 years by the IMD's *World Competitiveness Yearbook*. Both indices focus on the micro-level business perspective, and examine the extent to which nations provide an environment in which enterprises can compete. In line with this, rather than focusing on trying to calculate a measure of *actual* competitive performance, both adopt an approach of looking at a wide range of factors that could *affect* national competitiveness. To this end they use a large basket of variables (160 for WEF and 321 for IMD in 2003), which include both 'hard' published statistics and 'soft' data from surveys of businessmen. The sample size of these surveys is rapidly increasing with 7,741 responses to the WEF 'Executive Opinion Survey' in 2003, as opposed to 4,600 in 2001.

Both indices are widely used, gaining widespread media attention. They have also generated a wealth of empirical data. What light, then, can they shed on the competitiveness of small states? Unfortunately the answer is very little. Despite increasing its coverage from 80 to 102 countries, the WEF index only includes eight countries that are amongst the 47 small states in our study. The situation with the IMD index is even worse, with no small states amongst the 59 countries included. The precise reasons for this lack of coverage are unknown, and without discussion with the institutions involved any attempts to determine such reasons remain simple guesses. However, one of the most significant factors is likely to be that the very complexity of both the indices means that the data requirements simply cannot be met in small states. With small populations and often under-developed institutions there is simply not the capacity or demand to collect the data required.

The specific issues of small states may also mean that the general theory of competitiveness espoused by both the WEF and IMD is perhaps inappropriate for the measurement of competitiveness in the small states context. In small, developing economies, focus on the basic economic fundamentals (e.g. macroeconomic stability, outward-oriented trade policies, high levels of human capital, and efficient infrastructure) is perhaps more appropriate than worrying about the 200 sub-complexities found in the sophisticated multi-sectoral economies of the developed world.

Quite apart from the lack of attention given to small states, the WEF and IMD competitiveness indices have attracted criticism on technical grounds. Lall (2001, pp.1501–25) provides a comprehensive analysis of the WEF index of 2000 and finds flaws in its definition of competitiveness, model specification, choice of variables, identification of casual relations, and the use of data. He goes on to offer some insights into the construction of competitiveness indices, and whilst not writing with small states in mind, his comments are perhaps particularly relevant in the context of small states:

'To be analytically acceptable, however, all such efforts should be more limited in coverage, focusing on particular sectors rather than economies as a whole and using a smaller number of critical variables rather than putting in everything the economics, management, strategy and other disciplines suggest. They should also be more modest in claiming to quantify competitiveness: the phenomenon is too multifaceted and complex to permit easy measurement' (Lall, 2001, p.1520).

Wignaraja and Taylor (2003) also offers a critique of the theory and methodology used by WEF and the IMD, including a detailed exploration of the IMD index of 2001. In summary they find that the IMD rankings have:

- *Ambiguous theoretical basis* – The theoretical linkages between the input determinants and national competitiveness are weak. The 'fundamentals' of the IMD 2001 index (pp.43–49) which details the 'four fundamental forces of competitiveness' are more of a schema than a theory.

- *Problems of index construction* – The justification for the weightings given to each of the indicators is sometimes weak and often non-transparent. There also seems to be a lack of distinction between variables that indicate competitiveness and those that determine it, with both types used. This leads to problems in interpreting the results, and applying lessons to other countries.

- *Ad hoc data and proliferation of components* – The use of survey data can be problematic in that the perceptions of businessmen in one country cannot be directly compared with the views of businessmen in another country without some kind of moderation. The justification of the recent proliferation of indicators is also weak, with no explanation as to what is gained by their addition.

Building on this critique, and the argument that such indices need to be less ambitious and analytically simpler, recent work by UNIDO (2002) and Wignaraja and Taylor (2003) have emphasised the industrial competitiveness performance of developing countries.[1] This is a departure from the somewhat broader (and more vague) concept of national competitiveness implicit in the WEF and IMD work. The two newer indicies were developed from a general developing country perspective, rather than being small

Table 6.1. Features of recent competitiveness indices

Publication	World Economic Forum (2003)	Institute of Management Development (2003)	UNIDO (2002)	Wignaraja and Taylor (2003)
Name of index	'Growth Competitiveness Index'	'World Competitiveness Scoreboard'	'Competitiveness Industrial Performance Index'	'Manufactured Export Competitiveness Index'
Concept	Business school approach to measuring national-level competitiveness, using both performance and explanatory variables.	Business school approach to measuring national-level competitiveness, using both performance and explanatory variables.	Focused on industrial performance and national ability to produce manufactures competitively.	Focused on industrial performance and national ability to produce manufactures competitively.
Number of variables	160	321	4	3
Weighting system	Two-tier approach based on a concept of 'core' or 'non-core' innovator countries. Different aggregations and weightings apply to each group in the final index.	20 categories each weighted at 5%	Four variables, equally weighted	Three variables weighted at 30%, 30% and 40% (with technology intensity of exports weighted higher).
Data source type	Published data and entrepreneur surveys (7,741 responses)	Published data and entrepreneur surveys (over 4000 responses)	Published data	Published data
Country coverage (including small states)	Covers 102 countries (eight small states)	Covers 59 countries (0 small states)	Covers 87 countries (three small states)	Covers 80 countries (11 small states)
First published/ frequency	Yearly since 1979	Yearly since 1990	2002 and henceforth periodically	2003

states specific, but come closer to the methodology appropriate for the focus of this study, and in the context of data-sparse small states.

The UNIDO Competitive Industrial Performance Index focuses on the national ability to produce manufactures competitively, and is constructed from four basic indicators of industrial performance (see UNIDO, 2002).

- manufacturing value added (MVA) per capita;
- manufactured exports per capita;
- share of medium- and high-tech activities in MVA; and
- share of medium- and high-tech products in manufactured exports.

The UNIDO index provides valuable insights into the industrial record of the developing world. Unfortunately out of 87 countries listed in the index, only three are small states, as defined in our study. Again, the reasons are unclear, but perhaps even such a simplified index still poses data availability problems.

Wignaraja and Taylor (2003) have similar analytical underpinning to the UNIDO work and constructed a Manufactured Export Competitiveness Index (MECI) of 80 developing countries using three variables:

- manufacturing exports per capita (1999);
- average manufactured export growth per annum (1980–99); and
- technology-intensive exports (such as electronics, petrochemicals and chemicals, iron and steel, engineering, plastics and industrial ceramics) as percentage of total merchandise exports (1998).[1]

Of the 80 countries in the MECI, 11 are small states. The results for these economies are shown in Table 6.2 below. The top and bottom three results in the overall MECI are also shown in order to give put in context the data and index values for small states.

The 11 small states are fairly evenly spread through the middle section of the index, but even the highest performers have MECI values substantially below the East Asian tiger economies (such as Singapore, Malaysia and Taiwan) at the top of the rankings, putting the performance of small states into perspective. One of the reasons for this is perhaps the universally low level of high technology exports in the small states (whether due to lack of such productive capacity, or lack of data). Whilst the share of high-technology exports was an appropriate variable for the study of 80 developing countries, its applicability for work which focuses on small states exclusively is questionable, as it is either not available or not distinctive enough amongst a small states sample.

Significant differences in the performance of individual small states are visible. Trinidad and Tobago, Mauritius and Cyprus stand out among the sample of 11 small states in the MECI rankings. In contrast, smaller Caribbean economies (St Kitts and Nevis, Grenada, Belize and Guyana) and Tonga in the Pacific have performed poorly compared to the three leading small states.

Table 6.2 Summary of results from MECI

Overall rank	Country	MECI index value	Manufactured exports per capita, 1999 (current $US)		Average manufactured export growth % per year (1980–1999)		Technology-intensive exports (% of total merchandise exports), 1998	
			Rank	Value	Rank	Value	Rank	Value
1	Singapore	0.93	1	25,039	13	13.4	1	70
2	Malaysia	0.82	5	2,988	3	19.2	4	55
3	Taiwan	0.79	3	5,477	31	9.4	3	58
15	Trinidad and Tobago	0.52	16	645	37	7.7	14	23
24	Mauritius	0.45	12	984	15	12.8	43	3
26	Cyprus	0.45	15	684	62	3.1	23	17
30	Bahrain	0.42	13	953	19	11.6	65	0
38	Dominica	0.38	21	393	34	9.2	65	0
45	Jamaica	0.35	22	377	64	2.8	43	3
50	St Kitts and Nevis	0.33	26	300	57	3.8	65	0
55	Grenada	0.31	52	45	42	7.2	65	0
58	Belize	0.29	41	86	69	0.4	49	2
61	Guyana	0.27	53	37	67	0.9	43	3
67	Tonga	0.24	72	6	50	5.9	65	0
78	Congo, DR	0.15	76	1	74	-2.1	58	1
79	Nigeria	0.13	80	1	71	-1.2	58	1
80	Yemen, Republic of	0.00	78	1	80	-18.0	65	0

Source: Wignaraja and Taylor (2003)

3. A small-states-specific competitiveness index

Bearing in mind the limited coverage of small states in the mainstream competitiveness literature and the specific issues surrounding measurement of their performance, efforts to benchmark the export performance of small states requires a new small states specific index. As many of the existing methodologies are inappropriate for small states, the design of such an index and the interpretation of its results need to be handled with care. Building on the empirical work of Wignaraja and Taylor (2003), a simple, transparent small state manufactured export competitiveness index (SSMECI) was developed. The key features of this index are highlighted in Box 6.1 while the rest of the section presents the results by country and various aggregate categories.

3.1 Country-level findings

Country-level rankings of competitiveness generate considerable interest in academic and policy circles. Of particular interest are the top performers. Before considering the composite SSMECI rankings, it is useful to start with a brief look at the component variables. Table 6.3 shows the top ten performers for each of the three component variables in the SSMECI. It is noticeable that there is considerable difference in the ranking of the three tables, and that top performers in one component are not necessarily top in others. However, some countries rank consistently high, for example Estonia, which ranks 3rd, 3rd and 4th respectively. The Seychelles also figures in all three lists, albeit at the bottom end. Some countries which figure highly in two of the components, such as Mauritius in 'per capita manufactured exports' and 'manufacturing value added as a % of GDP', do not figure well in the third, 'average growth', and this ultimately leads to a lower overall ranking in overall SSMECI. At the same time, a particularly high ranking on a single variable can push up a country on the overall SSMECI rankings. Swaziland, which comes top of 'share of manufacturing in GDP', is a case in point.[2]

Table 6.4 shows the full SSMECI ranking for the 40 small states, with the component indices, the ranking in each individual variable, and the underlying data values.

As might have been expected two European countries, Malta and Estonia, occupy the first two places in the ranking, perhaps reflecting both their greater access to markets and the positive effect of sustained competitive pressure from their large European neighbours. (Calculations were also done for Singapore, Taiwan and Costa Rica, in order to check the robustness of the theory, and to put into context the SSMECI

Table 6.3. Country rankings for the three separate variables

Manufactured exports per capita 2001* (current $US)			Average manufactured export growth % per year (1990–2001)			Manufacturing value added as % of GDP (1999*)		
Rank	Country	Value	Rank	Country	Value	Rank	Country	Value
1	Malta	4469	1	Brunei	19.50	1	Swaziland	31.69
2	Botswana	2891	2	Maldives	17.07	2	Mauritius	24.56
3	Estonia	2203	3	Estonia	16.86	3	Namibia	15.45
4	Trinidad & Tobago	1666	4	Lesotho	15.70	4	Estonia	15.43
5	Qatar	1331	5	Trinidad & Tobago	13.25	5	Lesotho	15.13
6	Bahrain	1080	6	Bahamas	12.89	6	Belize	14.81
7	Mauritius	940	7	Fiji Islands	12.75	7	Fiji Islands	14.11
8	Brunei	773	8	Grenada	12.48	8	Jamaica	13.93
9	Cyprus	605	9	Seychelles	11.19	9	Seychelles	13.73
10	Seychelles	576	10	Suriname	10.36	10	Malta	12.03

Sources: See Table 6.4 for full description of sources and notes

Table 6.4. Overall SSMECI ranking

Overall rank	Country	SSMECI index value	Manufactured exports per capita 2001[1] (current $US)		Average manufactured export growth % (1990-2001)[2]		Manufacturing value added as % of GDP (1999)[3]	
			Rank	Value	Rank	Value	Rank	Value
1	Malta	0.72	1	4,469	16	5.36%	10	12.03
2	Estonia	0.71	3	2,203	3	16.86%	4	15.43
3	Swaziland	0.69	17	299	12	7.10%	1	31.69
4	Mauritius	0.65	7	940	22	3.14%	2	24.56
5	Trinidad and Tobago	0.59	4	1,666	5	13.25%	22	7.99
6	Brunei	0.58	8	773	1	19.50%	19	8.42
7	Seychelles	0.57	10	576	9	11.19%	9	13.73
8	Lesotho	0.56	24	113	4	15.70%	5	15.13
9	Botswana	0.55	2	2,891	25	2.25%	34	4.97
10	Fiji Islands	0.55	18	266	7	12.75%	7	14.11
11	Namibia	0.51	14	398	26	2.15%	3	15.45
12	Bahrain	0.51	6	1,080	21	3.25%	15	9.88
13	Qatar	0.49	5	1,331	28	1.73%	23	7.30
14	Guyana	0.49	19	207	11	10.02%	14	10.15
15	Grenada	0.49	16	319	8	12.48%	24	7.26
16	Maldives	0.49	23	116	2	17.07%	26	6.46
17	St. Kitts and Nevis	0.48	11	514	20	3.82%	13	10.33
18	Jamaica	0.48	26	105	18	4.51%	8	13.93
19	Bahamas	0.47	12	508	6	12.89%	38	3.20
20	Barbados	0.46	13	468	23	2.82%	16	9.32
21	Belize	0.46	22	122	30	0.00%	6	14.81
22	Bhutan	0.46	28	59	14	6.86%	11	11.56
23	Cyprus	0.46	9	605	31	-1.68%	12	10.54
24	Dominca	0.45	15	357	19	3.94%	17	8.48
25	Suriname	0.43	30	21	10	10.36%	21	8.12
26	St.Vincent/ Grenadines	0.41	25	111	17	5.16%	25	6.54
27	Gabon	0.39	29	48	13	6.89%	32	5.16
28	Solomon Islands	0.39	21	148	27	1.89%	33	5.12
29	Samoa	0.37	34	9	15	5.53%	28	6.02
30	Vanuatu	0.34	33	9	29	0.53%	27	6.35

Overall rank	Country	SSMECI index value	Manufactured exports per capita 2001[1] (current $US)		Average manufactured export growth % (1990-2001)[2]		Manufacturing value added as % of GDP (1999)[3]	
			Rank	Value	Rank	Value	Rank	Value
31	Papua New Guinea	0.32	32	10	33	-5.37%	20	8.28
32	Tonga	0.31	35	4	24	2.33%	36	3.89
33	St. Lucia	0.31	27	83	34	-9.79%	29	5.96
34	Cape Verde	0.30	31	21	36	-10.96%	18	8.45
35	Antigua and Barbuda	0.27	20	197	37	-13.97%	39	2.25
36	São Tomé and Príncipe	0.24	39	0	32	-3.65%	35	4.52
37	Djibouti	0.22	37	2	35	-10.90%	37	3.60
38	Gambia, The	0.20	36	2	38	-16.74%	30	5.60
39	Comoros	0.13	38	1	39	-26.09%	31	5.43
40	Kiribati	0.00	40	0	40	-29.07%	40	0.99

Sources: Data primarily from ITC, using COMTRADE Database, *World Development Indicators* (2001, 2002, 2003), and other regional and national sources. See Annex 1 for full details of data sources and methodology.

1 In some cases where data from 2001 was not available, 2000 or 1999 data was used. See Annex 1 for full details
2 Where data was not available for 1990 or 2001, the nearest available year was used. Growth rates were calculated using a compound method, adjusting for length of time period as appropriate. See Annex 1 for full details.
3 Where 1999 data was not available, 1998 or 2000 was used. See Annex 1 for full details.

figures. Not surprisingly, these three countries came out at the top of the index.) The rest of the top 10 is made up of some of the traditional small-state powerhouses of the various regions, such as Mauritius from the Indian Ocean, Trinidad and Tobago from the Caribbean, and Fiji Islands from the Pacific.

Of noteworthy interest is the performance of the 'BLNS' countries that make up the Southern African Customs Union (SACU) with South Africa. In the rankings all four score highly: Swaziland is 3rd, Lesotho 8th, Botswana 9th and Namibia 11th. This high performance may again be due in part to proximity to large markets, and the trade and investment stimulus that an agreement such as the SACU produces for its 'satellites'.

Some countries do not perform as well as might be expected. For example Cyprus, ranked 23, did not perform as well as the other European countries in the sample.

Box 6.1. The small states manufactured export competitiveness index (SSMECI)

The small states manufactured export competitiveness index (SSMECI) emphasises the ability to produce manufactures competitively in the world's smallest economies. It has been designed in light of the problems with data availability in some small states and the need to build in realistic data requirements in order to make the country coverage of the index as wide as possible. The SSMECI is composed of just three variables, each of which captures a different aspect of industrial competitiveness and which combine to create a simple but effective snapshot of the economy's overall international competitiveness in this area. The three factors captured are:

- current performance in world export markets scaled by size;
- the dynamism of this performance over time – i.e., growth rates; and
- the size of the manufacturing base in the structure of the wider economy.

The first factor captures an economy's actual record of competing in international markets rather than simply alluding to an ability to be competitive. The second captures how dynamic this performance is, and whether the economy's performance is on an upward or downward trend. The third looks at more structural issues, recognising that in a small state where economies of scale are such an issue, a larger manufacturing base is likely to reflect an advantage in achieving competitiveness. To reflect these three concepts and in light of the data issues, three specific variables were selected for the small states index. These were:

- manufactured export value per capita in 2001 (US$);
- average manufactured export growth per annum 1990-2001; and
- manufacturing value added as a % of GDP in 1999.

Using these variables, the SSMECI was constructed for 40 small states in the Commonwealth and IMF defined sample set. This sample size is sufficient to be representative and to permit basic statistical analysis of determinants. Calculations were performed to give each country a value between 0 and 1 for each of the three variables, and these were then weighted to produce a final index figure for each country, which could then be ranked. Higher values in the SSMECI indicate greater levels of competitiveness, thus for example, Malta, with a SSMECI of 0.72 is perceived to be more competitive than Djibouti, with a SSMECI of 0.22 in Table 6.3.

In interpreting the findings, readers should be aware of the sensitivity of results in small states. When the overall production base is so small, the establishment or closure of a single factory can substantially affect the overall figures for that year. The quality/reliability of the data obtained can also often be poor, due to underdeveloped/understaffed statistics institutions in small states. To a degree such factors may have influenced the overall rankings, and led to marginally higher or lower placement than would be expected. This needs to be taken into account when interpreting the results, though it is unlikely to change the basic patterns observed.

Full details of data sources, definitions, and the specific methodology used to construct the SSMECI are given in Annex 1.

Whilst it scored fairly highly in terms of per capita exports and manufactured value added, manufactured exports have actually fallen over the last ten years, possibly reflecting a fall in comparative competitiveness, and this negative average growth brings down the overall SSMECI ranking score.

3.2 Findings by region, income group and country size

In an attempt to establish patterns of performance and provide analytical insights, the 40 small states have been grouped into various categories as follows:

1. geographical region to facilitate comparisons across regions,

2. income per head to permit analysis of different income groups, and

3. population to enable analysis by country size.

In each case, the group values for each of the three variables have been calculated using weighted averages, which have then been indexed, using the same methodology as before. Simple averages are also shown for each grouping, calculated using average index values for each country in the group.

Table 6.5 aggregates the results according to geography, allowing the regional breakdown of the results to be analysed.

The high performance of the European region is probably to be expected, as discussed earlier. In comparison, the relatively high performance of the African region is more surprising, and closer inspection shows that there are in fact two tiers of performance within the region. At the top level, the four BLNS countries, Mauritius, and the Seychelles are all in the top 11 of the SSMECI rankings. At the other end, a number of African countries, particularly in Western Africa, occupy the bottom ten positions. Overall, the contributions of the top-tier performers are enough to produce a high average in comparison to the other regions.

Also of note is the particular poor performance of the Pacific region, which was not strong in any of the three variables, and significantly lower in the SSMECI rankings.[3] Apart from the Fiji Islands at 10 in the overall SSMECI, the other countries of the Pacific were all in the bottom 15.

Table 6.6 shows the performance by income grouping, which reveals some very interesting results. Rather than running from 'high income' down to 'low income' in a linear fashion, the performance of the four groups is more erratic. High-income countries perform only third best out of the four, with the lowest average growth rates in manufacturing exports, and the lowest manufacturing value added as a percentage of GDP. They do have the second-highest manufactured exports per capita though, which prevents them from being below the low-income countries. This pattern of results could reflect 'mature' economies who have developed a manufacturing export base, as shown in the high per-capita figures, but have then diversified their economies into other sectors such as services, particularly financial services and high-end tourism. In such a case, the per capita exports in manufacturing would still be relatively high, but growth in manufacturing exports would slow, and value added in manufacturing as a share of total GDP would fall.

Table 6.7 shows the SSMECI performance grouped by population size. This distinction is particularly important to capture the record of tiny, micro-states compared with

Table 6.5. SSMECI performance by region

Rank	Regional grouping[a]	No.	Weighted average SSMECI[b]	Simple average SSMECI	Manufactured exports per capita 2001 (current $US)		Average manufactured export growth % (1990–2001)		Manufacturing value added as % of GDP (1999)	
					Rank	Value	Rank	Value	Rank	Value
1	Europe	3	0.79	0.63	1	2,076	3	8.70%	2	12.24%
2	Africa	12	0.49	0.42	3	602	5	2.74%	1	12.86%
3	Asia	3	0.45	0.51	5	351	1	16.95%	5	8.46%
4	Caribbean/ Latin America	13	0.37	0.45	4	481	2	9.84%	4	9.04%
5	Middle East	2	0.28	0.50	2	1,200	6	2.41%	6	8.21%
6	Pacific	7	0.14	0.33	6	51	4	5.01%	3	9.53%

Sources: Table 6.4 and author's calculations
[a] Regional groupings according to World Bank (2003)
[b] Group values calculated from weighted components of sub-indices for members of each region. Where original data for manufactured exports for 1990 and 2001 was not available, data for these years has been extrapolated using average growth rates of that country. SSMECI values calculated using sample maximum and minimum levels.

Table 6.6. SSMECI performance by income grouping

Rank	Regional grouping[a]	No.	Weighted average SSMECI[b]	Simple average SSMECI	Manufactured exports per capita 2001 (current $US)		Average manufactured export growth % (1990–2001)		Manufacturing value added as % of GDP (1999)	
					Rank	Value	Rank	Value	Rank	Value
1	Upper middle income	11	0.84	0.52	1	1,520	1	6.23%	2	11.06%
2	Lower middle income	14	0.55	0.40	3	193	2	4.93%	1	13.98%
3	High income	8	0.36	0.50	2	1,308	4	3.80%	4	8.49%
4	Low income	7	0.13	0.33	4	38	3	4.62%	3	9.09%

Sources: Table 6.4 and author's calculations
[a] Income groupings according to World Bank (2003)
[b] Group values calculated from weighted components of sub-indices for members of each income group. Where original data for manufactured exports for 1990 and 2001 was not available, data for these years has been extrapolated using average growth rates of that country. SSMECI values calculated using sample Maximum and minimum levels.

larger small states. In the absence of a universally accepted definition of sub-categories by size, the sample was divided into countries with populations under 250,000 (micro-states), between 250,000 and 1 million, and over 1 million. The striking finding is that the micro-states record a particularly weak competitiveness performance. This suggests that even within the world's smallest economies, country size matters for industrial competitiveness. Perhaps unsurprisingly, the performance of the larger states was better than that of the two smaller population categories, though the magnitude of this is perhaps unexpected. Many factors probably explain the gap in industrial competitiveness performance between larger small states and micro-states These include the facts that larger small states have somewhat bigger markets than smaller ones; have access to a larger pool of technical and managerial skills; are more attractive to inflows of foreign direct investment; are better able to finance costly infrastructure project (e.g. setting up a national airline); and, possibly, are less susceptible to natural disasters.

3.3 Comparison with results from other indices

As stated earlier, one of the reasons for developing the SSMECI is the lack of coverage that existing work gives to small states. The IMD index contains none of the small states in the SSMECI, and so comparison of results is not possible. The WEF index,

Table 6.7. SSMECI performance by population size grouping

Rank	Population[a]	No.	Weighted average SSMECI[b]	Simple average SSMECI	Manufactured exports per capita 2001 (current $US)		Average manufactured export growth % (1990–2001)		Manufacturing value added as % of GDP (1999)	
					Rank	Value	Rank	Value	Rank	Value
1	More than 1m	11	1.00[c]	0.52	1	615	1	5.96%	1	12.42%
2	250,000 to 1m	16	0.63[c]	0.45	2	592	2	4.34%	2	8.72%
3	Less than 250,000	13	0.00[c]	0.36	3	123	3	0.48%	3	8.27%

Sources: Table 6.4 and author's calculations
[a] Population groups as per author's definition
[b] Group values calculated from weighted components of sub-indices for members of each population group. Where original data for manufactured exports for 1990 and 2001 was not available, data for these years has been extrapolated using average growth rates of that country. SSMECI values calculated using sample maximum and minimum levels.
c The extreme range of the weighted average SSMECI index values obtained (1.00 and 0.00) reflects the strength of the correlation. The group with population of over 1m was ranked first in all three variables, thus achieving an index value of 1.00 for all three variables. When weighted this gives an overall SSMECI of 1.00. For the group with a population under 250,000 the reverse is true, with last place rankings in each variable giving 0.00 index values, and an overall SSMECI of 0.00.

however, has eight common countries, and the MECI of Wignaraja and Taylor (2003) has 11 similarities. A comparison of the resulting rankings is given in Table 6.8.

Only three countries appear in all three indices, and so comparison across all at the same time is difficult. If the SSMECI is compared individually against each in turn, however, the results, whilst not identical, show some correlation. Against the WEF, the results are broadly similar, and whilst Botswana and The Gambia do slightly better in the WEF rankings than in the small states SSMECI, the rankings are otherwise fairly similar. The correlation with the MECI is somewhat surprisingly less strong, with a number of countries having significantly different rankings. However if these outliers, including Guyana, Cyprus and Dominica, are excluded, the overall pattern of correlation is again visible.

4. Explaining industrial competitiveness performance

Ranking inter-country patterns of competitiveness performance is only the first step in analysing competitiveness. A second and more interesting step is investigating 'What factors led to high, or low, performance?'. In other words, what are the determinants of manufacturing-export competitiveness and what lessons can be learnt for future policy development?

Table 6.8. Comparison of results from SSMECI, MECI and WEF Growth Competitiveness Index

Country	SSMECI ranking	MECI (Wignaraja and Taylor, 2003)	WEF growth competitiveness ranking 2003
Malta	1	–	19
Estonia	2	–	22
Mauritius	4	24	46
Trinidad and Tobago	5	15	49
Botswana	9	–	36
Namibia	11	–	52
Bahrain	12	30	–
Guyana	14	61	–
Grenada	15	55	–
St. Kitts and Nevis	17	50	–
Jamaica	18	45	67
Belize	21	58	–
Cyprus	23	26	–
Dominica	24	38	–
Tonga	32	67	–
Gambia, The	38	–	55

Sources: WEF (2003), author's calculations

4.1 T-test and variables

The analysis of the determinants of competitiveness in small states has been conducted using a simple statistical test, a two-sample t-test of the variable means.[4] It analyses whether the two sample means are equal, and thus whether the two groups are distinct in statistical terms. By using the top 20 performers in the SSMECI, and the bottom 20 as our two samples, we can determine whether the mean for a particular determinant is different in the two groups. If, for example, the mean value for a particular determinant (e.g. foreign investment) is higher in the top 20 sample to a level that is statistically significant, this would imply that high levels of foreign investment are associated with high SSMECI performance, and this thus implies it has an impact on competitiveness.[5]

Tests of this nature were conducted on 25 separate variables, to see which factors were statistically significant. The variables used are divided into seven sub-categories:

- *Macro-environment* – A stable and predictable macroeconomic environment, characterised by low inflation and interest rates, sustained GDP growth, and high levels of saving and investment, is widely accepted as a fundamental condition for business activity. Five variables are used in this category, covering a wide scope of macroeconomic variables.

- *Country size* – Recent literature has shown that country size is inversely correlated with susceptibility to economic, political and environmental risks. Traditional economic theory would also suggest that larger country size may allow greater economies of scale and scope. Population is used as the proxy for country size as this has been shown to have the same result as more complex indices based on variables such as total GNP, population and total arable land.

- *Trade and investment regime* – An open trade and investment regime exposes the business sector to overseas competition, encourages economies of scale through increased market access, and facilitates technological transfer. Three proxies of openness are used as well as inward FDI stock.

- *Vulnerability* – 'Vulnerability', whether in the form of susceptibility to natural disasters, or over-reliance on one commodity, may hamper the competitiveness of economies. Six variables are used to test this hypothesis, including both singular and composite measures of vulnerability.

- *Structural* – The overall structure of economic activity may impact competitiveness, with a move away from low-value-adding agriculture into manufacturing and services, freeing labour and benefiting the overall competitiveness of the economy. Conversely, at the opposite extreme, a lack of agricultural and mineral activity may prevent exploitation of potential for value-added industries based on natural resources. Two basic measures of economic structure are used.

- *Infrastructure* – Efficient and cost-competitive physical infrastructure allows businesses to compete in the global market without constraint, and for small states in particular modern ICT infrastructure allows the possibility to escape the 'tyranny of distance', and stay abreast of the latest technological innovation and production techniques. Three variables of modern ICT infrastructure are used.

- *Human capital* – A strong base of productive human capital is recognised as being the basis for industrial innovation and competitiveness. Education and training provides productive numerate workers with the skills to compete successfully. Four variables are used covering enrolment rates at different stages of education and adult literacy.

- *'Development'* – Whilst not strictly a 'determinant' of competitiveness, a country's level of development would be expected to correlate with its level of competitiveness, even if the direction of causality is complicated. As such three variables are used to proxy for overall 'development'.

4.2 The t-test results

Table 6.9 shows the results of the t-tests on the means of the variables for high-performing sample countries (top 20), and on the low performers (bottom 20). Data availability determined the sample size for a given t-test. In some cases the sample size would ideally have been higher, but all have enough for statistical relevance and are not low by cross national statistical analysis standards.

The main findings are as follows:

- *Macro-environment:* The higher performing sample countries had both significantly higher average savings ratios and lower interest rates (both at the 5 per cent confidence level). This may suggest that cost and availability of capital is a driver of SSMECI performance. The means of GDP growth of the two samples are statistically different at the 5 per cent level (5.6 per cent compared to 3.5 per cent between 1990-99). Whilst the high-performing sample countries do have a lower mean inflation rate, the difference is not statistically significant at the 10 per cent level. Nor was the gross capital formation ratio.

- *Country size* – Using the full data set the difference in the means of population size for the two samples were not statistically significant. However, if Papua New Guinea is not included in the sample (at 5.25 million, it is something of an outlier in the group), then the means are highly significant to the 1 per cent confidence level. This backs up the theory that size, even within the small states grouping, is a significant factor in SSMECI performance.

- *Trade and investment regime* – The higher performing sample countries have significantly greater means for FDI stock (at the 5 per cent confidence level), which would confirm the suggestion that FDI is a driver of competitiveness, through generation of export production and technological transfer. Unsurprisingly, openness as measured by exports/GDP ratio was significant, but imports/GDP and the combination of exports and imports to GDP were not significant. On the one hand

Table 6.9. T-tests to examine significance of determinants

Determinants	High performers top 20		Low performers bottom 20		t-stat	Significant at 5% (* also at 1% level
	Mean	Observations	Mean	Observations		
Macro fundamentals						
Inflation % (average 1996-2000) [b]	4.4	20	12.0	20	-1.10	
GDP growth % (average 1990-1999) [b]	5.6	17	3.5	19	1.75	✓
Interest rate % (1999) [b, c]	13.1	17	16.8	15	-1.75	✓
Gross domestic saving as % of GDP (1999) [b]	20.8	16	12.8	16	2.14	✓
Gross capital formation as % of GDP (1999) [a]	26.4	16	25.9	16	0.15	
Country size						
Population (2001) [a]	886,869	20	666,785	20	0.73	
Population (excluding PNG) [a]	886,869	20	425,429	19	2.49	✓*
Trade and investment regime						
FDI inward stock % of GDP (2000) [d]	75.4	18	42.8	18	1.86	✓
Imports as % of GDP (1999) [b]	62.5	20	66.1	20	-0.31	
Exports as % of GDP (1999) [b]	51.4	19	30.9	20	2.10	✓
Imports/exports as % of GDP (1999) [b]	111.3	20	97.0	20	0.92	
Vulnerability						
Vulnerability to natural disasters [e]	127	17	170	20	-0.72	
Composite vulnerability index [e]	7.55	17	7.41	20	0.21	
Export dependence [e]	64.66	17	43.49	20	2.66	✓*
UNCTAD Diversification Index (2000*) [f]	0.77	15	0.69	13	1.97	✓
UNCTAD Concentration Index (2000*) [f]	0.46	16	0.51	14	-0.76	
No. of commodities exported (2000*) [f]	81.9	16	25.3	14	3.62	✓*
Structural						
Agriculture value added % GDP (1999) [b]	7.9	18	18.4	19	-3.28	✓*
Services value added % GDP (1999) [b]	59.4	18	58.9	18	0.09	
Infrastructure						
Telephones/mobiles per 1,000 pop (2000) [a]	379	20	220	17	1.90	✓

Determinants	High performers top 20		Low performers bottom 20		t-stat	Significant at 5% (* also at 1% level
	Mean	Obser- vations	Mean	Obser- vations		
Internet users (2001) [a]	46,000	20	33,974	19	0.50	
Personal computers per 1,000 pop (2001) [a]	87.2	17	79.4	16	0.33	
Human capital						
Adult literacy as % population (1999) [a]	88.6	18	71.5	13	3.07	✓*
Secondary enrolment (2000) [a]	66.2	13	57.8	11	0.90	
Tertiary enrolment (2000) [a]	14.9	13	11.5	10	0.62	
Development						
GDP per capita 2001 (current US$) [a]	6,833	20	2,531	20	2.62	✓*
GDP per capita 2001 (PPP US$) [g]	10,203	20	5,145	18	3.07	✓*
HDI index value 2003 [g]	0.76	20	0.67	18	2.34	✓

[a] World Bank (2003)
[b] Commonwealth Secretariat (2002)
[c] IMF (various)
[d] UNCTAD (2002a)
[e] Atkins et al. (2001)
[f] UNCTAD (2002b)
[g] UNDP (2003)

this is surprising but perhaps reflects that all small states are by nature fairly reliant on imports, perhaps even more so if lacking competitiveness.

- *Vulnerability* – Some measures of vulnerability showed high levels of significance, particularly those relating to the structure and diversity of production. Dependence on exports, and the number of commodities exported, were both significant at the 1 per cent level, whilst the UNCTAD diversification measure was significant at the 5 per cent level. Perhaps surprisingly, the recent attempts to produce vulnerability indices were not significant, with neither the natural disasters vulnerability index nor the composite vulnerability index producing statistically significantly different means across the samples.

- *Structural* – The structural variable showed that higher performing SSMECI countries had a significantly lower mean for the share of 'agricultural value added in GDP' than the lower performing group (at the 1 per cent confidence level). Given the nature of the index this is perhaps not surprising, and represents the traditional shift from agricultural production to manufacturing and industry. The share of 'services value added in GDP' was not significant at the 10 per cent level.

- *Infrastructure* – In the area of modern infrastructure the difference in means for telephone connections (fixed lines and mobile) was significant at the 5 per cent level, suggesting that communication and information flow is a factor in competitiveness. The number of internet connections and PCs was not significant however, and this may be because it is too early for such new technology to be feeding through to the indicators found in the SSMECI.

- *Human capital* – The importance of human capital in determining competitiveness may be suggested by the high significance (at the 1 per cent confidence level) in the difference in means between samples for levels of adult literacy. For both secondary and tertiary-level education enrolment rates the higher performing SSMECI countries had greater means than the lower, however this was not statistically significant at the 10 per cent level. This lack of significance may have been effected by poor data availability in these data sets.

- *Development* – As expected the relationship between overall development and performance in the SSMECI was strong. Both measures of GDP per capita had significantly higher means in the top-performing SSMECI countries (at the 1 per cent confidence level), whilst for the Human Development Index the means were significantly different at the 5 per cent confidence level.

5. Conclusions

Exercises to benchmark competitiveness performance across countries, such as that undertaken here, have become increasingly popular in recent years, with the indices of the World Economic Forum and IMD in particular gaining popularity. The coverage of such work has recently broadened from including just-developed countries, to bringing in the developing world as well. To date, however, little attempt has been made to include small states, let alone focus on them particularly. This paper presents a first attempt at such an index, and develops a small-state manufactured-export competitiveness index (SSMECI) based on three sub-components, namely manufactured exports per capita, average growth in manufactured exports, and the share of manufacturing in GDP.

As ever with work of this kind, some results are expected and fit with a-priori expectations. However, other results take more analysis and explanation. The very size of the countries in question leads to increased data volatility, and this may affect the results, perhaps causing a few anomalies and raised eyebrows. This can never be avoided, but whilst one or two may have performed above or below expectations, the general pattern of results is sound, and provides insight.

Not surprisingly, the European small states (such as Malta and Estonia) perform well, as do other traditional regional small-state 'powerhouses', such as Mauritius, Trinidad and Tobago, and Fiji Islands. This shows that small states can successfully transit from a state of vulnerability to developing a viable, internationally competitive industrial sector. The high performance of the BLNS countries in the Southern African Customs

Union is of note, and perhaps points towards the benefits of integrated trade and investment relationships with larger neighbours. At the other end of the performance spectrum, tiny micro-states record a particularly weak competitiveness performance, suggesting that even within the world's smallest economies, country size matters for competitiveness. Factors like the lack of domestic markets, technical manpower, and foreign direct investment may help to explain the poor performance of micro-states.

Unfortunately, greater use of econometric techniques was hampered by the lack of data on key variables, and so the ability to analyse the determinants of competitiveness was constrained. However, simple t-test analysis indicates that the determinants of competitiveness include a number of variables, covering both the policy environment and supply-side factors. Higher performing small states had better macroeconomic conditions, higher levels of foreign direct investment, more trade openness, better levels of education, and modern infrastructure. This strongly suggests that the adoption of a coherent, market-oriented, competitiveness strategy in small states is vital to success on international markets (see Wignaraja (1997 and 2003) for more details of these and other elements of a coherent competitiveness strategy).

Ultimately, even with better data availability that would have enabled more complex econometric analysis to be undertaken, exercises of type can only begin to shed light on competitive performance and its drivers. The complex nature of factors involved in export competitiveness, and the particular circumstances and constraints of different countries, mean that the lessons that a particular policymaker can draw are normally only at the macro level. To truly understand the drivers of competitiveness, there is a need for a greater exploration of specific policy environments and institutional and firm-level competitiveness factors, which requires detailed case studies of individual small states.[6]

Notes

1. The UNCTAD/WTO International Trade Centre (ITC) also produces a Trade Performance Index, which benchmarks across developing countries at an industry/product level (see ITC, 2000). It is not discussed here due to our focus on national-level competitiveness, rather than individual industries/products. However, for policymakers interested in such detail it can be a valuable tool.

2. Swaziland's large share of manufacturing in GDP seems due to the following: (a) 26 garment factories established by Taiwanese investors to take advantage of the Africa Growth and Opportunities Act (AGOA) which provides ready access to the American market; (b) one of CocaCola's five worldwide plants which produces coke concentrate; (c) various sugar pulp factories; and (d) other light industries established by South African investors to take advantage of the South African Customs Union (SACU) market.

3. Out of the 47 small states in our definition, seven countries could not be included in the final MECI due to data reasons, and five of these were in the Pacific. As a result the sample for the Pacific is not complete and may be biased. However, lack of data is often correlated to poor performance, and it is unlikely that inclusion of these countries, if data was available, would significantly improve overall regional performance.

4. Recent attempts at statistical analysis of the factors affecting competitiveness in developing countries include Ul Haque (1995); James and Romijn (1997, pp.189-207); Wignaraja and Taylor (2003); and Wint (2003).

5. An important qualification about the testing procedure should be noted. The simple t-test shows significantly different means between two samples for individual variables. However, it does not indicate causality, and is thus less powerful than full econometric analysis. That said, it does provide insights into those underlying factors correlated with competitive success in comparisons of strong and weak national performance.

6. For recent examples of detailed competitiveness studies on small states see World Bank (1994); Harris (1997); and Lall and Wignaraja (1998).

Annex I

Construction of the SSMECI

This appendix covers the technical details of the methodology used to construct the small states manufacturing export competitiveness index (SSMECI), along with notes on data sources and definitions.

Data – definitions and sources

Definition of 'manufacturing'

The commonly used international definition of manufacturing is used throughout, which is defined using the Standard International Trade Classification (SITC) codes. The manufacturing sector is represented by the addition of the values for SITC code level 5, 6, 7, and 8, minus the value of code level 68.

The use of such a definition has both benefits and costs, but in light of the data constraints of small states, was the only realistic option. In order to put together data for as many countries as possible, a variety of sources had to be used (see below). The use of an international definition made this task both more accurate in terms of common definitions across multiple sources, and more realistic as far as availability is concerned.

Ideally, it would have been useful to define manufacturing to include more of the food processing industry, as this is often a large component of small states' export production. However, without access to dis-aggregated data for each country this was not possible, and in the interests of larger samples, a more standardised definition was more appropriate. Definition of small states and countries used

The standard Commonwealth definition of small states has been used throughout this paper, and is again used here. From this thirty-two small states are identified who are Commonwealth members. This includes four countries with small states characteristics despite their larger populations (Papua New Guinea, Swaziland, Lesotho and Namibia).

To increase the sample size slightly further, the IMF definition of small states was also used; this identifies forty-three small states, and when combined with the Commonwealth list, produces a final sample of forty-seven countries. Data sources

As mentioned above, given the difficulties of obtaining data in many small states, a number of sources were used. For the first two variables, the main source was the International Trade Centre, with data extracted from the COMTRADE database. This was supplemented using data from UNCTAD *Handbook of Statistics*, ITC's *PC-TAS*, and the World Bank *World Development Indicators*. National sources were also used where there were gaps in the data, or to verify erroneous-looking data. In certain circumstances, gaps in data have been estimated using standard imputation techniques from other data from that country. The specific sources of all data are detailed in the following table.

Table A6.1. Precise sources of all data in small states SSMECI

Country	Manufactured exports				Manufactured va as % GDP[f]
	Year	Source	Year	Source	Year
Antigua and Barbuda	1991 [1]	WTO [a]/ITC	1999	ITC	1999
Bahamas	1995	ITC [b]	2001	ITC	1999 [g]
Bahrain	1994	ITC	2001	ITC	1997
Barbados	1990	ITC	2001	ITC	1999
Belize	1992	ITC	2000	ITC	1999
Bhutan	1991	ITC	1999	UNCTAD HOS	1998
Botswana	1991 [1]	ITC/WTO	2001	ITC	1999
Brunei	1990	ITC	1998	ITC	1999 [g]
Cape Verde	1995	ITC	2001	ITC	1999
Comoros	1995	ITC	2000	ITC	1999
Cyprus	1990	ITC	2001	ITC	1999 [g]
Djibouti	1990	ITC	1995 [1]	UNCTAD/WTO	1999 [g]
Dominca	1990	UNCTAD [c]	2001	ITC	1999
Estonia	1995	ITC	2001	ITC	1999
Fiji Islands	1988	ITC	2000	ITC	1999
Gabon	1993	ITC	2000	ITC	1999
Gambia, The	1995	ITC	2000	PCTAS	1999
Grenada	1990	ITC	2001	ITC	1999
Guyana	1991 [1]	FTAA Web [d]	1998	FTAA Web	1999
Jamaica	1990	ITC	2000	ITC	1999
Kiribati	1990	ITC	1999	UNCTAD HOS	1998
Lesotho	1991	NATIONAL [e]	2001	NATIONAL	1999 [g]
Maldives	1995	ITC	2001	UNCTAD HOS	1998
Malta	1990	UNCTAD	2001	ITC	1999 [g]
Mauritius	1990	ITC	2001	UNCTAD HOS	1999
Namibia	1991	WTO/ITC	2001	ITC	1999
Papua New Guinea	1990	ITC	2000	ITC	1999
Qatar	1990	ITC	2001	ITC	1999 [g]
Samoa	1990	ITC	2001 [1]	ITC/WTO	1997
São Tomé and Príncipe	1995 [1]	UNCTAD/WTO	2001 [1]	UNCTAD/WTO	1999
Seychelles	1990	ITC	2001 [1]	WTO-ITC	1999
Soloman Islands	1990	WTO-HDI [e]	2001 [1]	HDI-WTO	1999 [g]
St. Kitts and Nevis	1988	UNCTAD HOS	2001	ITC	1999
St. Lucia	1990	ITC	2001	ITC	1999

Country	Manufactured exports				Manufactured va as % GDP[f]
	Year	Source	Year	Source	Year
St.Vincent/Grenadines	1993	ITC	2000	ITC	1999
Suriname	1990	ITC	2000	UNCTAD	1998
Swaziland	1990	WTO-HDI	2001	ITC	1999
Tonga	1991 [1]	ITC/WTO	2000	UNCTAD HOS	1998
Trinidad and Tobago	1990	ITC	2001	ITC	1999
Vanuatu	1990	ITC	2000	UNCTAD HOS	1999 [g]

1. Imputed from figure for alternative reference year (1990 or 2001), using total export figures from the WTO and using the assumption that the % of manufactured exports in total exports stays the same.

[a] WTO (2002)
[b] International Trade Centre using COMTRADE database
[c] UNCTAD (2003)
[d] Free Trade Agreement of the Americas (FTAA) website
[e] Data from national source, for example central bank or statistical office
[f] UNDP (2001)
[g] World Bank (2001)

Construction of the SSMECI

The small states manufactured exports competitiveness index (SSMECI) is a composite index constructed using a methodology similar to that used for the UNDP Human Development Index (HDI).[a]

Indexing the variables

For each of the three variables an index value was calculated using the following general formula:

$$\text{Index} = \frac{\text{actual value} - \text{minimum value}}{\text{maximum value} - \text{minimum value}}$$

A key consideration in such a calculation was determining the minimum and maximum values that were appropriate. In the absence of a theoretical rationale suggesting definite alternatives, the maximum and minimum values in the relevant sample set were used.

For example: 'Value added from manufacturing as a % GDP' of the Fiji Islands was 14.11 per cent in 1999, the sample maximum is 31.69 per cent in Swaziland, and the sample minimum 1 per cent in Kiribati. The index for Fiji is therefore:

$$\text{MVA Index} = \frac{14.11 - 1}{31.69 - 1}$$

$$= 0.43$$

This method was used for the 'Manufacturing value added' variable, and the 'Growth of manufactured exports' variable. However, for the 'manufactured exports per capita' variable the extreme high values of some countries in the sample meant that all bar three countries had an index value of below 0.4. This has the effect of introducing a large bias in the overall index in favour of the top three countries. In order to attempt to discount these extreme variables, logarithms were used in the calculations. However, this overcompensated for the bias, and even low performers were attaining index values of above 0.8. In order to even out the effect, an average of the two was used, that is the average of the two values produced from using logarithms and from not using them.

Rank correlation calculations were used to measure the effect of the use/non use of logarithms on the SSMECI order. The rank correlation between the SSMECI based on a logarithmic approach and the 'average' method above is 0.985. Whilst the rank correlation between the SSMECI based on a non-logarithmic approach and the 'average' method above is 0.993. Thus whilst the average method refines the index, its overall impact is relatively limited.

Weighting the indices

The three variables were weighted by percentages 40:30:30, with manufacturing exports per capita gaining the largest 40 per cent weight. This approach has been adopted, rather than perhaps the more obvious choice of equal thirds, given the particular interest in current performance, and the need to account for the varying sizes of the countries involved.

As above, the ranking is robust compared to the use of an equal weighting, with a rank correlation of 0.993 between the results of the two methods.

Annex notes

a. The HDI is an index produced annually by the United Nations Development Programme (UNDP). It uses a weighted sum of three indices representing life expectancy, educational attainment, and adjusted GDP per capita. For each country, each of the three variables is indexed to a value between 0 and 1, and then the three indices are combined with equal weights to form the HDI. See UNDP (2003).

Bibliography

Atkins, J., Mazzi, S. and Easterly, C.D. (2001) 'Small States: A Composite Vulnerability Index', in David Peretz, Rumman Faruqi and Eliawony J. Kisanga (eds) *Small States in the Global Economy* Commonwealth Secretariat, London.

Commonwealth Secretariat (1997) *A Future for Small States: Overcoming Vulnerability*, Report of a Commonwealth Advisory Group. Commonwealth Secretariat, London.

Gounder, R. and V. Xayavong (2001) 'Globalisation and the Island Economies of the South Pacific', *United Nations University – World Institute for Development Economic Research (UNUWIDER) Discussion Paper* No.2001/41. UNU WIDER, Helsinki.

Harris, D.J. (1997) *Jamaica's Export Economy: Towards a Strategy of Export-Led Growth, Critical Issues in Caribbean Development Series No.5.)*Ian Randle Publishers, Kingston.

IMD (2003) *The World Competitiveness Yearbook*. International Institute for Management Development, Lausanne.

IMF (various years) *International Financial Statistics Yearbook*. IMF, Washington DC.

ITC (2000) 'The Trade Performance Index: Background Paper'. UNCTAD/WTO International Trade Centre, Market Analysis Section, Geneva.

James. J. and H. Romijn (1997) 'Determinants of Technological Capability: A Cross-Country Analysis', *Oxford Development Studies*, 25:2.

Lall, S. (2001) 'Competitiveness Indices and Developing Countries: An Economic Evaluation of the Global Competitiveness Report', *World Development*, Vol.29, No,9.

Lall, S. and G. Wignaraja (1998) 'Mauritius: Dynamising Export Competitiveness', *Commonwealth Economic Paper No.33*. Commonwealth Secretariat, London.

Peretz, D., R. Faruqi and E. Kissanga (eds) (2001) *Small States in the Global Economy* . Commonwealth Secretariat, London.

Ul Haque, I. (1995) 'Introduction' in Ul Haque (ed.) *Trade, Technology and International Competitiveness*. World Bank, Economic Development Institute, Washington DC.

UNCTAD (2002a) *World Investment Report*. UNCTAD, Geneva.

UNCTAD (2002b) *Handbook of Statistics*. UNCTAD, Geneva.

UNCTAD (2003) *Handbook of International Trade Statistics*. UNCTAD, Geneva.

UNDP 2001. Human Development Report 2001: Making New Technologies Work for Human Development, United Nations Development Programme, New York

UNDP (2003) *Human Development Report*. Oxford University Press, New York.

UNIDO (2002) *World Industrial Development Report 2002/2003: Competing Through Innovation*. UNIDO, Vienna.

WEF (2003) *Global Competitiveness Report*. Oxford University Press for the World Economic Forum, New York. www.weforum.org

Wignaraja, G. (1997) 'Manufacturing Competitiveness With Special Reference to Small States' in *Small States: Economic Review and Basic Statistics*, Vol.3. Commonwealth Secretariat, London.

Wignaraja, G. (2003) 'Competitiveness Analysis and Strategy' in G. Wignaraja *Competitiveness Strategy in Developing Countries*. Routledge, London.

Wignaraja, G. and A. Taylor (2003) ' Benchmarking Competitiveness: A First Look at the MECI', in G. Wignaraja *Competitiveness Strategy in Developing Countries*. Routledge, London.

Wignaraja, G., M. Lezama and D. Joiner (forthcoming) *Small States in Transition: From Vulnerability to Competitiveness*. Commonwealth Secretariat, London.

Wint, A.G. (2003) *Competitiveness in Small Developing Economies: Insights from the Caribbean*. University of West Indies Press, Kingston.

World Bank (1994) *Mauritius: Technology Strategy for Competitiveness*, Report No. 12518-MAS. World Bank, Washington DC.

World Bank (2001) *World Development Indicators 2001*. World Bank, Washington.

World Bank (2003) *World Development Indicators*. Oxford University Press, New York.

WTO (2002) *World Trade Statistics 2002*. World Trade Organization, Geneva.

Part 4
REGIONALISM

7. The Establishment of the CSME: A Manifestation of Sir Arthur Lewis's Vision for the Caribbean

Claudius Preville

Although Sir Arthur Lewis never engaged in the debate for the creation of the CSME, since he unfortunately died in 1991 before it became an issue, efforts of intellectuals like him were the inspiration for pursuing deeper integration in the Caribbean and for the realisation of the CSME. Sir Arthur's direct involvement in exploring alternative forms of a constitution for the creation of a federation of Caribbean states was perhaps the deepest manifestation of his commitment to regionalism.

This chapter will focus on three themes. First, the CSME: what it is, how it is likely to affect our lives, and why Caribbean leaders are pursuing it at this stage of our development. Second, some of the works of Sir Arthur, in particular areas of relevance to the CSME. Third, a synthesis of the objectives of pursuing the CSME with some elements of Sir Arthur's work, to show that indeed a significant part of his work can be interpreted as an inspiration for the creation of the CSME.

I. The CSME: What is it? How is it likely to affect the lives of Caribbean people? Why pursue it at this time?

The CSME, when it comes into effect on January 1, 2006, will represent the strongest expression of CARICOM governments to deepen the integration process and strengthen the Caribbean Community in all its dimensions. CARICOM governments first expressed their intention to create the CSME at the 10th Conference of Heads in Grand Anse, Grenada, in 1989. At the 13th Conference of Heads in 1992, the necessary technical work for, and conceptualisation of, the CSME was completed and presented to the Conference of Heads for their endorsement. In many ways, the CSME was then seen as a vehicle for expanding the domestic markets in each member state.

But in addition to facilitating economic development of the member states of CARICOM, a driving exogenous force behind the need to create the CSME has been the increasingly liberalised and globalised international environment. When the endogenous and exogenous factors are taken together, the CSME can be seen as CARICOM's member states response to finding strategies for their growth and development in a global environment propelled by efficiency and competitiveness. Its key objectives include to:

- bring about full employment of all the factors of production;

- improve upon the standards of living and work for citizens of CARICOM;

- result in an accelerated, coordinated and sustained economic development for CARICOM member states;

- increase economic leverage and effectiveness of CARICOM in relation to other states, groups of states and entities;

- expand trade and economic relations with other Caribbean countries, and Central and Latin American countries;

- achieve increased levels of competitiveness; and

- result in more efficient organisation for increased production.

CARICOM member states had already all progressed beyond the creation of a Free Trade Area (FTA) and Common Market by 1992, as evidenced by the virtual elimination of intra-regional barriers to trade and adoption of appropriate Rules of Origin.[1] At the turn of the century more than 95 per cent of intra-regional trade was free from all restrictions. Additionally, member states committed themselves to implementing a Harmonised System (HS) based on Common External Tariffs (CETs) and a common trade policy. Completing the arrangements for a full customs union requires the implementation of uniform customs legislation and documentation that has been prepared and is under consideration by member states. Full implementation of harmonised customs legislation and further consideration of the issue of free circulation are the two outstanding actions required before all aspects of the customs union are complete.

Yet, realising the implementation of the CSME requires CARICOM member states to go a few steps beyond implementation of the customs union. These additional steps are as follows:

- add the free movement of services to free movement of goods within the existing Common Market;

- introduce the free movement of the factors of production, including particularly capital and labour;

- recognise the right of establishment;

- introduce measures to create a monetary union, such as co-ordination of macro-economic policies, monetary and fiscal policies, and a single currency, with a view to convergence of macro-economic performance of member states; and

- introduce support mechanisms, including institutions and structures, a scheme for disadvantaged countries, regions and sectors, and a public education initiative.

Recognising this, CARICOM member states embarked on the process of revising the Treaty of Chaguaramas in order to incorporate additional protocols that are necessary to realise the above objectives. The nine additional protocols that have been incorporated into the Revised Treaty of Chaguaramas cover the following areas: institutions and structures; establishment, services and capital; industrial policy; trade policy; agricultural policy; transport policy; disadvantaged countries regions and sectors; competition policy, consumer protection and dumping and subsidies; and disputes settlement (see CARICOM Secretariat, 2001).

In terms of how the CSME will affect the lives of ordinary CARICOM citizens, a few examples might best illustrate this. The right of establishment implies that any CARICOM citizen will have the right to set up a business in any other CARICOM member state under conditions no less favourable than those enjoyed in that member state by its own citizens. Similarly, capital mobility implies that any firm can source capital from any member state under terms no less favourable than those under which citizens of that member state can access capital. Additionally, labour mobility (for eligible categories) implies that labour will be free to move to any member state for the purpose of engaging in gainful employment under terms and conditions similar to those enjoyed by citizens of that member state. Notably, the requirements for work permits shall be abolished.

It is important to stress that ratification of the Revised Treaty of Chaguaramas by all CARICOM member states represents only the beginning of the process, that is provision of the Treaty-basis for the CSME. Full establishment of the CSME will only be realised when the nine new Protocols have been implemented, along with the supporting mechanisms and parallel initiatives. Whether or not the CSME is successful will depend in part on its potential for optimal production of goods, both quantity and quality, both of which are required for competitiveness in the global market. As such, whether or not firms in CARICOM member states can take advantage of opportunities in the increasingly liberalised global market will significantly determine the success of the CSME, given the relatively small size of CARICOM's internal market. Therefore, the external orientation of the CSME is critical. Such external orientation includes both its bi-lateral economic relations, with countries like Venezuela, Colombia, Costa Rica, Cuba and the Dominican Republic, and its inter-regional economic relations, such as those being negotiated too create the Free Trade Area of the Americas (FTAA) within the Western Hemisphere, and an Economic Partnership Agreement (EPA) with the European Union.

So, to summarise, whereas CARICOM's integration process has so far been inward and focused on trade in goods, the CSME focus is both inward and outward and will span trade in both goods and services. Moreover, in addition to treating with the free movement of goods and services, the CSME will incorporate free movement of the factors of production, particularly labour and capital, and in the case of land the right to its access by citizens of CARICOM for the purpose of establishing firms. Entrepreneurs will be allowed to trade freely without hindrance, to establish and service markets or clients in other CARICOM member states, to attract capital, invest, or otherwise use funds in another member state, to hire labour from or work in another member state, all with the objective of creating an internationally competitive system of production. Some of the works of Sir Arthur Lewis are particularly relevant to this subject.

2. Sir Arthur Lewis – A brief overview of literature

Sir Arthur was no ordinary scholar. In his own words he had 'never meant to be an economist', however, after obtaining first class honours in his Bachelor of Commerce degree at the London School of Economics and his subsequent receipt of a fellowship to do a Ph.D. there in Industrial Economics, his destiny had been defined for him. In his autobiography he explains how he emerged as an expert on British industrial organisation, the subject which had preoccupied him for his Ph.D., and on which he subsequently published a thesis at Manchester in 1948 (an update of his thesis, called *Overhead Costs*. Thereafter, Sir Arthur continued to build an academic career that culminated in the publication of ten books and approximately eighty other academic pieces. Included among these works are his Nobel Prize-winning classic *Economic Development with Unlimited Supplies of Labour* (1954); *Industrialisation of the British West Indies* (1951); *The Theory of Economic Growth* (1955); *Aspects of Tropical Trade 1883–1965* (1969); *The Evolution of the International Economic Order* (1977); *Growth and Fluctuations 1870– 1913* (1978); *The Agony of the Eight* (1965); and *Labour in the West Indies*; among others.

Perhaps it would be fair to describe Sir Arthur as an economist whose initial interest and mentorship was in industrial organisation, hence the direction he took for his Ph.D. However, it seems clear that throughout his life he was persistently concerned with the economic development of the so-called Third World – a concern that he appears to have addressed using two techniques. First, by analysing particular problems in the developed countries at the time and deriving explanations that could be generalised. Second, by undertaking empirical work in selected developing countries, out of which he was able to develop a model for development. An extension of the second is found in his very involvement in attempting to save the West Indies Federation, an analysis of which he subsequently wrote in his 'The Agony of the Eight'.

The Great Depression typifies the first of his analyses of world problems. In general, Americans appeared to have persuaded themselves that their economy was more prosperous than ever before in the second half of the 1920s. Hence, they found it difficult to understand why their economy had slipped into a recession in 1929, which would become so prolonged and acute that it is known as the Great Depression today. But Sir Arthur argued that such a contention could not be supported by statistics, which instead revealed only average performance for the American economy. The explanation that he advanced for the Great Depression is the convergence of a number of weaknesses in the world economy at the time. Three of these can be isolated, and are relevant to the CSME. First, prosperity in the US economy tended to coincide with a railway–construction–immigration–housing cycle. As such, when the US Congress restricted immigration from 1924 it resulted in a weak construction boom during the second half of the 1920s. Moreover, the abnormal weakness of the first half of the 1930s further weakened the entire economy. Second, both domestic and international agricultural prices had been in decline since the mid-1920s because capacity had been growing much faster than demand. Additionally, consumption in the rural areas was low and the US witnessed the failure of a number of rural banks. Third, countries abandoned the gold standard, replacing it with exchange controls and raised tariff levels which resulted in a 30 per cent reduction in the volume of international trade.

Another of the problems that preoccupied Sir Arthur's academic life and which is relevant to the creation of the CSME is the following. What determines the terms of trade between industrial and primary products? He proceeded to answer that question starting with the observation that a constant relationship existed between an index of world industrial production and an index of world trade in primary products.[2] Sir Arthur concluded that while the short-run determinants of the terms of trade for tropical crops had to be demand and supply, the long-run terms of trade were likely to be determined by the infinite elasticity of supply of tropical produce. He argued that such infinite elasticity of supply derives from the fact that tropical agricultural exports constitute only a small part (less than 20 per cent) of tropical agriculture output, which can be expanded or contracted at constant cost over a long time horizon. The implication of this finding, Sir Arthur argues, is that farmers would do better to grow more food than to put more resources into export crops. Such a recommendation derives from the very small cost of expanding exports given that the yield in food cultivation is very small.Let me now turn to the second of the techniques that Sir Arthur deployed in his pursuit of answers for the economics of development in the so-called Third World, that is the empirical work that he conducted on selected developing countries. First is his book *Labour in the West Indies*, in which he gives an account of the emergence of the trade union movement in the 1920s and 1930s. Among other things that book highlights the violent confrontations between the trade unions and government in the 1930s, and was inspired by Sir Arthur's resentment of the imperialistic order of the day. He was an exponent of the view that 'what matters most to growth is to make the best use of one's resources and that the exterior events are secondary'. Despite the accelerated pace of globalisation and greater trade liberalisation, his view is still relevant today. Globalisation and trade liberalisation might both be seen as hostile to especially small open economies. Yet, the extent to which small open economies might be adversely impacted by these processes depends in part on the efficiency of organisation of resources at the national level.

Another example to demonstrate the second of his techniques is found in what culminated in his Nobel Prize-winning classic. Sir Arthur was puzzled by the fact that although a number of developing countries had been developing for a very long time, the standard of living of the 'masses' remained extremely low. Conventional thinking at the time, the neoclassical doctrine, posited that the industrial revolution should result in an increase in urban wages as national income rises, since the share of profits in national income would remain constant. Yet, the observed evidence was that the share of profits in national income actually increased. The neoclassical doctrine was premised on the assumption that the elasticity of supply of labour was zero. Therefore, any increase in investment would result in increase in the demand for labour and wages would rise. Sir Arthur posited the contrary view – that in many developing countries the elasticity of supply of labour is infinite, and because of this growth raises profits for capitalists at the expense of persistent low wages for the urban 'sea' of proletariat. Sir Arthur's model is helpful in understanding the problem of migration, whether it be between the rural and urban parts of a country, or from a poor country to a rich country. Still another example is found in Sir Arthur's *The Agony of the Eight* in which he recalls how the Federation of the West Indies fell apart: first with the withdrawal of Jamaica and subsequently Trinidad and Tobago. Sir Arthur discusses how, after the withdrawal of Jamaica, he pursued the possibility of creating a federation guided by the principles that were enunciated in Dr Eric Williams' *Economics of Nationhood*. When that also failed with the withdrawal of Trinidad and Tobago, he pursued the possibility of a federation of Barbados and the Eastern Caribbean. But federation seemed doomed not to work at that time, and Sir Arthur's agony over its failure is captured in his statement 'If each little island goes off on its own, its people must suffer' (1965). The state of economic progress in the Caribbean today bears testimony to that statement.

So can the establishment of the CSME be seen at least in part as a fulfilment of Sir Arthur's vision for the Caribbean?

3. The CSME as a fulfilment of Sir Arthur's vision?

Unfortunately Sir Arthur died before any real debate on the CSME had begun, and as such there exists no direct reference to the CSME in any of his works. However, Sir Arthur's ideas can be revisited and recast in the context of some of the fundamental objectives for creation of the CSME.

We have seen that a fundamental pillar of the CSME is the freedom of movement of labour across member states of CARICOM. Although CARICOM member states do not envisage completely free movement of labour in the initial stages of the CSME, the labour market will be liberalised with respect to certain categories of employment: university graduates, media workers, sports persons, musicians, artistes, managers, supervisors and other service providers.[3] While this represents some attempt at liberalisation of the labour market, in reality it will constitute a very small percentage (perhaps less than 10 per cent) of the regional labour force. In other words, the vast majority of the 'masses' will not be in a position to benefit from the liberalisation opportunities created by the CSME, initially. What might have been Sir Arthur's view on this issue if he were still alive? In discussing the reasons why there was a Great Depression from 1929 into the early 1930s, Sir Arthur isolated restrictions imposed on immigration to the US as a major factor that contributed to the initial depression, as the vital 'construction sector' could not secure the much-needed labour to fulfil market demand. Experience in Caribbean economies typically suggests that these economies enter periods of 'boom' when there is intense construction activity and 'economic slowdown', or even slumps, after major construction periods are over. It would seem, therefore, that the logical direction to follow in the CSME would be to further liberalise at least labour attached to the construction sector.

Additionally, prior to developing his seminal piece, Sir Arthur was puzzled by the fact that despite significant sums of investment in several developing countries over several decades, the 'masses' simply could not lift themselves out of poverty, while the share of profits of capitalists in national income increased – something that he abhorred. Despite fluctuations in unemployment levels across the Caribbean, the region as a whole cannot be typified as a zone with unlimited supplies of labour. Instead, what seems to be more distinct is the demand for labour of certain types at certain times of the year, for instance for the sugar cane harvest in St. Kitts and Nevis and Barbados. That does not mean to suggest that structural unemployment is not on the rise in some states, like those that are being forced into adjustment as a consequence of banana trade liberalisation in Europe. It seems, however, that such structural unemployment problems can be overcome, or at least alleviated, if some Caribbean states were to specialise in production of agricultural produce both for immediate consumption and their associated industrial linkages (i.e., intermediate inputs) within the new regional economic space. If labour is fully liberalised then it can move freely to the member states that specialise in agricultural production, for instance. However, given the limited size of the regional labour supply relative to market demand for agricultural produce and its value added derivatives, as its use is intensified, i.e., as demand for its output increases, wages will rise.[4]

In consequence the CSME would simultaneously achieve two objectives that Caribbean states have long pursued. First, because the region's labour supply would be focused in the member states with a comparative advantage and higher levels of productivity, economies of scale can be realised. Thus national income will increase. Second, as labour is used more intensively its demand will increase, resulting in a higher wage, and thus a larger share of national income. Sir Arthur was very sympathetic to the rural poor and one of his concerns about economic development has been that its benefits should redound to the masses, that is their share of wages in national income should rise, as opposed to increasing the share of profits for the capitalist class. It is for these reasons that Sir Arthur, were he alive today, would have called for greater liberalisation of the labour market throughout the Caribbean than the regional leadership has committed itself to in the context of creation of the CSME.

Another pillar of the CSME is the liberalisation of trade in goods and services, i.e., elimination of all barriers that would make it difficult to move goods from one CARICOM member state to another, or to deliver or receive a service from one CARICOM member state to another. As mentioned earlier one of the causes of the Great Depression as far as Sir Arthur was concerned was that countries simultaneously increased tariff levels, resulting in a significant decline in international trade. This suggests that Sir Arthur saw a relatively liberalised trading environment as conducive to economic growth, although he was equally concerned that the terms of trade tended to move against the primary commodities supplied by developing countries. Trade in

However, liberalisation of trade in services across CARICOM member states is yet to be realised. When discussing what Sir Arthur refers to in his seminal work as surplus labour, he isolates not only labour to be deployed in agriculture, but also labour engaged is domestic work, including nurses and maids. Services had not yet evolved as a major concept in the literature on cross-border trade in Sir Arthur's time, hence the reason why he referred to the concept only in the context of trade within an economy. The CSME envisages the immediate liberalisation of trade in services of skilled labour, but what about the unskilled masses who are also service providers? Should not they too benefit from the creation of the CSME? The answer has to be yes. However, it seems to be a 'hard sell' for CARICOM leaders at this time, since the Revised Treaty of Chaguaramas only provides for self-employed persons and not employees (CARICOM Secretariat, 2001, Art. 32(3) - Prohibition of New Restrictions on the Right of Establishment).

The problem with the unskilled masses is not that they too would not like to make a contribution to regional development, but it is that they may not know how to do it. That problem is therefore one of failure of domestic policy – failure to train and educate the 'masses' for their employment in specific sectors of the economy. Hopefully, the protocols on: 'institutions and structures' and 'disadvantaged countries, regions and sectors' of the Revised Treaty of Chaguaramas can be implemented in a sufficiently creative manner to provide the much-needed solution to this problem.

CARICOM has made progress since its inception in 1973, but there remains much room for improvement. One of the pillars for success of any such integration movement is ensuring that some degree of convergence can be achieved between national economies. Such convergence can be achieved through the establishment of a structural convergence fund, perhaps the best example of which is found in the European Union. The Revised Treaty of Chaguaramas makes provision for a 'Development Fund' (CARICOM Secretariat, 2001, Art. 158 – The Development Fund), which might seem to provide the scope for serving that purpose. Among the CSME objectives reference is made to the need to create institutions and structures for 'disadvantaged countries'. One component of that definition of 'disadvantaged countries' is the less-developed countries of CARICOM as defined under Art. 4. It seems as if CARICOM sees some of its member states as being permanently disadvantaged (CARICOM Secretariat, 2001, Art. 4 – Less Developed Countries and More Developed Countries), a dangerous conception for the success of the CSME. In fact, such a conception is actually enshrined in the Revised Treaty of Chaguaramas, which nevertheless can be changed by majority decision of the Conference (CARICOM Secretariat, 2001, Art. 5 – Modification of the Status of Member States). Instead, the proper way to conceptualise member states is that they are at different levels of development initially, hence the need for structural convergence. It must not be forgotten from the lessons of federation that it was precisely such conceptual misunderstandings that led to the demise of the federation. However, success in achieving structural convergence requires clear objectives and targets for convergence. That necessitates the existence of a development plan for the region, on the basis of which industries can emerge.[5]

So, to conclude, there is little doubt that the present direction of CARICOM member states, that is the creation of a single market and economy, is in accord with Sir Arthur's vision for the Caribbean. Sir Arthur was an integrationist – he stuck to the cause of integrating the Caribbean through thick and thin, as one country followed by another left the federation in 1962. Rather than giving up on the idea prematurely, he shared in the agony of the smaller Eastern Caribbean States, exploring alternative constitutions for federation until the remaining states were too few to make it viable.

Sir Arthur was also genuinely concerned with the plight of the masses, and it was in his pursuit of a solution to that problem that he won the Nobel Prize for economics. The questions for CARICOM leaders today are, 'To what extent do they see the CSME as a mechanism for lifting the masses of humanity within the region out of poverty?'. If they do, what concrete steps do they envisage in that process and how do they plan to implement them? Not enough thought and attention has been given to these questions, notwithstanding the fact that they are the most important questions if the CSME is to be successful. Caribbean states continue to be insular: many of them seem to be concerned that liberalisation of the regional labour market will result in waves of migration from the relatively poorer member states to the relatively more affluent ones. However, such apprehensions are not borne out from the practical experience of integration in the European Union, for instance. In reality, providing there exist reasonable similarities between countries, legislation that provides for the free movement of their citizens does not result in massive migration. Those who are likely to migrate are the ones who perceive significantly superior opportunities in another member state and who know that they are sufficiently competitive to become gainfully employed. In practice, this means a concrete offer of employment in another member state. Certainly, this cannot be inimical to the interest of either the worker or the firm in the other member state in a competitive market: the firm receives the best qualified labour and has the best opportunity of maximising profits, while labour receives the wage that is commensurate with the demand for its skill.

If there exists an impediment to free movement of labour in the CSME then it is of our own making. Conceptually, the benefits to be realised from the creation of the CSME are realistic, but there is a need for a change in the mindset of Caribbean people to realise such benefits. Sir Arthur always contended that what matters most to economic growth is how well one exploits one's own resources. Increasingly, it seems the Caribbean's comparative advantage will lie in its ability to become an efficient service-oriented economy, at the core of which is its labour supply. Difference in levels of development of Caribbean states should not be seen as obstacles to the integration process, but opportunities. CARICOM leaders must initially minimise such differences through the creation and implementation of a programme for structural convergence, and should simultaneously realise that levels of development are dynamic and not static. Once a reasonable degree of structural convergence exists across member states, the regional labour market should be fully liberalised.

In terms of the future of Caribbean integration, Sir Arthur concluded his *The Agony of the Eight* with the optimistic phrase that 'It will begin with confederation rather than federation, a common nationality, a common currency and common representation abroad' (1965, p.37). Thus, the CSME is the first step in fulfilling of this prophecy.

Notes

1. In fact, this integration movement can be traced back to 1965 when the Caribbean Free Trade Association (CARIFTA) was created, followed by the signing of the Treaty of Chaguaramas, which established the Caribbean Community and Common Market (CARICOM) in July 1973.

2. The relationship was as follows: a 1 per cent increase in world industrial production was associated with a 0.87 per cent increase in world trade in primary products.

3. At a recent inter-sessional Conference of CARICOM Heads it was realised that the categories of labour need to be expanded to include several others. Work on this is still on-going, so a revised list is yet to be published and agreed.

4. The argument developed here is along the lines of the factor endowments (Heckscher, 1919, pp.497–512; and Ohlin, 1933) and factor-price equalisation theorem of Paul Samuelson (1948, pp.163-85).

5. CARICOM Heads reportedly identified this as a priority area for attention at their last Inter-Sessional Conference in Trinidad and Tobago, however work is yet to commence.

References

CARICOM (2001) Revised Treaty of Chaguaramas

Heckscher, E.F. (1919) 'The Effect of Foreign Trade on the Distribution of Income', *Ekonomisk Tidskrift*, pp. 497–512. Reprinted in H. S. Ellis and L. M Metzler (1950) *Readings in the Theory of International Trade*. Irwin, Homewood Ill, pp. 272–300.

Lewis, A. (1951) *Industrialisation of the British West Indies.*

Lewis, A. (1951) *Overhead Costs.* Allen and Unwin, London.

Lewis, A. (1954) *Economic Development with Unlimited Supplies of Labour.*

Lewis, A. (1955) *The Theory of Economic Growth.* Allen & Unwin, London.

Lewis, A. (1965) *The Agony of the Eight.* Advocate Commercial Printery, ND, Barbados.

Lewis, A. (1969) *Aspects of Tropical Trade 1883–1965.* Almqvist & Wiksells, Stockholm.

Lewis, A. (1977) *The Evolution of the International Economic Order.* Princeton University Press, Princeton.

Lewis, A. (1978) *Growth and Fluctuations 1870–1913.* Allen & Unwin, London.

Lewis, A. (1978) *Labour in the West Indies.* New Beacon Books.

Ohlin, B. (1933) *Interregional and International Trade.* Harvard University Press, Cambridge, Mass.

Samuelson, P.A. (1948) 'International Trade and the Equalization of Factor Prices', *Economic Journal*, 58(230), June.

8. Economic Integration in the Pacific: Review of Past Efforts and Future Prospects

T K Jayaraman

1. Introduction

Five decades ago, following the creation of the European Community, the first wave of regionalism spread across the world. Although European regionalism has blossomed into the realisation of the 'concept of an area without frontiers' as embellished in the Single European Act (1986), countries in other parts of the world, which had set regionalism as their goal, could not progress beyond the initial step. The emergence of the Association of Southeast Asian Nations (ASEAN) in the 1970s, which was hailed as another landmark, is yet to proceed beyond trade in goods and mobility in capital, not to speak of labour mobility. After being dormant for more than two decades, the wave of regionalism took off again. The United States of America, Canada and Mexico signed the North American Free Trade Agreement (NAFTA) in the 1990s. Noting this development, DeMello and Panagariya (1992) observed that regionalism was now being pursued on a larger scale, and it was no longer only among equals, since developing countries were seeking partnerships with specific developed countries.

The fear of net welfare losses due to preferential trading arrangements is real. The welfare losses arise from trade diversion: If the losses from preferential concession to a partner resulting from replacing imports from the cheapest source with expensive imports from the partner country are greater than gains from trade creation, there will be a reduction in net welfare. For this reason in particular, it was held that a preferential trading arrangement (PFTA), either among equals or with a few developed countries, was bad in principle as it is less optimal than multilateral free trade under the World Trade Organization (WTO). However, WTO-compatible PFTAs are now in vogue among small countries in different parts of the globe. It was felt that regional trading arrangements among small countries with complementary in nature, would result in lower net welfare losses as there would be fewer trade diversion possibilities. There are other gains as well: the small countries would be able to mobilise, nurture and exercise their collective market power; if the countries are socially and culturally similar, they would be better placed to get together and harmonise various policies including tax policies and product standards; trade diversion risks would be minimised; and, if the number of countries is small, a cooperative solution is more likely.

The term regionalism is not strange to a small number of the erstwhile, colonised island nations in the Pacific. Growing from a handful in the 1970s to 14 in the new Millennium, the Pacific island countries (PICs), with a current population of 7 million, established in 1971 their regional organisation the Pacific Islands Forum,[1] along with a secretariat known then as the South Pacific Bureau for Economic Cooperation, now called the Forum Secretariat. The objective was to promote co-operation among the island nations in trade and economic development. Progress has been slow, however, with setbacks in some spheres and successes in others. Regional integration has remained an elusive concept, despite various efforts in several directions during the past 34 years. The introduction of the single currency in Europe, together with the expansion of the European Union to 25 countries five years later in 2004, has set off a new wave spreading across the Pacific island countries. The Pacific island states are now considering the Pacific Plan, a document formulated by their leaders in a meeting held under the Forum auspices in Auckland in 2004.

Aside from reviewing the past efforts by PICs to promote regional co-operation, this chapter assesses the weaknesses and strengths of such efforts and explores the avenues now open to PICs, with a view to finding ways to exploit the opportunities without repeating past errors of omissions and commissions. This chapter is organised into three sections. The first section deals with various components of regional co-operation leading to ultimate integration, with specific reference to experiences in the Caribbean countries, with which PICs share many commonalities. The second section reviews the progress of integration efforts in the Pacific, while the third and final section discusses future strategies.

2. Regional integration: Relevant experiences from elsewhere

Integration efforts in Europe, culminating in a currency union (the exchange rates were set in 1999 and the notes appeared in 2002), have inspired several regional groups of aspiring developing countries in different parts of the globe. It is worth remembering, however, that it did take nearly fifty years to realise the grand vision of Jean Monnet and Robert Schuman for a United States of Europe without each country having to surrender its sovereignty. The first set of steps in Europe are the familiar ones, straightforward and simple: establishing unhindered trade in coal and steel by establishing the European Coal and Steel Community, which subsequently grew into a customs union with free trade amongst the members but a common tariff against the rest of the world. With increased mobility in labour and capital, the customs union became a common market, followed by other developments in monetary integration.[2] The European integration efforts were driven soon after World War II by an intense desire and collective will on the part of the war-ravaged nations to put aside the historical animosities and work towards recovery and reconstruction against yet another background of rising totalitarianism in the garb of an 'evil empire', the former Soviet Union. Such a passionate desire and sustained diplomatic efforts for integration were lacking in other regions in the post-cold-war years.

More recent experiences have shown that only perceivable economic gain is a powerful enough motivating force for small countries to come together to build a single economic space without barriers. The gains include larger economies of scale in production and distribution which are not realisable otherwise. A single economic space also attracts investment from overseas for producing goods for an assured market without any trade barriers. This is achieved by dismantling all barriers to trade in goods and services and promoting unhindered mobility of all factors of production, including labour and capital. Experiences have also shown that harmonisation of tax policies and product standards are also possible. Liberalisation of trade in goods has been more common than liberalisation in either services or labour movement. While progress towards promoting mobility of labour has been halting, remarkable progress has been achieved in many regions to deal with common regional problems – such as regional civil aviation and shipping services – to promote tourism and trade.

A comparative study on small island economies of countries of the South Pacific and the Caribbean (Fairbairn and Worrell, 1996) noted that the two regions do not command the range of information and skills needed for success in production for the international market, as domestic markets are very small. Even the best endowed have strengths in some areas and weaknesses in others. Noting that the requisite skills reside with government as well as the private sector, the two authors stress the need for pooling human resources so as to make available a wider range of skills, achieve synergies from the interaction of individuals within each profession, and attract and retain highly skilled personnel for whom a single country might not afford sufficient challenge or scope (Fairbairn and Worrell, 1996, p.95).

The experiences of the Caribbean islands, which share many commonalities with the PICs,[3] are highly relevant. Selected key indicators of countries in the two regions are presented in Table 8.1. The first initiative towards regional integration was taken by the Caribbean nations when they set up a Caribbean Free Trade Area (CARIFTA) as far back as in 1968. This was followed by a more definitive action when in 1973 they signed the Treaty of Chaguaramas establishing a Caribbean Community and Common Market (CARICOM). A secretariat was also set up. Among Caribbean countries[4] only the Dominican Republic is not a member (although it has a free trade arrangement with CARICOM).

The Treaty of Chaguaramas proved an inadequate mechanism for responding to various global developments, including intense competition among the rest of the world in regard to access to larger markets, as well as free movement of capital. The emergence of mega trading blocs and free trade areas in other regions necessitated the creation of a CARICOM Single Market and Economy (CSME). The 1973 Treaty of Chaguaramas was amended in 1989 with nine new protocols. The CSME is designed to pool resources to improve competition, mainly geared towards minimising both the

Table 8.1. Selected key indicators of Pacific island countries

	Population ('000)	Per capita GDP (Current prices) in US$ 2003	Human Dev Index Ranking	Aid per capita US$ (2002)	Aid % of GDP 2002	Average growth rate (%) 1990– 2003
Caribbean region						
Antigua and Barbuda	76	10,449	55	192.1	1.90	3.2
Bahamas	314	15,797	51	NA	NA	0.4
Barbados	270	9,423	29	12.8	0.10	0.4
Belize	256	3,382	99	88.6	2.60	6.7
Dominica	79	3,438	95	381.7	12.10	1.4
Dominican Republic	8,745	2,514	98	18.2	0.70	4.7
Grenada	80	4,060	93	117.5	2.30	3.6
Guyana	765	937	104	84.9	9.00	3.3
Haiti	8,132	415	153	8.9	4.50	-0.4
Jamaica	2,651	3,008	79	9.2	0.30	1.0
St.Kitts and Nevis	42	7,745	39	683.8	8.00	3.7
St.Lucia	1,419	4,124	71	226.5	5.10	1.7
St.Vincent and the Grenadines	120	4,060	87	40.1	1.30	3.2
Suriname	436	2,199	67	26.9	1.20	2.1
Trinidad and Tobago	1,303	7,384	54	5.6	0.10	2.9
The Pacific						
Cook Islands	19	2,651	62	490.9	28.00	3.3
Fiji	799	2,281	81	41	1.80	1.6
Fed States of Micronesia	114	1,864	120	702	37.40	1.8
Kiribati	85	530	129	203.3	18.60	2.9
Papua New Guinea	5,099	523	133	36.4	7..2	3.2
Republic of Marshall Islands	51	2,008	121	823.3	49.60	2.3
Samoa	175	1,484	117	214.2	14.50	0.5
Solomon Islands	418	541	124	56.8	11.00	0.1
Tonga	98	1,347	63	217.2	16.40	2.5
Tuvalu	11	345	118	254	45	3.8
Vanuatu	183	1,138	129	133	11.7	2.1

Notes: 1. Population and per capita GDP figures for the Caribbean are for 2003
2. Population and per capita GDP figures for the Indian Ocean and the Pacific regions are for 2001
3. Human Development Index for 2002
Source: ADB (2004), IMF (2004b), UNESCAP (2004)

Commonwealth Small States

problems of small states and structural deficiencies, with the target date set as January 1, 2006. CSME will be WTO compliant, and is also being prepared to be a platform for entering into a Free Trade Area of the Americas (FTAA), as well as to test the waters for more regional markets. Aside from the objectives of increasing competitiveness in the Caribbean region and facilitating the realisation of economies of scale, CSME is to create Pan-Caribbean product brands and companies specialising in such products, such as El Dorado (rum) of Guyana, Angostura (rum and sauces) and Chubby (a soft drink) of Trinidad and Tobago, and Appleton (rum) of Jamaica (World Bank, 2005).

The CSME, which is to be developed as a single economic space through the removal of all restrictions, is based on five pillars: (a) free movement of capital; (b) free movement of goods, services and people; (c) common trade and commercial policy; (d) harmonisation of economic, fiscal and monetary policies; and (e) a common currency (CARICOM, 2002). One of the most significant steps is to provide an institutional and legal framework by establishing the Caribbean Court of Justice (CCJ) for the region as a whole, with a view to ensuring an environment of economic stability and legal certainty in the CSME. In its original jurisdiction, the CCJ will interpret and apply the Revised Treaty of Chaguaramas. The Board of the Caribbean Development Bank has been authorised by the Heads of States to raise US$96 million, intended to be disbursed to a Trust Fund that will finance the budget of the Court out of its earned income.

Besides the CCJ, there will be other CSME institutions, including a standards organisation, a conciliation commission, a regional securities body, a regional intellectual property rights office, and a regional development fund. Most of these new community institutions are premised on the existence of national counterparts that actually do not currently exist.

Progress as of 2004 towards establishing the CSME by January 2006 is shown in Table 8.2. Notable events, aside from the creation of the CCJ, include (a) enacting the Treaty of Chaguaramas into domestic law by 12 members of the CARICOM; (b) setting up national standards bodies; (c) gradual removal of unauthorised import duties and non-tariff barriers; (d) removal of restrictions to provisions of services and mobility of skilled labour; (e) introduction of a CARICOM passport by member countries; (f) accreditation of institutions; (g) agreement on transference of security benefits; (h) free movement and integration of capital markets; (i) harmonisation of laws; (i) signing of intra-regional double taxation agreements; and (j) common external policies and sectoral programmes and common support services. As for the introduction of a common currency, it was agreed to have a set of convergence criteria[5] similar to the ones put forward by the Maastricht Treaty in Europe.

Before moving to the next section, which reviews integration efforts in the Pacific region, it should be noted that almost all initiatives came from the Caribbean nations, without any external goading or pushing. In a way, all the innovations were home-grown, although there were supportive studies by international bodies and academics. This is because CARICOM membership is open only to the Caribbean nations and no

Table 8.2. Status of key elements of CSME

Elements	Status
1. Treaty of Chaguaramas (Revised)	The 12 CARICOM countries who signed have ratified.
	Barbados, Belize, Jamaica, St.Lucia, and St Vincent & the Grenadines have enacted Treaty into domestic law.
2. National administration	All 12 member countries have arrangements (identification of a Ministry/Agency for implementation of requirements).
3. Enforcement, regulation and supporting institutions	Agreement has been signed and necessary legislation enacted for setting up the creation of Caribbean Court of Justice
	Agreement has been reached to establish CARICOM Regional Organisation for Standards and Quality (CROSQ).
	National Standards Bureaus are established in 11 member states.
	National Competition Bodies have been established in Barbados, Jamaica and St. Vincent and the Grenadines.
4. Free movement of goods	Task Force was established to review the existing non-tariff barriers against intra-regional trade. A schedule for removal of unauthorized non-tariff barriers has been prepared.
	Discriminatory taxes and charges have been identified on a number of goods of CARICOM origin.
5. Free movement of services	Schedules of Commitments for removal of Restrictions by Member States have been prepared for phased removal by 31 Dec 2006.
	Programmes for restrictions on international maritime and air transportation will be negotiated.
6. Free movement of persons	CARICOM Passport will be issued by all member countries. Core Elements for a CARICOM Port of Entry/Departure form have been agreed. Two lines at ports of entry will be introduced: one for CARICOM nationals and another for non-CARICOM nationals.
7. Mechanism for equivalency and accreditation	Establishment of National and Regional Accreditation Infrastructure has been agreed.
8. Agreement on transference for social security benefits	Agreement entered into force on 1 April 1997.

Elements	Status
9. Free movement of capital	Schedules of Commitments for removal of Restrictions have been approved.
10. Capital market integration	Regional Stock Exchange has to be established.
	Caribbean Credit Rating agency has been established in Trinidad & Tobago.
11. Intra-regional Double Taxation Agreement	11 Member Countries have signed and ratified.
12. Harmonisation of laws	Draft 20 Modules of model custom legislation have been reviewed.
	Model Competition Law has been prepared.
	Model Consumer Protection Law has been prepared.
	Model Financial Institutions Law has been prepared.

Source: www.caricom.org accessed on June 15, 2005

major powers outside the region have had any say. The sense of ownership of reforms by the member countries of the CARICOM has been a great strength in terms of legitimacy in pushing the integration idea thus far.

3. Regional Integration in the Pacific

Efforts to forge regional co-operation with the ultimate goal of economic integration began almost simultaneously when some of the island nations in the South Pacific were de-colonised in the 1970s. The erstwhile colonial masters of the Pacific region took the lead, unlike in the Caribbean where integration efforts were purely CARICOM driven. In the Pacific Australia, besides being a founding member along with New Zealand of the Pacific Islands Forum in 1971, has been bearing a major portion of the costs of running the Forum Secretariat (previously known as the South Pacific Bureau of Economic Cooperation). Further, the two advanced countries are major providers of external aid to PICs.

Pre-dating the Forum there is another organisation, known originally as South Pacific Commission but now called the Pacific Community (PC) after having been enlarged to include the northern Pacific island states, Republic of Marshall Islands, Federated States of Micronesia, and Palau in the mid-1990s. The PC was established in 1947 under the Canberra Agreement signed by the then six colonial powers in the region (Australia, France, New Zealand, Netherlands, United Kingdom and United States of America). The Secretariat of the Pacific Community (SPC), located in Noumea, New Caledonia, assists all Forum island countries (FICs) as well as the non-independent US Trust Territories, French and UK possessions, including the smallest island of

Pitcairn, by providing technical advice, training, and dissemination of information in social, economic and cultural fields.

The functions of the Forum Secretariat are similar to the CARICOM Secretariat: servicing the PIC governments; co-ordinating regional approaches in areas of common economic interest; overseeing areas of functional co-operation; and acting as the focal point for a range of associated institutions. Notably absent from the list of the Forum's objectives, as Fairbairn and Worrell (1996) observed in their comparative study on the South Pacific Caribbean island economies, are the issues of a single market and a common currency.

Table 8.3 presents the milestones of the long journey towards economic integration. Fry (2005) divides the 34-year old history of regional co-operation and integration into five more or less distinct phases, with some overlap: (i) 1971–75: comprehensive regional integration; (ii) 1975–80: sectoral integration; (iii) 1981–85: regional security; (iv) 1985–90: collective diplomacy; (v) 1991–2000: harmonisation of national policies; and (vi): 2001 onwards: new regionalism.

In the early period, comprehensive regional integration was the main focus on the grounds that small-sized economies, if they could not go it alone, would not be able to realise the economies of scale in manufacturing operations and in purchase of essential items such as fuel and medicines; and that national shipping lines, a university, and a development bank would also not be viable. The arguments, though valid, were not catchy enough for the young island nations, as they did not have any notable manufacturing capabilities, nor was there any immediate demand then for shipping services, as there were no products to be exchanged between them, nor any big demand for tertiary education.

Attention was turned to sectoral integration in the second half of the 1970s. The setting up of the University of the Pacific (USP) in Fiji and the creation of Air Pacific (with shares held by PICs), were some important achievements. However, there was some disillusionment with Air Pacific, on the grounds that Fiji gained more from the common airline. Over a period Nauru, Samoa, the Solomon Islands, Tonga and Vanuatu, while retaining shares in Air Pacific, set up their own national airlines to promote tourist arrivals direct from major airports in Australia and New Zealand and Honolulu in the US. With regards to the USP, there were some rumblings as well. Fry (2005) refers to the writings of Crocombe and Ueantabo (1983) which reflected the concerns of other island nations about whether the University was serving only Fiji's interests. Although the USP responded to these concerns by setting up Extension Centres and special campuses in Samoa (Alafua) and Vanuatu (Emalus), the impressions of yesteryear were not easily erased. Samoa went ahead and set up its own National University of Samoa. During the 2000 coup in Fiji, students enrolled at USP had to return to their respective island countries and their education was disrupted for a while. The dormant dissatisfaction surfaced again as some island nations, such as the Solomon Islands, indicated their desire to set up a university of their own.

Table 8.3. History of regional economic integration efforts in the Pacific

Years/Period	Events
1947	Establishment of South Pacific Commission (SPC) by six countries: Australia, France, New Zealand, Netherlands, the United Kingdom and the United States. SPC provided technical, consultative and advisory assistance in social cultural and economic activities. In 1998, with the inclusion of the Micronesian countries and northern Pacific States, which were former US Trust Territories, the name was changed to the Pacific Community. The acronym SPC is still retained and it stands for Secretariat of Pacific Community. There are 27 members. The programmes of SPC consist of three sectors: land resources, marine Resources, and socio-economic sectors. The functions are provision of technical assistance, education and training, and information/communication. SPC is located in Noumea, New Caledonia.
1968	The University of the South Pacific was established to provide higher education and training that reflects the aspirations and needs of the Pacific islands. The main campus is in Suva, Fiji, and there are two other campuses, one in Samoa, which hosts the School of Tropical Agriculture and in Vanuatu, which hosts the Law Unit and Language Unit. There are University Extension centres in other island states.
1971	Establishment of South Pacific Islands Forum by seven founding members (Australia, Cook Islands, Fiji, Nauru, New Zealand, Tonga, and Samoa). Expanded later to include in all 16 states, covering the Northern Pacific region. The name was changed to Pacific Islands Forum (PIF). It is popularly referred to as the Forum, which serves as the premier regional policymaking body of the of the self-governing states. The Secretariat is known as the Forum Secretariat and its objective is to service the Heads of Government meeting, to foster and promote regional economic cooperation, particularly on political, economic and trade issues.
1972	Establishment of the South Pacific Applied Geo-Science Commission (SOPAC). Started as a UN Project for mineral prospecting in offshore areas, it assists member countries in identifying, assessing, and developing mineral and non-living resource potential of extensive marine resources.
1974	Establishment of South Pacific Regional Environment Programme (SPREP). SPREP aims to provide assistance to the member states in the areas of protecting and improving the environment and ensuring sustainable development for the present and future generations.
1977	The Pacific Forum Line was founded for regional cooperation in shipping. It is a private company wholly owned by nine members of the Forum. The shareholding members are: Cook Islands, Fiji, Kiribati, Nauru, New Zealand, Papua New Guinea, Solomon Islands, Tonga and Samoa.
1979	Establishment of the Forum Fisheries Agency (FFA). It provides technical assistance in the development of fisheries management policies and in negotiations on the issue of licenses. Collection of fees, and surveillance of zones; collecting and dissemination of information on prices; shipping, processing and marketing of fish and fish products; focusing on management procedures legislation, and

agreements within and outside the region. FFA is based in Honiara, the Solomon Islands.

Establishment of South Pacific Trade Commission (SPTC) in Sydney to promote trade and development and encourage Australian investment in island countries, through joint ventures, the SPTC holds exhibitions.

1980   Establishment of Pacific Island Development Program (PIDP) in Honolulu under the East–West Center. Membership covers all island countries regardless of political status. PIDP conducts research on topics identified by Pacific island leaders.

1980–1989   Period of Collective Diplomacy
Successful negotiations with European Community on Lome Conventions.
Negotiations on Law of the Sea
Anti-nuclear dumping campaign against Japan's proposal to dump radioactive wastes in the Marianas Trench, demonstrating collective action. Anti-drift netting campaign against Japan and other environmental initiatives.

Institutionalisation of understandings:
South Pacific Nuclear Free Zone Treaty (1985)
The Convention for the Protection of the Natural Resources and Environment of the South Pacific Region (1986)
The Convention for the Prohibition of Fishing with long driftnets in the South Pacific (1989)

1990–1999   Period of Harmonisation of Policies
Structural reforms
Policy dialogues
Donor-led reform programmes Funded by Asian Development Bank
Melanesian Spearhead Group (Trade Agreement between four Melanesian countries: Fiji, Papua New Guinea, Solomon Islands and Vanuatu for freer trade.)

2000   Pacific Island Countries Trade Agreement (2002) for free trade among the Pacific Island Countries by 2010.

Pacific Agreement on Closer Economic Cooperation (2002) for forging greater cooperation and negotiations by Pacific island countries with Australia and New Zealand to start in 2011.

Preparation of Working Draft on Pacific Plan by Task Force for review and approval by Pacific island Leaders in December 2005.

Source: Fairbairn and Worrell (1995), Fry (2005)

Sectoral integration did not proceed beyond USP and Pacific Forum Lines (the shipping service). As Fry (2005) notes, not only would sectoral integration in other areas require substantial outlays, but also PICs were not prepared to sacrifice their autonomy and they did not like that regional institutions were being located in well-off PICs such as Fiji. The differences between Fiji and other PICs quickly revealed the growing rift between them. So sectoral integration was replaced by a more practical approach of collective diplomacy in many soft areas of co-operation, where conflicts were less likely to surface. The Lome negotiations with the European Community in the 1980s, the Law of the Sea Negotiations, and environmental protection arguments at the Rio Conference were some outstanding examples of success (Table 8.3). Along with these achievements, the regional security concerns of Australia and New Zealand to contain Soviet influence in many PICs led to new initiatives to meet situations such as Kiribati granting the Soviet Union legal access to fish in Kiribati waters and similar overtures by Vanuatu. This gave rise to resentment in PICs against Australia, that while Australia and New Zealand had kept diplomatic relations with the Soviet Union, the foreign policies of PICs were needlessly dictated by the metropolitan states. Fry (2005) observes that the late 1980s witnessed a shift in the approach of Australia. Its foreign policy pronouncements of 1988 indicated 'a constructive commitment' emphasising partnership rather than an agency of western interests or Australian hegemonic aspirations (which represented past Australian diplomatic thrusts).

In the 1990s, the Melanesian countries (Fiji, Papua New Guinea (PNG), Solomon Islands and Vanuatu) forged a trading bloc under the Melanesian Spearhead Group (MSG) Trade Agreement for free trade in select goods. Since there was no common secretariat to oversee implementation of MSG Trade, progress was slow as the PICs involved took time to prepare a list of agreed items, instead of drawing a negative list, which would have been simpler. Under MSG trade, Fiji and PNG built up trade surpluses with Solomon Islands and Vanuatu, with the result that the latter two decided to suspend free trade in early 2002 and re-imposed trade restrictions on imports from Fiji and PNG.

On a wider regional level, during this period efforts were made towards harmonisation of national policies. The emergence of 'neo-liberalism' and wider acceptance of the Washington Consensus of fiscal and monetary restraints, financial sector liberalisation, and public sector reforms paved the way for Australia and New Zealand to tie the goals of fiscal discipline and financial sector liberalisation and other related goals into their bilateral assistance programmes. The Asian Development Bank (ADB) funded several structural adjustment reforms that allowed a great deal of participation by Australian experts in public sector reforms and financial management through technical assistance components. Australian consultants implemented the donor-led ADB-funded agenda of privatisation, investment promotion and tariff reforms. The Comprehensive Reform Programme (CRP) in Vanuatu, which was implemented in large measure by Australian and New Zealand expertise during the second half of the 1990s (with ADB funding) came to be criticised on the grounds that it failed to take into account the sensitivities of the local populace. In fact, when the government changed, the first thing the new prime minister of Vanuatu did was to put the CRP in cold storage (Jayaraman, 2003). The unwillingness of the governments, who had been helped with loans from international funding agencies and grants from bilateral agencies, to accept obligations imposed by the legal agreements of loans, frustrated the Australian and New Zealand governments.

The frustration and disappointment with the poor progress regarding structural reform implementation led Australia and New Zealand to reconsider the past approaches. The terror attacks of 9/11 in 2001 on the United States imposed new responsibilities on Australia to make the Pacific safer from the newly emerging risks of terrorism as well as the already known risks of money laundering and gun-running. Additionally, ethnic strife and civil disorder in the Solomon Islands since the late 1990s and the overthrow of an elected government in 2000 in Fiji caused fresh worries to Australia and New Zealand. Furthermore, a study by Hughes (2003) described some PICs as 'failed states', since they could not effectively use their aid funds, and funds may have been diverted for personal use, amounting to corruption and wastage.

Taking the cue from Hughes (2003), an Australian Senate Committee (the Committee) held hearings on Australia's Relations with Pacific island States in 2002 and in their report *A Pacific Engaged: Australia's Relations with Papua New Guinea and the Island States of the Southwest Pacific* (Australian Senate Committee, 2003) concluded that a *Pacific Economic and Political Community*, along similar lines to the European Union circa 2003 should be a consideration in the medium to long-term future of the region. The Committee also considered the region adopting a common currency, preferably the Australian dollar, to promote fiscal and monetary discipline. Noting the observations (made in another context) by Mike Moore, the former WTO Director General, that studies showed that the countries preparing for entry to the EU do better than those without such objectives and that economic discipline brings with it growth, social progress and better governance (Feizkhah, 2003), the Committee observed that 'If PNG and PICs see benefit to their economies and their overall economic development by adopting the Australian dollar or using the potential for an integrated region as an incentive to reform and address the necessary structural and other issues, the Australian Government should not discourage this' (Australian Senate Committee, 2003, p.79).

Following the Australian Senate Committee's observations in July, the Prime Minister of Australia floated the idea of a single regional currency during the Leaders' Meeting in Auckland.[6] Since the subject was not included in the Agenda, it was not formally discussed. However, the indications were clear: in the event of regional integration in the medium to long-term future, dollarisation would be a logical conclusion.

In the meantime, increased globalisation has already thrown up some new challenges. Both the phased discontinuance of preferential treatment by the EU for the products of PICs and the end of the Sugar Protocol for Fiji's sugar exports under the Cotonou Agreement by 2007 required PICs to restructure their export industries to compete with the rest of the world for access to EU markets. The Cotonou Agreement is likely to be replaced by a new agreement, known as an Economic Partnership Agreement (EPA), on the condition that PICs should speed up and promote regional integration, at least on the lines of the MSG. Further, access to Australia under the South Pacific Regional Trade and Economic Cooperation Agreement (SPARTECA) was also seen as becoming less and less significant as the Australian tariffs on imports of products such as coconut cream from cheaper sources in other regions were also being reduced. In the face of rising stiff competition from competitor economies, PICs had to take quick action to restructure their economies and increase their bargaining position. Further, having found themselves unable to attract foreign direct investment in the immediate past, they wanted to come together and offer an assured regional market of 7 million people. The EU's offer of a new EPA to improve production capabilities and marketing skills means that PICs have to sign the Pacific Island Countries Trade Agreement (PICTA), ushering in a free trade area (FTA) among the 14 PICs, by 2010.

However, the PICs who were nervous about the prospect of any immediate removal of barriers because of both the impact on local consumer goods industries as well as the impact on government finances of the resulting loss of tariff revenue (Scollay, 2005), decided to leave Australia and New Zealand out of the FTA arrangement and keep it among themselves. Persuaded by the arguments of PICs that they looked upon PICTA as a stepping-stone for an eventual closer relationship with the two advanced Forum members, including free trade in goods and services as well as mobility of labour, Australia and New Zealand tacitly agreed to be kept out. They did all sign another agreement, however, known as the Pacific Agreement on Closer Economic Relations (PACER) with them. PACER requires PICs to start negotiations for freer trade in goods with Australia and New Zealand by April 2011. PACER would be triggered earlier than 2011 if any PIC, in its negotiations with the EU on Economic Partnership Agreements to replace the Cotonou Agreement, gives reciprocal access to the EU leading to FTA. Under the Road Map, it is expected that EPA negotiations will trigger PACER by 2006 (Grynberg, 2005). PACER covers only goods and there is no obligation on any PIC to extend negotiations beyond trade in goods.

Studies by Scollay (1998, 2005) and Grynberg (2005) show that free trade in goods with Australia and New Zealand would impose far higher adjustment costs than would the EPAs with the EU, as the trade volume with Australia and New Zealand is much higher than with EU (Australia being the more dominant partner) (see Table 8.4). The revenue loss from the abolition of tariffs on imports from two advanced Forum members has to be replaced by other taxes, including VAT, and Vanuatu in particular has to consider introducing income tax and other direct taxes. The only way to avoid triggering the PACER negotiations is to also avoid free trade in goods and deny access to the EU until 2011 (Kelsey, 2004), which is just not possible. As Kelsey herself admits, the mere opening of EPA negotiations with the EU would trigger PACER (as noted earlier) (Grynberg, 2005). Thus, PICTA may not ultimately give PICs enough 'breathing space', as PACER negotiations will have to commence sooner than contemplated. A more drastic remedy, suggested by Kelsey (2004, 2005), would be to withdraw from PACER, which will prove disastrous to all efforts towards regional integration.

On the other hand, a more practical solution has been suggested by Narsey (2003), which is to enter into a free trade area arrangement with Australia and New Zealand right away, although there will be revenue loss and higher adjustment costs involved. These adjustment costs would be much less now than they would be after 2011, assuming PACER is not triggered until then. During the interim period, any production capability built in the consumer good industries to increase trade exclusively among PICs will be rendered useless when free trade eventually commences with Australia

Table 8.4. Intra-regional exports and imports of PICs

Countries		Intra-regional exports (% of total exports)	Imports (% of total imports)	Intra-regional (% of trade total trade)	Intra-regional trade (% of GDP)	Exports to Australia (% of total exports)	Imports from Australia (% of total imports)	Exports to NZ (% of total exports)	Imports from NZ (% of total imports)	Total trade (% of GDP)
Cook Island	Average of 1994-1997	—	10.26	9.52	4.9	21.07	7.19	25.51	70.94	51.43
		—	11.76	10.83	5.6	28.3	9.75	10.4	68.2	52.45
		—	10.44	9.82	5.2	9.32	8.2	25.2	68.94	54.85
		—	18.49	15.68	12.03	33.91	5.97	25.13	60.58	76.73
		—	11.12	9.74	6.77	29.12	6.1	8.2	74.83	74.4
	2001	—	6.2	5.6	3.41	22.08	6.85	13.9	79.07	61.5
Fiji	Average of 1994-1997	0.31	0.07	0.38	0.505	26.67	39.86	6.99	15.50	76.87
		4.73	0.12	2.13	0.73	33.79	44.84	4.31	15.11	86.84
		6.84	0.1	2.81	0.64	33.02	41.09	4.47	13.10	90.62
		7.11	0.14	3.35	0.94	25.67	48.71	3.53	13.04	89.62
		8.33	—	3.7	0.07	19.74	44.26	3.46	14.88	82.5
	2001	7.21	—	3.02	0.06	19.43	37.31	3.76	17.15	89.26
Kiribati	Average of 1994–1997	—	7.8	5.15	11.67	3.02	18.11	—	3.94	88.78
		—	10.01	8.7	17.06	4.05	21.82	—	1.69	102.74
		—	14	11.37	16.31	2.59	33.08	—	3.02	98.02
		—	14.21	10.7	22.26	0.24	34.12	—	4.75	80.98
	2001	—	20.8	11.87	21.53	0.39	37.16	—	2.91	91.87
	2002	—	12.67	9.14	20.69	0.38	26.6	—	3.58	124.74
RMI	Average of 1994-1997	—	0.97	0.71	0.46	—	1.31	—	1.01	83.41
		—	0.78	0.7	0.35	—	2.01	—	0.71	67.93
		—	1.16	1.02	0.5	—	1.42	—	0.85	68.94

Countries		Intra-regional exports (% of total exports)	Imports (% of total imports)	Intra-regional (% of total trade)	Intra-regional trade (% of GDP)	Exports to Australia (% of total exports)	Imports from Australia (% of total imports)	Exports to NZ (% of total exports)	Imports from NZ (% of total imports)	Total trade (% of GDP)
FSM	2001	—	1.25	1.05	0.54	—	1.46	—	0.89	68.33
	Average of 1994-1997	0.01	NA	NA	NA	NA	NA	NA	NA	61.3
		0.19	NA	NA	NA	NA	NA	NA	NA	67.62
		0.2	—	0.01	0.01	NA	2.62	—	—	65.61
		NA	—	0.02	0.01	NA	4.02	—	—	64.71
		NA	—	0.02	0.01	NA	19.79	—	—	64.39
		NA	NA	NA	NA	NA	NA	NA	—	73.07
	2001	NA	NA	NA	NA	NA	NA	NA	NA	53.05
		NA	NA	NA	NA	NA	NA	NA	NA	52.01
PNG	Average of 1994-1997	0.03	0.03	0.06	0.11	27.68	51.43	1.39	4.01	88.89
		0.21	0.24	0.45	0.21	18.72	52.41	0.69	4.12	94.70
		0.18	0.30	0.44	0.23	26.29	53.01	0.16	4.1	114.12
	2000	0.21	0.36	0.57	0.29	29.98	49.54	0.73	3.8	116.45
	2001	0.1	0.21	0.25	0.2	24.62	51.29	1.35	4.02	94.42
	2002	0.10	0.13	0.31	0.18	23.74	49.26	1.32	4.4	95.81
Samoa	Average of 1994-1997	—	10.49	7.70	6.50	84.18	19.18	6.17	35.15	47.89
		—	18.08	11.9	11.6	48.96	16.23	2.74	22.59	51.74
		—	16.67	12.27	11.52	58.95	14.59	3.68	23.01	57.34
	2000	—	9.48	13.02	9.48	57.36	27.31	2.37	13.89	38.69
	2001	—	12.6	9.98	13.64	60.98	13.12	1.42	17.32	59.9
	2002	—	20.33	14.17	13.43	59.5	15.75	2.05	4.25	56.2
Sol. Is.	Average of 1994-1997	0.38	0.66	1.04	1.92	1.38	40.92	0.26	7.43	94.27
	1998	1.07	4.3	5.1	2.66	1.97	42.96	0.35	5.26	108.46
	1999	1.29	3.7	4.36	2.81	1.34	38.53	0.47	6.29	110.78

Countries		Intra-regional exports (% of total exports)	Imports (% of total imports)	Intra-regional (% of trade total trade)	Intra-regional trade (% of GDP)	Exports to Australia (% of total exports)	Imports from Australia (% of total imports)	Exports to NZ (% of total exports)	Imports from NZ (% of total imports)	Total trade (% of GDP)
	2000	2.1	6.1	8.2	3.7	2.79	27.5	0.74	5.63	85.89
	2001	—	7.46	4.4	NA	1.69	29.27	0.28	5.0	NA
	2002	—	9.1	5.10	NA	0.88	31.31	0.25	5.02	NA
Tonga	Average of 1994-1997	3.08	7.65	6.97	3.76	4.72	33.56	9.66	38.47	51.67
	1998	6.12	7.41	7.26	4.04	4.53	24.68	13.98	36.17	52.4
	1999	2.0	9.96	8.79	4.98	3.21	19.98	8.74	37.22	65.7
	2000	1.65	12.2	9.73	6.65	1.98	10.27	3.68	23.99	79.2
	2001	2.55	19.73	17.1	12.98	1.56	11.24	4.41	33.21	102.9
	2002	2.14	21.42	17.0	13.61	1.44	13.2	3.55	30.83	133.7
Tuvalu	Average of 1994-1997	1.04	30.49	45.5	29.23	—	39.41	—	6.31	81.63
	1998	1.61	59.81	58.39	41.24	—	20.21	—	6.31	70.06
	1999	5.14	63.84	57.18	45.67	—	18.1	—	5.27	79.87
	2000	11.39	58.58	56.01	58.77	—	19.57	—	4.57	104.93
	2001	13.92	65.19	62.48	69.7	—	16.28	—	7.68	52.10
	2002	9.16	54.32	51.1	NA	—	12.9	—	5.21	NA
Vanuatu	Average of 1994-1997	0.01	0.93	0.94	2.67	4.05	21	0.47	5.19	85.58
	1998	1.41	5.67	7.08	3.92	0.60	21.67	0.39	4.76	92.32
	1999	1.19	4.12	5.31	3.98	0.68	17.95	0.44	4.13	122.87
	2000	4.84	8.55	13.39	5.75	0.54	25.08	0.44	6.93	79.24
	2001	—	4.72	3.17	3.58	3.01	25.37	1.12	6.57	53.72
	2002	—	7.11	1.88	4.13	3.20	23.48	0.64	10.69	52.41

NA: Not available
"—": negligible
Source: Asian Development Bank (2003)

and New Zealand, as all consumer industries in PICs will be wiped out. Narsey (2003) also suggests that during the PACER negotiations with Australia and New Zealand PICs, for their part, should seek relaxation of immigration restrictions for both skilled labour from PICs, enabling them to move freely to seek jobs in Australia and New Zealand, as well as for limited annual intake of unskilled labour with temporary work permits for employment in farms and other areas where the two countries currently experience shortages.

While the PICs are being confronted with these problems of bewildering complexities involved in trade agreements, the Group of Eminent Persons appointed by the Forum went around the region in 2003 and met numerous leaders in different walks of life and prepared their report. The PIC leaders met in Auckland in April 2004 to consider the Report of the Group, on the basis of which they agreed to evolve a Pacific Plan. A task force, called Pacific Plan Task Force (PPTF) was set up with specific terms of reference and consultation procedures and a timeframe for preparing the final document for endorsement at the next PIC Leaders Meeting, scheduled to take place in Port Moresby (PNG) in December 2005.

The PPTF's Working Draft has laid down the framework of the Pacific Plan, which will be built upon the four pillars of (i) economic growth; (ii) sustainable development; (ii) good governance; and (iv) security. Specifically with regards to economic growth, the Working Draft indicates that the Pacific Plan would seek to integrate trade in services, including the temporary movement of labour, in the PICTA/PACER negotiations and create bulk purchasing capacity for essential items such as fuel and medicines. While the second item of bulk purchase has been on the agenda ever since 1971 without any progress, the inclusion of trade in services indicates the willingness of PICs to consider deeper integration, of course for 'a price'. Thus, the ball is now in the court of the advanced Forum member countries to consider relaxing immigration laws. The other three items, namely sustainable development, good governance and security are familiar ones. They are now part of Australia and New Zealand's heavy involvement in the region: provision of experts in financial management, public sector reforms and strengthening legal machinery and the placement of prosecutor's services to bring to justice the perpetrators involved in the civilian coup of 2000, which led to the overthrow of the duly elected government, all of which will contribute to better governance and sustainable development; and the provision of a Regional Assistance Mission to Solomon Islands (RAMSI) to improve law and order in the ethnically divided nation. The draft Pacific Plan is now before the PICs and expected to be finalised by December 2005.

The way ahead

Before looking at the short and long-run strategies to promote deeper economic integration among the Forum countries, it would be worthwhile taking stock of developments in the two regions: the Caribbean and the Pacific. The Caribbean is more integrated than the Pacific region. Commitments on CSME have been extensive and considerable progress has been made in terms of free trade, although some obstacles remain in terms of the exclusion of some agricultural products and the continuance of quotas. While observing that a significant agenda still remains to be implemented, a recent World Bank study (2005) notes that there has been significant progress in liberalising trade in labour services among CARICOM countries.[7]

Progress in the Pacific, however, has been slow. There has been no serious commitment to regional integration of the kind envisioned in the original Treaty of Chaguaramas or the revised Treaty to usher in CSME. The main reason behind this, which is also the basic difference between the efforts towards economic integration in the Caribbean and the Pacific regions, is that while CSME is totally CARICOM driven, this is not the case in the Pacific. It is apparent that the draft Pacific Plan has been influenced by the Australian and New Zealand governments' concerns about regional security and stability. Although the title of Pacific Plan is obviously different from the earlier one, a *Pacific Economic and Political Community*, written by the Australian Senate Committee, the ingredients of Pacific Plan, which are called four pillars (i) governance; (ii) security; (iii) growth and (iv) sustainable development, are just the same. They reflect the particular concerns of the two major metropolitan powers, who also happen to be the founding members of the Forum. Since the two advanced Forum members are also major aid providers, PICs feel that any step towards integration of the region would mainly confer benefits on Australia and New Zealand, and hence there is a reluctance to go along the full way with them. 'What's in it for me?' is the question that has been haunting PICs.

It is the perceptions of small PICs that any deeper regional integration, as in the past, would benefit only major PICs, such as Fiji, and hence their apparent unwillingness to show of support. The failure of the regional airline and the poor performance of the regional Pacific Forum Shipping Line and the resulting tensions were pointers. Recently a major breakthrough was achieved in promoting tourism, in the successful conclusion of the Pacific Islands Air Services Agreement (PIASA). However, Fiji, to the disappointment of the others – in particular the small PICs – was reluctant to join PIASA. A centrally operated scheme to bulk purchase essential goods such as fuel and medicines, which has been talked about ever since 1971, was never put into place. Once again, bulk purchase figures in the draft Pacific Plan document. Small PICs, such as Tuvalu have expressed concerns that in the absence of more concrete support by bigger PICs for regional air services, bulk purchase of commodities and other regionally related needs, the envisaged Pacific Plan would not be any different from the previous efforts.[8]

PICs who chose to participate in free trade and deeper integration would naturally weigh up their gains and costs. Even among a subset of PICs, the Melanesian group, both the Solomon Islands and Vanuatu feel that the MSG Trade Agreement benefited only Fiji.[9] Group perceptions of small PICs have been that past efforts including the MSG Trade Agreement have benefited only bigger PICs. On the other hand, all PICs have the feeling that all of the past regional integration moves were in the interest of and influenced by Australia and New Zealand. These suspicions surface from time to time including very recently, when the Solomon Islands, much to the disappointment of Australian interests, voted along with Japan on June 21, 2005 for a resumption of commercial whaling, which has been consistently opposed by Australia and New Zealand, the two developed member countries of the Forum.[10]

Looking back, both Australia and New Zealand did the right thing by stepping aside when the PICs decided to have a separate trade agreement aiming for a FTA amongst themselves by 2010. It would be most appropriate again for Australia and New Zealand to consider not rushing into negotiations with the PICs, although legally they can do so, if PICs in their negotiations for EPA trigger PACER earlier than 2011. The objective of PICTA is to foster trade and closer relations amongst PICs themselves without the two advanced countries, so that they can use it as a stepping stone. Both Australia and New Zealand will do well to let that happen. Eventually negotiations for closer relations, paving the way for free trade and ultimately regional integration, will have to begin under PACER after 2011. In the meantime, both Australia and New Zealand can have a look at their immigration laws and provide special access and temporary work permits for unskilled farm labour to work on their farms. Any substantial gestures of this nature will be of immense help in building trust.

Both a single market and a single currency are advanced concepts for which PICs are not yet ready. Although they were adopted as the goals of CARICOM a long time ago, the progress is understandably slow, as they involve sacrifices of some measure of sovereignty.[11] Aside from sovereignty issues, empirical studies on the feasibility of a common currency for PICs, either on their own or by adopting the Australian dollar, have indicated there has been no convergence observed in any economic real variables, such as gross domestic products, inflation, and real exchange rates of the PICs and Australia and New Zealand (Bowman, 2004, pp.115–32; Jayaraman, 2001, 2005b).

External shocks experienced by PICs and Australia and New Zealand in the past have been asymmetric, and hence they are unsuitable candidates for a common currency at this stage since common fiscal, monetary and exchange rate policies would not be appropriate either for PICs or for the union as a whole (Bunyaratavej and Jayaraman 2005, Jayaraman 2005a, 2006, Jayaraman, Ward and Zu 2005). Although it could be argued that most of the real economic variables such as real exchange rates are endogenously determined and hence a common currency could be adopted (Duncan, 2005), one has to recognise the presence of inherent risks, which are likely to be far greater than the anticipated gains. There will be no easy exit from a common currency arrangement once established, and it will only be at a very high cost (Worrell, 2003; Farrell and Worrell, 1994). Having been aware of the high risks involved in a currency union, the Heads of Governments of CARICOM did not want to take any chances and they prescribed the pre-union convergence criteria similar to those imposed by the Maastricht Treaty for adopting the common currency, the Euro.

Economic integration efforts in Europe began by promoting unhindered trade and were speeded up by labour and capital mobility. The CARICOM is just doing the same, by dismantling trade barriers and facilitating intra-region mobility of labour. The PICs at this stage should concentrate on these essentials, leaving the other ambitious goals aside for a while.

Notes

1. The Pacific Islands Forum comprises 14 Pacific island countries: Cook Islands, Fiji, Kiribati, Republic of Marshall Islands, Federated States of Micronesia, Nauru, Niue, Papua New Guinea, Samoa, Solomon Islands, Tonga, Tuvalu, Vanuatu and the region's two developed countries, namely Australia and New Zealand. Australia, which is the biggest aid giver to the PICs, bears nearly 80 per cent of the operating costs of the Forum as well. The current Secretary General is an Australian citizen, whose nomination in 2003 by Australia and subsequent election to the office was controversial, even though it was, in the end, by consensus, as it marked a departure from the past practice of having a citizen of one of the 14 PICs as the Secretary General.

2. There were several notable milestones. These include: the setting up of the European Coal and Steel Community in 1950, aimed at free trade in coal and steel by 1954; establishing the European Economic Community under the Treaty of Rome signed in 1957, the European Free Trade Association in 1960, and several regional institutions; and harmonising measures for facilitating movement of capital and labour under the Single European Act of 1987. The creation of a single market was achieved in 1992. Along with these measures, there were parallel efforts in monetary integration. These included introduction of the European Monetary System in 1979 to create an area of exchange rate stability among members by ushering in the Exchange Rate Mechanism and the European Currency Unit, paving the way for Monetary Union within the European Community. In 1989, the Delors Report recommended the introduction of a single currency by setting out the stages, including the establishment of the European Central Bank System. The stages included the signing of the Maastricht Treaty of 1991, which laid down the criteria for reaching convergence and enacting the Growth and Stability Pact of 1996. The latter levied a fine of 0.1 per cent of GDP on members in case of fiscal deficits in excess of the 3 per cent of GDP ceiling. These measures, which were introduced and implemented through political consensus, eventually prepared the members to become eligible for adopting the single currency. The Euro was ultimately born on 1 January, 1999.

3. These include: (i) Remoteness and insularity: being located far from major markets and comprising widely dispersed multi-island micro-states, resulting in high international and domestic transportation costs, arising from both the distances to be covered and the low volume of cargo. Further, the development of even a small domestic market is constrained by distances between settlements and infrequent internal transport services. (ii) Susceptibility to natural disasters: being frequently affected by adverse climatic and other natural events that typically affect the entire population and economy. (iii) Small population size: being limited by small population size affects institutional capacity and increases unit costs of services, and also restricts the potential for private sector growth and investment. (iv) Limited diversification: having a narrow resource base and small domestic markets necessarily results in being relatively undiversified in production and exports, and also limits capacity in the private sector. (iv) Openness: relying heavily upon external trade and foreign investment to overcome inherent scale and resource limitations, which leaves states vulnerable to external economic and environmental shocks (Urwin, 2004).

4. The members of CARICOM are: (i) Antigua and Barbuda; (ii) Anguila; (iii) Barbados; (iv) Belize; (v) Dominica; (vi) Grenada; (vii) Guyana; (viii) Haiti; (ix) Jamaica; (x) Montserrat; (xi) St.Kitts and Nevis; (xii) St. Lucia; (xiii) St. Vincent and Grenadines; (xiv) Suriname; and (xv) Trinidad and Tobago.

5. The convergence criteria for accession to the monetary union, which were laid down in the Decision of the Conference of the Heads of Governments of the Caribbean Community on Caribbean Monetary Integration, Port of Spain, Trinidad and Tobago, July 1992 are as follows: The prospective member must have (i) maintained an unchanged US dollar value of its currency for at least 36 consecutive months; (b) maintained a minimum of foreign exchange reserves equivalent to three months of imports, for at least 12 consecutive months; and (iii) recorded a ratio of external debt service ratio to exports of goods and services of no more than 15 per cent (Farrell and Worrell, 1994, pp.244-46).

6. Chand (2003) notes that while New Zealand and small PICs chose to remain silent, the Prime Minister of Fiji snubbed the idea of a regional currency.

7. This includes free movement for graduates, media workers, musicians, artists and sportspersons, in all member countries of CARICOM, except two, Antigua and Barbuda, and St. Kitts and Nevis Jamaica, Trinidad and Tobago, and Barbados further extended the free movement of architects and engineers. The full CSME is now expected to come on stream in 2008, with complete dismantling restrictions on labour movements within CARICOM (World Bank, 2005).

8. The Tuvalu High Commissioner observed in an interview with Jemima Garret on Radio Australia's Pacific Beat: 'If bigger PICs such as Fiji are keen on markets for goods under Pacific Plan, Tuvalu, which cannot export goods, would be looking for markets for labour'(Finiakaso, 2005). This opens the possibility of considering the intra-PIC labour movement, for skilled labour to start, as part of Pacific Plan.

9. The ongoing 'biscuit war' (Vanuatu banning the exports of Fiji's biscuits) is a glaring example of the difficulties involved in implementing a PFTA.

10. The Australian government accused the Solomon Islands of assuring one thing and doing something else. It happened at the best of times when relations between the Solomon Islands and Australia were cordial, as the RAMSI, largely funded by Australia, restored normalcy to the strife-torn country. It also strangely coincided with the Solomon Islands conferring the highest honour of the nation – the Star of Solomon Islands – on the prime ministers of Australia and New Zealand.

11. William Demas. A former Governor of the Central Bank of Trinidad and Tobago, who later became the first Secretary General of CARICOM observed that: 'A single independent currency entails a single set of economic, monetary, financial and fiscal policies designed to influence the balance of payments. Such a single set of policies is possible only with a high degree of economic union tantamount to political union' (Demas, 1974, p.54).

References

Asian Development Bank (ADB) (2003) *Key Indicators of Asian and Pacific Developing Countries 2003*. Asian Development Bank, Manila.

Australian Agency for International Development (AusAID) (2001) *Pacific: Program Profiles: 2000–01*. Australian Government Overseas Aid Program, Canberra.

Australian Senate Committee Report (2003) *A Pacific Engaged: Australia's Relations with Papua New Guinea and the Island States of the Southwest Pacific.* Commonwealth of Australia, Canberra.

Bowman, C. (2004) 'Pacific Island Countries and Dollarisation', *Pacific Economic Bulletin*, 19(3).

Bunyaratavej, K. and T.K. Jayaraman (2005) 'A Common Currency for the Pacific Region: A feasibility study', *Working Paper No.4*, Economics Department, University of the South Pacific, Suva.

CARICOM (2005) Caribbean Community and Common Market. www.caricom.org

Chand, S. (2003) 'An Assessment of the Proposal for a Pacific Economic and Political Community', *Pacific Economic Bulletin*, 18 (2), p.117-24.

Crocombe, R. and M. Meleisea (1988) 'Achievements Problems and Prospects: The Future of University Education in the South Pacific' in R. Crocombe amd M. Meleisea, (eds) *Pacific Universities, Achievements, Problems and Prospects.* Institute of Pacific Studies, Suva.

Crocombe R. and N. Ueantabo (1983) 'Options in University Education for the Pacific Islands', *Pacific Perspective*, 12(1), p.5-17.

Demas, W. (1974) *West Indian Nationhood and the Caribbean Integration.* CCC Publishing House, Barbados

DeMello, J. and A. Panagaria (1992) 'The New Regionalism', *Finance and Development*, December. p.37-40.

Duncan, R. (2005) 'A Common Currency for the Pacific Island Economies'. Paper presented at the International Workshop on Pacific Integration and Regional Governance, Asia Pacific School of Economics and Government, Australian National University, Canberra, June 2005.

Fairbairn. T and D. Worrell (1996) *South Pacific and Caribbean Island Economies: A Comparative Study.* The Foundation for Development Cooperation, Brisbane.

Farrell, T. and D. Worrell (1994) *Caribbean Monetary Integration.* Caribbean Information System and Services, Port of Spain.

Feizkhah, E. (2003) 'Hands Across Water', *Time*, 7 July.

Finikaso, T. (2005) 'Radio Interview to Pacific Beat', www.abc.net.au/ra/pacbeat/stories/s1398190.htm, accessed on May 12, 2005.

Fry, G. (2005) 'Pooled Regional Governance in the Island-Pacific: Lessons from History'. Paper presented at the International Workshop on Pacific Integration and Regional Governance, Asia Pacific School of Economics and Government, Australian National University, Canberra, June 2005.

Grynberg, R. (2005) 'PICTA, EPA, PACER and the Pacific Plan: Discussion Paper'. Forum Secretariat, Suva.

Hughes, H. (2003) *Aid has Failed in the Pacific*, Issue Analysis No.33. The Centre for Independent Studies, Sydney.

International Monetary Fund (IMF) (2003) *International Financial Statistics Yearbook 2003.* IMF, Washington, DC.

Jayaraman, T.K. (2001) 'Prospects for a Currency Union in the Pacific: A Preliminary Assessment', *The Journal of Pacific Studies*, 25(2), p.173-2001[201?]

Jayaraman, T.K. (2003) *Financial Sector Development and Private Investment in Vanuatu.* Macmillan Brown Centre for Pacific Studies, Christchurch.

Jayaraman, T.K. (2005a) 'Patterns of Shocks and Regional Currency for the Pacific Islands', *Journal of Economic Integration*, 21 (1). Center for International Relations, Seoul, Korea.

Jayaraman, T.K. (2005b) 'Dollarisation of Pacific Island Countries: A Feasibility Study', *Perspectives in Global Development and Technology*, 4 (2). University of Toledo, Toledo, Ohio.

T.K. Jayaraman (2006) 'Patterns of Shocks and Regional Currency for the Pacific Islands', *Journal of Economic Integration* 21(1), pp.99–119.

Jayaraman, T.K, B. Ward and X. Zu (2005) 'Are the Pacific Islands Ready for A Currency Union? An Empirical Study of Degree of Economic Convergence', *Working Paper No.4*. Economics Department, University of the South Pacific, Suva.

Kelsey, J. (2004) *Big Brothers Behaving Badly: The Implications for the Pacific Islands of the Pacific Agreement on Closer Economic Relations*. PANG, Suva.

Kelsey, J. (2005) *A People's Guide to the Pacific Economic Partnership Agreement*. World Council of Churches, Suva.

Narsey, W. (2004) 'PICTA, PACER, and EPAs: Where are we going? Tales of Fags, Booze, and Rugby', *Working Paper No:6*. Economics Department, University of the South Pacific, Suva.

Pacific Islands Forum Secretariat (2005) *Working Draft: The Pacific Plan for Strengthening Regional Cooperation and Integration*. Forum Secretariat, Suva.

Rosales, J.R. (2001) Macroeconomic Policy and Financial Sector Stability in Pacific Island Countries. Paper presented at the Conference on Financial Sector Stability and Development, Apia, 2–21 February.

Scollay, R. (1998) 'Free Trade Options for the Forum Island Countries'. Report prepared for the South Pacific Forum Secretariat, Suva: Forum Secretariat.

Scollay, R. (2005) 'Deeper Integration with Australia and New Zealand? Potential Gains for Pacific Islands'. Paper presented at the International Workshop on Pacific Integration and Regional Governance, Asia Pacific School of Economics and Government, Australian National University, Canberra, June 2005.

United Nations Economic and Social Commission for Asia and the Pacific (UNESCAP) (2004) *Economic and Social Survey 2004*. UNESCAP, Bangkok.

Urwin, G. (2004) *Economic Development of Pacific Island Economies and Regional Cooperation*. Public Speech at the University of the South Pacific, May 18, 2004. www.forumsec.org.fj

World Bank. (2005) *A Time to Choose: Caribbean Development in the 21st Century*. World Bank, Washington, DC.

Worrell, D. (2003) 'A Currency Union for the Caribbean', *IMF Working Paper WP/03/35*. IMF, Washington, DC.

9. Development of a Regional Strategic Plan for Fisheries Management and Sustainable Coastal Fisheries in Pacific Island Countries

Michael King, Ueta Fa'asili, Semisi Fakahau, and Aliti Vunisea

During the period April 2002 to August 2003 the Commonwealth Secretariat collaborated with the Secretariat of the Pacific Community (SPC), the lead regional organisation on coastal fisheries management and development in the South Pacific, to work with fisheries agencies and other stakeholders to develop a Strategic Plan for the sustainable management and development of coastal fisheries in Pacific island countries (PICs).

The methodology included obtaining pre-meeting information on key problems in coastal fisheries management through questionnaires. The results were presented and discussed at the SPC Regional Policy Meeting on Coastal Fisheries Management held in Nadi, Fiji, from 17 to 21 March, 2003. The purpose of the Nadi meeting was to provide a forum for country representatives to address common problems in coastal fisheries and suggest how the SPC Coastal Fisheries Programme and other agencies could assist countries to take remedial actions. Of the 22 SPC member countries and territories, 17 were represented at the meeting. Participants and resource people shared experiences and used problem–solution tree techniques to suggest actions that could solve the problems identified.

A subsequent field study in selected PICs was conducted during May and June 2003 to assist fisheries agencies to review their needs and their capacity to address the problems in fisheries management identified at the Nadi meeting. The field study was restricted to thirteen countries and other member countries were contacted by fax or email and invited to supply similar information.

During the field study, advisers were mindful to make the distinction between needs and wants; care was taken to relate stated needs to those activities required to address the most pressing problems in managing fisheries resources and protecting marine habitats.

In June 2003, the advisers used the outcomes of the Nadi meeting and the field study to compile the first draft Strategic Plan and submit it to the SPC management. The management then tabled it at the SPC Heads of Fisheries (HOF) Meeting held at its headquarter in Noumea, New Caledonia on 18–22 August, 2003. The HOF endorsed the Strategic Plan and it became the key fisheries management component of the SPC Coastal Fisheries Programme Strategic Plan 2003–05. This represents a significant step forward in the management and development of fisheries in the South Pacific region, as the Strategic Plan becomes the very first formal regional expression of there being a mechanism to promote the greater harmonisation of national policy regarding the management of coastal fisheries in PICs.

Like most developing fisheries situations in the Commonwealth, PICs coastal fisheries are managed and developed for two main purposes: export and domestic consumption.

PICs export a small number of products aimed to very specific markets. They include: sea-cucumber (beche-de-mer); trochus shell; mother-of-pearl shells; black pearl; red

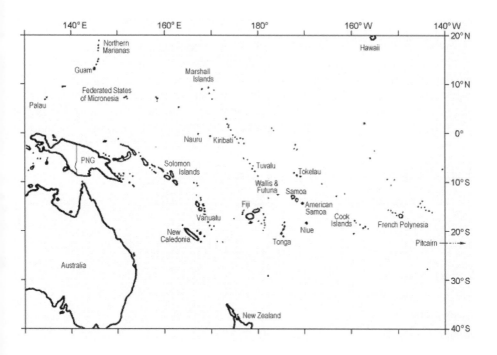

Figure 9.1. The Pacific island region showing the 22 member countries of SPC. Australia, New Zealand and Hawaii are included for geographic reference.

snapper (deep-slope eteline snapper); giant clam; and live aquarium fish and fish for caged fish farming. There is no accurate information available on the volumes being extracted, but Table 9.1 provides an estimate of current exports of major coastal products from PICs.

Fishers' catches are sold to middlemen or exporters either processed or fresh, depending on the type of product. For example, sea-cucumber (beche-de-mer) is sold and exported in dried form, deep-slope red snapper is exported chilled, and aquarium fish are exported live. Shells of mother-of-pearl collected from the wild and cultivated wild stocks (*Trochus niloticus, Pinctada margaritifera, Turbo marmoratus*, in decreasing order of volume) are exported for natural shirt buttons and traditional furniture inlays. Only a few PICs have so far been successful in producing black pearl on a commercial basis for export. Again, only a few PICs catch and chill red snapper and other species prior to export. The supply of live fish for aquarium and caged fish farming is becoming important to an increasing number of PICs.

Increasingly, PICs are concerned about the sustainability of these fisheries. Some organisms (such as trochus, smaller aquarium fish, and shallow-water holothurian species) are resilient enough to adapt to the seasonal fishing practices. However, other species (such as grouper, giant clam, green snail and pearl oyster) are often fished far beyond their capability for short-term recovery. PICs also acknowledge that reef fishery resources are vulnerable to overfishing and cannot be sustainable if subjected to uncontrolled foreign investment and pressure from the cash economy.

In most, if not all, PICs, the total weight of seafood caught in subsistence, or village, fisheries is greater than that from commercial fisheries. And when a nominal value per kilogram is put on the subsistence catch, it is found to be of greater value than commercial catches. This is particularly so if one considers the net profits from commercial fisheries, many of which rely on imported boats, equipment, and even bait. Subsistence fisheries on the other hand, are labour-intensive but generally low in other

Table 9.1. Current annual exports of major coastal fisheries products from Pacific island countries (data from SPC)

Commodity	Amount
Sea-cucumber	1,500 tonnes (dried, equivalent to 15,000 tonnes live weight)
Trochus shell	2,000 tonnes of shell
Mother-of-pearl shell	400 tonnes (mainly spent farmed shell)
Black pearls	US$100 million value
Eteline snapper (mainly Tonga)	300 tonnes
Giant clam (mainly Fiji)	20 tonnes of adductor muscle
Live serranids (i.e. live fish for aquariums and caged fish farming)	Unknown

fishing costs. In addition, the catches from coastal areas result in health benefits and cost savings beyond their intrinsic value.

Traditionally, seafood has been the most important source of protein in PICs, and this is particularly so in low-lying islands and coral atolls where soils are too poor to support agriculture. In some atolls the per capita seafood consumption is as high as 180kg, compared with the world average of about 12 kg per/capita (see Table 9.2). Even in high islands where agriculture is well developed, seafood consumption often approaches 50kg per person per year.

It is estimated that about 80 per cent of the coastal fishery production of around 100,000 tonnes annually (excluding the export commodity production described above) do not enter the cash economy.

Because of the small size of the islands, almost all Pacific islanders live within the coastal zone. In rural areas, virtually every person fishes and women do most of the shoreline fishing and reef-gleaning. A great variety of marine organisms are consumed. In Fiji, for example, over 100 species of finfish and 50 species of invertebrates are consumed locally. Although there is an increasing concern about the apparent overfishing of certain fish and shellfish stocks around national capitals, the marine food base of most PICs appears to be currently secure. Nearly all PICs have the sustainable resource capacity to feed their populations, even at the present high rates of consumption. The domestic coastal fisheries production in Table 9.3 is estimated from data from a wide range of sources with a wide range of reliability.

However, in many PICs densely populated towns' catches of the most accessible seafood – the fish, seaweed and shellfish of the lagoons and reefs – have been declining in

Table 9.2. Per capita fish consumption (1990s), present population (2003) and the total fish requirement at 1990s consumption levels

Country	Per/capita intake (1990s)	Population (2003)	Fish requirement* (Mt)
Cook Islands	68	18,400	1,250
Kiribati	182	90,000	16,380
Marshall Islands	61	63,000	3,843
Nauru	50	11,200	560
Niue	62	2,500	155
Palau	108	18,500	1,998
Tonga	35	100,000	3,500
Vanuatu	27	170,000	4590
Samoa	32	170,000	5,440

Source: Gillet et al (2001)
*Total fish requirement based on the level of per capita consumption in the 90s.

Table 9.3. Domestic coastal fisheries production (data from SPC)

Country or territory	Production		
	Commercial	Subsistence	Total
American Samoa	52	215	267
Cook Islands	124	858	982
Federated States of Micronesia	637	6,243	6,880
Fiji	6,653	16,600	23,253
French Polynesia	2,352	3,691	6,043
Guam	118	472	591
Hawaii	10,206	2,000	12,206
Kiribati	3,240	9,084	12,324
Marshall Islands	369	2,000	2,369
Nauru	279	98	376
New Caledonia	981	2,500	3,481
Niue	12	103	115
Northern Marianas	141	2,825	2,966
Palau	736	750	1,486
Papua New Guinea	4,966	20,588	25,554
Pitcairn	0	8	8
Solomon Islands	1,150	10,000	11,150
Tokelau	0	191	191
Tonga	1,429	933	2,362
Tuvalu	120	807	927
Vanuatu	467	2,045	2,512
Wallis & Futuna	296	621	917
Western Samoa	208	3,281	3,489
Total	34,534	85,914	120,448

some island countries over many years. Reductions in the availability of seafood from inshore areas and changes of lifestyle have created a greater reliance on unhealthy diets (consisting mainly of imported low-quality protein food) that are contributing to the high incidence of heart disease, diabetes and other diet-related diseases in PICs. Growth in population sizes (approaching 4 per cent per year in some islands) is continuing to place pressure on coastal ecosystems and their resources. And as demand for seafood species increase, the ability of the marine environment to sustain them is likely to decrease. The coast is in increasing demand for housing and development. And the sea that supports coastal ecosystems is being polluted by silt and by chemicals and waste from towns, forestry, agriculture, and industry.

Concern over such problems by member countries and territories at the second SPC Head of Fisheries meeting in July 2001 prompted a recommendation for a broadly based regional consultation on fisheries management. In response, SPC and the Commonwealth Secretariat undertook to arrange for a participatory examination of issues and concerns in relation to coastal fisheries management in PICs.

Lifestyle changes and the requirements of a growing cash economy in PICs will continue to result in further shifts from subsistence to commercial fishing. Fisheries managers in PICs have to address the implications of this, not only in terms of development and income generation, but in terms of sustainability and food security. This Strategic Plan will help develop the capacity of island governments, and the region as a whole, to achieve both the Millennium Development Goals (MDGs) on poverty reduction and the outcomes of the 2002 Johannesburg World Summit on Sustainable Development (WSSD, 2002). The relevant ones are:

- Implement strategies for sustainable development by 2005

- Reverse the loss of environmental resources by 2015

- Maintain or restore fisheries stocks on an urgent basis and where possible by 2015

The impact of globalisation on socio-economic development and the sustainable use of fisheries resources in the region emphasises the use of international instruments under both the United Nations Convention on the Law of the Sea (UNCLOS, 1982) and the United Nations Conference on Environment and Development (UNCED, 1992). In particular, Chapter 17, Agenda 21 of UNCED provides a basis for national policies and strategies on the sustainable development and management of coastal fisheries.

The outcomes of the policy meeting and field study identified the following key fisheries management problems and possible solutions:

1. The reduction in catches of inshore marine species was of most concern. Catches of the most accessible seafood – the fish, seaweed and shellfish of the lagoons and reefs – have been declining in some island countries for many years. In Guam, for example, catch rates have decreased by 70 per cent during the past 15 years.

2. The main reasons for the decline in inshore catches include overexploitation; a shift from subsistence to commercial fishing; the use of overly efficient and destructive fishing methods; and environmental degradation. Growth in human populations (approaching 4 per cent per year in some islands) is placing increasing pressures on coastal ecosystems and their resources. In response to the declining stocks of inshore species, fisheries agencies need to change their focus from development to conservation in order to allow fish stocks to recover. Whereas in the past the emphasis has been on making exploitation more efficient (e.g. by encouraging the use of modern boats and fishing gear), at present the emphasis is on reducing fishing mortality (e.g. by controlling fishing effort and by restricting the use of certain fishing gear).

3. There is a need to control the use of overly efficient gear – gill nets in lagoons, underwater torches to spear fish sheltering on reefs at night, and scuba gear to spear fish and lobsters are all examples of bad practice. The use of destructive fishing methods, including the use of explosives and poisons, needs to be eradicated.

4. Local fisheries agencies need sufficient resources and expertise to assess and manage coastal fisheries.

5. Fisheries agencies' staff need training as well as attachments to regional organisations and to the national programmes of other countries in order to enhance their expertise. In particular, skills are required to assess the status of fish stocks and to collect catch and effort data from subsistence fisheries. There is a widespread need for a simple method (using household surveys) of collecting fisheries data, including sociological information, from fishing communities.

6. PICs' fisheries regulations are in need of review in order to improve their effectiveness in terms of restricting both fishing (input controls) and the catch (output controls), and protecting the marine environment.

7. The involvement of stakeholders is increasingly regarded as essential. Some fisheries agencies are promoting community-based fisheries management (CBFM), often with SPC assistance, and many others have expressed interest in receiving help to do so. Gender issues in this respect are regarded as particularly important and efforts are being made to involve women and untitled men in management decisions ('untitled' meaning mean without chief status in societies where all decisions are made by chiefs).

8. Currently, public support for the aims of fisheries management and the necessity of fisheries regulations is weak. The situation is serious and calls for training and other assistance in the production of publicity material, including the preparation of media releases and information sheets to increase public awareness.

9. The degradation of fish habitats including coral reefs, lagoons and wetlands and the decline of inshore fish stocks requires a broader ecosystem approach to fisheries (EAF) to replace the narrower target-species approach to fisheries management. In some PICs, the problems of achieving EAF are exacerbated by the lack of coordination between the two separate government authorities responsible for fisheries and the marine environment. PICs should be encouraged to establish marine protected areas (MPAs) to provide refuges in which invertebrate and fish stocks can grow and reproduce without interference. Although the number of MPAs, both nationally and community-owned, is growing, throughout the region some countries are encountering problems in establishing workable MPAs. Both attachments to countries with successful MPAs and training is required.

The Strategic Plan consists of six main goals and strategies that represent its main objectives and encapsulate both the recommendations from the Nadi meeting and from the needs expressed by fisheries agencies during the subsequent field visits, and the overall objectives.

Goal 1: To enhance the capacity of fisheries agency staff to manage sustainable fisheries.

Proposed strategies to achieve the above goal are:

1.1 Provision of in-country assistance to review or develop an organisational structure and an HRD plan for requesting fisheries agencies. The assistance could vary from three to six weeks in-country depending on requirements. At the top end of requirements, assistance would include working with fisheries staff and stakeholders to develop a mission statement, goals, activities, outputs and an annual work plan for the agency. A review of staff and training needs should be included. At the low end of requirements, assistance would involve a participatory review of the existing organisational structure and functions.

1.2 Provision of support for attachments of individuals from fisheries agencies to relevant SPC programmes and to successful national programmes of other countries for the purposes of training and capacity building. Individuals will be attached to an experienced mentor and required to translate reports, working documents and publicity material into his or her national language.

1.3 Provision of short courses in the preparation of fisheries management plans. Each two to three-week course could be run either at SPC or another central location. The course would take into account the need for a broader ecosystem approach to fisheries (EAF) to replace the narrower target-species approach to fisheries management. The course could also address alternative and innovative ways of applying fisheries controls (see discussion in Section 3.3 and Strategy 3c).

1.4 Provision of short courses on *practical* fisheries management issues for staff of fisheries agencies in Pacific island countries. Each course would be suitable for new recruits to fisheries agencies and as refresher training for more experienced staff. Each course, of perhaps two to three weeks, could be run either at SPC or another central location for up to 12 participants per course.

1.5 Provision of short courses on the preparation of proposals for funding, designing projects, report writing, and the preparation of papers for publication. Each two-week course could be run either at SPC or another central location for up to 15 participants per course. Follow-up activities (written assignments, etc.) could be conducted by email via a trainer/tutor based at SPC.

Other strategies relating to capacity-building are included under other goals.

Goal 2: To assist fisheries agency staff in their efforts to collect, store, retrieve and analyse basic fisheries data and/or indicators to monitor the status of fish stocks.

Proposed strategies to achieve the above goal are:

2.1 Provision of a manual, database and training for the collection and storage of fisheries data from subsistence fisheries. The assistance would include the preparation and provision of a step-by-step manual and a simple database on compact disc. Workshops based on using the manual and the database could be conducted at a central location for staff of fisheries agencies. An in-country visit by an adviser would be necessary for an initial trial run in each requesting country.

2.2 Provision of short courses on the use of basic fisheries data in assessing the status of fish stocks. Several fisheries agencies are presently collecting catch and effort data and require training in their use. Others plan to collect data from subsistence fisheries (see 2a) and require similar training. Two-week workshops (using sample data) could be conducted at a central location for relevant staff of fisheries agencies.

Goal 3: To assist countries to review, update and/or develop practical and enforceable fisheries regulations.

Proposed strategies to achieve the above goal are:

3.1 Provision of legal expertise to assist island countries in drafting or reviewing legislation related to coastal fisheries. The assistance could be related to both national fisheries regulations and community by-laws. An in-country visit by a legal adviser and a fisheries management adviser is required; the latter to advise on the practicality and enforceability of proposed laws.

3.2 Provision of recommendations on size limits for important species on a regional basis to assist countries in the preparation of fisheries regulations. This assistance could be in the form of a booklet containing recommended size limits from studies in the Pacific and elsewhere. Ideally, differences in growth and in attaining reproductive age in different latitudes and environments would have to be considered.

3.3 Provision of a workshop on the application and enforcement of fisheries regulations.

The one-week course could be run at a central location and address alternative and innovative ways of applying fisheries controls. As an alternative, this workshop could be attached to other workshops – e.g. on the preparation of management plans.

Goal 4: To assist countries to involve fishers and other stakeholders in fisheries management and to assist with the development of property-use rights.

Proposed strategies to achieve the above goal are:

4.1 Provision of training and continuing assistance to enable fisheries agencies to establish community-based fisheries management (CBFM). Training in community motivation techniques and facilitation may be conducted in a central location for nominated participants from several countries. Both women and men will participate, as gender-sensitive approaches will be used when working in communities.

Each requesting country will require several visits of an adviser. An initial visit is needed to assess existing laws, policies, and the agency, as well as to design a culturally acceptable process for a national CBFM programme. A second visit is required to conduct a 'train the trainer' exercise for fisheries agency staff. A third visit (and subsequent visits) will be needed to review progress and help solve any problems that are encountered.

4.2 Provision of assistance in developing community by-laws to be used as tools for fisheries management. An in-country assignment of one to two weeks in each requesting country would be required to review existing laws and to recommend requirements.

4.3 Provision of assistance with the formation of fisheries management advisory committees (F-MACs) and to promote the involvement of other stakeholder groups in the management of specific inshore fisheries (e.g. on deepwater bottom-fish or sea-cucumbers). At least one in-country assignment for an adviser is required to recommend the composition of the committee(s) and to assist in devising terms of reference.

Goal 5: To assist countries in raising public awareness of the need for conservation, fisheries management and fisheries regulations.

Proposed strategies to achieve the above goal are:

5.1 Provision of training in preparing non-technical publicity material to raise public awareness of the need for conservation, food security, fisheries management and fisheries regulations. A gender-sensitive approach will be emphasised in training, which would include the preparation of media releases (press and radio), information sheets, and fisheries newsletters. A two or three-week course (or courses) could be conducted at SPC with participation preferences given to information officers from agencies responsible for fisheries and the marine environment.

5.2 Provision of non-technical publicity material to raise public awareness of the need for conservation, food security, fisheries management and fisheries regulations. This material, including information sheets and posters, could be prepared in draft form at SPC in English and/or French. This material would be printed in the relevant country languages after translation by local counterparts.

5.3 Provision of assistance in conducting socio-economic assessments of subsistence fisheries in requesting countries. Such assessments are believed necessary in order to raise government awareness of the direct and indirect value of subsistence fisheries and the work done by fisheries managers in this regard. Assessments should include estimates of catch value (based on market prices), import substitution value (in reducing the need to import low-quality protein), and health-care value (in reducing the long-term health costs of treating diet-related diseases such as diabetes and heart disease).

Goal 6: To assist countries to site, survey and monitor marine protected areas and to assist with an ecosystems approach to fisheries management

Proposed strategies to achieve the above goal are:

6.1 Provision of assistance to countries by providing training in methods used to assess the suitability of sites for MPAs and to monitor MPAs. Requirements vary from country to country, but assistance could be provided to requesting countries.

6.2 Provision of assistance to conduct socio-economic surveys to determine the benefits of MPAs in requesting countries. This assistance would require in-country work in requesting countries.

6.3 Provision of assistance to countries pursuing an ecosystems approach to fisheries (EAF). Initially, this could involve a workshop for two counterparts (one from a fisheries agency and the other from an environmental agency) from each requesting country. The workshop, perhaps a week long, could be held at SPC or in another central location. The workshop would involve discussing ways in which environmental issues threatening inshore fisheries could be addressed in a cooperative manner.

6.4 Provision of training in environmental impact assessment (EIA) techniques. Some fisheries agencies are now being required to conduct EIAs involving the marine environment. Depending on final demand, a workshop, perhap a week long, could be designed and conducted at SPC or in another central location.

The Strategic plan contains high-priority fisheries management activities under strategies related to the six goals. It is estimated that a total of US$891,000 (£536,747) is required to fund these activities. Although it is impossible for SPC to directly address all of the identified needs, those that can will be incorporated in the work plan of the Coastal Fisheries Management Section. In others, SPC will undertake to identify available sources of assistance and seek donor funds. On many issues, SPC will play the role of an advocate or facilitator in the provision of assistance and capacity building. The Commonwealth Secretariat will continue to support the work of the SPC and its member countries in order to achieve the goals set out in the Strategic Plan.

References

Gillet, R., McCoy, M., Rodwell, L., and Tamate, J. (2001) *Tuna: A Key Economic Resource in the Pacific.* ADB, Manila.

UNCED (1992) Report of the United Nations Conference on Environment and Development, Rio de Janeiro, 3–14 June, 1992.

UNCLOS (1982) United Nations Convention on the Law of the Sea, signed at Montego Bay, Jamaica, 10 December 1982.

WSSD (2002) The United Nations World Summit on Sustainable Development, August 26 to September 4, 2002, Johannesburg, South Africa.

Part 5
GOVERNANCE

10. Democracy and Good Governance in Small States

Paul Sutton

The Commonwealth has taken a leading role among international organisations in the promotion of good governance and democracy in small states. The principles guiding these actions were formulated at successive Commonwealth Heads of Government Meetings (CHOGMs), beginning with the Declaration of Commonwealth Principles in 1971, the Harare Declaration in 1991 (which defined democracy and fundamental human rights as core values), and the Millbrook Declaration in 1995, which established a mechanism, the Commonwealth Ministerial Action Group on the Harare Declaration, to recommend action in the case of 'serious or persistent violations of the principles'. The 2003 CHOGM in Nigeria reaffirmed the commitment to democracy and development made in the Aso Rock Declaration which declared, among other things, the objectives of promoting 'a participatory democracy characterised by free and fair elections', 'an independent judiciary', 'machinery to protect human rights', and the 'active participation of civil society, including women and youth'.

The Commonwealth has also been at the forefront in promoting the cause of small states. Thirty-two of its 53 members are classified as small states[1] and in 1993 it established a special mechanism, the Commonwealth Ministerial Group on Small States (CMGSS), which meets immediately prior to CHOGMs, to discuss the special needs of small states and set out guidelines for future action in their interest. The various reports of CMGSS to CHOGM have highlighted economic, environmental and security issues as major concerns and identified capacity building and institution building to be of particular importance. They have also commended the work of the Commonwealth Secretariat in promoting fundamental political values in small states; in providing technical assistance and observer missions for national elections; and more specifically in helping to resolve difficult situations through the good offices role of the Secretary General. In recent years this has involved actions in Lesotho, Solomon Islands, Antigua and Barbuda, Fiji, Papua New Guinea, Guyana, The Gambia, Swaziland and Tonga.

It has also meant a wider commitment to supporting and deepening democracy throughout the Commonwealth. In May 2000 a workshop on 'Democracy and Small States' was held in Malta, jointly organised by the Commonwealth Secretariat and the Commonwealth Parliamentary Association. Government ministers, parliamentarians, public servants and representatives from civil society in 28 small states examined key aspects of the democratic process, including the role of the executive and the legislature, accountability and transparency, elections and electoral processes, the role of civil society, and sovereignty and democracy. On many of these issues different views were expressed but there was also general agreement that democracy was essential to the future of small states as a means of offsetting their inherent vulnerabilities and ensuring their well being (Commonwealth Secretariat, 2000a). In support of small states the Commonwealth Parliamentary Association has since 1981 run a small countries conference for its smallest members (including non-independent territories) in conjunction with the main annual parliamentary conference.

This chapter examines democracy and good governance in small states under three main headings. In the first part describes some general characteristics of politics in small states, providing the background to processes which support and challenge democracy. In the second part the record of democracy in small states is examined, in particular those features that help to sustain as well as challenge democracy. The third part considers some aspects of good governance of particular relevance to small states. It is followed by a brief conclusion.

Some characteristic features of political systems in small states

While the different historical, regional and cultural contexts of small states ensure that there is distinctiveness among them, there are some political features that many small developing Commonwealth states share. In respect of domestic politics these have been identified in one study as institutional fidelity, governmental pervasiveness, exaggerated personalism, concerted social harmony, and pragmatic conservatism (Sutton, 1987, pp.8–19).

Institutional fidelity

Most small countries have emerged into statehood through the tried and tested procedures of tutelary devolution of responsibility and the adoption or adaptation of the Westminster–Whitehall system of government and administration. The parliamentary system is the preferred method of government and this draws on the experience of the UK in particular. A two-chamber legislature is common, although among the smaller countries there is a preference for single-chamber legislatures, either wholly elected or combining an elected and nominated element. Most countries have political parties which regularly compete for office in multiparty systems, although again among the smallest territories many candidates for office are independents and durable political parties have only recently begun to emerge. Central government tends to be modelled on the Whitehall pattern of single ministries and a specialised public service. There have been significant and growing departures from this practice in recent years, but these are more often than not the result of incremental change rather than fundamental restructuring, ensuring that much continuity in procedures and practices remain.

Governmental pervasiveness

Government is said to dominate in small states. It is often the largest employer of labour and is frequently the most important agency for identifying political issues and seeking their resolution. As Nobel laureate Sir Arthur Lewis, himself a St Lucian, has noted, 'in a small island... everyone depends on the government for something, however small, so most are reluctant to offend it' (Lewis, 1965, p.16). Government patronage is therefore an important and ubiquitous part of the political system. Government is also said to be subject to fewer constraints from countervailing sectors, pressure groups, and non-governmental organisations, although this is in part a contestable proposition, particularly since the number of these have grown in recent years. Nevertheless, the autonomy of government from civil society (e.g. churches, professional associations, trade unions, chambers of commerce, etc.) is a crucial issue and is an important feature in securing liberal democracy. More generally, governmental pervasiveness in small states, where anonymity is not possible and pressures toward partisanship are considerable, means that special attention must be paid to mechanisms ensuring impartiality of administration and justice. These include various constitutional provisions for human rights and fundamental freedoms as well as administrative features such as public service commissions and the offices of ombudsmen.

Exaggerated personalism

The importance of personality in politics is the most commonly cited attribute of small states. Early studies identified these as the role of the individual takes on greater significance; the individual, as a member of a group, is more susceptible to pressures, both internal and external; politicians exercise greater influence over administrators, frequently based more on personal than on party factors; senior administrative and political office holders have more direct contact with the man in the street, and accordingly there is less of the aloofness traditionally associated with a bureaucracy; top political leaders are more likely to communicate directly with one another and directly to oversee the actions of their lieutenants; there is less functional specialisation among politicians and both they and senior administrators are likely to accumulate roles; politics may be less than a full-time job, constituting either a means to promote other interests or an avenue of mobility into other areas in a situation of limited economic opportunities; and criticism of political leaders and senior administrators may be muted, often informal, but where it does appear is likely to be personal in form and strident in tone (UNITAR, 1971, pp.52-3; Dahl and Tufte, 1973, pp.87-8).

These features can have positive and negative effects. Among the former it is likely that leaders, being personally accessible, are more likely to be in direct touch with affairs; more directly accountable for their actions; and their suitability for office better known by citizens. Among the latter the record shows that small states can be dominated by one or several individuals and that they can be difficult to remove from office, particularly when they have assembled powerful patronage machines and/or have concentrated the coercive power of the state in their hands. The question of 'who guards the guardians?' is as relevant for small states as it is for large ones, although small states have the option, not always open to large states, of maintaining only small paramilitary forces or dispensing with them entirely.

Concerted social harmony

Small states have a lower incidence of serious civil disorder than larger ones. Several reasons are given for this fact, the most important of which is the observation that small states are more homogeneous than larger countries. There is less alienation, higher degrees of system legitimacy, and a basic consensus of values. Recent research has shown this is both wrong and right. It is wrong to attribute to small states any greater degree of homogeneity than larger states if the measurements used are ethnic and religious diversity. After all, some small states are plural societies with very high levels of diversity. At the same time if attitudinal diversity is measured (i.e. the extent to which there is a strong sense of local community which binds members together in mutual solidarity) then very small states do show less diversity than large states (Anckar, 1999). These findings point to the need to be aware of the specific circumstances of each small state. In highly diverse plural societies, for example, there is a risk that conflicts among groups will be politicised and spill over to polarise the whole community. The breakdown of the political system in such a situation is an ever-present danger. Fortunately, the comparative rarity of such events underlines the general rule that small states manage to limit unduly divisive conflict. Among the more important contributing factors are elite consensus and institutional adaptiveness, which, when coupled with parliamentary systems and proportional representation, encourage the emergence of multiparty coalition government and political inclusiveness (Lijphart, 1991, pp.146-58). To this can be added those features of size which give greater opportunity for citizens of small democracies to participate effectively in making decisions and to perceive a relation between their own self-interest, the interests of others, and the public or national interest.

Pragmatic conservatism

Small states tend to cluster on the centre-right of the political spectrum. They do so for reasons Lowenthal (1987) has identified as 'managed intimacy' and 'conservatism and tradition'. The former is similar to the feature of 'concerted social harmony' and relates to the fact that small state inhabitants 'learn to get along, like it or not, with folk they know in myriad contexts over their whole lives...they minimize or mitigate conflict. They become expert at muting hostility, deferring their own views, containing disagreement, avoiding dispute, in the interest of stability and compromise' (ibid, p.39). It follows that dissenting opinion and radical views are generally muted and that criticism and innovation are limited and often suggested by 'outsiders'. This is reinforced by the fact that 'those who live in small states cling tenaciously to familiar patterns of life. Their settled conservatism stems from a caution born of long experience with resources whose exploitation is severely limited by scale, by isolation, and by physical and economic hazards beyond their control. These constraints incline residents toward the maintenance of continuity, the practice of conservation, and the hedging of bets by taking on multiple occupations' (ibid, p.35). While this observation applies most to the smallest and/or least-developed small states, it highlights why many small states value stability and tradition. The persistence of local monarchy and/or a special role for chiefs within their political systems is one expression of this fact, as is the limited part women play in political life as traditionally conceived. It also acts as a restraint on development which is, by necessity, 'destabilising' and therefore to be introduced, at best, incrementally.

None of these five characteristics are exclusive to small states and can be found in larger states. They are, however, more pronounced in small states, and constitute a syndrome of interrelated characteristics which help shape political life. They also qualify the practice of democracy and good governance in small states, pointing to possibilities and constraints which are not found in quite the same proportion in larger states.

Democracy

Democracy is an elusive concept. There are many types of democracy (e.g. direct democracy, guided democracy, liberal democracy, social democracy) and no agreed definition. However, what has emerged in the last ten years has been a convergence toward and a relative privileging of 'liberal democracy' as the most desirable form of democracy. This can be defined as 'a type of political regime in which binding rules and policy decisions are made not by the entire community but by representatives accountable to the community. This accountability is secured primarily through free, fair and competitive elections in which virtually all adult men and women have the right to vote and stand for elective office. Citizens within a liberal democracy have the right: 'to express themselves without the danger of severe punishment on political matters broadly defined, including criticism of officials, the government, the regime, the socio-economic order, the prevailing ideology' and 'to form relatively independent associations of organisations including independent political parties and interest groups' (Potter et al, 1997, p.4; Dahl, 1989, p.221).

Defined in this way many small states can be considered liberal democracies. The most recent annual survey (2004) by Freedom House confirms the relative high degree of freedom that continues to be enjoyed by most small developing states. In a sample of 48 small developing states (32 Commonwealth and 16 non-Commonwealth, all with a population of 1.5 million or below), 28 states were classified as free (21 Commonwealth); 14 as partially free (eight Commonwealth); and six as not free (three Commonwealth).[2] The strong position of the Commonwealth small states is also confirmed over time. Taking the individual rankings of states into account (and ignoring a minor change in either direction), 22 Commonwealth states have a better ranking now than at independence or in 1972/73 when the first rankings were made, and 10 have a worse record (Freedom House, 2004). Such figures compare very favourably with larger states and suggest a relationship between size and democracy that is favourable to small states.

The presumption of such a relationship can be traced back to the Ancient Greeks. Aristotle thought that a small polis encouraged participation and discouraged tyranny. In the Enlightenment, Rousseau and Montesquieu argued that democracy and civic virtue were most likely to be sustained in small or medium-sized states. In the early 1970s Dahl and Tufte (1973) explored the relationship between size and democracy at length and while they found no specific relationship they provided numerous theoretical speculations as to why small states (which they defined rather generously to include medium-sized states) may be more supportive of democracy in certain circumstances. Although arguments linking small size with democracy often appeared plausible, it is only very recently that the relationship between size and democracy has been explored empirically for small developing states with some interesting (and disputed) findings indicating that small size is indeed conducive to democracy.

One of the most widely quoted studies is that by Hadenius (1992). In a review of 132 developing countries he found that small island states (population up to one million) were much more likely to be democratic than other countries. In his top ranking (those scoring 9 or more points) 17 out of 28 were small island countries, the majority being Commonwealth small states. These findings were corroborated and extended by Ott (2000). In a study of 237 nations in the period 1973–95 she found that using measures for political freedom, political rights and civil liberties 'small states (population under 1.5 million) are more likely to be democratic than large states **at any single point in time**' (ibid, p.117, author's emphasis) across all income levels (i.e. irrespective of levels of economic development). Other findings were 'that small states are more likely to remain democratic over time than large states' (ibid, 122); that 'very small states are consistently less likely to be authoritarian than large states' (ibid, 124); and that 'being an island country has a consistent and positive impact on the likelihood of political democracy' at all levels of income (ibid, 128). A similar finding on islands is reported in a study on the political regimes of 146 countries from 1960–94[3] by Clague, Gleason and Knack (2001), when they show 'that islands are more democratic and less autocratic than the average less developed country' (p.25) and 'islands are more democratic than non-islands' (p.31). More contentiously, they also argue 'that small size itself is not conducive to democracy, while being an island is' (p.31).

However, the most consistently rigorous empirical research programme on democracy in small states (population under 1 million) has been undertaken by the Anckars over the last twelve years. In it they have demonstrated that 'country size is an important determinant of the degree of democracy, party fragmentation and choice of electoral system' (Anckar, 2004a, p.379). Dag Anckar has also examined the British connection. Several features stand out. First, in a sample of 36 states (excluding Tonga but including 25 countries that were former colonies of the United Kingdom or with strong British connections) he unsurprisingly finds parliamentary regimes to be dominant

(20 cases), followed by absolute regimes (nine cases), presidential regimes (six cases) and semi-presidential (one case). These figures diverge significantly from the global total where only one quarter of the world have parliamentary regimes, just over one third presidential regimes and just under one third absolute regimes, leading Anckar to conclude that in small states 'there is clearly more parliamentarism, less presidentialism and less absolutism' (Anckar, 2004b, p.214). Second, colonial heritage is an important consideration of regime choice with most small states (72 per cent in the British case) adopting the regime of the former metropolitan power. Lastly, regime stability is a conspicuous feature, with most regimes remaining with the model of government adopted at independence. These observations underline the characteristics of 'institutional fidelity' and 'pragmatic conservatism' identified earlier. At the same time the degree of importance attached to the British connection is disputed. Clague et al find 'that being a former colony of Britain or one of its four settler colonies increases the probability of democracy by 0.368, being an island increases it by 0.203' (2001, p.27). Anckar disagrees, laying greater emphasis on small size, with both the colonial connection and insularity being contributory factors helping to embed democracy rather than the crucial consideration in determining democracy (Anckar, 2002). That aside, the general consensus among political scientists remains that the institutional legacies of British colonialism as embodied in the Westminster–Whitehall system of government, coupled with small size and insularity, have supported democracy in Commonwealth small states (Srebrnck, 2004, pp.300–32).

Some democratic issues for small states

While all small states begin with the advantage of size, this does not necessarily mean that democracy is any easier to achieve or to sustain than elsewhere. Some of the features earlier identified as typical of small developing Commonwealth states can constrain or erode democratic practice. Those featured below are not exhaustive, but suggestive of some of the more important considerations.

Head of State and Head of Government

Although most small states are parliamentary democracies, they are evenly divided as to their practice in determining the head of state. Twelve recognise Queen Elizabeth II as head of state and appoint governor-generals; 10 divide the position between locally hereditary monarchs or elected presidents as head of state and prime minister as head of government; and 10 combine the office of head of state and head of government (Commonwealth Secretariat, 2003b). While in the first two categories there have been occasions in which the prime minister has been dismissed by the governor general or hereditary monarch, the reality of all three categories is the power that is potentially concentrated in the hands of the prime minister or executive president. Politics revolves around the prime minister or executive president and his/her office is the linchpin of government. The extent to which any individual will seek to dominate the office to the exclusion of all others will vary with circumstance, but bearing in mind the characteristic features of small states cited earlier there are likely to be fewer constraints than in larger states. Considerable attention should therefore be placed in small states in defining the constitutional powers of the prime minister and executive president and in developing informal political practices that can hold him/her to account. Attention could also be paid to incumbency. The recent history of small states gives many examples of political leaders who dominated the affairs of the country for many years. There is also some limited evidence that ministers and heads of government remain longer in office than in larger countries (Sutton, 1987, p.16). Some constitutional limitation on the number of consecutive terms for a head of government may redress this situation, although this would need to be balanced by a consideration of whether the 'pool of talent' is large enough in small states to provide sufficient outstanding candidates for political office.

Elections

While elections are important in all states, in small states the relatively greater importance of government in both daily affairs and development invest them with particular significance. Good electoral practice is essential if the outcome of the election is to be accepted. The framework and mechanisms for election should be carefully set out, preferably within the constitution. The delimitation of boundaries is an important question given the small number of voters in many constituencies. There is also the issue of overseas voters. Many small states have substantial numbers of citizens working overseas. In various countries different sorts of provision is made to count their vote and in the past this has often proved contentious since they can make a difference to outcomes. This is a matter which has so far not been commented upon by various Commonwealth studies, but is clearly of importance for small states given the emphasis now being put on engaging the support of migrant overseas communities in small state development.

The number of candidates allowed to stand is again a question, as small states imply relatively small constituencies and under some electoral systems e.g. first-past-the-post, a candidate can be elected by a very small proportion of the ballots cast if there are multiple candidates contesting. The provision of finance for elections is also a concern in small states, many of which have few or no regulations on this issue but remain vulnerable to large donations (from suspect local or foreign donors) which could result in undue influence over, or capture of, government by criminal elements (Pinto-Duschinsky, 2001, pp.23-24). Rules governing finance and Codes of Conduct can be very helpful in ensuring free and fair elections and their importance for small states has been underlined in the reports of the various Commonwealth Observer Missions to elections in small states. Regard must also be paid to the counting of ballots. For example, in archipelagic small states, the voting preferences of isolated communities can easily be determined after the vote unless there is some effort to combine their ballots with those of other polling districts. In itself, this then raises further questions about the security and transport of the ballot once the polls are closed and the impartial observation of elections in places that may be difficult to reach. The Commonwealth recommends that 'in order to be credible domestic observers must ensure that they are genuinely non-partisan and are perceived as such' (Commonwealth Secretariat, 1999, p.6). This is sound advice, but more difficult to achieve in small states where individuals and their viewpoints are known. In such small states it may be necessary to employ regional and/or international observers. As of March 2004, the Commonwealth had sent observers to elections in 10 small states throughout the Commonwealth (some on several occasions) and it is clear from their reports that their presence has added to the credibility of results. The reports also contain a wealth of practical advice that would be useful to all small states if collected together and disseminated as examples of 'good practice'.

Finally, there is the question of electoral systems. The first-past-the-post system is to be found in nearly three-quarters of Commonwealth states, and it is by far the most common system in small states. It is not without its critics, particularly the distortion that may occur in the number of votes cast nationally and the proportion of seats obtained in the legislature. For example, recent elections in small states have returned landslide governments with the opposition of only one or two members on under 50 per cent of the national vote. However, relatively few small states have sought an alternative system and those that have done so have generally been plural societies, when their interest has been to ensure that all groups are represented. This has usually involved some form of proportional representation in mixed systems, or multiple constituencies, or combinations of both. The merits and deficiencies of these systems (and others such as the use of the single transferable vote or best-loser) have not been systematically investigated for small states. It is now time to examine whether such electoral systems have lessons for other small states and whether the first-past-the-post system best suits smaller societies, particularly the smallest where adversarial politics can lead to unnecessary division and exclusion of those with talent from government service. Attention could also be focused on if, and how, electoral systems could encourage greater participation by women. The percentage of seats in the legislature held by women is below 20 per cent in 21 small states (out of a total of 26) (Commonwealth Secretariat, 2003B, Appendix C), demonstrating the need for rapid improvement, particularly given the high level of educational qualifications women hold proportionate to men in some small states.

Accountability

Exaggerated personalism and governmental pervasiveness put a premium on executive accountability in small states. Fortunately, serious and prolonged abuse is comparatively rare. Outside of Africa, the human rights record for most small states is good and for the Commonwealth small states very good.[4] Political instability is relatively infrequent[5] and the incidence of coups, the collapse of states, and external intervention is low, though not unknown. The real issues that are to be addressed are not these exceptions but structural and behavioural features which routinely weaken accountability.

The dominance of personality in small states makes collective decision-making in cabinet more difficult and political parties more centralised. The prime minister or executive president is more than *primus inter pares* and dominates both, leaving those who are critical little option but to be silent or to leave. The exit option is not uncommon in small states and the recent history of small states is full of new political parties formed by those who were once the trusted lieutenant of the political leader. This tendency to multiplication is in itself indicative of the power of personality, which makes combination in opposition difficult and renders electoral success more uncertain. As noted above, the prime minister or executive president may find themselves with substantial parliamentary majorities and a weakened or practically non-existent elected opposition. When combined with small size this has important consequences. One is that parliamentary opposition, as it is conventionally conceived in the Commonwealth, is limited (Commonwealth Secretariat, 1998). The leader of the opposition may speak only for himself/herself or at best a few others. He/she will find it difficult to credibly present their party as an alternative government. The opposition as a whole will find it difficult to staff committees and to contribute positively and constructively to legislative debate. The temptation of government in such circumstance is to ignore the opposition altogether – a not infrequent practice in small states.

The issue of accountability must therefore be addressed through additional avenues other than parliamentary election. One way forward would be to limit the number of ministers to 50 per cent or less of elected members, leaving the remainder to occupy the backbenches and serve on parliamentary committees. Another is nomination. Most Commonwealth small states provide for either a nominated second chamber (Commonwealth Secretariat, 2002, p.11) or a nominated element in a unicameral chamber (ibid, p.8). While the prime minister or executive president has the power in such cases to nominate the greatest number, the possibility of nomination by the leader of the opposition boosts the opposition and, importantly, opens the way for inclusion (e.g. by nomination by the head of state) of 'non-partisan' elements from civil society speaking for a range of interests. Yet another avenue is extra-parliamentary institutions such as human rights commissions, auditor-generals, and ombudsmen. The real effect of these institutions varies from country to country but the fact that they are established provides opportunities for accountability which might otherwise go by default.

However, by far the most important factor is an active civil society in which the norms of government accountability are embedded. Scale is here significant. In small societies the public and the private are blurred and private interests are often associated with the interests of particular individuals. It is also the case that the political sympathies or antipathies of prominent individuals are often well known and their motive for action or inaction thus often suspect. The involvement of non-governmental organisations is also defined as narrowly political when it may be for purely professional or national reasons. Scale also matters in the media. News travels by word of mouth in small states and it is notoriously difficult to keep anything secret. At the same time, coverage of political affairs is often limited. The government may dominate the broadcast media and the press, making it difficult for opposition views to get a hearing. The amount of investigative journalism is small and since foreign media will be uninterested in such countries the availability of alternative views non-existent. To these constraints can be added some of the features of scale identified earlier that support a political culture in which tradition and respect for authority mute or limit criticism and independent voluntary action.

None of this suggests that civil society cannot be actively engaged and the record in a number of small states contradicts any presumption of impotence. But it does argue that the overall impact of civil society may be less than in larger liberal democracies. This puts a duty on government and on the judiciary. In respect of the former, it is one of consultation. In the smallest countries, where face-to-face contact among the political elites and non-governmental organisations is frequent and informal, such consultation does occur, often at local level. The problem then becomes one of ensuring that local interest (the parochialism for which small states are famed) does not become confused with national interest. In the 'larger' small states some institutionalisation may be necessary. In some countries there is already a practice of involving employers' organisations and trade unions in a dialogue with government to determine development priorities. This could be followed in other areas, with gender equality being among the foremost topics to discuss.

In respect of the judiciary it is maintenance of the rule of law. While in some small states there have been complaints of political interference in the administration of justice, the principle of the separation of powers is firmly established and the record in most instances is one small states can be proud of. It is incumbent on the judiciary to maintain it, particularly since the safeguard adopted in some small states of appeal to the Judicial Committee of the Privy Council will be removed.

Good governance

Democracy is an essential prerequisite for good governance. It is, however, only one element of a more comprehensive vision that the concept of good governance embraces. Although the term itself is imprecise, with different emphasis put on different aspects of it by different agencies (for example the World Bank has a narrow view, the United Nations Development Programme a wide view) there is a general consensus that it includes a sound and responsive administration, the rule of law, and respect for human rights as well as the promotion of democracy. The Commonwealth vision is consistent with such a view but also with its own particular emphasis on institutional development. This it interprets broadly to include not only the organisation of government but also the values and legal systems that infuse and sustain it. Commonwealth programmes operate in all these areas. Two, however, have been particularly important: the promotion of effective and efficient delivery of public services through public sector reform, and the fight against corruption.

Public sector reform

Many Commonwealth small states are actively engaged in public sector reform programmes. A recent publication, for example, describes reform efforts in 20 small states from across the Commonwealth (Ayeni, 2002). The experience to date appears rather mixed. The need for reform is not in doubt, but in small states the approach has been selective (Collins and Warrington, 1997). Among the reasons for this are the greater importance of the public sector in small states, organisational environment, and the bureaucratic process.

Small independent states have to provide an irreducible number of services at a relatively greater cost than larger states. The public sector therefore looms large in terms both of the number employed within it and its share of the economy. This is reinforced by the weakness of the private sector in many small developing countries, in part because of the difficulty of realising economies of scale. The government of a small developing country is thus likely to find itself in a position of supplying not only the normal range of administrative and public services, but also elements vital to the productive and commercial life of the country, including ownership of (or substantial participation in) production enterprises as well as transport and financial services.

The new public management paradigm, with its insistence on fundamental reform and downsizing of the state, potentially constitutes a large-scale shock to a small-scale society with ramifications well beyond those of larger states. It is therefore not surprising to find small states questioning the benefits of privatisation (which may result in the substitution of a private foreign-owned monopoly for a locally owned one); of contracting out services when there is weak capacity in the private sector; or of enforcing redundancy in the public service when alternative employment opportunities are limited and the number of well-qualified and enterprising migrants is already too high, to mention but a few considerations. This suggests that the adoption of public sector reform is not only an administrative question but, above all, a political question – which should be debated widely and on which a wide measure of general consent should be achieved before large-scale changes are implemented.

The organisational environment of the public services in small states has been the subject of a number of studies. They usually begin with the observation of a mismatch between the universalistic and achievement criteria of Weberian models of bureaucracy and the particularistic and ascriptive characteristics of small state society (for example Baker, 1992). This makes the fit between inherited systems, such as the Westminster–Whitehall model, and political reality less than perfect. In administrative terms it means the individual often defines the role rather than vice versa, making a functionally differentiated public service more difficult to achieve. There can be problems of recruitment through merit and competition because of family and local concerns. (The widespread adoption of public service commissions in small states is an attempt to mitigate this problem.) There are difficulties in rewarding good and disciplining poor performance, particularly in very small societies where face-to-face interaction and local values hold sway. The prevailing ethos also acts to stifle change;

and to reinforce a tendency to measure the effectiveness of the public service in terms of procedures and compliance rather than focus on outcomes. For these and other reasons, a substantial body of opinion argues that public sector reform in small states must be more aware of local cultural factors and design systems appropriate to them, particularly in the smallest states. It also suggests that successful public sector reform must start with (or at least embrace) attitudinal as well as organisational change.

In many small states the politician is said to dominate the bureaucrat; and in others the bureaucrat the politician. Whatever the case, the relationship between the executive and the public service is at the core of public policy in small states. Most policy is initiated by a small directorate of senior ministers and officials, and while there may be consultation with various groups and people in formulating policy, the temptation and the reality in many small states is for the executive to centralise authority at the top. Issues all too often get referred upward and the prime minister/executive president becomes involved in the minutiae of decision-making. This may be deliberate, particularly in those political systems where patronage is the key to maintaining power, but the effect is to politicise administrative decision and compromise the autonomy of the public service. Senior public servants find themselves closely identified with particular leaders, parties and policies, creating difficulties when there are changes of government and/or direction. Lower down in the public service, initiative is discouraged and partisanship in the delivery of services often overlooked. The fact that these features are reported in so many small states (Baker, 1992) suggests they are generic to small scale (though not exclusively confined to small states). Their resolution is thus difficult and stands in the way of the recommendations for reform that spell out the importance of more autonomous decision-making in the delivery of services at middle and lower levels.

Corruption and integrity

There is no evidence that small states are any more corrupt than larger ones.[6] Indeed, the opposite is the case, with a general impression that some small states have a not far from exemplary record of integrity (e.g. none of them are listed among the 32 states subject to particular attention in the most recent survey of Transparency International (2004) which focused on political corruption). However, this does not mean that small states are free from corruption and political abuse or that being small does not carry special risks to the security of small states.

The importance of robust accountability and transparency to limit the dominance of personality in politics and in administration in small states, as well as to oversee the proper exercise of the powers of patronage, has been made on several occasions. It needs to be underlined once again. The formal mechanisms available to do so include the office of ombudsman, auditor general, chair of the public accounts committee, chair of various service commissions (the public service, judicial service, teaching service and protective services), and the disciplinary rules exercised within the public sector. Most small states have provision for such mechanisms, although evidence presented in various Commonwealth workshops on their operation often shows serious deficiencies in funding and staffing, as well as delays in procedure and reporting. There are also informal mechanisms within the political system to limit abuse and corruption, including independent political associations, a vigorous investigative media, and an active civil society. Again many small states have a good record in establishing such bodies, but weaknesses are not uncommon, allowing government to go unchecked. Lastly, the separation of powers between the legislature, executive, and judicial system constitutionally protects the independence of the judiciary and the powers and prerogatives of the legislature from the political executive. Fortunately, many small states are well served by their judiciary who are not afraid to rule against the government. The independence of the legislature – particularly in the Westminster model – is more difficult to ensure. The recent adoption of the 'Latimer House Guidelines' for implementing the principles of responsibility, transparency, and accountability in the three branches of government constitute a step forward in this regard and are commended to small states.

None of the above, however, will work effectively unless there is 'a culture of integrity' in small states. This concept makes it clear, among other things, that the general requirements of accountability, as well as the more specific requirements of public scrutiny and institutional oversight, demand 'that national governments accept their responsibility to promote a system-wide commitment to public integrity among leading decision makers' and civil society nurture a sense of 'civic responsibility' among citizens to 'honour their obligations to help others manage their own affairs' (Uhr, 2003, p.35). In short, the battle against corruption needs to be engaged by everyone to ensure that the public interest prevails over those individuals in small states who see public office as an opportunity to serve private interests, when the proper distinction between the two in situations of familiarity may sometimes be difficult to determine. The promotion of citizenship education in developing a 'civic culture' in small states has an important part to play.

Lastly, there is an important link between corruption and the national interest in small states. Twenty-one Commonwealth small states are host to tax havens. These provide valuable revenues for development. They also provide opportunities for money laundering and tax evasion; and fertile ground for corruption. The financial rewards for facilitating such criminal action are very tempting: they are also very damaging to the security of the state, especially when linked to drug trafficking and international criminal syndicates. These issues have attracted a great deal of attention in recent years and sometimes put small states unfairly under suspicion. There is, however, a limit to what small states can realistically be expected to do. One is the vigorous prosecution of corrupt officials when they are caught, bearing in mind the costs of such corruption to the political and economic reputation of the state. Another is regional co-operation in intelligence and policing. But above all international action is needed as the Commonwealth Secretariat made clear some years ago (Commonwealth Secretariat, 2000b). The promotion and enforcement of international conventions on corruption, which was then proposed, are very much in the interests of small states and should be supported by them, not only to further their own 'good governance' but that of 'global good governance' as well.

Conclusion

In their submission to the Commonwealth Secretariat/World Bank Task Force the Caribbean states wrote: 'the costs of poor governance in a small society is very large, given the extreme difficulty in recovering from the consequences of inappropriate policies and practices sustained over a long period. A national consensus on the importance of government is needed in many small states, as is an appreciation of the ease with which the system can go off-track as a result of both domestic and external shocks' (Commonwealth Secretariat/World Bank, 2000, p.40). Small states are vulnerable but they are also in the main democratic. More to the point, the political system is crucial to their survival and development. In its 1997 report *A Future for Small States: Overcoming Vulnerability*, the Commonwealth Advisory Group identified the resilience of small states as a positive attribute that offsets some of the disadvantages of small size. At the core of resilience are the political and social systems. In recognition of this fact a recent workshop on small states set out as its first recommendation the proposal that small states should 'take steps to promote good governance by pursuing appropriate policies to ensure political stability and the enforcement of the rule of law, to address issues of corruption, as well as to promote accountability, transparency and efficiency in the delivery of public services' (Commonwealth Secretariat, 2004). A few months before this meeting, in his 'opening remarks' to the CMGSS prior to the Abuja CHOGM, the Commonwealth Secretary General, Don McKinnon, pointed out that 'a country is more likely to achieve sustained development if it inspires confidence and it will only inspire confidence if it is founded on a strong democratic culture'. He also noted that 'democratic institutions are often more costly to establish and maintain for small states (which is) why the Commonwealth provides support in promoting good governance and assists in the process of civil service reform' (Commonwealth Secretariat, 2003b). It follows that 'getting the politics right' and 'smart government' are essential in small states. The record to date is generally good and most small states are following sound policies, but there is always room for improvement, and deepening democracy and promoting good governance are not incidental to, but essential for, their future well-being.

Notes

1. The Commonwealth defines small states as those with a population under 1.5 million. Twenty-seven countries currently meet this criterion. Five larger countries are also considered as small states since they share some or all of the characteristics of small states. In this chapter reference to Commonwealth small states includes all 32 states.

2. The Freedom House surveys are not universally accepted, although they are by far the most common measure used in empirical studies of democracy. In this instance the surveys provide a guide since they employ a methodology that gives particular weight to features that are essential to liberal democracy. The status of 'free', 'partly free' and 'not free' are obtained by

averaging political rights (rights to participate meaningfully in the political process) and civil liberties (rights to free expression, to organise or demonstrate, as well as rights to a degree of autonomy such as is provided by freedom of religion, education, travel and other personal rights).

3. The study unfortunately excludes five small states (Nauru, Tonga, Tuvalu, the Federated States of Micronesia, and the Marshall Islands).

4. Amnesty International's *Amnesty International Report* for 2002, for example, lists 23 small developing states (16 Commonwealth). While the *Report* emphasises that exclusion of a state does not mean it does not have a human rights problem (and it is evident that information on small states may be difficult to obtain) the situation is nevertheless generally positive. Many of the reports for Commonwealth countries focus on retention of the death penalty, poor prison conditions, and police brutality, rather than the more gross violations such as torture, political detention and disappearance, and restriction of political freedoms.

5. Ott challenges this finding but accepts that further empirical work is necessary to confirm or refute it (Ott, 2000, pp.125-7).

6. The most recent Transparency International Corruption Perceptions Index (2003) carries reports on only 12 small developing countries, nine of which are from the Commonwealth, out of a total of 133 entries. The sample is (a) too small to draw any real inference and (b) demonstrates a bias towards the exclusion of small states from consideration. The methodology of the index is also subject to challenge.

References

Amnesty International (2002) *Amnesty International Report*. Amnesty International, London.

Anckar, Dag (1999) 'Homogeneity and Smallness: Dahl and Tufte Revisited', *Scandinavian Political Studies* Vol.22, No.1.

Anckar, Dag (2002) 'Why are Small Island States Democracies?', *The Round Table* No.365.

Anckar, Dag (2004a) 'Direct Democracy in Microstates and Small Islands', *World Development*, Vol.32, No.2.

Anckar, Dag (2004b) 'Regime Choices in Microstates: The Cultural Constraint', *Journal of Commonwealth and Comparative Politics* Vol.42 No.2.

Ayeni, Victor (2002) *Public Sector Reform in Developing Countries: A Handbook of Commonwealth Experiences*. Commonwealth Secretariat, London.

Baker, Randall (ed.) (1992) *Public Administration in Small and Island States*. Kumarian Press, West Hartford.

Clague, Christopher, Suzanne Gleason and Stephen Knack (2001) 'Determinants of Lasting Democracy in Poor Countries: Culture, Development and Institutions', *The Annals of the American Academy of Political and Social Science* Volume 573.

Collins, Paul and Edward Warrington (1997) *The New Public Administration: Lessons from the Experiences of Small and Island States*. A report on The Seychelles/CAPAM/IASIA Conference.

Commonwealth Advisory Group (1997) *A Future for Small States: Overcoming Vulnerability*. Commonwealth Secretariat, London.

Commonwealth Secretariat (1998) *The Role of the Opposition*. Commonwealth Secretariat, London.

Commonwealth Secretariat (1999) *Domestic Election Observers*. Commonwealth Secretariat, London.

Commonwealth Secretariat (2000a) *Democracy and Small States*. Commonwealth Secretariat, London.

Commonwealth Secretariat (2000b) *Fighting Corruption: Promoting Good Governance*. Commonwealth Secretariat, London.

Commonwealth Secretariat (2002) *The Commonwealth Yearbook*. Commonwealth Secretariat, London.

Commonwealth Secretariat (2003a) 'Opening Remarks by the Commonwealth Secretary General, Rt. Hon Don McKinnon', *Meeting of the Commonwealth Ministerial Group on Small States*, Abuja, Nigeria, 4 December, 2003.

Commonwealth Secretariat (2003b) *Making Democracy Work for Pro-Poor Development*. Commonwealth Secretariat, London.

Commonwealth Secretariat (2004) 'Conclusions of the International Workshop on Economic Vulnerability and Resilience of Small States', Malta, 1–3 March, 2004.

Commonwealth Secretariat/World Bank Joint Task Force on Small States (2000) *Small States: Meeting Challenges in the Global Economy*. Commonwealth Secretariat, London.

Dahl, R. (1989) *Democracy and its Critics*. Yale University Press, New Haven.

Dahl, R. and E.R. Tufte (1973) *Size and Democracy*. Stanford University Press, Stanford.

Freedom House (2004) *Freedom in the World*. www. freedomhouse.org.

Hadenius, Axel (1992) *Democracy and Development*. Cambridge University Press, Cambridge.

Lewis, Sir Arthur (1965) *The Agony of the Eight*. Advocate Commercial Printery, Bridgetown.

Lijphart, Arend (1991) 'Constitutional Choices for New Democracies' in Larry Diamond and Marc Plattner (eds) *The Global Resurgence of Democracy*. The Johns Hopkins University Press, Baltimore.

Lowenthal, David (1987) 'Social Aspects' in Colin Clarke and Anthony Payne (eds) *Politics, Security and Development in Small States*. Allen and Unwin, London.

Ott, Dana (2000) *Small is Democratic: An Examination of State Size and Democratic Development*. Garland Publishing, Inc., New York and London.

Pinto-Duschinsky, Michael (2001) *Political Financing in the Commonwealth*. Commonwealth Secretariat, London.

Potter, David and David Goldblatt, Margaret Kiloh and Paul Lewis (1997) *Democratization*. Polity Press and the Open University, Cambridge.

Srebrnik, Henry (2004) 'Small Island Nations and Democratic Values', *World Development*, Vol.32, No.2.

Sutton, Paul (1987) 'Political Aspects' in Colin Clarke and Anthony Payne (eds) *Politics, Security and Development in Small States*. Allen and Unwin, London.

Transparency International (2004) *The Global Corruption Report*. www.transparency.org.

Uhr, John (2003) *Creating a Culture of Integrity*. Commonwealth Secretariat, London.

UNITAR (United Nations Institute for Training and Research) (1971) *Small States and Territories: Status and Problems*. Arno Press, New York.

11. Public Sector Reform in Small States: Cases from the Commonwealth Caribbean

Paul Sutton

In the last two decades the role of the state in development has come under challenge. The reasons for this include the fiscal crises that hit most developing countries in the 1980s, weakening the ability of the state to fund development programmes; the stabilisation and structural adjustment policies that followed, which imposed reductions in the role and size of government and an increase in the scope and activities of the private sector; and the elaboration, from the beginning of the 1990s, of programmes of 'good governance' that aimed to build 'an effective state' through matching a state's role to its capability, which required a sharper focus on fundamentals, and raising state capability by reinvigorating public institutions. In the achievement of these last set of activities sweeping public sector reform was to be encouraged.

The impact of such programmes on the developing world has been the subject of much comment. In the case of small states[1] it raised particular difficulties. The public sector tends to be proportionately bigger and its responsibility for delivering services across a wide range of activities is greater than in many larger countries. There were thus serious questions about any proposal to reduce the role of the state. At the same time the need for public sector reform was acknowledged in many small states. Within the Commonwealth, for example, the majority of its small states (20 in a recent partial listing) implemented programmes of public sector reform (Ayeni, 2002). Among them are seven from the independent Commonwealth Caribbean – a region which has been undergoing public sector reform in many guises since the beginning of the 1990s (and in some cases earlier).

This chapter examines that experience in four of these – Barbados, Jamaica, St Lucia and Trinidad and Tobago. In order to do so, however, and to situate the analysis within the context of small states, it first sets out some characteristics of public administration in small states. It then considers the reasons behind and the shape of reform in the Commonwealth Caribbean in general before looking in more depth at the four countries. The final part returns to the question of public sector reform in small states, raising some issues for further research and consideration.

The administration of small states

There is a small but growing literature on public administration in small states. It has identified certain characteristics that influence the structure and processes of government and shape the political culture and behaviour of their citizens. This review is not intended to be exhaustive of such features but rather considers some of the more important and formative ones.

The theory of public administration tends to assume that small states are 'scaled down' versions of larger states. The dominant way of thinking about public administration in larger states has therefore shaped the analysis of small state administrative behaviour. At its core has been the Weberian model of the modern public service 'characterised by a clearly defined division of labour, an impersonal authority structure, a hierarchy of offices, dependence on formal rules, employment based on merit, the availability of a career, and the distinct separation of members' organisational and personal lives' (Turner and Hulme, 1997, p.83). This pattern, in turn, has been buttressed by the process of decolonisation that have left many small developing states, and especially those in the Commonwealth, with a derived 'Westminster-Whitehall' model of government in which a clear distinction is drawn between the political and administrative dimensions of government. The function of the bureaucrat is to implement policy in a value-neutral way with due regard to political instructions.

The impact of this dominant Weberian model on the political behaviour of small states has been mapped in a number of studies. These have identified certain features that most small states have in common and which bear directly on their administrative behaviour. Four of them - exaggerated personalism, limited resources, inadequate service delivery, and donor dependence - appear to show that size does matter. They are drawn from several of the most recent studies of the public service in small states (Ghai, 1990; Baker, 1992; Warrington, 1994) and underpin earlier studies by UNITAR (1971) and Jacobs (1975).

Exaggerated personalism

The importance of personality in politics is the most commonly cited attribute of small states. The individual takes on greater significance and their opinions are often known among a wide circle. Ministers and public servants may be more accessible to the public and open to informal contact. Within the public service the person often defines the post, rather than the reverse; senior administrators can dominate politicians (although the opposite is also cited); decisions tend to get taken by a few people or only one person at the top (and those who take the decisions are known); recruitment is often influenced by personal (or patronage) factors; and appraisal, promotion and disciplinary proceedings may be unduly influenced by personal considerations.

Limited resources

There are limited manpower resources and problems of scale in administration and infrastructure. Sovereign states are expected to supply a range of public goods and services including central government, education, health and social services, a judicial system, foreign relations and security. The infrastructural costs of these are high when spread among a small population, especially when they have to be duplicated in remote islands of archipelagic states. Such facilities need to be staffed, making economies of scale in administration difficult to effect, particularly among less-developed countries where expatriates need to be employed to cover for services that cannot be provided by local staff. Staffing difficulties are often met by the creation of multiple portfolios among senior staff, leading to lack of specialisation, motivation, and career mobility. There are also problems in providing local training, especially at the higher levels of administration, with the result that staff will often be sent for training abroad which is not always appropriate (in particular the training will not necessarily prepare them to work in such a small state) and which can encourage subsequent 'brain drain', compounding the problem it is meant to resolve.

Inadequate service delivery

The combination of exaggerated personalism and limited resources influences the way the public service functions and affects the quality of service delivery. The public service is frequently the largest employer, especially in the very smallest states, and salary levels and productivity are often low. The lack of alternative employment and appropriate training mean innovation and entrepreneurship are not encouraged, instead there is a reliance on routine administration and compliance (following instructions) along with a proclivity for non-decision-making (buck passing) at middle management levels. Limits on opportunity means there is limited mobility, low job satisfaction, and frequent absenteeism. While the public sector is expected to achieve a great deal there is in reality a growing gap between demands on it and its capability to deliver, particularly in areas where there is inadequate or no spare capacity, indicating a low overall ability to adapt to changing conditions.

Donor dependence

Many of the above problems were identified years ago. They have led to long-running programmes to redress them in the Commonwealth Secretariat supported by the Commonwealth Fund for Technical Co-operation (CFTC), which currently disburses some 60 per cent of its funds in favour of projects in Commonwealth small states. Bilateral donors have also been active in the Caribbean (UK and Canada) and the South Pacific (Australia and New Zealand) in support of public sector development, providing the basis for much of the higher per capita level of official development assistance (ODA) that small developing states receive compared to larger developing states. The result is a well-established and continuing metropolitan input into both the definition of the problem and the proposals for solution in small states, reinforcing the metropolitan model of administration, metropolitan procedures (e.g. in budgeting and accounting), and metropolitan proposals for reform. In turn, this can lead to distorted development priorities, with an emphasis on what the donor is willing to provide rather than what is best for local development, stifling local initiative and adding to cost and inefficiencies through inappropriate programmes and projects.

The dominant discourse is thus clearly focused on the constraints that scale imposes on small states, particularly the smallest among them. While this is a question of resources it is also a question of the appropriate model of administration. In a much cited article, Murray (1981) contrasts the informal working methods he encountered in the South Pacific with conventional attempts to apply scaled-down standard prescriptions for effective development in such countries, pointing to the successes of the former compared to the inadequacies of the latter, thereby indicating the need for what he terms 'ordinary knowledge' in developing the public service. The same point has been reiterated more recently for small states in the North Atlantic area. Baldacchino and Greenwood (1998, pp.10–11, author's emphasis) distinguish between '**common sense** – counsel dictated by established expertise and typically supported by international organisations, state bureaucrats, and policy makers' and '**good sense** – often a haphazard collection of intuitive, home-grown, resilient, and environmentally proven and sustainable ideas' which takes a more imaginative approach to development in small states. The question of what is appropriate theory and practice for development administration is therefore an important issue for small states.

So also, and allied to it, is the question of reform. Most efforts in the past have been directed to overcoming resource constraint through ODA and some very limited restructuring. Little thought or attention has been given to more fundamental reform. At independence most (if not all) Commonwealth small states simply inherited (or on occasion adapted) existing public service departments in an ad hoc manner without consideration of the new demands that would be placed on them in an era of independence. Since then innovation has on the whole been relatively limited and the 'machinery of government' in small states has proved remarkably durable, with the most far-reaching departures from the 'Westminster–Whitehall' system to be found in the smallest states (Wettenhall, 1999). It can, of course, be argued that piecemeal change has been all that has been needed since most small states have weathered independence reasonably well. However, even if this is conceded, the demands now being placed on small states from the international environment are impelling change (Commonwealth Secretariat/World Bank Joint Task Force on Small States, 2000). There are also significant and mounting challenges to democracy in small states (Commonwealth Secretariat/Commonwealth Parliamentary Association 2000). The question before most small states is thus not whether change is desirable in itself, but the extent of change that is needed to compete in the international system and secure 'good governance'.

Public sector reform in the Commonwealth Caribbean

The signal for change in the Commonwealth Caribbean first came with the stabilisation and structural adjustment programmes implemented in several states in the 1980s. It was strengthened in the 1990s with the report of the influential West Indian Commission, which recommended 'that Governments should become less and less involved in the direct production of goods and services, and should increasingly concentrate on catalytic, facilitating, supportive and regulatory functions. This means different government. It does not mean no government' (West Indian Commission, 1992, p.100); and in the CARICOM Ministerial Roundtable on Public Management in the Caribbean held in Jamaica in February 1992. In the Kingston Declaration on Public Management issued at the end of the conference Caribbean governments were urged, among other things, to promote the development of human resources; 'confront structural inefficiencies and determine the proper dimensions of their administrative machinery'; become more proactive in their approach to macroeconomic policy and financial management; and 'implement a new managerial orientation and strengthen the competencies in the public sector' to encourage responsiveness, efficiency and creativity in the delivery of public services (Kingston Declaration, 1992).

The broad guidelines on how to proceed were mapped out by a Working Group on Public Sector Reform and Administrative Restructuring established by the CARICOM Heads of Government in 1993 and reporting to them in 1995. This identified principles and practices under four heads:

- redefining the role of the state, during which 'those in authority [should] be prepared to examine all our institutions, procedures and systems of decision-making in the light of new paradigms and understanding of human behaviour and the need for personal satisfaction and creativity in the discharge of professional obligations';

- the primacy of human resource development, which would entail introducing into the public service the principles of promotion by merit not seniority, training at all levels, remuneration according to skills and responsibilities, and delegation of authority;

- greater dedication to service provision under which public employees would be customer focused and 'more responsive, timely and business-like in dealing with the public'; and

- a strong commitment by the political directorate and senior public servants to public sector reform in a clearly articulated public sector reform programme, institutionalised in government and involving as 'stakeholders' public employees at all levels and their staff associations and trade unions (CARICAD, 1995).

The Report was approved by the CARICOM Heads, signalling a major shift in the direction and priorities of public sector reform.

The proposals for reform were strongly influenced by the New Public Management (NPM) paradigm which had come to dominate management thinking on public service reform in a number of advanced industrialised countries (including Australia, Canada, New Zealand, and the United Kingdom). Many of its principles were taken up by major bilateral donors in their programmes in support of 'good governance' in the developing world and by organisations such as the Commonwealth Association of Public Administration and Management (CAPAM). This was a professional association founded in 1994 with the aim of 'exchanging experiences in government reforms and working toward the practice of the new public administration' (CAPAM, 1999). The 'defining characteristics' of the NPM model have been summarised 'as its entrepreneurial dynamic, its reinstatement of the market as a potentially more proficient provider of services than the state, and its proclaimed intention to transform managerial behaviour' (Minogue, 2001, p.6). The Commonwealth version of NPM was developed in several major conferences and numerous workshops organised with the support and active participation of the Management Training and Services Division (MTSD) of the Commonwealth Secretariat. According to its then Director, Dr Mohan Kaul, its specific characteristics were as follows: it (1) redefines the role and functions of government (consistent with the idea of the catalytic, effective and facilitating state); (2) involves thinking differently about service users (consistent with the idea of the public as customers); (3) means thinking differently about administrative structures (consistent with the idea of distinguishing policymaking from policy implementation); (4) seeks to create synergy between the public and private sectors (consistent with the idea of introducing competition into the public service through internal and external markets); (5) improves financial planning and control systems (consistent with the idea of curbing corruption and ensuring value for money); and (6) harnesses information technology (consistent with the goals of efficiency and effectiveness) (Kaul, 1996; Kaul, 1997). Dr Kaul concluded that 'The broad objectives of such reform have been to shift the emphasis from developing plans to developing key strategic areas, to shift emphasis from inward-looking systems to developing partnerships, to shift emphasis from inputs and processes to outputs and outcomes, and to shift emphasis toward managing diversity within a unified public service' (Kaul, 1997, pp.25-26).

The NPM model has proved particularly influential in the Commonwealth Caribbean. Beginning with Trinidad and Tobago in 1991 it has informed the strategy for public sector reform in that country and in Jamaica, Barbados, St Lucia, Belize and Guyana. Other countries that have embarked on reform such as The Bahamas, Dominica and Grenada have also drawn on aspects of the model..

Jamaica

The Jamaican government has been pursuing public sector reform through various initiatives since 1984. The current phase began in 1996 and has focused on the Public Service Modernisation Project (PSMP), which is jointly funded by the government, World Bank, European Union and the UK's Department for International Development (DFID). The PSMP is directed by the Cabinet Office and located in the Office of the Prime Minister. It is therefore directly driven by senior members of the government and constitutes, in the view of Dr Carlton Davis, the Cabinet Secretary charged with implementing the programme, the most sweeping change introduced in the public sector since independence (Government of Jamaica, 2001).

The various elements of the programme are difficult to summarise but most importantly include: the establishment of Executive Agencies on the UK model; emphasis on improved customer service by selected public agencies, including the introduction of citizen's charters; a financial management and improvement programme involving extensive computerisation of records and service delivery; improved efficiency, value-for-money and transparency in government procurement and contracting; the implementation of a performance management system for permanent secretaries; the close monitoring of public expenditure to reduce costs; and the general reform of the public service through human resource development programmes, the introduction of strategic planning, and decentralisation of decision-making and service delivery (Government of Jamaica, 1999/2000; Government of Jamaica, 2000/2001). The general objectives of such reform has been to create a small, effective, efficient and accountable public sector capable of providing high quality service.

The element of reform which has attracted the most attention inside and outside the region is the creation of Executive Agencies. To date nine have been established. The primary aim of such Agencies is to improve service quality and achieve cost effectiveness by introducing business principles into their organisation and operation. The Agencies operates at arms length from government under the direction of a Chief Executive Officer (CEO) to whom substantial authority is given to manage its affairs on a contractual basis. The CEO agrees performance targets with the appropriate ministry and he/she has control over both finance and personnel. Any savings generated from the efficient use of resources can be retained and used to provide bonuses or benefits and/or improve working conditions. The quality of services given is regularly monitored. The introduction of such Agencies is a substantial departure from the traditional operation of the Westminster–Whitehall system of public administration in Jamaica and required specific legislation (the Executive Agencies Act 2002). Importantly, however, they are seen as a success and have won cross-party support from the Opposition, ensuring their continuation in the future if there is a change of government.

The other main elements of the PSMP have included the modernisation of selected ministries, in part along lines already pioneered by the Executive Agencies; the continued rationalisation of the public sector through specific privatisation measures; strengthening government procurement procedures to improve efficiency, accountability, transparency and value for money; and improving the quality of financial and personnel management through computerised information systems. To date, the indications are that the PSMP is delivering better quality services in the reformed sector. The government therefore remains committed to further public sector reform. In June 2002 a national consultation on public sector reform was held subsequent to which a comprehensive Ministry Paper was approved, mapping the course of future reform (Government of Jamaica, 2002). This set out the strategic priorities for reform, which built on the existing strategy, and promised accelerated 'agencification' and further modernisation of key ministries, along with a continued focus on customer service, information technology, human resource development and financial management systems. It also created a Permanent Reform Unit in the Cabinet Office with the mission of 'driving forward the implementation of the agenda for modernising government, improving the quality, coherence and responsiveness of public services, and for promoting a strong and professionally well-managed Public Sector, capable of enabling and facilitating the achievement of the national goals' (Government of Jamaica, 2002, p.12). In all, the Ministry Paper confirms the 'institutionalisation' of the reform process in Jamaica, overcoming some of the problems associated with earlier reform efforts that were essentially 'short term'. It also points to the continued importance of the public sector in delivering sustainable development and 'good governance', which the Paper identifies as core national goals.

Trinidad and Tobago

In December 1991 a new government was elected in Trinidad and Tobago. It soon embarked on an ambitious programme of public sector reform under the overall direction of Gordon Draper[2] as Minister in the Office of the Prime Minister with responsibility for Public Administration and Public Information. The programme drew directly on the NPM paradigm and sought to deliver decentralised management, improved morale and productivity, improved human resource management, improved quality of service and delivery, and improved budgeting and accounting systems (Draper, 1995, pp.87–98). The details of the programme were set out in detail in a publication of the MTSD as A Profile of the Public Service of Trinidad and Tobago (Commonwealth Secretariat, 1995a). It covered seven areas, three of which were elaborated in some detail. The first was 'making the most of staff' through training and development, the establishment of 'change teams' within ministries to lead reform, new systems of performance appraisal, and improving work performance by upgrading accommodation and developing an employee assistance programme. The second focused on 'making government more efficient' through the introduction of strategic planning, improving productivity via computerisation, contracting out services, redundancy management, and conducting comprehensive audits. The third area, 'improving policy analysis and co-ordination', was to be achieved by creating standing committees of Cabinet in vital areas for national economic development, improving policy presentation in the media, and creating more mechanisms for public consultation on national development. The other areas addressed the quality of public services, partnerships with the private sector and non-government organisations, effective management and the management of finance.

It was a comprehensive vision and some of the ideas, mechanisms and procedures set forth in it have since been adopted by other Caribbean countries in their programmes of reform. In Trinidad and Tobago, however, it ran into difficulties. One was over the powers and responsibilities of the Public Service Commission (PSC). The reforms proposed reducing and rationalising these powers and responsibilities, with many of them being exercised by ministries and other public agencies in accordance with the more decentralised management principles of NPM. This was resisted by the PSC, which claimed that the government was unfairly blaming them for failures in the public service. They also questioned the introduction of private sector values into the very different ethos of the public service (Government of Trinidad and Tobago, 1995). Another was the proposal to establish human resource units in ministries, which would have seriously weakened the Personnel Department. A number of ministries submitted plans but there was much delay in implementation, reducing the effectiveness of the reform. Other changes in this area, such as performance appraisal, also met employee resistance, suggesting a strong cultural resistance to change. In a major survey of public servants conducted at the time (ibid), this was both confirmed and denied. On the one hand, public servants supported change which was beneficial to them 'such as training, pay increases, systems of career path planning and enhanced opportunities' (Bissessar, p.149). On the other, they were 'afraid of change' which was in any way radical, rather than incremental, since they equated it with 'retrenchment and downsizing' (ibid, p.148) which would threaten their jobs and erode their tenure. In such circumstances it is not surprising that many were 'openly hostile to suggestions for further reform' (ibid, p.149). In the face of such opposition, and also a lessening of commitment to micro-manage change by the political leadership, the reform programme slowly ground to a halt.

Was it then a failure? In 2000 Dr Roland Baptiste of the University of the West Indies in Trinidad published a short study using the checklist for sustainable public sector reform developed by the MTSD (see Commonwealth Secretariat, 1995, p.14). His conclusion was that 'the reform effort in Trinidad and Tobago between 1992 and 1995 more or less satisfied the Commonwealth Secretariat's nine point 'best practices' list in so far as methodology is concerned. However, it is difficult to identify any concrete outputs of the programme' (Baptiste, 2000, p.73). At the same time, he points out that when there was a change of government in November 1995 the incoming government did not depart radically from the programme and initiatives already undertaken. Indeed, in some ways it was an even greater adherent of NPM as was very evident in its development of a policy agenda for the public service in the policy document *Towards a New Public Administration* (Government of Trinidad and Tobago, 1997) that directly drew on, and deepened the theory and practices of, the previous government. Other continuities were the continuation of the job classification exercise, the extension of the new performance and appraisal system, the introduction of regional health authorities, and modest legal amendments strengthening parliamentary oversight of the PSC. Beyond this, however, no really new initiatives were introduced and in December 2000 a decision was taken to disband the Ministry of Public Administration. Although it was reconstituted in December 2001 under yet another new government the drive for reform had by then been truly blunted. The aims now were to be modest, and they focused on modernising the human resource management function, improving public management systems, creating value for money initiatives, and promoting a results-based management culture (Government of Trinidad and Tobago, 2002). Expectations were also lower, with the realisation now that reform would be a long slow process requiring carefully crafted incremental change.

Barbados

The imperative of public service reform was raised by the winning political party in the general elections of September 1994 and set out in detail in the *Draft White Paper on Public Sector Reform* published the following year (Barbados, 1995). It essentially presented a case for modernisation, arguing that the structure and the organisational culture inherited at independence (based on the Weberian model) held back development and limited operational efficiency. In common with experiences elsewhere it therefore sought a different type of public service, one focused 'less on procedures...and more on outcomes or outputs consistent with the policy intentions of government. A management style of getting results rather than consistency in following traditional procedures...' (ibid, p.33). In order to achieve this it was proposed to develop: a vision to which all subscribe; mission statements for all government departments; strategic planning at ministry and agency level; organisational review and restructuring as appropriate; decentralisation and devolution to encourage greater autonomy in the management of ministries and departments; new systems of human resource management involving rationalisation and review of institutions, new performance appraisal systems, and new emphasis on training and development; improved financial management; and raising the standard of performance with a focus on the public as customer through citizen's charters and better information management systems (ibid, pp.45–100). In line with the new thinking on development, the paper envisages a different role for government than in the past – as catalyst and facilitator – implying review and rationalisation of the role and functioning of statutory boards (ibid, pp.101-3) and the greater engagement of the private sector in the delivery of services (ibid, p.104). It also comments on the role of trade unions and staff associations in the process of change and suggests the need for legal reform in the shape of a Public Service Act (ibid, pp.105-8). Lastly, it proposes the creation of a Public Sector Reform Unit (PSRU) to provide advice and assistance to the internal reform teams that were to be established in each ministry, department and agency as the 'drivers' of reform.

The detailed proposals on how to implement public sector reform were discussed and approved at the highest level in August 1996. They drew directly on the White Paper and set an ambitious agenda for comprehensive and thorough reform over the next three years (Government of Barbados, 1996). The Office of Public Sector Reform (OPSR) was established in 1997. In September 2000 it drew up a report of its activities for consideration by Cabinet (Government of Barbados, 2000). The results of reform were judged as disappointing. It identified substantial difficulties in strategic planning and organisational review, with a reluctance by ministries and departments to go beyond the review process; very limited progress in the adoption and promotion of customers' charters (only three had been launched); and the failure of many of the internal reform committees to sustain activities (while 52 had been created most were regarded as 'dormant'). It also pointed to the lack of support given to reforms, including by senior managers, and to the existence of 'a public service culture that condones behaviours, attitudes, practices and values that are negative, non-productive and anti-reform'.

The situation toward the end of 2000 was thus one where ownership of the reform process was limited and implementation at best piecemeal. It was also clear that the political commitment to reform had weakened. In the face of such difficulties the emphasis changed from fundamental reform to specific improvement – doing things a bit smarter. An example of this is the continued computerisation of financial and personnel records. The programme also became more focused on human resource development and management. To this end a job evaluation exercise was begun at the end of 2000 and a performance review and development system launched in 2001. A relatively generous budget was also set aside for training and staff development, includ-ing provision for education in business administration. The OPSR also continues to promote reform through various activities and publications. However, it is clear that the process now lacks any meaningful central direction or co-ordination. The most telling example here is the failure to date of the government to provide for a new Public Service Act, which was called for in the White Paper, and around which a measure of consensus has been reached with 'stakeholders' regarding it as import for the modernisation of the public services (Government of Barbados, 2002).

St Lucia

Public sector reform was one of the main priorities of the new government elected in 1997. Shortly after taking office it established the Office of Public Sector Reform and later in the year a Public Service Reform Commission. In 1999 a Green Paper on Public Sector Reform was published. This set out the rationale and philosophy guiding public sector reform as well as some of the strategies to achieve it. In so doing it contrasted previous attempts at reform with the current attempt. Earlier reforms, it noted, were largely directed at restructuring and reclassifying the service and strength-ening skills and financial management, i.e. were relatively limited in scope. This initia-tive was to be much broader and high profile: 'The Government plans to take the process further and at a quicker pace by taking a more embracing approach to Public Sector Reform and has therefore placed Public Sector Reform as one of its many objectives to be attained during its term of office' (Government of St Lucia, 1999, p.3).

The Green Paper was released for public consultation in August 1999 and in April 2000 a White Paper was completed, developing the arguments and setting out in detail the reform process as outlined in the Green Paper. The philosophy guiding reform was one where the state continued to fulfil important functions and would remain a key player in some economic areas. At the same time, and reflecting the growth of the private sector and civil society, the state would relinquish some functions to these sectors but would do so only in the context of 'the political, social and economic realities confronting St Lucia' (Government of St Lucia, 2000, p.12). This suggested more than a minimal state and was in line with previous thinking by the Prime Minis-ter on this subject where he indicated that while a reduced state was desirable it was not always politically feasible and should not be at the expense of social justice (An-thony, 1998). The White Paper also extolled the virtue of a neutral and impartial public service and set out four principles that would guide it: professionalism, accountability, impartiality and efficiency.

The greater part of the White Paper was directed to consideration of the strategies and means by which reform would be delivered. The main areas covered were planning, monitoring, budgeting and evaluation; organisational review; human resource management and development; values and cultural change; and supporting processes. The final part set out a plan of action. At the top were the Cabinet, which provided guidance and leadership, and the Committee of Permanent Secretaries, which 'will serve as a consultative forum for discussions on reform initiatives which call for common action and solutions' (Government of St Lucia, 2000, p.119). The Ministry of the Public Service and the Office of Public Sector Reform were given various oversight and co-ordination roles, although they were not to be the prime agents for implementation. This was to be the responsibility of internal reform committees that would be 'broad based' and established in every ministry. External assistance would be sought from the Commonwealth Secretariat, CARICAD and DFID.

The White Paper is both comprehensive and ambitious. It provides a detailed blueprint for action and it reflects the theory and practice of good public sector management, drawing especially on the NPM paradigm. Of particular value was its identification of many of the weaknesses of the public sector in St Lucia. It did not, however, provide any rationale as to why some strategies and actions were recommended and it appears to give little credence to issues of small size and the ability of the public service to implement and sustain such a sweeping programme of reform. These omissions were later to have an important bearing on the progress of reform.

This has been hesitant and spasmodic at best. For example, while the White Paper was approved by Cabinet in October 2000 it was not published until 2002. Similarly, the retreat of ministers and permanent secretaries listed in the White Paper to take place in May 2000 was delayed until May 2002. The Public Sector Reform Unit was also disbanded immediately the White Paper was completed and not re-established for a year. The Prime Minister gave several reasons for procrastination in his 'address' at the retreat on public sector reform: the novelty of government for a party out of office for 15 years requiring a period of 'getting to know the public service' and 'understanding the ways of public officers/public servants and decision-makers generally'; the difficulty of determining how to deal with difficulties inherent in the Westminster–Whitehall model of government, such as the proper role and responsibilities of ministers and permanent secretaries and the concept of neutrality for the public service in the face of demands for open, transparent and accountable government; and the confusion in the mind of the public between the operations of government and the delivery of public services, which were in practice distinct but not perceived as such (Anthony, 2002). In short, he implied that precipitate comprehensive reform could have met with substantial problems, not to say opposition, and that the government needed to tread warily to avoid unnecessary political costs.

Nevertheless, some reform has been initiated. Several examples can be given. The first was a pilot project at the Post Office implemented with the support of DFID in 2000. This included the appointment of a change team and a diagnostic review that focused on customer service. The second is the experience of the Ministry of Education, Human Resources Development, Youth and Sport, which has been engaged with aspects of reform at the micro-level since the late 1990s. A plan involving island-wide consultation has been developed, a mission statement drafted, the ministry restructured, a new appraisal system adopted, and strategic planning introduced in schools along with various novel measures to encourage extra-curricular activities and motivate staff and students. Another is the convening in December 2003 of a workshop for senior policy officials on policy research, design and analysis, which indicates that the reform process is still under way. However, it is difficult to avoid the conclusion that the overall thrust of reform is much diminished, requiring major commitments in political direction and resource allocation if it is to be successful.

The Caribbean Experience of Reform: Some Conclusions for Small States

The Commonwealth Caribbean clearly has a mixed record of reform, with some successes but also many problems of implementation and of sustained political commitment. In itself, this is not unusual in the developing world. The study on public sector reform in Commonwealth developing states (covering 40 jurisdictions) reports a similar conclusion: 'The outcome of reform has been mixed at best: limited and often scattered successes; several pockets of uncertainties; and persistent economic and governance crises. The best success stories remain those countries that had made appreciable strides in any case before the current swell of reforms' (Ayeni, 2002, pp.5-6). The last sentence would also stand for the Caribbean where Jamaica is the example.

Beyond these generalisations, however, there is the more particular question of what the Caribbean experience provides for other small states. Taking as a guideline the characteristics set out at the beginning, the following points appear relevant.

Political leadership

In all the cases given above political leadership has been the key element in both introducing reform and sustaining it. When it has waned reform has slowed down and when it has lapsed reform has all but come to a halt. The commitment of top political leaders is therefore essential to successful public sector reform in small states. Delegation downwards, for example to public sector reform units, is understandable, but unless they have the explicit and continuing support of the top leadership their prospect of leading public sector reform is diminished. Similarly, internal reform committees, consisting largely of middle- and junior-level management, may have many good ideas but will lack credibility. None of this is to suggest that reform cannot be attempted without such explicit support, but where it has been done it is by exceptional individuals and on further examination it is seen that they often have very close links to the political leadership.

Resource issues

All the reform programmes have been ambitious. They have attempted to fundamentally change the way the public service operates. To this end they initially set out sweeping programmes of reform. In practice, however, these are very costly to implement, in both time and money, which resource-poor small states can ill afford. In some cases external funding has been sought, which has provided useful support, but even then important questions of capacity can arise. Overworked senior administrators have little time for training or familiarising themselves in any depth with new ways of delivering effective and efficient management. The private sector is no substitute and may be even more ineffective and inefficient, or even incapable, of taking over the provision of services from government. All this suggests that a careful and deliberately incremental strategy of reform is more likely to succeed. In reality, this is what has happened in all the cases above, but in only one of them was it a deliberate element of the reform process, in the other cases it has been more of a 'fall-back position' occasioned by difficulties encountered once the reform process has begun.

Service delivery

The provision of better public services has been at the heart of all reform. In some cases this has resulted in genuine innovation – as in the creation of agencies and the development of citizen/customer charters. But the most favoured approach to reform has been through human resource development strategies. These have focused on various forms of decentralised management, performance appraisal, employee assistance programmes, training programmes and information technology. They thus directly address the commonplace observation on small states that human resources are the greatest resource possessed by such countries, with the associated conclusion that their full development is essential to any successful reform. At the same time, they also point to another and more entrenched problem of the culture of the public service. In all cases there has been resistance to change, which in some cases has slowed down or stalled reforms. Such opposition is not unreasonable given the limited opportunities for employment in small states, so it will be difficult to overcome. It will require a patient and innovative approach in which employee opportunity becomes recognised as the most likely outcome of reform rather than immobility or loss of relative income and/or secure employment.

Foreign models

All the reforms have drawn on NPM for theory, inspiration and example. In some cases the process has been more selective than in others, but the provenance of most of the reforms can easily be authenticated. In this Caribbean small states are no different from many other developing countries, but it has led to a deepening of dependence, especially when major international donors and their consultants have been actively engaged in various forms of 'policy transfer'. In itself, this would not matter if 'policy transfer' is sympathetic to local conditions. The evidence is that by design, accident or oversight it is not. The issue here is the distinction between 'common sense' and 'good sense' identified earlier. The argument is that small states should favour the latter and be more innovative in reform programme design and implementation. Of course, this does not stop small states from borrowing from the NPM menu or adapting it for their purpose. There are good examples of it in the Commonwealth Caribbean – but they should be better known in the region (and outside) and should be the norm in the reform process as a whole.

The Commonwealth Caribbean needs a modern, efficient and effective public service. It has recognised the need for public sector reform and is in the process of implementing it in nearly every state. There are many lessons that can be learnt from the experience so far. One of the most important is the need to take small size more fully on board. The literature on small state public sector reform in developing countries is sparse and scattered and comparative evaluation practically non-existent, even within regions.[3] This omission now needs to be rectified for two reasons. The first is theoretical, although with practical consequences. The existing literature on small state administration has concluded whether size is an independent variable in its own right or simply an important qualifying feature that has a bearing on the governance of small states. If it is the former then clearly more care must be taken than has been the practice so far in fashioning reform in small states. The second is practical. Public sector reform is expensive and carries substantial economic, social and political costs if it fails. The political culture of most small states tends to be conservative and considerable weight is placed on continuity in administrative practice. The difficulties of successfully introducing reform must not be underestimated. The policy environment is no less complex than in larger states. What works in one small state may not work in another. In these conditions the management of change is not simply a technical matter but one that requires a full appreciation of the cultural, historical and socio-political context peculiar to each small state. In short, a better understanding of what produces success. Only then will the political leadership of small states be persuaded to undertake and stay with the public sector reforms they need for 'good governance' and development.

Notes

1. There are 43 independent developing countries with a population of 1.5 million or less, of which 27 are in the Commonwealth. The Commonwealth also includes as small states five developing countries with a population above this figure.

2. Gordon Draper had played an important role in furthering public sector reform in the Commonwealth and the Caribbean as an academic, consultant, minister and official. He was closely associated with CAPAM in its early years.

3. Draper makes the point that up until 2001 there had 'generally been no systematic attempt to evaluates the results of reform' in the Caribbean (2001). That remains the case.

References

Anthony, Kenny (1998) *Feature Address at the Conference on Restructuring the State: Managing Tensions between Economic Reform and Social Equity*. Mimeo, Barbados.

Anthony, Kenny (2002) Address by Hon. Dr. Kenny D. Anthony, Prime Minister, at the Retreat of Cabinet Ministers and Public Sector Managers, May 21, 2002. Mimeo, St. Lucia.

Ayeni, Victor (2002) *Public Sector Reform in Developing Countries: A Handbook of Commonwealth Experiences*. Commonwealth Secretariat, London.

Baker, Randall (ed) (1992) *Public Administration in Small and Island States*. Kumarian Press, West Hartford.

Baldacchino, Godfrey and Robert Greenwood (1998) 'Introduction' in Godfrey Baldacchino and Robert Greenwood (eds), *Competing Strategies of Socio-Economic Development for Small Islands*. Institute of Island Studies, Prince Edward Island, Canada.

Baptiste, Roland (2000) 'The New Public Management and the Public Service of Trinidad and Tobago' in John LaGuerre (ed.) *Policy Change, Governance and the New Public Management*. University of the West Indies, Trinidad and Tobago.

Bissessar, Ann Marie (2001) *The Forgotten Factor: Public Servants and New Public Management in a Developing Country*. University of the West Indies, Trinidad and Tobago.

CAPAM (1999) *Reflections on the First Four Years: CAPAM 1994-1998*. Commonwealth Association for Public Administration and Management, Toronto.

CARICAD (Caribbean Centre for Development Administration) (1995) *Report of a Working Group on Public Sector Reform and Administrative Restructuring in the Caribbean Community*. CARICAD, Barbados.

Commonwealth Secretariat (1995a) *A Profile of the Public Service of Trinidad and Tobago*. Current Good Practices and New Development in Public Service Management: The Public Service Country Profile Series No.4. Commonwealth Secretariat, London.

Commonwealth Secretariat (1995b) *From Problem to Solution: Commonwealth Strategies for Reform*. Managing the Public Service: Strategies for Improvement Series No.1. Commonwealth Secretariat, London.

Commonwealth Secretariat/Commonwealth Parliamentary Association (2000) *Democracy and Small States*. Report of a Commonwealth Workshop on Deepening Democracy, Valetta, Malta, May 2000.

Commonwealth Secretariat/World Bank Joint Task Force on Small States (2000) *Small States: Meeting Challenges in the Global Economy*. Commonwealth Secretariat, London.

Draper, Gordon (1995) 'A transition in outlook for government: A culture of success (Trinidad and Tobago)' in CAPAM *Government in Transition*. The Inaugural Conference of the Commonwealth Association for Public Administration and Management, Canada, August 1994. Commonwealth Secretariat, London.

Draper, Gordon (2001) 'Situation and Future Challenges: The Caribbean Perspective'. *The Civil Service in Latin America and the Caribbean*, Draft Working Paper, August 2001.

Ghai, Yash (ed) (1990) *Public Administration and Management in Small States; Pacific Experiences*. The Commonwealth Secretariat and the University of the South Pacific, London.

Government of Barbados (1995) *Public Sector Reform*. Draft (revised) White paper on Public Sector Reform. Ministry of the Civil Service.

Government of Barbados (1996) *Blueprint for Public Sector Reform in Barbados*. Ministry of the Civil Service. Report of Meeting of Cabinet and Permanent Secretaries and Officers of Related Grade, Barbados, August 21 1996.

Government of Barbados (2000) *Public Sector Reform Activities 1995-2000: Progress Report/ Review*. Office of Public Sector Reform, September 2000.

Government of Barbados (2002) *Brief on Policy Framework for Public Service Act*. Office of Public Sector Reform, October 2002.

Government of Jamaica (1999/2000) *A Defining Year*. Annual Report of the Cabinet Office, Kingston, Jamaica.

Government of Jamaica (2000/2001) *The Change has Taken Root*. Annual Report of the Cabinet Office, Kingston, Jamaica.

Government of Jamaica (2001) Cabinet Secretary and Head of the Public Service, Jamaica, 'The Public Sector Reform Agenda in the Caribbean'. Luncheon Speech by Carlton Davis at the Conference on Changing Governance and Public Sector Reform in the Americas, Ottawa, Canada, May 2001.

Government of Jamaica (2002) *Government at your Service: Public Sector Modernisation Vision and Strategy 2002-2012*. Ministry Paper No.56, September 2002.

Government of St Lucia (1999) *Green Paper on Public Sector Reform*. Office of Public Sector Reform, St Lucia.

Government of St Lucia (2000) *White Paper on Public Sector Reform*. Office of Public Sector Reform, St Lucia.

Government of Trinidad and Tobago (1995) *Position Paper on the Role of the Service Commission in the Context of Public Service Reform in Trinidad and Tobago*. Service Commission Department.

Government of Trinidad and Tobago (1997) *Towards a New Public Administration:; A Policy agenda for the Public Service of Trinidad and Tobago*. Ministry of Public Administration and Information.

Government of Trinidad and Tobago (2002) 'Public Service Transformation Division: Strategic Intent and Organisational Structure'. Ministry of Public Administration and Information, 8/9/2002.

Jacobs, B.L. (1975) 'Administrative problems of small countries' in Percy Selwyn (ed), *Development Policy in Small Countries*. Croom Helm, London.

Kaul, Mohan (1996) 'Civil Service Reforms; learning from Commonwealth experiences', *Public Administration and Development* Vol.16.

Kaul, Mohan (1997) 'The New Public Administration: management innovation in government', *Public Administration and Development* Vol.17.

Minogue, Martin (2001) 'The internationalisation of new public management' in Willy McCourt and Martin Minogue (eds), *The Internationalization of Public Management: Reinventing the Third World State*. Edward Elgar, Cheltenham.

Murray, David (1981) 'Microstates: public administration for the small and the beautiful', *Public Administration and Development*, Vol.1.

The Kingston Declaration on Public Management in the Caribbean, 1992, Ministerial Roundtable on Public Management in the Caribbean, February 21st, 1992.

Turner, Mark and David Hulme (1997) *Governance, Administration and Development*. Macmillan, London.

UNITAR (United Nations Institute for Training and Research) (1971) *Small States and Territories: Status and Problems*. Arno Press, New York.

Warrington, Edward (guest editor) (1994) 'Symposium on the Governance of Small and Island States', *The Asian Journal of Public Administration*, Vol.16, No.1, 1994.

West Indian Commission (1992) *Time for Action*. Report of the West Indian Commission, Barbados.

Wettenhall, Roger (1999) 'Machinery of Government in Small States: Issues, Challenges and Innovatory Capacity'. Paper for the International Conference on the Governance of Small Jurisdictions, University of Malta, Valetta, November 1999.

Part 6
EDUCATION

12. A Summary of 'Teaching at Risk': Teacher Mobility and Loss in Commonwealth Member States

Kimberly Ochs

'Teachers' interaction with learners is the axis on which educational quality turns.'
VSO, 2002, p.10

1. Introduction

The link between effectiveness in education and the quality of teachers is undisputed. Teachers play a pivotal role in the education system of any country, but the role of the teacher is even more relevant in developing countries and in areas where the educational environment is challenged and learning resources are limited.

Teacher loss is a phenomenon of many Commonwealth countries, both in industrialised and in developing nations, and can be classified into five broad categories, each of which must be addressed with careful consideration of the contextual issues of the education system:

* teacher loss to developed countries;

* teacher loss to neighbouring and other developing countries;

* teacher 'drifting';

* teacher disaffection and loss due to career change; and

* teacher attrition.

This research, supported by the Commonwealth Secretariat, was designed to:

* determine the extent of teacher loss, whether for reasons of recruitment by other countries, disaffection with the teaching environment leading to career change, or death due to the HIV/AIDS epidemic;

* understand the impact of teacher mobility and teacher loss; and

- investigate practices of teacher recruitment to inform the discussion of the Draft Protocol for the Recruitment of Commonwealth Teachers.

The second section explores the following questions related to the international context: What are the important contextual issues of supply and demand in the teaching profession throughout the Commonwealth? How has the Commonwealth addressed teacher mobility and teacher loss to date? What can be learned from the work on the Commonwealth Health Code of Practice? What might be applied to the establishment of a Protocol for the Recruitment of Commonwealth Teachers?

Section 3 reports results from a Pan-Commonwealth survey of teacher loss, and includes responses from 24 per cent of the Commonwealth member nations. In addition, personal experiences of teachers were shared in focus groups with teachers from Commonwealth member countries who had been recruited to work in the United Kingdom. Important and general themes were identified in the focus groups, although the scope of this study was limited to discussions with teachers in London.

The fourth section looks more closely at the teaching profession and the dimensions of teacher loss due to recruitment, teacher disaffection, career change, and HIV/AIDS.

Section 5 draws on findings from other reports and data related to teacher loss, and focuses more specifically on the issue of teacher recruitment.

The concluding section identifies key questions for further research and gaps in the findings of this study. In addition, the Annex has an overview of key educational facts for each of the Commonwealth nations, where provided.

2. The context of teacher loss and teacher mobility

2.1 What are the important contextual issues of supply and demand in the teaching profession throughout the Commonwealth?

According to UNESCO, teachers represent some 1.6 per cent of the world's population in the age group of 15–64-year-olds, and by some estimates the largest single group of professionals in the world. More than two-thirds of these teachers are employed in developing countries (Siniscalco, 2002, p.7). In examining the context of teacher loss in all countries in the Commonwealth, it is important to address the contextual issues that drive labour mobility among teachers. Although the effects may vary from country to country, all education systems are impacted by globalisation, GATS, and the universal initiative towards Education for All. HIV/AIDS must also be addressed, given its tremendous impact on labour in certain regions of the world, particularly Africa, and its impact on specific Commonwealth countries such as Uganda, Zambia, Botswana, The Gambia, South Africa and Swaziland among others.

2.2 Globalisation

As defined by Joseph Stiglitz, globalisation is 'the removal of barriers to free trade and the closer integration of national economies' (Stiglitz, 2002). Information about work, opportunities and life experiences has become much more widely disseminated. This has encouraged the exchange of goods and services, and has inevitably influenced individual curiosity and aspirations. According to Harvard University professor Dani Rodrik, 'even a marginal liberalisation of international labour flows would create gains for the world economy' far greater than prospective gains from trade negotiations' (Fidler and Marsh, 2002, p.9). It is estimated that the benefit to workers in poorer countries would yield $200bn for the developing world, with the benefits going into workers' pockets.

One of the strategies used by developed countries to adapt to and survive in the new global economy is to improve the education system. Investment in the educational infrastructure, teacher training, and the creation of incentives to lure people to the teaching profession are common practice in many countries. School systems need good talent in the classrooms and in managerial roles to prepare pupils effectively. International studies, such as the OECD PISA study, have helped to encourage the cross-national comparison of education systems and student achievement. Such discourse is frequently related to economic prosperity, and may continue to fuel competition and the notion that teachers are crucial to train pupils and build long-term economic capacity.

2.3 GATS and teacher mobility

The General Agreement on Trade in Services (GATS) is the first multilateral agreement to provide legally enforceable rights to trade in all services, including cultural ones. It recognises four modes of service delivery:

- Mode 1: *Cross-border supply* of services supplied from one country to another (e.g. banking or architectural services provided through telecommunications or mail);

- Mode 2: *Consumption abroad* by consumers or firms using a service in another country (e.g. tourism or aircraft maintenance work);

- Mode 3: *Commercial presence* of a foreign company setting up subsidiaries to provide services in another country (e.g. insurance companies or hotel chains); and

- Mode 4: *Presence of natural persons* who travel from their own country to supply services in another (e.g. auditors, physicians, executive officers of multinational corporations, or teachers).

However, there is an important distinction to be made between liberalising the permanent movement of labour versus the temporary movement of labour. It is also a fine distinction to bring to the discussion teacher loss, which leads this author to ask 'Does the mobility of teachers and experience abroad help them to develop skills which can be brought home, or does mobility merely drain skills and create problems of inadequate human resources?'.

The economic principle behind Mode 4 of GATS is that larger differences in the prices of factors of production in international trade bring larger potential gains from opening up international trade. More specifically, the principle is that if medium and less-skilled workers, who are relatively abundant in developing countries, move and provide their services in developed countries, then potentially larger returns would be available. A team of economists led by L. Alan Winters of the University of Sussex, using an equilibrium model, suggest that if quotas were increased by an amount equal to 3 per cent of developed countries' labour forces, there would be an increase in world welfare of $US156 billion per year (Winters et al, 2002). The team argues that as the population's age and the average levels of training and education rise in developed countries, they will face a growing scarcity of less skilled labour. They advocate a Temporary Movement of Natural Persons (TMNP) to provide a strong commonality of interest between developing and developed countries (Winters et al, 2002).

Mobility among teachers, and labour in general, is not new. In developing countries, migration became more profound following independence in response to political turmoil, economic hardships, and repressive dictatorships. For others, mobility brings the opportunity of more qualifications and, in theory, more career stability. In the Caribbean region, 'microstate educators are themselves invariably trained abroad in the metropolis and usually return home imbued with the theory and content of courses which they generally seek to duplicate or reproduce, laced with the glamour accorded to international credentials' (Fentey, 2001, pp.245-56).

As the director of the Refugee Study Centre at Oxford University, Stephen Castles, points out, migration has been associated historically with periods of high growth in destination countries: 1875-1914, the 1960s and 1990s. Today, in most countries, there is a shortage of teachers. Recruitment, however, is now being done in a more organised way by governments, targeting more experienced teachers with special skills in return for 'better' compensation. Teachers from Guyana are going to Botswana and The Bahamas where remuneration is more lucrative (Guyana Chronicle Online). Teachers from India are moving to the United States, Canada and the UK.

Recruitment agencies have identified 'education' as a high-growth area in the recruitment business. The issue of teacher loss, the ramifications in the source country, and the suitability of skill transfers across different countries must be considered carefully. An important finding of this study is that when careful consideration is not given to the needs of the students, schools and teachers, recruited individuals return home, incurring greater costs and lost revenue to the recruitment firms.

2.4 'Education for All'

A worldwide commitment to 'Education for All' was first made in 1990 in Jomtien, Thailand and reconfirmed in Dakar, Senegal at the World Forum on Education of 2000. These commitments are outlined below. According to Education International, an estimated five million primary teachers will be needed to deliver the commitment on primary education in Africa alone. According to UNESCO/ILO, the population of official primary school age children has grown by more than 16 per cent in the African region south of the Sahara and 3.5 per cent in the Caribbean and Latin American regions, with an average of 9 per cent in developing countries (Siniscalco, 2002, p.7). Hence, issues around the performance of teachers, retention, training and recruitment will become very important matters of concern. The Dakar Framework for Action, issued in 2000, mentioned specifically the 'pre-eminent role' of teachers in providing quality basic education, and that this 'must entail measures to respect teachers' union rights and professional freedoms and improve their working conditions and status, notably in respect of their recruitment, initial and in-service training, remuneration and career development possibilities, as well as to allow teachers to fulfil their aspirations, social obligations and ethical responsibilities. However, fears are emerging that the 2002/03 World Bank plan has the potential to undermine governments' ability to formulate rational, appropriate national policy in this vital sphere. For example, the World Bank Action plan recommends capping teacher salaries as a percentage of per capital GDP.

As Voluntary Service Overseas (VSO) discusses in its 2002 report *What makes teachers tick?*, donors are now moving away from the paradigm of the 1980s and 1990s, providing project-based interventions and regarding education as an arena for cost-reduction (VSO, 2002). VSO also points out that the issue of access to education overshadows the issue of quality education. Recruiting new teachers will help to mitigate the issue of access, but the importance of initial training, along with on-going training and experience, must also be addressed as it relates to the quality of education received so that it is relevant to the local needs of students and the community (VSO, 2002).

2.5 HIV/AIDS

It is estimated that by the end of 2001 there were over forty million people infected by HIV/AIDS. About one-third of the people living with HIV in the world are between 15 and 24. It is estimated that about 36 per cent of Botswana's 15–49 year olds live with

---

Box 12.1. 'Education for All' commitments – Dakar 2000

- Expand improving comprehensive early childhood care and education, especially for the most vulnerable and disadvantaged children

- Ensure that by 2015 all children, particularly girls, in difficult circumstances and those belonging to ethnic minorities have access to and complete free and compulsory primary education of good quality.

- Ensure that the learning needs of all young people and adults are met through equitable access to appropriate learning and life skills programmes.

- Achieve a 50 per cent improvement in levels of adult literacy by 2015, especially for women, and equitable access to basic and continuing education for all adults.

- Eliminate gender disparities in primary and secondary education in 2015, with a focus on ensuring girls' full and equal access to and achievement in basic education of good quality.

- Improve all aspects of the quality of education and ensure excellence of all so that recognised and measurable learning outcomes are achieved by all, especially in literacy, numeracy and essential life skills.

---

the disease while Lesotho, Swaziland and Zimbabwe, all members of the Commonwealth, have 25 per cent of their population in this same age group similarly afflicted (de Rebello, 2002).These are merely estimates, as the collection of statistics on HIV/AIDS is extremely problematic. In areas of the world where testing is limited, it is difficult to verify who are infected with HIV and in many countries HIV/AIDS is not recognised as a cause of death. Rather, an affiliated illness might be reported as the cause of death, which obscures our understanding of the epidemic. HIV/AIDS has the potential to affect education, throughout the world, in several ways, as set out in the following framework by Michael Kelly (1999) of the University of Zambia, within the Commonwealth. HIV/AIDS affects:

- demand for education;

- supply of education;

- availability of resources for education;

- potential clientele for education;

- process of education;

- content of education;

- role of education;

- organisation of the school;

- planning and management of the education system; and

- donor support for education.

2.6 The context of small states

Thirty-two of the countries in the Commonwealth are classified as small states - those with a population of less than 1.5 million. The depletion of the human resource in education has the greatest immediate and prolonged impact on small states. This includes the territories in the Caribbean that are frequently targeted today as sources for teacher recruitment. Colin Brock (1988, pp.167-79) described small states in some instances as relatively remote, dependent and constrained. Mark Bray (1992) identified six factors that pose problems and challenges for small states for planning, developing and managing their systems. These are:

(1) Resource capacity: Many small states lack adequate water supplies and mineral resources, or the qualified human resources to meet their needs.

(2) Natural disaster: Hurricanes, volcanoes, earthquakes and cyclones have devastated island economies, such as Antigua.

(3) Foreign capital: Many small developing states rely on external grants and loans, and most of their available capital is owned by foreign multi-national corporations.

(4) Transport and communications: Small developing countries pay more for transportation since they do not generate sufficient volume. There are often problems generated by terrain, multi-island management, and connecting transport links.

(5) Domestic and external markets: Small country economies are dependent on foreign trade.

(6) Expenditure on administration: The achievement of an economy of scale is rarely possible.

In discussing the development of educational personnel, Charles Farrugia acknowledges factors such as a fragile infrastructure, limited resources, and a volatile economic base. However, an advantage of a small population is a wide network of personal relationships.

As Fentey Scott found in his study of head teachers, despite generous spending on educational services in the eastern Caribbean – Anguilla, Antigua, the British Virgin Islands, Dominica, Grenada and the Grenadines - it is difficult to provide for adequate training of head teachers. Most of the allocated funds go towards the expansion needs of primary and secondary level education, and to the training of primary teachers. Unlike Barbados, Trinidad and Tobago, and Jamaica, these islands do not have sufficient resources to send their heads to be trained in Barbados, which is the campus more convenient to them geographically (Scott, 2001, pp.245–56).

2.7 How has the Commonwealth addressed this issue to date?

The Draft Protocol for the Recruitment of Commonwealth Teachers (2003) emerged after a series of initiatives by Commonwealth member nations to take a holistic approach to addressing the global problem of teacher loss and a shortage of teachers.

On 14 June, 2001, a joint statement of co-operation on education and training between the government of the UK and the government of South Africa was issued to address teacher recruitment, higher education, further education and training, recognition of qualifications, and school twinning. It was signed by the then UK Secretary of State for Education and Skills Estelle Morris (MP) and Professor Kadar Asmal, Minister of Education for the Government of the Republic of South Africa. This agreement was important in setting a precedent for key areas that are also addressed in the Draft Protocol for The Recruitment of Commonwealth Teachers.

In May 2002, following a major upsurge in the recruitment of Caribbean teachers (from Barbados, Guyana, Jamaica and Trinidad) by North America and the United Kingdom, the then Minister of Education of Jamaica, Hon. Burchell Whiteman, requested the assistance of the Commonwealth Secretariat to address the problem of teacher recruitment in the Caribbean.

On 2 July, 2002, the Ministers of Education of the Commonwealth Caribbean held a meeting at the Savannah Hotel in Barbados, including representatives from Barbados, Jamaica, Grenada, St. Lucia, Cayman Islands, Trinidad and Tobago, Antigua and Barbuda and Guyana. The purpose of the meeting was to develop a uniform approach to deal with the issue of the recruitment of teachers from the Caribbean by developed countries, particularly the United States (New York) and the UK. Not all of the Caribbean islands have yet been affected by the migration of teachers, but as Jamaican Minister Whiteman stated, the problem would eventually touch each of the islands.

Issues addressed included:

- 'Brain Drain' – this is of concern particularly in specialised areas such as mathematics and science, where the local area needs to benefit from local talent in the region.

- Teachers who migrated to the US and the UK still remained Caribbean nationals. Minister Whiteman commented that their policies and systems should address matters such as job security.

Between August 2002 and February 2003, as requested in the Savannah Accord, meetings were held with the High Commissioners and a consultant was contracted to prepare the draft protocol. In September, all 54 Commonwealth member nations were surveyed to report data on teacher loss. In March 2003, the first draft of the protocol was reviewed at a meeting in the Seychelles and it was agreed that the protocol should go forward to the 15th Conference of Commonwealth Education Ministers (15CCEM). In June 2003, the draft Protocol was circulated to all members of the Commonwealth. Between July and September, this study was conducted to analyse the data gathered on teacher loss in the Commonwealth member states and to understand the dimensions of this issue in preparation for a planned discussion of a code of practice for the international recruitment of teachers, similar to the initiative championed by the health section with regard to the recruitment of health care workers.

3. Findings of the study 'Teaching at Risk in the Commonwealth'

This study was designed to satisfy two action items that were specified in the Savannah Accord:

- Conduct national research to determine the extent of teacher loss and the short and long-term impact on each country's education system and provide the outcomes of this national research to the Commonwealth Secretariat.

- Support the conduct of a Pan-Commonwealth study of the problem.

Both qualitative and quantitative research strategies were used to achieve these objectives. On 30 September, 2002, a survey was sent out to all 54 Ministers of Education within the Commonwealth, along with a copy of the report of the meeting of Ministers of Education of the Commonwealth Caribbean held in July 2002 and of the Savannah Accord. Countries were asked to provide the following data:

- total numbers in teaching force (2001–2): males, females and total;

- percentage turnover of teachers in years 2000, 2001, and 2002; and

- teacher loss in numbers due to overseas recruitment, career change, death and retirement in the years 2000, 2001, and 2002.

The analysis includes data from 13 countries and territories. Reponses were received from twelve countries and territories: Australia, Bahamas, Barbados, Canada, Jamaica, Malaysia, Montserrat (UK), New Zealand, St. Lucia, Seychelles, Swaziland, and Zambia. Canada responded to the request for information but was not able to provide data. Data for the United Kingdom were incorporated into the study and are publicly available on the website of the Department for Education and Skills and in various Office of Standards in Education (Ofsted) reports.

Focus groups were also conducted with teachers who had been recruited from developing Commonwealth countries to teach in schools in London. Due to time constraints and the feasibility of the study, in-person focus groups were only conducted in London, but included a wide sampling of teachers from different Commonwealth countries to offer insights and reflections about their career aspirations, potential disaffection with teaching in their home countries, and general commentary on the state of the education system and teaching profession in their home countries. The first of these focus groups met on 11 August at the offices of the National Union of Teachers in London. Eight Jamaican qualified teachers (five men and three women) attended the group. Their median age was 28 and they had a median of five years teaching experience in Jamaica. The second focus group met on 15 September at Hurlingham and Chelsea School in Fulham, South London and included eight teachers from South Africa, Australia, India, Canada, Ghana, and Jamaica.

3.1 Survey results from Commonwealth member nations

Whilst accepting that teacher loss and turnover are not identical, as some teachers may leave the system for a time and return later, the summary table reporting the size of the teaching force and teaching turnover is presented in Table 12.1. The data provided by the ministries of education that responded to the survey is presented with the understanding that such data is not easy to capture, but is nonetheless the most accurate that member countries have been able to provide for this study.

The highest reported turnover rate among those surveyed was in Australia. In 2001, the reported turnover rate in Australian secondary schools was more than 16 per cent. For the same year, the total turnover rate for primary and secondary schools was 14.33 per cent. Since data are not available for the UK for the year 2001, and 'the information requested is collected neither by governments nor by teacher federations' in Canada, further research would need to be conducted to make a definitive comparison (Cappon, 2002). In the findings, a distinction is made among the types of teacher loss, classifying them according to: disaffection/ career change, recruitment to developing countries, recruitment to developed countries, retirement, death, HIV/AIDS, and teacher 'drifting'. Quantitative information was not available for all respondent countries which delineated these distinctions, but the focus group discussions provided valuable information to further understanding of this situation.

Over half of the respondents did not directly answer the questions. Some provided data for 1999, and additional information such as the impact of teacher loss on certain subjects and the gender composition of teachers. This information is included in the individual country summaries, along with relevant commentary from the Savannah Meeting of education ministers, and relevant information gathered from secondary sources where available.

3.1.1 Australia

The Australian Education Union has reported that there are already shortages in regional schools and specific subject areas such as science and technical studies, but by 2005, there will be a national shortfall of 5,000 teachers (Goodfellow, 2003).About 200,000 full-time equivalent teachers were employed in schools in 1990.

Australia has also reported a tremendous loss in the teaching profession, as supported by these research findings. As stated in a recent document from the Australian Education Union: 'Across Australia there is a growing teacher shortage. Unless this issue is addressed now with a comprehensive and national approach, we will have more classrooms without teachers and a decline in the standard of the teaching profession. The

Table 12.1. Number of teachers working and percentage turnover for Commonwealth countries, 1999–2002

Country	Total population	Teaching force (2001-2002)			Percentage turnover			
		Male	Female	Total	1999	2000	2001	2002
Australia *	19,138,000	77,137	172,492	249,629	n/a	n/a	13.03	n/a
Australia **					n/a	n/a	16.15	n/a
Bahamas	304,000	969	3,384	4,353	3.70	4.10	5.50	n/a
Barbados	267,000	906	1,965	2,871	2.58	1.78	3.52	n/a
Canada	30,007,094	n/a	n/a	n/a	n/a	n/a	n/a	n/a
Jamaica	2,576,000	4,825	16,807	21,632	5.50	2.90	9.80	n/a
Malaysia	22,218,000	99,298	180,689	279,987	n/a	0.89	1.10	1.75
Montserrat (UK)	8,437	11	48	59	n/a	5.00	8.00	3.00
New Zealand	3,855,400	13,185	33,023	46,208	11.60	12.50	12.90	12.80
Seychelles	80,000	450	1,165	1,615	n/a	7.10	5.80	6.00
St Lucia*	148,000	485	1,781	2,266	6.10	6.00	4.40	n/a
St Lucia**					10.50	8.80	7.20	n/a
Swaziland	925,000	3,913	6,983	10,896	n/a	5.50	3.60	12
United Kingdom	58,789,194			438,800	14.30	15.30	n/a	n/a
Zambia	10,421,000	n/a	n/a	n/a	n/a	3.10	3.40	2.50

*primary
**secondary

solution of looking overseas to recruit is no longer possible as the shortage is a world-wide problem' (AEU, no date). The union explains teacher loss by increased disaffec-tion among teachers who have left the job early due to the increased complexity and difficulty of the job, lack of career progression, and the loss of support from employers. Real wage value for teachers has declined over these years, leaving teachers paid less than people in professions with similar training requirements. In addition, there is great concern about the retirement of teachers. Today, the average age of an Australian teacher is 43 and it is projected that the nation faces a potential loss of 30,000 teachers in the next decade (Hutchinson, 2003).

An Australian member of one of the focus groups provided additional insights into the issue of teacher migration. According to him, it was common practice for university graduates to seek a two-year holiday visa to go and explore, travel, and seek short-term or long-term employment opportunities in conjunction with teaching. In this opinion, however, this was a more common practice among younger teachers. A work permit and experience abroad was not thought to significantly impact a teacher's salary, or help a teacher get a better job, because the experience was itself so common.

3.1.2 Bahamas

The Bahamas are a small island chain close to Cuba with a population of 304,000 and where over 90 per cent of people live in urban areas. Education in the Bahamas is free and compulsory from age five to sixteen. The Bahamas reported on the absolute num-bers of teachers in schools, providing a breakdown between teachers in government schools and teachers in private schools.

Data were provided on percentage of absolute turnover, but no data were provided that explained the causes for turnover, as requested.

3.1.3 Barbados

Barbados is the most easterly of the islands group of the Caribbean, with a population of only 267,000. Barbados provided information on the total size of the teaching force. As of June 2002, there were 2,871 teachers in Barbados, 68 per cent of whom were female and 32 per cent were male. Between 1999 and 2001, there was a slight increase in the number of teachers who left the system, from 2.58 per cent in 1999 to 3.52 per cent in 2001. Barbados also reported very useful data on where leaving teachers went to work, and on the number of teachers in each of these locations:

Subject areas that experienced losses were: Business, English, General Studies, History, Fine Arts and Foreign Language. M.A. Bryan, responding for the Permanent Secretary

	Male	Female	Total
Teachers in government schools	632	2404	3036
Teachers in private schools	337	980	1317

1999	3 – Cayman Islands
	1 – Botswana
	1 – British Virgin Islands
2000	5 – Cayman Islands
	1 – British Virgin Islands
	1 – Saba
	1- Bermuda
2001	3 – Cayman Islands
	22 – New York

added, 'Generally, the Ministry has not been supporting requests from overseas recruiters where the teacher is assigned to subject areas such as Mathematics, Sciences (Chemistry, Biology, Physics), Geography and Special Education and other priority areas as may be determined from time to time'.

In Barbados and Jamaica in 2001, the largest number of teachers who were recruited went to New York State, closely followed by the UK. Although the purpose of this report is to address the issue within the Commonwealth, it is clearly a global issue. Additional data provided on the impact on subject areas, particularly teacher loss in the sciences, provided insight as to important areas for human resource development.

3.1.4 Canada

Canada responded to the request for information, but did not provide any data. Paul Cappon (2002), Director General of the Council of Ministers of Education, Canada, stated, 'It is with regret that I must inform you that Canada is unable to complete the questionnaire, since the information requested is collected neither by governments nor by teacher federations. I am aware of the importance of gathering this kind of data for Commonwealth countries, but unfortunately at this time Canada is unable to provide a report'.

Similar to Australia, Canada is particularly concerned about the demographics of the 'baby boom' generation and the retirement of teachers. For example, Ontario anticipates that it will need 3,000 secondary school mathematics and science teachers in the next ten years to replace those expected to retire. It expects to hire 9,000 – 10,000 teachers per year for the next seven years (Canada Newswire, 2003).

3.1.5 Jamaica

Jamaica has a longstanding tradition of losing its teachers to other islands in the Caribbean, such as The Bahamas, Turks and Caicos Islands, Cayman and the Virgin Islands, and in more recent times to African countries such as Botswana and Ghana (PARU, 2002). Today, there is much more concern about recruitment to the US and to the UK, and as of March 2002 it was reported that more than 600 Jamaican teachers had gone to work in US and English schools (*Daily Mail*, 2002). With a total population of 2,576,000, this is of great concern to Jamaica. Recruitment firms are, of course, targeting the most talented and experienced teachers, which is leading to even greater 'brain drain'. According to a report compiled by the Policy Analysis and Research unit, in reference to one cohort of recruits, 'Over 40 per cent of the 337 recruits [in one year] had between five and ten years' teaching experience while 30 per cent has between 10 and 20 years. Of the 116 primary school teachers, 57 per cent had over 10 years experience' (PARU, 2002).

In response to the survey for this study, Jamaica also reported on the total size of the teaching force at early childhood, primary and secondary levels by age and gender. The majority of teachers are over 30, and 46.5 per cent are over 40 years of age, indicating that the issue of retirement will become a concern in the very near future.

In addition, Jamaica reported (see Table 12.3) results on the number of teachers by subject area who left the system in 2001 in all regions, except region one.

Table 12.2. Teachers in Jamaica, by age and gender

Age	Male	Female	Total	%
18-20	36	120	156	0.7
21-30	1,666	4,837	6,503	30.0
31-40	1,162	3,753	4,915	22.7
41-50	1,328	5,340	6,668	30.8
51-60	598	2,650	3,248	15.0
61 and over	20	85	105	0.5
Missing age	15	22	37	0.2
Early childhood to secondary level	4,825	16,807	21,632	99.0

Table 12.3. Teachers leaving the system in Jamaica, by subject area

English	22.0%
History / social studies	14.4%
Science	12.8%
Mathematics	10.4%
Primary teachers	10.4%
Business education	8.8%
Industrial art	4.4%
Art & craft	3.6%
Home economics	2.4%
Agriculture	2.4%

New York state has targeted specifically to hire teachers from Jamaica. In 2001, 51 per cent of the international teacher recruits in New York came from Jamaica. In the report from the Policy Analysis and Research Unit, it was stated that:

> Many teachers in Jamaica may love their country and want to contribute to its development, but their personal situation forces them to work in the US and UK schools, which should result in an improved standard of living for them. The basic gross salary for a diploma trained teacher starts from J$406,977 to J$621,167 for a master teacher. In comparison, in 2001, teachers recruited by VIF, would have received an annual salary of between US$26,000 – 35,000 and those recruited by the NY Board of Education, a minimum salary of US$31,910 [J$1,691,230]. Presently, the Jamaican dollar is being traded at J$53 to US$1 and it takes over J$87 to buy one UK pound.

There was a significant increase in turnover among Jamaican teachers from 2.9 per cent in 2000 to 9.8 per cent in 2001. The Jamaican government has since then engaged in discussions with NY State to limit the number of recruits, but data were not available for 2002.

3.1.6 Malaysia

As reflected in the data, the total size of the teaching force increased from 267,758 to 279,987 between 2000 and 2002. However, the percentage turnover had also increased sharply, from 0.89 per cent in 2000 to 1.75 per cent in 2002. Malaysia provided figures for teacher loss due to optional retirement, resignation and compulsory retirement, but was unable to provide statistics indicating death. Shahrol Padiman, in a letter of response from the Educational Planning and Research Division commented, 'Regretfully, we are not able to identify the reasons why teachers in Malaysia resigned and chose optional retirement as they are not required to state specific reasons other than to cite 'personal reasons' for leaving the profession. Likewise, statistics indicating death among teachers are also not available as the data is not reported to our ministry'.

3.1.7 Monserrat (UK)

Monserrat is an island in the Caribbean and a protectorate of the UK, with a very small population of just over 8,000 people (2002) of which 59 are teachers. Much of the island was devastated and destroyed by a volcano in July 1995 which has continued to emit pyroplastic flows as recently as 2003. The population size – hence the teaching force – varies and has been as high as 12,000 (June 1995) and as low as 3,000 (1997) as the volcano activity continues. The country is largely engaged in rebuilding its infrastructure. In 2000, a total of two teachers left for a career change and one left for retirement. In 2001, one teacher left to go overseas and three retired. Most recently, in 2003, one teacher retired.

3.1.8 New Zealand

New Zealand responded by providing absolute numbers for teachers as of March 2002, and a breakdown of teacher loss by designation and school type for the May to May academic years ending in 1999, 2000, and 2001. Figures were startling, and indicated total attrition rates escalating from 11.6 per cent in 1999 up to 12.8 per cent in 2002. These numbers reflected teacher loss in primary, secondary, special, composite and correspondence schools. In addition, New Zealand provided information on losses among school principals (headteachers) and management. Although the trends were the same, the absolute percentages of teacher loss were lower.

3.1.9 Seychelles

Seychelles provided all of the information required. Data indicated a total of 1,615 teachers in the teaching force in 2001–2 (72 per cent female, 28 per cent males), and a decline in turnover from 7.1 per cent in 2000 to 6.0 per cent in 2002.

In absolute numbers, the greatest loss of teachers was due to career change (62 teachers), followed by overseas recruitment (20 teachers) in 2002. The absolute number of teachers who left due to career change has changed very little, whereas there was a drastic drop in the overseas recruitment between the years 2000 (43 teachers recruited) and 2003 (20 teachers recruited).

3.1.10 St Lucia

St Lucia was able to provide aggregate information on teacher loss, and also provided a breakdown of teaching force by gender and school level (2001/02) and teaching force by age for primary and secondary schools (2002). In total, 76 per cent of their teachers are female. However, the gender distribution is radically different across the school levels. 100 per cent of the primary school teachers are female, but the participation of men gradually increases with the school level, to the point where men make up 45 per cent of the teaching force in tertiary institutions. The age range of teachers is fairly evenly distributed between the ages of 20 and 50.

St Lucia was unable to provide reasons for teacher loss. As the respondent stated, 'All teachers request study leave without pay to pursue studies. No teacher thus far has indicated that the reason for requesting leave is for overseas recruitment'. St Lucia claims to have experienced no impact on teacher loss by subject. 'It has been noted by the Human Resources Management department that all teachers on their records have

Table 12.4. New Zealand teacher loss rates by designation and school type, May to May

% Loss	1998/99			1999/00			2000/01			2001/02		
	P	S	T	P	S	T	P	S	T	P	S	T
Principal	6.0	6.5	6.1	6.8	9.5	7.2	8.1	8.1	8.1	8.1	12.3	8.7
Management	6.4	7.4	7.1	6.6	7.0	6.9	7.2	7.6	7.5	8.1	8.9	8.6
Teacher	11.2	12.3	11.6	12.4	12.7	12.5	12.7	13.1	12.9	12.1	14.0	12.8
Total	9.4	9.3	9.4	9.9	9.4	9.8	10.4	9.9	10.2	10.2	11.1	10.6

P= Primary; S= Secondary; T= Total

Table 12.5. Teachers in St Lucia, by gender and teaching level

School level	Male	%	Female	%	Total
Pre-school	0	0	362	100	362
Primary	170	16	892	84	1062
Secondary	256	36	454	64	710
Tertiary	59	45	73	55	132
Total	485		1781		2266

Table 12.6. Teachers in St Lucia, by age group

Age group	# of teachers
20 years or less	10
>20 and <=30	524
>30 and <=40	503
>40 and<=50	559
>50	176
Total	1,772

left at the end of the school years. Thus no loss by subject is experienced. Replacements are normally found for the next school year.' This question was interpreted slightly differently by the St Lucian representative than it had been by other respondents.

3.1.11 Swaziland

There are 10,896 teachers in Swaziland. 64 per cent of these teachers (6,983) are female, and 36 per cent (3,913) are male. There has been a large increase in the percentage of turnover, from 5.5 per cent in 2000 to 12 per cent in 2002. Nearly four times as many teachers were lost due to death or retirement in 2002 than to career change. A very likely explanation for this reason is the impact of HIV/AIDS, but more information would need to be gathered to confirm this hypothesis. Also, it is difficult to say if sick teachers retired in anticipation of death from HIV/AIDS. In general, it is difficult to capture accurate data on HIV/AIDS- related death, particularly in countries which do not report HIV/AIDS as an actual cause of death, but instead report the symptomatic illnesses.

3.1.12 United Kingdom

As of 22 May, 2002, there were 4,480 vacancies for nursery, primary, secondary and special schools in England. According to Joy Nichols, Director of Nichols Recruitment Agency, conservative estimates state a shortage of 2,500 teachers for London schools, and possibly up to 40,000 nationally. It is anticipated that there will be a shortage of teachers with experience in the UK, since 60 per cent of current teachers are over 40.

The current rate of retirement and premature retirement in the UK is 6,100 per year, which is expected to rise to over 14,000 per year within five years (Hutchings et. al., 2002, p.182–3).

According to an Ofsted report, 'In primary schools inspected during 2001/02, an average of 32 per cent of teaching staff had left during the previous two years, while for secondary schools the equivalent figure was 30 per cent. The greatest turnover of teachers in primary and secondary schools was in inner and outer London LEAs, where about 40 per cent of teachers changed. High staff turnover is often found in schools where a high proportion of pupils are entitled to free school meals. Peter Butler, president of the National Association of Schoolmasters/Union of Women Teachers (NASUWT) believes that the shortage of teachers in Britain has been caused by inadequate pay, poor working conditions, increased workload, and violent and disruptive pupils. As Ofsted acknowledged, 'strategies to support the recruitment of teachers are more firmly established than those designed to retain teachers. Most of the LEAs surveyed have suitable induction programmes and other arrangements for newly qualified teachers and new headteachers. Few, however, have clear policies for quality assurance through providing teachers with a coherent set of programmes to extend teachers' and headteachers' professional knowledge and skills. The best LEAs recognise that there is a need to develop an attractive career package for school staff.'

In an effort to manage staffing shortages, many schools recruit temporary (supply) teachers. In primary schools in England, about 7 per cent of the teachers were on temporary contracts at the time they were inspected; the corresponding figure in secondary schools was 5 per cent. In both primary and secondary schools, the greatest proportion of temporary teachers was in inner and outer London LEAs: 10 per cent in London primary schools and 7 per cent in London secondary schools. 'A third of LEAs surveyed during the year have been actively pursuing the recruitment of overseas teachers. In London, in particular, the recruitment of overseas teachers has been vital to fill teacher vacancies. This has brought problems as well as solutions. Such teachers are not usually familiar with the National Curriculum or the national strategies, and some have significant problems with classroom management and control. Some LEAs do actively follow up schools unable to meet the training and induction needs of these teachers. In one of these LEAs, approximately one primary teacher in every six had been trained overseas.'(GoUK, 2002) According to Mr. Butler, if it had not been for teachers from Australia, New Zealand and South Africa, schools in London would have faced 'wholesale' closure (Omar, 2002).

Joy Nichols, director of Nichols Employment Agency, cites some additional reasons why the teaching profession is a less attractive profession in the UK: long and antisocial working hours, increase in administration work, high transportation costs, an erosion of authority in the classroom, limited access to affordable accommodation, and poor pay and benefits. Schools in England are interested in recruiting teachers to motivate under-achieving Afro-Caribbean children. As Labour MP Diane Abbott stated, 'It's good in a way to bring in supply teachers from the Caribbean into schools where there are large numbers of Caribbean children. It's better than bringing them in from

Eastern Europe because they've never taught in multi-cultural schools' (Omar, 2002). Percentage-wise, there are very few black teachers in Britain's schools, even in schools where the student population exceeds 80 per cent black or other ethnic minority groups (Voice, 2002). It is reportedly difficult for the DfES to gauge exactly how many overseas-trained teachers there are working in the UK, as teachers can be employed on either a work permit or working holiday visa. Most schools record personnel data independently, so that there are no central figures about where teachers received their training. In 2001, Britain issued nearly 6,000 work permits to teachers from outside the European Union, mostly to South Africa, Canada, Australia, New Zealand and the US. This number is nearly three times as many as those who were recruited in 2,000. Table 12.8 delineates the breakdown of the permits.

3.1.13 Zambia

Zambia provided data based on 20 districts out of 72, with an added note 'that even if more districts submitted, the overall picture in terms of percentages would not change much' (Chilangwa, 2002). Teacher loss was reported as per Table 12.7.

The percentage of teacher loss is on the decline. Not surprisingly, Zambia's largest cause of teacher loss is death, which is most likely strongly associated with HIV/AIDS. According to UNAIDS, as of 2001, the adult HIV infection rate is 21.5 per cent and there are an estimated 570,000 current living orphans who have lost their mother or father or both parents to AIDS and who were alive and under the age of 15 at the end of 2001.

4. Qualitative research findings – The stories of teachers through focus groups

Due to time and other constraints of this study, we were only able to examine the experiences of teachers from Commonwealth member nations who work as teachers in the United Kingdom. Two focus groups were conducted in the London area, organised by a postgraduate student at the University of Brighton.

Table 12.7. Percentage of teacher loss in Zambia, by gender

	2000			2001			2002		
	Total	Male	Female	Total	Male	Female	Total	Male	Female
Overseas recruitment	0.0	0.1	0.0	0.1	0.1	0.1	0.1	0.1	0.0
Career change	0.3	0.4	0.2	0.3	0.4	0.2	0.1	0.2	0.1
Death	2.0	2.2	1.8	2.2	2.1	2.3	1.7	1.6	1.7
Retirement	0.8	1.2	0.4	0.9	1.0	0.7	0.6	0.7	0.5
Total % Loss	3.1	3.8	2.4	3.4	3.6	3.3	2.5	2.6	2.2

Table 12.8. UK-approved work permits where job includes teacher, January 2001 to January 2003, by country of origin.

	Total population	2001	2002	2003	Total
South Africa	43,309,000	2010	2542	150	4702
Australia	19,138,000	1011	1528	140	2679
New Zealand	3,855,400	609	887	52	1548
Jamaica	2,576,000	381	530	63	974
Canada	30,007,094	348	513	37	898
Zimbabwe	12,627,000	194	325	28	547
India	1,008,937,000	130	317	10	457
Ghana	19,306,000	53	123	13	189
Nigeria	113,862,000	60	90	2	152
Kenya	30,669,000	39	77	4	120
Trinidad & Tobago	1,294,000	43	50	4	97
Pakistan	141,256,000	22	43	5	70
Mauritius	1,161,000	19	45	2	66
Uganda	23,300,000	16	22	2	40
Zambia	10,421,000	16	22	-	38
Malaysia	11,308,000	16	17	1	34
Guyana	761,000	8	21	1	30
Sri Lanka	18,924,000	10	16	-	26
Barbados	267,000	15	9	-	24
Singapore	4,405,000	9	10	-	19
Cameroon	14,876,000	10	5	-	15
St. Lucia	148,000	5	10	-	15
Namibia	1,757,000	8	6	-	14
Malawi	11,308,000	3	10	-	13
Malta	390,000	5	8	-	13
Seychelles	80,000	2	10	1	13
Sierra Leone	4,405,000	4	8	1	13
Cyprus	784,000	7	3	-	10
St. Vincent	113,000	2	5	1	8
Bangladesh	137,439,000	1	3	1	5
Tanzania	35,119,000	3	1	1	5
Swaziland	925,000	-	3	-	3
Antigua	65,000	1	1	-	2
Botswana	1,541,000	-	1	-	1
Papua New Guinea	4,809,000	1	-	-	1
Samoa	159,000	1	-	-	1
St. Kitts	38,000	1	-	-	1
Vanuatu	197,000	1	-	-	1
TOTAL		5,064	7,261	519	**12,844**

Source: Work Permits (UK) section of Home Office

A series of open-ended questions were asked to address the issue of teacher loss due to teacher disaffection, retirement, and recruitment. For these particular groups, the issue of HIV/AIDS was not relevant, it seemed, and was not mentioned in the context of the discussion. A brief survey was also administered to understand more about their personal background, and the circumstances that brought them to the UK. Twelve of the 16 who participated in the focus group completed the survey, as four had to leave the session early.

The composition of both focus groups and key findings are summarised in Table 12.9 below:

Participants spoke of their reasons for leaving their home countries and ambitions for seeking employment in the UK, their experiences with recruitment firms, and general comments about their experiences teaching in London and in their home countries.

4.1 Reasons for coming to teach in the United Kingdom

In the first focus group, a number of the Jamaicans stated that they wanted to teach in the UK as a means to get higher education. This was not a theme which emerged in the second focus group, containing teachers from South Africa, India, Canada, Australia, and Jamaica.

Almost everyone identified travel and economic opportunity as other primary reasons. Several people mentioned the relevance of the working visa. One dimension was that

Table 12.9. Composition of teacher focus groups in the UK, and some findings

# Men	9
# Women	7
Country of origin	Jamaica – 9
	South Africa – 3
	Ghana – 1
	India – 1
	Canada – 1
	Australia - 1
# Teachers who were qualified at home prior to arrival	12/12
# Teachers who would like to return home	12/12
# Teachers who would like to return home (but not to teach)	5/12
Way in which UK teaching position was identified	Internet – 4
	Newspaper - 4
	Teaching agency - 1
	Friend - 1
	Not identified - 2

it served as a good means to find relatively well-paying part-time employment as a supply teacher, and an opportunity to travel. Immediately after university, it was appealing to people in the focus groups from Australia, Ghana and South Africa. It seemed as if teaching was linked to personal development, and to the desires to learn and to experience a different culture.

Some focus group respondents did not see the opportunity to work as a teacher in England as an opportunity to further their career back home. For others, such as one teacher from India, it was essential in helping to further his opportunities when he returned home. A teacher from South Africa added: 'I think it is a springboard from here to Canada, or Australia or the United States...'

All of the people in the focus groups resigned from their positions at home as teachers, and were willing to take the risk in moving to England without having an opportunity waiting for them back home. Although for some working in England was not thought to help further their individual career, everyone agreed that working in England would help their financial status. A South African teacher added that there was a distinction between people from developing countries and developed countries as it related to financial risk and reward:

> 'I think the experience of people coming from developing countries is probably different in that sometimes we don't want to go back because the financial constraints at home are.. a lot worse and it is so nice being in a place where there is so much money, it's easy to live, financially secure, and much more stable. Whereas South Africa, every time I go back home it's more expensive. Inflation is skyrocketing. It is quite scary as a teacher when you don't get paid very well teaching...'

4.1.1 Teacher disaffection

Some teachers spoke of their frustrations with teaching conditions back home, while others spoke of their frustrations with teaching in London. All of the teachers included in the focus group were teaching in 'tough inner-city' London schools, where students have a general reputation for behavioural problems. Examples of teacher disaffection that motivated teachers to leave their home environments and seek employment in the UK included low pay and low status of the profession.

4.1.2 Discipline problems

Every individual spoke up, or nodded in agreement, on the topic of the poorly behaved and unruly children in London schools. According to one Australian teacher, 'n comparing Australian schools to London schools, 'but you call it challenging compared to here, is like a walk in the park.'

Teachers were shocked by the lack of discipline that they saw amongst the students in the inner-city London schools. One teacher spoke of being hit three times by students in his school. He continued to say that, 'When a discipline action occurs, I complete all this paperwork and nothing seems to happen. It is best not to call the child's home in some cases because you might be adding insult to injury.... My main issue back home was violence... students fighting each other, but not the teacher. Yes, you are being pressured to manage your classroom, but how can you manage your classroom if students observe you being disrespected?' According to one Jamaican teacher:

'I have been hit by students three times in my school. Three times. I remember in Jamaica standing among three boys who were throwing fists in every direction, using pens at each other, and none of them tried to hit me or stab me or anything like that...'.

Many of the teachers did not feel prepared or trained to handle the behavioural management issues simply because they did not exist at home. Both the Indian and Ghanaian participants commented that you would not have such behaviour at home. Some attributed this to the lack of parental involvement.

4.1.3 Recruitment agencies

The majority of individuals interviewed had been recruited through an agency, although some were recruited directly by a school in the Chelsea area of London. TES and Eteach.com were mentioned as websites that recruited teachers and were contracted directly by the boroughs. Recruitment agencies used several methods to recruit teachers, including advertising on the internet, recruiting via telephone, and advertising in the local Jamaican Sunday newspaper. Individuals also spoke about friends being asked to recruit individuals to take up teaching opportunities. One woman alleged that her school went to South Africa to recruit teachers, some of whom were unqualified teachers who had never spent any time in the classroom.

The following items in the Commonwealth Teacher Recruitment Protocol, adopted in 2004, show ways in which the document seeks to address the need for ethical recruitment practices on the part of recruitment businesses:

Protocol Article 3.8: The recruiting agency has an obligation to contact the intended source country in advance, and notify it of the agency's intentions. Recruiting countries will inform recruiting agencies of this obligation. Recruiting countries should inform source countries of any organised recruitment of teachers.

Protocol Article 3.9: Prior agreement should be reached between the recruitment agency and the government of the source country, regarding means of recruitment, numbers, and adherence to labour laws of the source country. Recruitment should be free from unfair discrimination and from any dishonest or misleading information, especially in regard to gender exploitation.

Protocol Article 3.15: As a targeted and responsive mode of reciprocation, bilateral agreements will provide for specific professional development opportunities or experiences for recruited teachers, who are about to return to the country of origin after a fixed term.

4.1.3.1 Information needs

The majority of recruits were given little information before coming to the United Kingdom. One Jamaican teacher was given some information on the cost of housing and other expenses, but it proved to be inadequate. As he stated,

> After I was in the job, they sent me another package about what my salary would be and the cost of living... about £200-300 a month in London. What they did not state, though, they did not tell you about council tax, and other expenses that you would incur.

It should be mentioned that the UK government initiated Quality Mark – a joint initiative between the Department of Education and Skills and Recruitment and Employment Confederation – to improve recruitment standards, but one must also address the issue of compliance with this standard (see Annex). It would appear that at least one agency which subscribes to Quality Mark, based on the focus group feedback, lapsed in its compliance to the standards and provided information which was incomplete and inadequate to at least one recruited teacher at the time of his recruitment.

4.1.3.2 Response to the needs of recruits

Teachers spoke about inconsistencies between the information they received in their home (source) countries and the information that they received upon arrival. Before arrival in the country, they were uncertain about their contractual terms. Also, qualification issues, and qualification requirements for teaching in the destination country, were unclear before arrival.

> They did not tell you about council tax, other expenses, TV licence. It just says about shopping and dining out, and that sort of thing, it doesn't give you any in-depth information. (Jamaican E)

> I arrived in this country with £100. No one told me how far the money would stretch. I arrived, met some friends, and slept on their floor for four weeks. (South African)

> One of the things I remember is that we were told that for us in our circumstances, there would be a tax-holiday type of situation where if you agree and are coming to teach for the two years, you will not be paying any taxes. Even after being here, they were still saying it – you are not supposed to be paying taxes. (Jamaican D)

Protocol Article 3.10: Wherever appointed, recruited teachers shall enjoy employment conditions not less than those of nationals of similar status and occupying similar positions.

Protocol Article 3.11: The recruited teacher is bound and subject to rules of national labour law and is also governed by any legislation or administrative rules relating to permission to work and suitability to work with children in the recruiting country.

Protocol Article 3.12: Further, where a complaints mechanism and procedure in relation to teachers' contracts of employment does not already exist in national legislation or administrative provision, one should be established for the purpose. The recruiting agency shall inform recruited teachers of the names and contact details of all teachers unions in recruiting countries.

Protocol Article 3.13: Recruited teachers should be employed by a school or educational authority. Only schools and education authorities should obtain work permits to enable the employment of recruited teachers.

Protocol Article 3.14: A recruiting country shall ensure that the newly recruited teachers are provided with adequate orientation and induction programmes, including cultural adjustment programmes, with a focus on the school and its environment.

4.1.3.3 DISCRIMINATION IN THE RECRUITMENT PROCESS

Evidence of cultural discrimination in the recruiting process was identified.

> *They wanted black teachers to work with the black children. But they were getting South African teachers to work with the Caribbean children who could not understand what they were saying. (Jamaican E)*

One black South African teacher was told by a recruitment agency that she should change her accent to make it sound more British. Her white and Indian South African colleagues had not received a similar request.

4.1.3.4 QUALIFICATIONS AND QTS REQUIREMENTS

Teachers were given very little guidance about the qualifications they would need to have to teach in the UK, or the QTS scheme, or tax issues related to pay. All of them arrived in the country as qualified, experienced teachers and were not made aware of the process required to become qualified in the UK to teach after the first four years, and the limitations of salary associated with levels of qualification.

Currently, the system is focused on the qualifications of teachers, rather than the equivalency of training and skills as a teacher.

> *I heard a story that a man... was trained like us in Jamaica, went through the rigorous training in a teacher's college, had about 15 or 16 years teaching experience, to a point where he was made head of the department. Upon arriving in the UK and contacting his school for a job, not through an agency he wanted to find a job on his own, who told him listen here now: According to our standards you are not a qualified teacher. I think it would best suit you if you seek a job as a classroom assistant. He was so angry. He said, ' How dare you tell me that! I am a teacher.' (Jamaican B)*

Not one of the people interviewed received detailed information about the QTS requirements before arriving into the UK. They were given little guidance about the process, their entitlements, and the longer term expectations about the profession.

> *It was not until recently that I started to put together the pieces of the jigsaw (South Africa)*

Protocol Article 3.10: The recruiting countries should also provide dedicated programmes to enable such teachers to achieve fully qualified status in accordance with any domestic requirements of the recruiting country.

Protocol Article 5.1: The recruited teacher has the right to transparency and full information regarding the contract of appointment. The minimum required information includes information regarding complaints procedures.

Protocol Article 5.2: Recruited teachers are in turn expected to show transparency in all dealings with their current and prospective employers, and to give adequate notice of resignation or requests for leave. Teachers also have a responsibility to inform themselves regarding all terms and conditions of current and future contracts of employment, and to comply with these.

4.1.4 Comparison of classroom standards

Inevitably, teachers spoke about their experiences teaching at home and compared them to those they have had teaching in London. Some teachers felt that they had become better teachers since they arrived in the UK and while others felt that the national curriculum has restricted their teaching to a point of deterioration and has caused them more frustration with teaching.

> *I used to get up and teach from a textbook, and no one ever worried about me. I was a terrible teacher and I have come here and realised how much more there is to teaching and how much more effort you can really put into it. (South African)*

> *The resources here compared to our resources? [There] we had one tenth of the resources. (Jamaican C)*

Both of these teachers have had positive experiences, using different resources in the classroom and learning different techniques. Others, however, have had the opposite experience:

> *I used to have students do poetry evenings. I do not feel compelled or have the interest to do that kind of thing because of the way the curriculum has you confined to certain (things) and all of that makes my job... I feel like my standard has dropped in that respect. I feel that I am conforming to the curriculum, the requirements of the curriculum rather than (being) a teacher to my students. (Jamaican D)*

This was an important finding. One of the general assumptions is that teacher mobility will lead to greater job satisfaction, not more disaffection and frustration with the profession. The Jamaican teachers, in particular, have found the British system of examinations to be very restrictive, and also have not been able to use effectively their own skills from teachers' college. The irony is that Jamaican teachers are especially sought because of the similarities between the Jamaican and English systems of education.

4.1.5 Class size

Class size was discussed briefly, but was not raised as a point for teacher disaffection per se. One teacher did make the association between classroom size and linked it to behavioural problems and the difficulty the teacher has in monitoring larger classes. For the teacher from Ghana, the class size in England was a drastic improvement.

> You are in a class of 30 whereas at home there were 20. You [have] ten less kids [in a London classroom]. (Australian)

> I think a class of 20 is just excellent because we used to have 50 or 60 back in Africa. If your class was 30 you were lucky. It would be a very posh private school to get 30 kids in a classroom. The thing is, if you tell a kid to sit down and put a pen down, he does it. He'll do it straight away. (Ghanaian)

4.1.6 Administration requirements

Besides behavioural problems among the students, teachers also mentioned administrative requirements as a key reason for job frustration.

> I also feel sometimes... you also have lots and lots of administrative work... it takes as much of my time, every day two or three hours spending on this, rather than improving my lesson. (Indian)

> Every form you fill out is not teacher-friendly. At this school... you don't get the time to sit down and prepare a good lesson. (Australian)

One teacher mentioned his previous working environment where certain staff were appointed specifically to handle the administrative tasks, which enabled the teachers to devote time to their lesson plans, working with students, and improving their methods as teachers. Others commented on the potential advantages of such a system.

4.2 Summary

This review of both quantitative and qualitative data has resulted not only in the discovery of reasons for teacher disaffection and teacher loss, but also revealed methodological issues in assessing the impact of teacher loss. The pan-Commonwealth survey and statistics available from other sources, particularly from the UK, helped us to understand the scope of the problem and determine some of the frequent paths of mobility across countries. The focus groups helped provide insight into teachers' perceptions about the profession, factors contributing to frustration, and long-term ambitions. In determining the impact of teacher loss, one needs to more fully understand both the immediate and the long-term impact of teacher loss. Are the ramifications different in losing a newly qualified teacher who wishes to obtain a working holiday permit than in losing an experienced one who is planning to retire?

Two factors are very important to consider: What is the overall population of the source country? What are the age demographics of the source country? Clearly, small states will suffer most in trying to replace already scarce human capital. However, more needs to be understood about the needs and ambitions of those teachers who choose to leave small states, and about the means which will be required to retain them. The mass retirement of experienced teachers, primarily in Canada, Australia and the US, is fuelling demand for teacher recruitment. However, in an era of globalisation and information technology, what type of teachers is needed to replace this lost capital? Do we fully understand the skills, talent, and cultural backgrounds of the teachers needed? Do they fully understand the implications of their move, the cost of living in what seems to be a new place full of opportunity? These are all areas for further research.

Additional articles in the Commonwealth Teacher Recruitment Protocol address some of these issues:

Protocol Article 3.1: It is the responsibility of the authorities in recruiting countries to manage domestic teacher supply and demand in a manner that limits the need for resort to organised recruitment in order to meet the normal demand for teachers. At the same time the right of any country to recruit teachers from wherever these may be obtained is recognised.

Protocol Article 3.2: It is recognised that the organised recruitment of teachers may be detrimental to the education systems of source countries, and to the costly human resource investments that have [been] made in teacher education. Recruiting and source countries should agree on mutually acceptable measures to mitigate any harmful impact of such recruitment. Where requested by source countries, recruiting and source countries shall enter into bi-lateral discussions and make every effort to reach an agreement which will provide for such measures. Consideration will be given to forms of assistance such as technical support for institutional strengthening, specific programmes for recruited teachers, and capacity building to increase the output of trained teachers in source countries.

Protocol Article 3.3: Recruiting countries shall make every effort to ensure that departure of recruited teachers is avoided during the course of the academic year of the source country, to prevent the disruption of teaching programmes.

5. The teaching profession and the dimensions of teacher loss due to recruitment, teacher disaffection, career change, and HIV/AIDS

Based on the findings of the data, some general statements can be made about teacher recruitment, teacher disaffection and career change. Unfortunately, due to the nature of the sample, HIV/AIDS did not come up as a point in any of the focus groups. Similarly, retirement also did not feature in the discussion apart from one Jamaican teacher briefly mentioning that he would plan to retire soon.

5.1 Recruitment agencies play a key role in teacher mobility

As the founder of one recruitment agency stated, 'International recruiting is nothing new. In the corporate world, the most sought-after position is engineers; in education, it's teachers.' The recruitment business is based on the principles of industry, and can be very profitable. The mobility of labour is a global reality and the demand for teachers remains very high throughout the world. Just as one must analyse the impact of lost resources on the organisation, one must also consider the impact of the loss of a teacher to the school and community. In the developing world, where one teacher may teach up to 70 students in a community where a teacher's role extends beyond the role of instructor to that of supervisor, HIV/AIDS counsellor, disciplinarian and community leader, the impact of teacher loss has wider implications than in industrialised societies where the teacher's role may be more limited to classroom duties.

5.2 Teacher qualifications

There is also an important distinction to be made between the qualifications needed to do 'supply teaching' (or to be a 'substitute teacher') and the requirements to teach full-time in the classroom. The different requirements of these two jobs is affecting the supply and demand for teachers and impacting on the labour issue. In the focus groups, several teachers spoke of having holiday visas, having the opportunity to travel, and earn money as supply teachers for two years. Should the qualifications and long-term ambitions of the individual teacher both be factors in the recruitment process and targeted position? These are also areas for further research.

Also, how can UK NARIC and other organisations in other countries correctly evaluate the equivalency of teacher qualifications? Anomalies exist in the current schedules for the remuneration and status of teachers from recruiting countries when they are compared to those recruited from source countries. A teacher with over ten years of experience in Jamaica may arrive as an unqualified teacher in the United Kingdom and be subjected to a different pay scale before obtaining the QTS. How can ten years of experience be assessed and understood in the new (in this case English) context?

5.3 Teacher disaffection

Several reasons were cited as to why teachers wish to migrate. These include personal ambitions to improve their financial standing, travel, gain experience, and learn from elsewhere. However, when expectations were not met, compensation was not fully understood, and conditions were worse than anticipated, teachers became disaffected in their new environments.

5.3.1 Compensation should be made clear

Teachers are tempted by recruiting agencies with offers of daily rates for teaching of between £100 and £130. For example, the average principal in Jamaica earns about J$40,000 a month (nearly £600) while the average class teacher earns in a month J$24,000 or close to £350, which is less than they would earn in a week in Britain (The Voice, 2002). However, if these supply teachers become ill or must be absent for the day, they are not paid.

5.3.2 Teachers must be motivated

Teacher mobility does bring advantages of experience and gives teachers a different perspective in the classroom. Allowing teachers to experience other teaching environments can help improve their attitudes toward teaching at home in the Caribbean region. For example, Caribbean teachers have found a lack of discipline in the New York classrooms. In theory, teachers could gain extra qualifications and beneficial experiences from their overseas experiences. However, steps need to be taken to secure such benefits. In this study, we found evidence of teachers frustrated by the requirements of qualifications, frustrated by constrictive teaching methods, and bogged down in administrative work. If they had already been frustrated about the profession before moving abroad, it is likely that they became more frustrated after moving.

Trinidad and Tobago engaged in improving teacher development programmes, sabbatical leave, assistance programmes, a revision of school management systems, and a compensation review. Guyana is pursuing a policy of teacher training and continuing efforts to improve the compensation of teachers.

As Burchell Whiteman, former Jamaican Minister of Education points out, Jamaica and the rest of the region cannot compete in terms of money, but there are other initiatives that can be undertaken. In Jamaica, scholarships were being offered to aspiring teachers and plans are being put into place to train all teachers to graduate level.

Policymakers and organisations such as VSO have encouraged people to think of teaching not as a career for life but as an occupation which might be undertaken for a period of years, before turning to or returning to another profession. Several people who were interviewed had that perception for themselves, or for their friends – that teaching was a way to travel, contribute, explore, gain better financial security, as well as serve in the classroom.

The 15th Conference of Commonwealth Education Ministers has chosen the conference theme 'Closing the Gap – Access, Inclusion and Achievement'. Similarly, the Dakar (2000) framework of 'Education for All' focused on access, equity and elimination of gender disparities but put less emphasis on the quality of education. The evidence from this report alludes to a difference between access to education, and access to quality education. The role of the teacher is paramount in providing this quality. Securing teachers requires securing their position, another motivation, and providing them with the best means to enable them to teach.

6. Recommendations for further investigation

The findings of this study provide insights into how Commonwealth countries could work together to potentially minimise the gap between teacher demand and teacher supply and counter unethical practices in the recruitment of teachers. They also helped to identify important areas requiring further investigation:

1. Further investigate the consequences of teacher mobility at home.

2. Further explore the definitions of 'teacher' and the 'teaching profession'.

3. Further explore the practices of recruitment firms, and compliance with initiatives such as the Quality Mark.

4. Explore in detail the issue of qualification requirements, and the compatibility of requirements based on the needs determined by certain jobs.

5. Investigate the true requirements for supply and permanent teachers.

References

AEU (Australian Education Union) (no date) www.aeufederal.org.au/Campaigns/teachersupply.pdf

Anderson, Omar (2002) 'More teachers set to leave', *The Weekly Gleaner*, April 10-16.

Bray, M. (1992) *Educational Planning in Small Countries*. International Institute for Educational Planning, UNESCO, Paris.

Brock, C. (1988) 'Beyond the Fringe? Small States and the Provision of Education', *Comparative Education*, 24, 2.

Canada Newswire (2003) 'Regulating body works with post-secondary institutions to respond to teacher shortage', July 16.

Cappon, Paul (2002) Letter from the Council of Ministers of Education, Canada, dated December 10, 2002 and signed by Paul Cappon, Director General.

Chilangwa, Barbara Y. (2002) Email of response addressed to the Commonwealth Secretariat, dated 30 December 2002 from Barbara Y Chilangwa, Permanent Secretary of the Ministry of Education.

Commonwealth Secretariat (2003) *DRAFT A Protocol for the Recruitment of Commonwealth Teachers*. See www.thecommonwealth.org.

Commonwealth Secretariat (2004) *Commonwealth Teacher Recruitment Protocol*. Adopted by Ministers of Education at Stoke Rochford Hall Conference Centre, Lincolnshire, United Kingdom, September 1st Commonwealth Secretariat, London.

Coulthard , M. and C. Kyriacou (2002) 'Does teaching as a career offer what students are looking for?' in Ian Menter et al (eds.) *The Crisis in Teacher Supply research and strategies for retention*. Trentham Books, Stoke on Trent, UK.

Daily Mail, Saturday March 16, 2002

de Rebello, D. (2002) Presentation to Section for Education for Sustainable Development, UNESCO, Paris, 19 February.

Degazon-Johnson, R. (2003) *'Teachers at Risk'. The Response of Commonwealth Small States to the depletion of Human Resources in their Education Sectors.* Commonwealth Secretariat, London.

Farrell, J.P. and J.B. Oliveira (1993) *Teachers in Developing Countries: Improving effectiveness and managing costs.* World Bank, Washington, DC.

Goodfellow, Nhada. (2003) 'SA heading for teacher crisis', *Adelaide Advertiser*, 16 August.

GoUK (2002) Annual report of Her Majesty's Chief Inspector of Schools: Standards and Quality in Education 2001/02, section on 'Teacher training, development and supply'.

Guyana Chronicle Online (2002) Editorial 'Finding a solution to teacher migration', 4 April 2002.

Hutchings, M., I. Menter, A. Ross, and D. Thomson (2002) 'Teacher supply and retention in London – Key findings and implications from a study carried out in six boroughs in 1998/1999' in M. Huchings et al (eds) *The Crisis in Teacher Supply research and strategies for retention.* Trentham Books, Stoke on Trent, pp.182–3.

Hutchinson, Sascha (2003) 'Ageing workforce hits home', *The Australian*, 25 August.

Kelly, M.J. (1999) 'What HIV/AIDS Can Do to Education, and What Education Can Do to HIV/AIDS'. Paper presented to the All Sub-Saharan Africa Conference on Education for All – 2000, Johannesburg, 6-10 December, 1999.

Fidler, S & Marsh, V. (2002) 'Sense of crisis as migrants keep moving', *Financial Times* 25 July, p.9.

Nichols, J. (2002) *From The Perspective of A Recruiter.* Brief prepared on 20 May, 2002.

PARU (The Policy Analysis and Research Unit) (2002) 'Recruitment of Jamaican Teachers by Overseas Agencies'. October.

Postlethwaite, T.N. (ed.) (1995) *International Encyclopedia of National Systems of Education.* Pergamon, Oxford.

Scott, F. (2001) 'Developing human resources for effective school management in small Caribbean states', *International Journal of Educational Development*, 21.

Siniscalco, M.T. (2002) *A statistical profile of the teaching profession. International Labour Office (ILO) and United Nations Educational Scientific and Cultural Organization.* UNESCO, Geneva.

Stiglitz, J. (2002) *Globalization and its Discontents.* Penguin, London.

Voice (2002) 'Plugging the Caribbean brain drain', May 20.

Voluntary Service Overseas (2002) *What makes teachers tick?* VSO, London.

Winters, L. Alan, Terrie L. Walmsley, Zhen Kun Wang, and Roman Grynberg (2002) *Negotiating the Liberalisation of the Temporary Movement of Natural Persons*, University of Sussex at Brighton, Discussion Paper 87, October.

ANNEX I

The Savannah Accord

Whereas Ministers of Education of the Commonwealth Caribbean, meeting at the Savannah in Barbados, on this the second day of July, 2002, are deeply concerned about the loss of teachers from our education systems (whether for reasons of recruitment by other countries, disaffection with the teaching environment leading to career change, or death due to the HIV/AIDS epidemic), and are in accord that swift action is needed to address this situation; conscious nevertheless of the potential opportunities for our countries available through a structured and well-managed programme of teacher exchange and of trade in skills;

We call upon our colleague Commonwealth Ministers of Education in general, and the thirty-two Ministers of Education of Small States in particular, on whose countries the depletion of the human resource in education has the greatest immediate and prolonged impact, to:

- Conduct national research to **determine the extent of teacher loss** and the short and long-term impact on each country's education system and provide the outcomes of this national research to the Commonwealth Secretariat within a three-month period from this day.

- Intensify the **sharing of information on best practice** within the member states in relation to human resource and performance management strategies affecting our teachers and our schools.

- Support **the conduct of a Pan-Commonwealth study** of the problem, findings of which shall be presented at a special session of the 15CCEM in Scotland, 2003, entitled 'Teachers at Risk'.

- **Mandate the Commonwealth Secretariat to develop a draft protocol/code of practice for the recruitment of teachers** in the Commonwealth which should include:

  - A development assistance programme by recruiting countries to compensate for the loss of human capacity.

  - Regulatory guidelines and controls for recruiters which will address the standards and quality of the recruitment process from contracting stage through orientation and induction of teachers.

- **Invite the collaboration of diplomatic representatives of Small States-** Consuls General, High Commissioners and Ambassadors – in negotiating with representatives of recruiting agencies, states and countries.

Annex 2

The Quality Mark

[*Source:* http://www.rec.uk.com/press-centre/qm.htm]

The Quality Mark is a joint initiative between the Department for Education and Skills (DfES) and the Recruitment and Employment Confederation (REC), which is an industry body for employment agencies and businesses. It is hoped that it will improve the standards of supply teachers for both the supply teachers themselves and the schools that use them.

The Quality Mark sets the minimum standards for agencies and local education authorities in such areas as the way they recruit and interview supply teachers, the way they check and manage their supply teachers, and the way they stay at the forefront of changes in the teaching sector. The REC administers and awards the Mark, in close co-operation with the DfES. All LEAs and agencies (trading for at least one year) which provide temporary teachers are eligible to apply for the Quality Mark. They will be required to submit written evidence to show that they meet the standards as outlined. Checks will be made.

The main objectives of the Quality Mark are:

- To recognise private sector supply agencies and LEAs who are able to demonstrate that they meet standards of good practice in managing and providing supply teachers for schools.

- To enable schools and temporary teachers to feel confident about the quality of the agencies and LEAs with which they are dealing.

- To raise the standards and status of supply teaching.

- To recognise the contributions made by supply teachers, agencies and LEAs in supporting schools.

As of September 2003, the following organisations have been awarded the Quality Mark:

Academy Supply Agency Ltd; Capita Education Resourcing; Celsian; Dream Education; Focus Education; GB Recruitment (Staffs) Ltd; GSL Education; ITN Teachers; Kelly Educational Staffing; Link Education Ltd; Louis Paul Recruitment; Protocol Teachers; Quay Education Services; Reed Education Professionals; Renaissance Education; Select Education Plc; SOS Education Services; Standby Teacher Services; Supply Desk; Supplynet Recruitment Ltd; Teach London; Teachers Workline; Teaching Personnel Ltd; TimePlan Education Group Ltd; and UK Teaching Appointments Ltd.

The Quality Mark Selection and Referral

Standard	Referral
1. All relevant checks are undertaken. Schools notified in writing of checks not completed.	Statement of selection and referral policy; registrations with CRB; standard check forms (e.g. for identity, permission to work, GTC registration, references, and qualifications checks); standard medical declaration.
2. A personal face-to-face interview is conducted by a trained interviewer.	Standard letters (or invitations to attend an interview); interview notes; recruitment policy statement; CVs / training records of interviewing staff.
3. Relevant induction materials are provided in writing, including a clear statement of arrangements for pay, conditions or employment and pension entitlements.	Copy of standard teacher's contract. Joining / introduction pack.
4. At least two references are followed up in all cases, including previous agencies/LEAs with whom the teacher may have been registered and Headteachers.	Standard letters. Recruitment policy statement.
5. Where an agency/LEA recruits overseas, local recruitment requirements are satisfied. Overseas teachers are familiarised with key aspects of English education provision. And, where appropriate, the standards of this Mark are fully adhered to for overseas teachers, including home country reference and criminal record checks.	Statement of policy on overseas recruitment. Exemplar induction materials for overseas teachers, to include explication of National Curriculum requirements and Key Stage standards.
6. Solicits feedback on teachers' performance from schools.	Feedback forms/ policy statement.
7. Acts on schools' comments by giving regular feedback to teachers and assists in identifying development needs.	Feedback forms/ policy statement.
8. Has procedures in place for terminating the engagement of teachers where appropriate.	Statement of management policy including child protection/discipline/complaints statement. Details of procedures for making referrals to GTC, DfES, police in cases of incompetence/ misconduct.
9. Where appropriate (i.e. LEAs), facilitates the appraisal of supply teachers who are eligible for the performance pay threshold.	Statement of management policy.
10. Provides information about opportunities for professional development.	Statement of management policy. Examples of information circulars.

Standard	Referral
11. To assist and support teachers' preparation, provides access to CPD and curriculum materials and equipment as required.	Inventory of available materials, opportunities and equipment.
12. Takes all reasonable steps to ensure teachers are provided with relevant information about schools (e.g. time table; directions; details of the class(es) they will be teaching; information about any pupils with special educational needs; other adults (i.e. teaching assistants); line management arrangements.	Induction pack. Information sought from schools.
13. Contributes to the compilation of a personal portfolio of training and development for each teacher, recording: training undertaken; assessments; qualifications; and appraisals.	Example of a personal portfolio; training policy statement.
14. Maintains knowledge and awareness of current initiatives in education.	CVs of all educationally qualified personnel (e.g. Qualified teachers).
15. Provides opportunities for specific personal development for NQTs (opportunities for induction); and overseas trained teachers (opportunities to pursue QTS through employment based training routes).	Statement of policy on Induction for NQTs and overseas teachers.
16. Provides schools with accurate teacher profile information (i.e. outlines how it will meet the school's requirements, endeavouring to provide teachers with appropriate skills and qualifications).	Copy of material sent to schools.
17. Communicates recruitment policy to schools.	Policy statement on contacts with schools.
18. Transparency in dealing with schools is important, especially in relation to charges. Agrees charges with schools and pay with teachers and informs schools in advance of any significant changes to previous rates.	Statement of policy on fees and charges. Information provided to schools on fees and charges (if difference). Copy of Terms of Business.
19. Follows up complaints and concerns (from schools and teachers) arising from the placement of teachers according to a formal complaints procedure.	Copy of complaints procedure.

Annex 3

Qualitative research interview guides

Questions by Jacqueline Clark

1. Did you have information needs, and if so, what are they?
2. What info would you have liked to have had? What surprised you?
3. Did the information that you receive change when you arrived in the UK?
4. Where were you placed?
5. If you were placed in inner-city schools, were you told about the situation?
6. What were you told about the classroom environment of the students?
7. How did you find out about QTS?
8. Whose responsibility is it to provide you with information?

Additional questions (as appropriate)

Related to above:

1. Do you have the job that you thought that you would get?
2. Are you getting the remuneration that you expected (in salary and in benefits)? How does this compare to what you were earning at home?
3. Please talk about your experience with your recruitment firm and the various people responsible for your employment.

Additional questions

1. Please describe your background and experiences as a teacher.
2. Please describe the teaching conditions in your home country.
3. What were some of your reasons for coming to the UK?
4. Does your current compensation package (including any benefits, or opportunities for further training) meet the expectations you had before you came to the UK?
5. Please describe how you learnt about the job in the UK and your process to come to the UK to teach.
6. How are you finding your job and the teaching profession in the UK?
7. How are you finding the students and the school environment?
8. Please compare what it is like to work in a school in your home country and to work in a school in England.
9. Are you pleased that you decided to move to the UK? Why or why not?
10. Would you like to go back your country? If so, why and when?

Probing questions for wider group (as suggested by Commonwealth Secretariat)

1. Can you please compare and contrast your experiences working in a developed country vs. working in a developing country?
2. Did you feel that you had adequate training to meet the needs of your new position?
3. Have you worked with the teachers union in your country of employment? If so, how?
4. Are you currently receiving any subsidies for training? Any external bursaries?
5. In your home country, did you pay for your teacher training? Did you receive any subsidies? If so, are you expected to pay back anything, in service or fees?
6. Did your contracts at home give you the option to return to your position after working abroad?

Annex 4

Estimated number of current living orphans

Estimated number of current living orphans, by country, total, from 2001 to 2001
Source: UNAIDS/WHO/UNICEF Epidemiological Fact Sheets on HIV/AIDS and STIs, September 2002

The presentation of material on the maps contained herein does not imply the expression of any opinion whatsoever on the part of the World Health Organization concerning the legal status of any country, territory, city or areas or of its authorities, or concerning the delineation of its frontiers or boundaries.

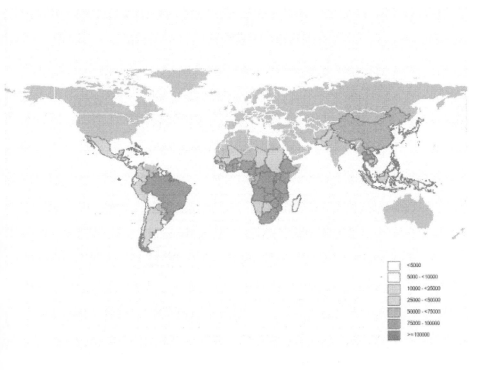

	<5000
	5000 - <10000
	10000 - <25000
	25000 - <50000
	50000 - <75000
	75000 - 100000
	>= 100000

Annex 5

Start of school year in Commonwealth countries (primary or secondary)

[*Sources:* Commonwealth Secretariat, International encyclopedia of national systems of education]

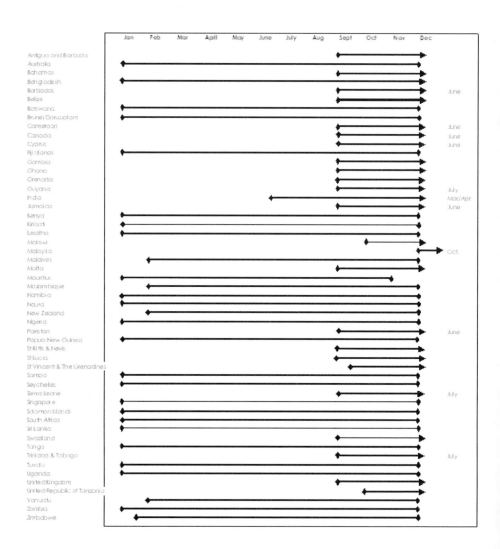

Part 7
DEVELOPMENT

13. Small States and Graduation

Eliawony J Kisanga and Carl L Mitchell

1. Introduction

The Commonwealth Secretariat (COMSEC) has played a seminal role in work associated with the vulnerability of small states and has been involved with the issue of graduation of small states from the United Nations' list of Least Developed Countries (LDCs) (Mitchell and Kisanga, 2002). Generally, these states view graduation as a shock that will have adverse repercussions on their development. As a result of this, and concomitant with the problems that small states have coping with globalisation and trade liberalisation, they offer considerable resistance to graduation.

Globalisation and trade liberalisation have accentuated graduation as an important issue for developing countries. The concerns surrounding this issue extend beyond being transferred from the list of LDCs to the list of 'more-developed countries' (MDCs) by the UN's graduation process; MDCs are also affected by graduation through the removal of special considerations with respect to financing, trade, and aid. Cognisant of the problems that graduation could impose, the UN's Economic and Social Council (ECOSOC) and its Committee for Development Policy (CDP) is in the process of developing a policy and measures for the smooth transition of graduating countries, and has indicated its willingness to work with and seek the views of other agencies in this process.

This submission presents to the CDP the views of the Commonwealth Secretariat on the graduation of small states. Small states are dominated by small island developing states (SIDS), and in this chapter these two terms are used interchangeably. The chapter examines the graduation issues of small vulnerable states, indicates future policy direction for graduation, and identifies a programme for their smooth transition. It covers:

- the graduation process and experience;

- current issues affecting the graduation of small states; and

- policy implications and measures for a smooth transition.

2. The graduation process and experience

There are two main types of graduation: graduation of countries from the UN category of LDCs to the category of MDCs; and graduation with respect to the loss of preferential treatment by International Financial Institutions (IFIs), such as the World Bank/ IMF and regional development banks (RDBs) and bi-lateral aid organisations. This chapter concentrates on the first, the graduation of countries from the list of the least-developed countries to the list of MDCs. However, some of the arguments advanced are relevant and applicable to the second type of graduation, which affects countries in the low middle–income, or more-developed category of countries (MDCs). This type of graduation is exemplified by the World Bank's graduation of countries from concessional financing of the International Development Association (IDA). This section will therefore deal with both the UN and World Bank's policies and experience with graduation.

2.1 The UN's experience with graduation

The responsibility for graduating a country rests with ECOSOC and the UN General Assembly. The Committee for Development Policy (CDP) has been mandated over the past thirty years to identify which developing countries should be considered 'least developed' and which countries should be graduated. The first set of criteria for the identification of LDCs was established by the former Committee for Development Planning in 1971. In 1991 these criteria were substantially revised and consisted of gross domestic product (GDP) per capita, Augmented Physical Quality of Life Index (APQLI), and a composite economic diversification index (EDI). A rule was recommended by the CDP that in order to be graduated a country must meet two of the three criteria for at least two consecutive triennial reviews. In 1991, the General Assembly of the UN, in resolution 46/206, endorsed the criteria and the graduation rules of the CDP. The General Assembly, aware that for some countries graduation could result in a loss of welfare, incorporated the welfare principle of optimality in the resolution, which states that a graduating country should at least be not worse off than before as a result of graduation; and stressed that there was 'a need for a smooth transition of the countries graduating out of the list of LDCs with a view to avoiding a disruption of their development paths, and invited governments and international development partners to take appropriate action for a smooth transition' (UN CDP, 2001, p.47).

Based on the application of the revised criteria, Botswana was graduated from the list of least-developed countries in 1994. In a 1997 review, four countries – Vanuatu, Samoa, Cape Verde and the Maldives – were found to be eligible for graduation. In July 1998, the Committee for Development Planning was reconstituted as the Committee for Development Policy. In its first session in 1999, the CDP proposed that the least-developed category should include countries with a low per capita income, a low level of human resource development, and a high degree of economic vulnerability. The Committee therefore replaced the EDI with an economic vulnerability index (EVI). Thus, the criteria for graduation now consist of: GDP per capita; the Augmented Physical Quality of Life Index (APQLI); and an Economic Vulnerability Index (EVI). Present requirements are: a GDP per capita of over US$1,035; an APQLI score greater than 64; and an EVI score of less than 34.

In 2000, the four countries eligible for graduation were re-examined by the CDP on the basis of the newly adopted graduation rules. Only the Maldives was recommend for graduation, while the graduation of Cape Verde was postponed for reconsideration at the next triennial review in 2003. The CDP also recommended that Senegal be added to the list of least-developed countries. ECOSOC (Resolution 2000/34) endorsed the recommendation for Senegal but decided to defer the recommendation for the Maldives to its next substantive session in 2001. At this session, it was found that the Maldives met two of the criteria, GDP and the APQLI, and therefore was eligible for graduation. However recognising the vulnerability of the Maldives, the CDP recommended to ECOSOC that the transition period for the graduation of the Maldives be extended until the next triennial review in 2003 and to consider what special assistance might be provided for that country. ECOSOC requested the CDP 'to continue its work on the methodology to be used in the identification of the least-developed countries, where appropriate in association with other international organisations working on environmental and economic vulnerability issues' (ibid, pp.44-5).

In 2000, ECOSOC had requested (Resolution 2000/34) the UN Secretary-General to make recommendations for additional measures that could be taken to ensure a smooth transition for graduating countries. A concern affecting the measures was the likely treatment of development partners, such as the World Trade Organization (WTO), the funding organisations of the UN system, the regional development banks, and the bilateral aid agencies. None of these organisations was able to say whether its policy would change and if it did change in which respect it would do so.

In 2001, the CDP recommended that ECOSOC should request relevant development partners and multilateral organisations to make available the relevant information on their likely response to a country's graduation and to urge bilateral donors to respond to the issue of 'smooth transition' before the fourth session of the CDP in 2002. These requests, it was hoped, would enable the CDP to be in a position to evaluate the potential consequences of graduation and to identify concrete measures that could be taken to ensure a smooth transition from the least-developed country status after graduation (ibid, p.52) and to make recommendations to ECOSOC for the triennial review in 2003. However, based on discussions of the progress on work done with the UN, the CDP is not expected to put in place in 2003 a package of measures for the smooth transition of graduating countries. Nevertheless, the Maldives and Cape Verde are slated for graduation in the 2003 review.

2.1.1 Botswana, a special case

The UN's experience with graduation has demonstrated flexibility and an evolutionary approach. It is obvious from this experience that the UN does not intend to penalise countries for demonstrating good economic management by graduating them if this will result in their being worse off after graduation than before. Consequently, only one country, Botswana, has been graduated, and it has become, because of its post-graduation performance, a model for graduation. Botswana, however, is a special case. Although the country has a high level of output volatility and a high degree of susceptibility to natural disasters, its relatively large landmass with extensive mineral and agricultural resources, along with good economic management, has more than compensated for its high degree of vulnerability. (With respect to COMSEC's environmental vulnerability index, Botswana rates in the higher medium vulnerability category of countries.) The IMF has pointed out that abundant diamond resources, coupled with sound macroeconomic policies, have enabled Botswana to achieve one of the highest rates of growth in the world. Over the past 30 years, real per capita GDP growth averaged more than 7 per cent a year, allowing Botswana to move from being one of the poorest countries in the world to a position of a middle–income country (IMF Article VI, 2002 consultation). Botswana also graduated in 1994, when the process of globalisation and trade liberalisation were less advanced. Thus, Botswana is not a good model or 'representative country' for graduation because of its national circumstances and changed external environment.

2.2 World Bank graduation experience and policy

The World Bank provides assistance to poor countries to enable them to reduce poverty by growing faster, more equitably, and on a sustainable basis by means of concessional lending from the International Development Association (IDA) and eligibility-to-borrow at market rates from the International Bank for Reconstruction and Development (IBRD). When countries reach certain levels of development, they are graduated from these forms of financing.

There are currently 78 IDA-eligible countries, of which 10 are small island states (Cape Verde, Dominica, Grenada, Kiribati, Maldives, Solomon Islands, St. Lucia, St. Vincent and Vanuatu). A total of 31 countries graduated during the period 1961–99. Because of adverse developments subsequent to their graduation, eight of these graduates have been granted renewed access to IDA, leaving the total net graduates during these years at 23.

A country's eligibility for IDA resources is determined by its level of poverty and its level of creditworthiness for market borrowing from both commercial sources and from the IBRD. Per capita income, as defined by the World Bank Atlas, is IDA's basic indicator for poverty, and credit worthiness is defined as 'the ability to service new external debt at market interest over the long run'. In 2000, the ceiling for IDA eligibility, which has been revised since 1964 to account for inflation, was a per capita income of $1,445. There are two exceptions to the per capita income operational cut off for graduation: (a) 'gap countries' – countries with incomes above the operational cut-off but which are not creditworthy for IBRD lending, and might therefore find themselves without access to either IBRD or IDA resources for their development; and (b) small island countries which face special size-related problems and which have little or no access to bank group assistance because of their limited creditworthiness for IBRD lending. These countries are eligible for full concessionary treatment by the World Bank.

Less concessional terms are given to a third category: 'blend countries', which are countries that are IDA-eligible on the income criterion, but which have also been creditworthy for limited IBRD lending. These countries have access to IDA but are also able to borrow from the IBRD. Currently the four small islands of Dominica, Grenada, St. Lucia, and St.Vincent and the Grenadines are blend countries. IDA credits to blend countries have had 35 years maturity and 10 year's grace in comparison with 40 years maturity and 10 year's grace for IDA-only countries. This has created only a marginal difference (3 per cent) in concessionality between IDA-only and blend countries.

The process of graduation from IDA is normally triggered when a country exceeds the operational per capita income guideline. Because income levels fluctuate, countries normally begin a graduation process that lasts several (three to five) years. This approach avoids situations in which income fluctuations could allow intermittent access to IDA financing and recognises that a sudden termination of IDA would not be desirable from a developmental point of view. When IDA determines that a country should graduate, a graduation programme is formulated consisting of:

- a phase-out for IDA lending;

- a phase-in for IBRD lending;

- special economic and sector work (ESW) and technical assistance to help address transition issues, such as improving access to commercial sources of lending;

- increased role for the Multilateral Investment Guarantee Agency (MIGA) and the International Finance Corporation (IFC) to improve private sector capital inflows; and

- application of triggers to accelerate the repayment of IDA credits.

Each of these measures, with the exception of the last one, is tailored to suit the particular circumstances of the country.

2.3. A comparative analysis of the UN and the World Bank approaches to graduation

The experience with graduation from both the UN and the World Bank perspectives indicates that the decision to graduate a country is not an automatic one and rests on a combination of factors. There are some similarities and differences, however, between the UN and the World Bank's approaches to graduation. A comparison of both approaches reveals that the World Bank:

- has a higher per capita threshold for graduation ($1,445 in comparison with $1,035);

- provides special treatment for small island states and 'gap' countries (that include small states) by exempting them from the per capita cut off for graduation;

- makes provision for a longer transition period for graduation (three to five years in comparison with three for the UN); and

- has a specific programme for a smooth transition.

The World Bank has graduated many more countries than has the UN, and its experience has demonstrated that graduation can be transient in nature – about one third of the countries graduated had their old status reinstated. This comparative analysis exposes three main inadequacies of the UN's approach to graduation: (a) the criteria for graduation are limited to economic vulnerability and do not make provisions for environmental vulnerability; (b) it presently lacks a programme for a smooth transition; and (c) the transition period of three years is too short.

The criteria for graduation are evolving because of the new economic forces in the world economy and the recognition that vulnerability is an important factor in determining the development prospects of nations. The LDCs are regarded as the most vulnerable countries and so have the most difficulties coping with global exogenous factors. The UN has attempted to compensate for the effects of the new forces by extending the confidence limits on the criteria for graduation and by a consideration of special circumstances in an environmental profile of the country on the threshold of graduation. The threshold limits are 15 per cent above those for inclusion on the list. In the case of per capita GDP, this still results in a threshold that is 28 per cent lower than the World Bank's threshold for graduation.

Despite the environmental profile, the question of vulnerability is still not satisfactorily tackled. The UN's vulnerability index is an economic index (EVI) and does not capture ecological fragility. It is based on population data, the share of manufacturing and services in GDP, export concentration, agricultural instability and export instability. Despite not taking environmental vulnerability into consideration, the results from the EVI place all the states slated for graduation into the vulnerable and highly vulnerable category of countries. The UN rates countries with EVI scores between 31 and 36 as vulnerable and those over 36 as highly vulnerable. Scores for the graduation candidates were as follows: Cape Verde 56.89; Samoa 52.45; Vanuatu 41.31; and the Maldives 32.18.

3. Current issues affecting the graduation of small states

The major issues of graduation for small states emanate from: (a) the loss of preferential treatment for trade, aid, and financing associated with LDC status; and (b) their vulnerability, which could jeopardise their post-graduation growth and hinder their sustainable development. These issues have been identified by SIDS as follows: (a) graduation can hinder the process of coping with and benefiting from globalisation and trade liberalisation, since the two sectors most affected by graduation are the trade sector, particularly commodity exports, and the government sector, because of the adverse effects of graduation on Official Development Assistance (ODA); (b) graduation can exert adverse influences on sustainable development; and (c), given (a) and (b), graduation could impose an added shock to their already vulnerable economies.

3.1 Globalisation and trade liberalisation and integration

SIDS are experiencing serious problems adjusting to the global forces of trade liberalisation and economic integration. These two forces have brought about a new world economic regime characterised by the following.

- The creation of large world market blocs covering North America (NAFTA) and its extension to the Free Trade Area of the Americas (FTAA), Europe (EU), and Asia (APEC – the Asia-Pacific Economic Co-operation Forum).

- The decrease of external trade protection brought about by the Uruguay Round of the General Agreement on Tariffs and Trade (GATT) and the international regulation of trade by the World Trade Organisation (WTO).

- The new worldwide economic orthodoxy, advocated and championed by the World Bank and the International Monetary Fund (IMF), whereby there is a greater reliance on market forces and private enterprise for development.

For most SIDS, trade was conducted under protected and preferential trade regimes, a legacy of their colonial past. As a result of their protected trade regimes and their economic vulnerability, SIDS have been most affected by changes in the global trading regime, particularly by the global forces of trade liberalisation and economic integration, which have been instrumental in creating the large world market blocs (Mitchell and Hinds, 1999, pp.235–44).

The liberalising of trade involves employing measures to increase international competitiveness – such as the removal of trade restrictions, the unification of effective rates of protection, and, if necessary, currency devaluation. These measures, combined with the new economic orthodoxy of curtailing government expenditure and placing a greater reliance on private enterprise for development, severely constrain the capacity of SIDS to implement actions that would solve their problems effectively. Graduation, by its effects on trade, adds another dimension to the adjustment problems faced by SIDS.

3.2 Graduation and sustainable development

It has been internationally accepted that small states, because of their economic and environmental vulnerability, have peculiar developmental problems that severely affect their ability to implement the measures necessary for attaining sustainable development as recommended in UNCED's Agenda 21. This has been recognised by the Commission on Sustainable Development (CSD), and in 1994, the Barbados Programme of Action (BPOA) was developed. The BPOA called for national, regional and international action in 14 priority areas. These range from sectoral concerns such as freshwater, climate change, biodiversity, marine resources and tourism, to cross-cutting issues such as human resource development, and financing and support needed to put the plan into action (UN, 1999).

In 1999, the UN General Assembly Special Session on SIDS found that although there had been international acceptance of the BPOA, its implementation was disappointing. SIDS had established national environmental action plans (NEAPS), and there was considerable progress in strengthening regional indigenous institutions for sustainable development. At the international level, however, the level of funding necessary never materialised. The Assembly therefore called on the Secretary General to improve the existing institutional arrangements in the UN to effectively support SIDS in a more proactive way. It highlighted the impact of globalisation, trade liberalisation and the erosion and/or loss of preferential treatment in economic relations (UN, 1999b). It appealed to the highly developed countries (HDCs) to provide more tangible support to the BPOA. At the World Summit on Sustainable Development (WSSD) in Johannesburg in August–September 2002, it was acknowledged that more support was necessary for the BPOA, but there were no concrete measures to ensure that this support was forthcoming. However, there was a decision for a comprehensive review of the programme in 2004, its tenth anniversary.

The economic performance of small states has worsened with globalisation, trade liberalisation, and the pursuit of sustainable development. This can be realised by a comparison of growth rates for small states before and after 1995. From 1995-2001, World Bank/IMF data (World Bank, 2001; IMF, 1995-2001) indicated that the growth rates of GDP for most SIDS declined significantly in comparison with the growth rates for the period 1985-1994; and there was a deteriorating balance of commodity trade as growth rates for SIDS exports declined in comparison with imports. This evidence indicates that SIDS have not profited from the gains made in world trade as a result of trade liberalisation. However, graduation can exacerbate trade difficulties and growth problems for small states. Thus graduation can affect sustainable development in two ways: it can reduce growth; and it can retard growth by making it more difficult for economies to be resilient in the face of external shocks. Given the economic shocks from globalisation and trade liberalisation and from the requirements of sustainable development, there are legitimate concerns from countries selected for graduation that this will impose another serious shock on their economies.

3.3. The economic impact of graduation

Graduation affects trade, aid and financing, and development. Thus its economic impact is felt most acutely in the trade and government sectors of the economy, two sectors that play leading roles in the economic development of SIDS.

3.3.1. The impact of graduation on commodity trade

Under the GATT and the WTO, developing countries enjoy special treatment from the Generalized System of Preferences (GSP) and the Global System of Trade Preferences (GSTP). Under the GSP, developed countries offer non-reciprocal preferential treatment to products originating in the developing countries. Under the WTO there is special and differential treatment for the LDCs over and above the special provisions for developing countries, and the WTO also assists the LDCs with measures to facilitate their greater participation in its deliberations and in building up their trade capacity. The UN and its agencies, such as UNCTAD and UNDP, provide special and differential treatment to the LDCs, such as lower membership fees and financial assistance for LDCs' representation at critical international meetings. UNCTAD provides technical assistance and market intelligence for niche markets to the LDCs.

Graduation will therefore affect the trade in goods or commodities and not the trade in services. With respect to the trade in goods, graduation will affect exports rather than imports. This will worsen the terms of trade situation, since imports generally have a high-income inelasticity, with serious ramifications for the balance of trade and payments.

3.3.2. The impact of graduation on the government sector

The impact of graduation on the government sector will be due to its effects on external sources of funding for the financing of the government's current and capital account. Donor agencies have demonstrated a preference for serving the LDCs in their programmes as the recipients most in need and deserving of aid, and many have aid programmes that offer more concessional terms to LDCs than to MDCs. There are also special programmes devoted to the LDCs by UN agencies and other bodies subsidiary to or related to the UN (e.g., IMO, ITU, UNESCO, UNCTAD, UNDP and ESCAP), by other multilateral institutions, and by bilateral donors and some international NGOs. Some of these institutions also facilitate the participation of LDCs in international conferences, seminars, and training programmes, and help donor agencies in coordinating assistance to the LDCs. With respect to assistance from UN agencies, these agencies will have to conform to UN policies for MDCs that impose more stringent conditions than do policies for the LDCs.

With the loss of concessionary financing from foreign aid, graduated countries will have to rely on non-concessionary financing and on the open market. Higher interest rates and shorter repayment periods will significantly increase the cost of capital and lower capital efficiency in the economy. In turn, this will increase the debt burden and increase the capital account deficit.

These effects will depend on whether or not there is a high dependence of government finances on trade, aid and grants and concessional loans. If there is a high dependence, graduation can adversely affect the overall government financial situation and the budget's deficit or surplus situation. SIDS are highly dependent on aid and are the highest per capita aid recipients in the world.

3.3.3. The impact of graduation on the economy

The total costs of graduation, due to their impact on trade, government operations, and the growth rate of the economy, could be significant and, even if they were not, could lead to deterioration in the economic fundamentals and place a damper on long-term growth. Graduation can push a country off its long-term growth path, from which recovery might be difficult, particularly in the short run. In fact, the main implication of graduation is that it can impose an external shock on the graduating economy that will adversely affect future growth. **One of the major lessons emanating from the World Bank's experience with graduation is that a country should graduate when its economy is on an upturn with respect to growth of GDP. If the country is on a downturn, then the economy could slide back to its non-graduation category.**

The adverse effects of graduation are dependent on the magnitude and diversity of exports and ODA, which differ among states. SIDS, with their narrow export trade base, large government sector (with trade and government being the largest source of employment), and a relatively high aid:dependence ratio, are most likely to be adversely affected by graduation than are other countries.

The Commonwealth Secretariat's work in assisting with the preparation of the Maldives Memorandum on graduation to the UN (Appendix 1) revealed that graduation would dampen growth, and given the fact that the economy had been in a downturn in recent years, this would be a most inopportune time for graduating this country. All the countries slated for graduation, with one exception, had experienced slower and more volatile growth rates during the 2000s than before (Table 13.1).

The recent economic performance of these countries suggests unstable growth, with a resulting high probability that if these countries are graduated they could experience negative growth rates and revert to their pre-graduation status. The World Bank's experience with graduation certainly exemplifies that this phenomenon is possible.

4. Policy implications of graduation and measures for a smooth transition

The main implication of graduation is that it can impose an external shock on the graduating economy that will affect future growth. This is the reason why there has been resistance to graduation by the countries recommended for it. This resistance indicates the need for the UN to re-examine and rethink its graduation policy, as well as the requirements and measures for a smooth transition. Graduating countries also have to develop a policy and strategy for graduation and a capacity for implementing measures for a smooth transition.

Table 13.1. Growth rates in real GDP, graduation candidate countries, 1988–2002

	1998	1999	2000	Est. 2001	Est. 2002
	Per cent				
Cape Verde	7.4	8.5	6.8	3.3	4.5
Maldives	9.8	7.2	4.8	3.5	4.3
Samoa	3.4	5.6	6.8	6.0	n.a
Vanuatu	3.0	-2.1	2.5	-1.9	-0.3

Source: IMF Article IV consultation reports

4.1. The need for rethinking UN graduation policy

The resistance to graduation indicates the need to revisit the whole issue of LDC status and graduation, particularly in light of the problems that LDCs have and are encountering as a result of globalisation and trade liberalisation that transcend the UN classification of states. To weather the effects of globalisation, developing countries will have to increase their international competitiveness and rely more on market forces and private enterprise for development. Small states suffer from some disadvantages in this regard. There are few areas in which small states can be internationally competitive; and a recent study by COMSEC has highlighted the problems that small states have in attracting private foreign investment (Commonwealth Secretariat (2002a). This combination imposes serious constraints on small states in terms of improving their international competitiveness, particularly in the short run. Yet, the future of small states in a global context is at stake unless they can be competitive in the global marketplace. This accentuates the role of graduation and the UN's future approach to this issue.

It is recognised by international organisations, including the WTO, that developing countries will require a longer transition period for making these changes than will the developed countries. The WTO allows transition periods of 10 years' duration in certain cases. The UN's transition period for graduation is only three years, and graduation will affect the sectors that will be most vulnerable to the global forces (trade and investment). This, and other aspects of the UN's policy on graduation, suggests that the UN should change its policy on graduation. The change in policy should involve special treatment for small vulnerable states since it is essential that the UN should view small states' vulnerability as an operational rather than a theoretical concept. The two major elements of the policy change are: (a) increasing the threshold requirements for small vulnerable states by amending the criteria for their graduation, and (b) introducing measures for a smooth transition.

4.1.1. Amending the criteria for graduation of small states

The need to amend the criteria for graduation is based on the differential treatment accorded small vulnerable states in comparison with larger ones. The measures required are the following: (a) increase the per capita income threshold for small states, and; (b) establish a composite vulnerability index by combining the results of economic and vulnerability indices.

(a) The UN's per capita income threshold for graduation of all states should be increased to the same level as the World Bank's and a higher rate should apply to small vulnerable states. The two-tier levels should be amended on a triennial basis by ECOSOC.

(b) The UN should replace the EVI by a composite vulnerability index based on economic and environmental indices. The Commonwealth Secretariat has developed and applied a composite vulnerability index (CVI) to developing countries (Commonwealth Secretariat (2000b). It is based on sound economic precepts and appropriate statistical procedures and consists of two main components: a vulnerability impact index (VII); and a resilience indicator. The vulnerability impact index covers three broad areas: economic exposure, remoteness and insularity, and susceptibility to environmental events and hazards. The Commonwealth Secretariat also provided an environmental index for developing states and island states (Aitkins et al, 2002, Annex IV) based on a number of environmental indicators selected to capture the pressures that exist on the natural environment of a particular state. These Commonwealth indices provide models for or can be adopted by the UN to establish a more comprehensive vulnerability index for graduation.

4.2. UN measures for a smooth transition

The transition constitutes a critical period in the graduation process, and this has been recognised by the UN. The two requirements for this period are for the UN to increase the transition period to five years, and to introduce specific measures to ensure a smooth transition during that period. The specific UN measures for a smooth transition are:

1. Fiscal and budgetary support. Support to governments to prevent budget deficits over the transition period will go a long way toward cushioning the effects on the government sector.

2. Access to soft funding from the World Bank/IMF and from IFIs (similar to treatment for 'countries in transition').

3. Provision of a social safety net. This could include retraining programmes if employment and job dislocations occur.

4. Encourage the participation of the international community, particularly IFIs and bilateral aid agencies, in transition programmes by establishing specific policies and programmes that are directed to the transition period.

These measures need not be universal and their applicability will depend on the particular problems faced by individual graduating states. However, a UN graduation transition programme covering a five-year period will help to allay the fears, whether real or imagined, that countries have of graduating.

4.3. National measures for the smooth transition

Recognising that graduation can impose an economic shock on graduating countries, the UN has accepted the need for a transition period. This period is currently a three-year one, and the CDP is in the process of examining measures that can be taken to ensure a smooth transition for graduating countries. However, it is not expected that these measures will be presented or put in place in the next triennial review this year. Nevertheless, the requirements for a smooth transition are those that will address the major issues of graduation. Essentially, they should enable the greater integration of the graduating countries with the global economy by means of trade liberalisation and development assistance. Since graduation will affect trade, government, and aid, the requirements will be both external and internal. They should also make allowances for any internal dislocation in the trade and other sectors of their economies that might ensue from graduation.

With respect to trade, the need is to maintain access to traditional markets or secure access to new markets on terms that will not be disruptive to the country in transition. The national objective is that of improving international competitiveness with measures designed to attain greater efficiency in the export industries. Trade policy has to aim at increasing exports of goods and services, with services featuring prominently since this is an area in which small states can be internationally competitive. Small states will require the capacity to participate actively in trade negotiations and in the WTO.

With respect to government, the loss to government revenues from the reduction in trade and aid or in access to concessionary financing can adversely affect the budget and balance-of-payments situation. Thus it is essential that the government should pursue a sustainable development strategy, accompanied by progressive fiscal policies and measures. These policies and measures should provide for an enabling environment for private sector development which would play a crucial role in the developmental process and during the transition period.

With respect to aid, governments should make a concerted effort to attract more aid from bi-lateral and multi-lateral donor agencies. It would be useful if aid agencies viewed the transition as a period requiring special attention and were prepared to assist countries on the threshold with special programmes to assist in the transition, such as the formulation of a strategy and plan for this period. This could be patterned after disaster assistance, including short-term, specific-to-graduation issues.

These requirements for trade, government revenue and aid indicate that countries declared eligible for graduation will have to develop a strategy and programme for graduation. From a small states standpoint, it is evident that an appropriate programme for tackling graduation-related problems will require: improved negotiation capacity for small states in trade, aid and development; improved institutional capacity to plan for the effective implementation of graduation measures; and the effective implementation of measures to effect a smooth transition. These constitute further costs of graduation but they can be tempered by UN measures for a smooth transition.

4.4. Strengthening the capacity to negotiate and implement graduation

The most effective case a country can make for postponing graduation will be based on whether or not the country will be worse off as a result, in the medium and long run. If the country will be worse off, then graduation will contravene the principle of optimality in UN resolution 46/206. It is essential, therefore, that countries recommended for graduation should have an objective assessment made of the economic impacts of graduation. The UN has not developed a methodology to do so but the approach should be based on measuring the benefits and costs associated with graduation and then analysing their impact on growth and employment over the short and medium term.

In the planning phase, the country should undertake a study on the environmental and economic impact of graduation to determine the negotiating strategy and the measures to be taken to minimise the detrimental effects. In the past, UN agencies such as the UNDP have conducted impact studies on countries eligible for graduation on behalf of ECOSOC. It is important, however, that an eligible country should do its own study and, based on its findings, present its case and negotiate favourable conditions for graduating with the ECOSOC. Funds from UN or donor agencies could provide financing for this study. In the case of the Maldives, a study was done for the GOM under COMSEC's Technical Assistance Programme.

Small economies have had serious problems with effective representation at international fora due to the lack of professional negotiators and the costs involved. This has been realised by UN agencies and the WTO and they have made provisions for both participation and training. There should be similar arrangements for providing assistance for improving the negotiating capacity of small economies slated for graduation, particularly since graduation issues are so strongly related to trade issues and concerns.

4.5. Main findings and recommendations

The main findings from the analysis of the graduation issues for small vulnerable states are the following.

1. Graduation places countries in the category of 'countries in transition' but without the supporting provisions, mechanisms and services accorded these countries.

2. Graduation should be considered within the context of globalisation and trade liberalisation (WTO agreements). Although the trade in goods will be the most affected, the trade in services will also be affected by OECD regulations against harmful taxation. Small states may well be told that they cannot give concessions to attract foreign investment.

3. The UN criteria for graduation are still flexible and evolving. It is recognised that the EVI does not account adequately for vulnerability and that environmental considerations should be taken into account. The UN should combine its EVI with an appropriate environmental index for this purpose.

4. A comparison of the transitional arrangements for trade by the WTO (and for graduation by the World Bank/IMF) indicates that they are more favourable than the UN's in terms of the length of the transition period, threshold requirements, and supportive mechanisms.

5. It is obvious from the experience with graduation that the UN does not intend to penalise countries for demonstrating good economic management by graduating them, if this will result in their being worse off after graduation than before. Hence the concerns about a smooth transition. However, the CDP is not expected to put

in place, in 2003, a package of measures for the smooth transition of graduating countries. Given this situation, countries should not be graduated before these measures are in place.

6. Graduating countries have to develop a strategy to cope with graduation and with the transition period. This will require increased capacity to negotiate, manage and implement measures that will assist with a smooth transition.

Based on the above findings, the following recommendations are made by the Commonwealth Secretariat to the UN.

1. Amend the criteria for the graduation of small vulnerable countries to reflect more appropriately the constraints of their vulnerability. Specifically, their threshold requirements should be raised.

2. Extend the period of transition to five years or more.

3. Provide a transition programme based on the measures identified in this submission.

4. Seek ancillary support for the transition period from the World Bank/IMF, multilateral development banks, and bilateral donor agencies.

Selected bibliography

Commonwealth Secretariat (2002a) *Lowering the Threshold: Reducing the cost and risk of private investment in least developed, small vulnerable economies.* Commonwealth Secretariat, London.

Commonwealth Secretariat (2002b) *International Tax Competition: Globalisation and Fiscal Sovereignty,* R. Biswas (ed.). Commonwealth Secretariat,, London.

Commonwealth Secretariat/World Bank (2002), *Small States in the Global Economy,* David Peretz, Rumman Faruqi and Eliawony Kisanga (eds.). Commonwealth Secretariat, London.

Aitkins, J.P., S. Mazzi and C.D. Easter (2002) 'Small States: A Composite Vulnerability Index', in *Small States in the Global Economy,* David Peretz, Rumman Faruqi and Eliawony Kisanga (eds). Commonwealth Secretariat, London.

Easterly, W. and A. Kraay (2000) 'Small States, Small Problems? Income, Growth and Volatility in Small States', *in Small States in the Global Economy,* David Peretz, Rumman Faruqi and Eliawony Kisanga (eds.). Commonwealth Secretariat, London.

IMF (1995-2001) *Direction of Trade Statistics.* IMF, Washington.

Mitchell, C.L. and L.O. Hinds (1999) 'Small island states and sustainable development of ocean resources', in *Natural Resources Forum* Vol.23, No.3.

Mitchell, C.L and E.J. Kisanga (2002) 'The Graduation Issue for Small States' in *Small States: Economic Review and Basic Statistics* Volume 7. Commonwealth Secretariat, London.

South Pacific Applied Geoscience Commission (2002) *Towards Managing Environmental Vulnerability in Small Island Developing States.* Concept Paper. South Pacific Applied Geoscience Commission, Fiji.

UN (1999a) *Small Island States: Programme of Action.* UN, New York.

UN (1999b) *Vulnerability and Poverty in a Global Economy.* UN, New York.

UN CDP (2001) *Participatory Development and Governance: Africa's Special Needs.* Report of the Committee for Development Policy on the third session (2-6 April, 2001), New York.

World Bank (2001) *Atlas 2001.* World Bank, Washington.

Appendix I

The Maldivian experience with graduation

The UN recommended in 1997 that The Maldives be graduated from the list of Least Developed Countries (LDCs). Because of a conjuncture of circumstances, namely changes in the criteria for graduation and representation from the Government of the Maldives (GoM) against the recommendation for graduation, the graduation of the Maldives was postponed until 2003. However, the UN had indicated that the period from 2001 to 2003 might be the transition period for graduation of the Maldives. This appendix examines the case made by the GoM's Memorandum to the UN against graduation and the possible impact of graduation on future growth. It covers the following: (1) the economic background to graduation; (2) vulnerability and sustainable development; (3) the costs of graduation; and (4) the implications for sustainable development and growth.

1. The economic background to graduation

The economic performance of the Maldives slowed down during the 1990s in comparison with the growth that was experienced during the 1980s. The average rate of real growth (constant 1995 Rufiyaas) for the period 1990–2000 was 7.1 per cent in comparison with 10 per cent for the 1980s. The overall economic performance increased per capita incomes and improved economic conditions. This growth was unbalanced regionally, its effects being felt mainly in Malé, leading to the perpetuation of serious regional disparities accompanied by an increased dependence on expatriate and foreign labour.

The two sectors of the economy that will be most affected by the graduation issue are trade and government operations, both of which are critical to growth and development in the Maldives.

1.1 Trade and government performance, 1990-2000

The trade situation during the period 1990–2000 reveals that: (a) there is a substantial imbalance in the trade of goods in the Maldives, with imports far exceeding exports; (b) there is a very favourable balance in the trade of services, where tourism predominates, but this is insufficient to bring about a favourable current account of the balance of payments; and (c) the overall balance of payments, which was positive for most of the period, relies on the inflow of capital in the form of grants, loans and remittances.

The merchandise trade of the Maldives is dominated by imports rather than by exports. Imports increased at an average rate of growth of 10.4 per cent a year during the period. In comparison, domestic exports increased at an average rate of growth of 3.6 per cent a year. This is indicative of a worsening of the terms of trade during the period, the resulting imbalance not being compensated for by the trade in services, in which tourism plays a significant role. The export trade consists of only two major commodities: fish products and textile (garments) products. The major markets are Europe and the US, respectively, and the exports enjoy preferential treatment because of LDC status.

Government plays a commanding role in the development of the Maldives, and good developmental policies and sound financial management have been largely responsible for the exceptional growth performance. The government is the largest employer of labour in the economy: over 20,000 people are employed, including security personnel. Government's total revenues and grants increased from $46.4 million in 1990 to $210.3 million in 2000, at an average rate of

15.1 per cent a year; and total expenditures and net lending increased from $60.9 million to $235.8 million, at an average rate of 13.5 per cent a year. The government sector has relied heavily on foreign assistance for the implementation of many of its programmes. However, there are problems associated with aid, which have been identified as follows: withdrawal of donors, reduction in the level of multilateral assistance, an increasing reliance on a small number of donors, and unpredictability of aid programmes.

2. Vulnerability and sustainable development

The UN decision to graduate the Maldives was the result of the application of new criteria for graduation. The new criteria were: GDP per capita; the Augmented Physical Quality of Life Index (APQLI); and an Economic Vulnerability Index (EVI). The Maldives met all these criteria. However, of critical concern to the Maldives is its EVI rating, which does not adequately reflect its environmental fragility. This fragility, if taken into account, would indicate that the Maldives is one of the most vulnerable countries in the world. This vulnerability has important implications for sustainable development, to which the Maldives is committed.

2.1 The implications of sustainable development

The pursuit of the objective of sustainable development has imposed greater responsibilities on SIDS, because of their small size and fragile environments, than on other countries. The Maldives consists of the smallest populated islands in the world, the largest island being only 5.8km². With regard to the Maldives, the major challenges of sustainable development are the following.

1. *Protecting the marine environment.* Protecting the marine environment is critical in the Maldives because this environment constitutes the largest natural resource base for the economy. Threats to the environment arise from the activities of man and/or nature. For example, reef deterioration due to bleaching is a problem that only nature will solve, but the reefs can be protected from other threats, e.g., coral mining. Also critical is enhancing the marine infrastructure of sea defences against expected hazards – swells, rough seas, and beach erosion due to climate change.

2. *Sustainable fisheries management and development.* The fishing industry, the most productive natural resource industry, faces many problems of a biological and economic nature. Sustainable development, with its emphasis on management that is based on the precautionary principle, will impose new constraints on the industry. However, an ocean management regime, which integrates fisheries management, management of the marine environment, marine transportation, and tourism, will be essential in the Maldives where the marine industries together constitute the most important economic sector.

3. *Implementing a long-term programme for combating the effects of sea-level rise due to climate change.* It is economically impossible to save all the islands from the effects of the sea-level rise expected this century. The strategy for counteracting or minimising these effects involves concentrating on protecting strategic islands, increasing their land space where possible by sea defences and dredging, and fostering island-cluster development.

4. *Developing the financial sector and creating the enabling environment for private enterprise.* The financial sector in the Maldives is underdeveloped, dominated by four state-owned banks. Lack of competition has resulted in both little depth and inefficiencies in the sector. The GoM has recognised that the lack of a capital market and of long-term finance institutions, especially for development finance, are major constraints to private sector develop-

ment and to the establishment of a more enabling environment for private sector activity that will be crucial for future development.

5. *Good governance and strengthening the social safety net.* One of the planks of sustainable development is that of good governance. Good governance implies greater involvement of the people in the political process, and honesty, transparency and accountability in government. In the Maldives, the requirements are for administrative, fiscal and legal reform, continued improvements in the social services of education and health, and the introduction of a National Insurance scheme.

It is apparent that these challenges cannot be met without sustained economic growth, accompanied by extensive external capital, technological, and technical assistance. This has been realised by the GOM, which has developed a National Vision 2020 for the purpose of providing a long-term sustainable developmental perspective and strategy for the Maldives.

2.2 Medium-term growth prospects, 2001–2005

The Sixth National Development Plan constitutes the first five-year plan to be implemented under the National Vision 2020. The Plan emphasises: (a) regional development by means of population concentration in regional North/South growth centres consisting of four Atolls each, and the establishment of a national transportation grid to serve these centres; (b) the role of the private sector in development and the necessity to create a more enabling environment in the Maldives for encouraging greater private sector activity; and (c) good governance by fiscal, administrative and legal reform and human resource development.

The IMF has recently made medium-term growth prospects for the Maldives that indicate a real growth rate of 6.1 per cent for the period 2001–05. This is well below the average real growth rate of nearly 10 per cent for the twenty-year period 1980–99. The IMF projections are postulated on the basis that graduation will take place during the period and that it will adversely affect the flow of ODA, particularly grants. However, the projections indicate that growth will be accompanied by deficits in the balance of payments, the current account and the overall balance, which is indicative of poor economic fundamentals that can affect the stability of the currency and the resilience of the economy to overcome external shocks. These aspects indicate that graduation comes at a very inopportune time for the Maldives: a period of lower growth rates and decreased resilience.

3. The costs of graduation

The costs of graduation have been identified as follows.

(a) Loss of preferential treatment to trade and access to markets

Under the GATT and the WTO, developing countries enjoy special treatment from the Generalized System of Preferences (GSP) and the Global System of Trade Preferences (GSTP). Under the GSP, developed countries offer non-reciprocal preferential treatment to products originating in the developing countries. Under the WTO there is special and differential treatment for the LDCs over and above the special provisions for developing countries, and the WTO also assists the LDCs with measures to facilitate their greater participation in its deliberations and in building up their trade capacity.

(b) Decline in foreign aid (ODA)

Donor agencies have demonstrated a preference for serving the LDCs in their programs as the recipients most in need and deserving of aid, and many have aid programmes that offer more concessional terms to LDCs than to MDCs.

(c) Increased debt burden

With the loss of concessionary financing from foreign aid, the Maldives will have to rely on non-concessionary financing and on the open market. Higher interest rates and shorter repayment periods will significantly increase the cost of capital and lower capital efficiency in the economy. In turn, this will increase the debt burden and increase the capital account deficit.

(d) Loss of access to other special arrangements

There are special programmes devoted to the LDCs by UN agencies and other bodies subsidiary or related to the UN (e.g., IMO, ITU, UNESCO, UNCTAD, UNDP, ESCAP programmes in the Maldives), by other multilateral institutions, and by bilateral donors and some international NGOs. Some of these institutions also facilitate the participation of LDCs in international conferences, seminars, and training programmes, and help donor agencies in co-ordinating assistance to the LDCs. With respect to assistance from UN agencies, these agencies will have to conform to UN policies for MDCs that impose more stringent conditions than those for the LDCs.

The costs of graduation are therefore significant, impacting on trade (aid) and government operations. The macro effects of these on the economy are simulated over the medium term, i.e., the period from 2001 to 2005, assuming that graduation has taken place in 2001.

4. The impact on growth and development

4.1. The impact of graduation on commodity trade

Graduation will affect the trade in goods or commodities and not the trade in services, which is far more important in terms of value to the Maldives. With respect to the trade in goods, graduation will affect exports rather than imports. Fish products and garments are the only major products exported, and they accounted for 99 per cent of the value of domestic exports during the period 1990–2000. Estimates of the effects of graduation on exports from the fishing and garment industries show that the loss in export earnings from graduation could increase from $6 million in 2001 to $15 million in 2005. These losses will reduce the growth rate of total exports from 6.1 per cent a year to 4.8 per cent a year for the period.

4.2. The impact of graduation on the government sector

The impact of graduation on the government sector will be due to its effects on external sources of funding and on the current account to compensate for these and other disruptive influences such as government financial support to fisheries (MIFCO). These effects will reduce the projected surplus on current account and increase reliance on loans. It is estimated that the costs of graduation to the GOM would average over $7 million a year and amount to $37 million for the period.

4.3. The impact of graduation on the economy

The total costs of graduation for the Maldives, from the reduction in export revenues and costs to government, will increase from $11.1 million in year one to $26 million in year five. These costs have significant ramifications for the balance of payments and the government's overall balance. The impact of these costs on the growth rate of the economy is not significant, the change in the growth rate being only a 0.1 percentage point. However, graduation will lead to deterioration in the economic fundamentals and place a damper on the long-term growth of the economy.

5. Main findings of the analysis

The main findings from the analysis are as follows.

1. The timing for graduation could not be more inopportune for the Maldives. It comes at a time when the main challenge facing the Maldives is how to maintain high levels of growth in the face of existing external shocks from globalisation and trade liberalisation. The economy is displaying signs that it is on a point of inflection whereby the rate of growth of GDP is declining. It is apparent, however, that the challenges posed by sustainable development in the face of global forces cannot be met without sustained economic growth accompanied by extensive external capital, technological, and technical assistance.

2. The analysis of the costs of graduation indicate that the Maldives will be worse off from graduation because of its adverse effects on trade, primarily on exports of fisheries products and garments, and on government finances. This contravenes UN General Assembly Resolution 46/206, which states that graduation should not make a country worse off than before. The simulated graduation scenario indicated that although the average growth rate of GDP projected by the IMF for the period 2001–05 would not change significantly because some of the effects of graduation were taken into account in making the projections, the direct costs to the economy are estimated to be $88.6 million for the period, or an average of $17.7 million a year; and the increasing nature of these costs indicates that graduation will place a damper on growth in the economy over the long term.

These are the reasons why graduation is so threatening for the Maldives. Graduation could place a damper on the long-term growth path, cause severe dislocation and adverse structural transformation, and seriously impede progress on the environmental front, without which sustainable development is just not possible. Given these probabilities, the main concern is to minimise the disruptive effects of graduation and to ensure a smooth transition from LDC to MDC status for the Maldives.

5.1 The requirements for the smooth transition

The UN had indicated that the period from 2001 to 2003 might be the transition period for graduation of the Maldives. However, during this period, the UN will be in the process of examining measures that can be taken to ensure a smooth transition for graduating countries. To ensure that the Maldives would be able to benefit from these measures, it is desirable that the UN should not graduate the Maldives before the termination of the Sixth National Development Plan, i.e., 2005. In the meantime, there are measures that can be taken for a smooth transition of the Maldives that pertain to trade, government operations, and aid.

With respect to trade, the need is to maintain access to traditional markets or secure new markets on terms that will not be disruptive. In the Maldives, there are only two commodities that are threatened: fish products and garments. With regard to fish, the need is to tackle the problem externally and nationally. The national measures are to attain greater efficiency in the fishing industry by sustainable management, privatisation, and the reduction of post-harvest losses by improved fish handling and storage. Internationally, joint-venture marketing arrangements could circumvent tariff and non-tariff barriers in major markets.

With respect to government, fiscal reform, involving a broadening of the tax base and direct taxation, is essential in order to reduce the reliance on indirect taxation, primarily tariffs on imports. The GoM should also formulate a trade policy aimed at increasing exports of goods and services, with services featuring prominently since this is an area where the Maldives can be internationally competitive because of an educated labour force.

With respect to aid, the Maldives has to make a concerted effort to attract more bilateral and multilateral donor agencies based on its policy for sustainable development and good governance. It is essential that the Maldives be treated as an ACP country by the EU because of a historical connection to three European states: the UK, Portugal, and Holland. It would be useful if aid agencies viewed the transition as a period requiring special attention and be prepared to assist countries on the threshold with special programmes to aid the transition.

Arguably, the greatest benefit of graduation is that it makes it imperative that the GoM quicken the process of fiscal and administrative reform and concentrate more on the priorities for sustainable development. In essence, to make structural adjustments that will place the economy on a firmer foundation for growth and future development. These are in conformity with the objectives of the Sixth National Development Plan and of Vision 2020.

5.2 Recommendations

Based on the findings and implications of this memorandum, the following recommendations are made to the Economic and Social Committee (ECOSOC) of the UN.

1. The Maldives should not graduate from the list of LDCs until 2005 because graduation before that time will disrupt growth and sustainable development and because the period to 2005 is a more meaningful one for attaining a smooth transition to MDC status.

2. The measures that will be most beneficial in the transition are those that concentrate on minimising the real costs of graduation. In essence, they pertain to strengthening and diversifying trade, preserving access to grants and concessional financing, and assistance (financial and technical) with the preparation of a programme and plan for graduation (with the objective of reducing the disruptive effects).

14. Progress Towards Achieving the Millennium Development Goals in the Small States of the Commonwealth

Andrew S Downes

1. Introduction

In September 2000, member states of the United Nations adopted the Millennium Declaration at a meeting of the General Assembly. This Declaration consisted of a set of development goals that reflect the need to eradicate poverty and promote human development throughout the world. These goals, which have been branded as the Millennium Development Goals (MDGs), focus on the following eight areas of human development:

1. the eradication of extreme poverty and hunger;

2. the achievement of universal primary education;

3. the promotion of gender equality and the empowerment of women;

4. the reduction of child mortality;

5. the improvement of maternal health;

6. the control of HIV/AIDS, malaria and other diseases;

7. the promotion of environmental sustainability; and

8. the development of a global partnership for development.

These goals are associated with 18 targets and 48 social, economic, political and environmental indicators. It is expected that the goals would be achieved over the 1990–2015 period. The adoption of these goals heralds the return of strategic long-term development planning which was largely abandoned in the 1970s when several developing countries were concerned with short-run macroeconomic management and stabilisation policies required to deal with economic shocks such as increases in oil prices and interest rates. The MDGs have prompted countries to adopt an integrated development planning framework incorporating the social, economic and environmental dimensions of development. The goals are broadly specified so that individual countries can prioritise their own goals and pursue associated strategies and policies for achieving them. The goals have both qualitative and quantitative features which enable progress towards their achievement to be monitored and evaluated.

This chapter examines the progress which the small states within the Commonwealth have made towards the achievement of the MDGs since their adoption in the year 2000. Some of these small states have attained a relatively high level of human development which can make the MDGs achievable within the planning period. However, several of these states face serious resource and capacity constraints which can curtail progress towards the achievement of the MDGs. The chapter first examines the basic features of the small states in the Commonwealth which provide the context within which planning and policymaking for the MDGs will take place. The chapter then discusses the progress with the eight MDGs in the 32 small states of the Commonwealth. The quantification of goal achievement is presented where information is available. An overall assessment of progress towards the achievement of the goals is presented in terms of the main challenges that will be encountered over the next decade, the nature of the supporting environment needed, the data needs to monitor progress, and the priorities for development assistance. The chapter concludes with suggestions on the way forward for these small states and on the role of the Commonwealth in helping these small states to meet their development needs and goals.

2. Features of Commonwealth small states

The Commonwealth consists of 50 independent developing countries, four developed countries and 24 associated states and dependencies, which are nearly all developing countries. Using an upper limit of 5 million people to denote a 'small' country, approximately 60 per cent of the Commonwealth can be regarded as being 'small'. Furthermore, nearly all of the associated states and dependencies are 'small' or 'micro' states. In effect, the Commonwealth consists largely of 'small developing countries' (SDCs).

The characteristics of SDCs have been well documented (see, for example, Demas, 1965 and Commonwealth Secretariat/World Bank, 2000]. Some of these features are critical to the achievement of the MDGs over the planning period. Small states are highly dependent on external economic relations for their survival. Dependence can be examined from two perspectives: structural and functional (see McIntyre, 1971, pp.165-83). Structural dependence derives from the smallness of the domestic markets and resource bases of these economies. Small countries will inevitably be opened to international trade and capital flows. Functional dependence relates to the ability of the small country to formulate and implement autonomous economic policies.

The historical legacy of small states has left them both structurally and functionally dependent. Several, if not all, of these countries have very concentrated production structures involving one or two main areas of economic activity - sugar, bananas, bauxite, tourism, and fishing. Although there have been attempts to engage in production diversification, these have been constrained by both resource availability and international trading constraints. Some small states in the African, Caribbean and Pacific regions have been dependent on remittances from migrant labour in order to help maintain decent living standards. In other cases, they have depended on overseas development assistance to supplement domestic financial resources.

The effects of external economic events on small countries represent one dimension of their vulnerability. Small undiversified countries pay higher costs after an external shock than large diversified countries. Several factors contribute to the economic vulnerability of small states: a high degree of openness to trade and financial flows; export concentration and reliance on foreign development and technical assistance, along with underdeveloped financial markets and undiversified production structures. Such vulnerability has been a major argument for special consideration (special and differential treatment) for small countries in international trade negotiations (see Downes, 2004, pp.416–421). The high volatility and instability in export prices, external markets and capital flows have adversely affected the performance of small economies.

The geographical location of several small countries makes them vulnerable to natural disasters such as hurricanes/cyclones, volcanic eruptions, floods brought about by sea level rise and landslides. These natural phenomena can severely disrupt the functioning of the economy and cause a significant amount of damage to the physical environment as evidenced by the recent tsunami in the Indian Ocean. The need to eke out a living in a small physical environment also puts pressure on the ecological environment of small countries. In some cases, the activities of a major producer in a small country can have adverse effects on the physical and ecological environments of small countries. Such effects are particularly pronounced where chemical and waste products are involved or where significant quantities of vegetation have been removed from the land to accommodate 'luxury' housing, hotels and similar physical structures. In addition to being economically and environmentally vulnerable, small states are also affected by social and political events. Several small states have been targets of criminal activities (invasion, drug trade, money laundering and piracy) which have not only changed the social fabric of these countries but have also re-oriented the nature of economic production. Where people see substantial potential net gains from criminal activities, they are tempted to participate - especially when traditional areas of economic activity are not prosperous. Furthermore, small states, singularly, have little or no power to influence the course of major political events which may have a significant impact on the lives of their inhabitants. The international mass media and promotion of tourism have had a profound influence on the cultural lives of the people of small states. In several cases, skilled people have emigrated from these countries to the more developed countries of North America, Europe and Australasia in search of work and a different cultural experience. Although remittances from such migration have been beneficial to small countries, the cultural fabric of these countries has been changed significantly. In addition, the loss of skilled human resources adversely affects the provision of high quality services in some of these small countries (for example, health and education).

The limited financial and human resources associated with small states constrain their ability to manage the development process in an efficient and effective manner. Small states usually have the same range of public services as several large states, but a much lower capacity to manage the administrative systems. For example, the inability to police their maritime shores has made some small states havens for drug traders. The complexity of some contracts with large companies can be a challenge for small states. In addition, the limited human resources in small states restricts the degree to which they can meaningfully engage in international trade negotiations and undertake specialised tasks (for example, medical procedures, legal representations, engineering feats). Although regional collaboration has helped to overcome some of these problems, there are still major shortcomings in such arrangements. The inability to develop good surveillance and enforcement systems has prevented several small states from fully benefiting from the sale of services associated with intellectual property and cultural industries.

In the case of the Pacific area, issues of remoteness and isolation raise questions about the viability and survival of several very small (micro) states. Remoteness not only raises the cost of doing business but keeps these states in a perpetual state of dependence (see Winters and Martins, 2004, pp.347–83). While developments in transportation and information and communications technologies (ICTs) have eased the problems of remoteness and distance, the limited capacity of small states restricts their ability to take full advantage of the opportunity to develop new areas of economic activity, for example, electronic commerce and remote data processing.

In summary, the small states of the Commonwealth are characterised by a high degree of openness; structural and functional dependence; remoteness and isolation; limited production diversification and small domestic markets; vulnerability to natural and man-made disasters and external economic shocks; export concentration; limited power in the economic and political arenas; high cost of development administration and 'doing business'; limited financial and human resources; vulnerability to criminal activities; and cultural penetration and volatility of export income and prices. These features limit the ability of small states to achieve all of the MDGs within the specified time frame (1990 to 2005). While the achievement of these goals can be perceived as an international priority, the economic management authorities of small states have to prioritise their own goals in keeping with the resources available to them.

3. The MDGs in small states

One of the challenges in monitoring the progress towards achieving the MDGs in the small states of the Commonwealth is the lack of data on several of the indicators. While data on several economic variables are available for several countries, social and environmental data are difficult to obtain. It can be argued that given the universality of the goals and indicators and the recent adoption of the MDGs, it would be difficult to collect and assess data on the MDGs especially where there have been no well-developed data collection systems in small states. Furthermore, the MDGs were adopted in the year 2000 but require data on some indicators as far back as the year 1990, which may not be available. The problem is compounded by the lack of human and financial resources to collect data on a range of economic, social and environmental indicators. It is well known that statistical departments in several small developing countries are severely understaffed and there is no consistent process of collecting key development statistics. Central banks and some government departments (especially financial-related ones) are the main producers of data in several small countries. International agencies such as the International Monetary Fund, World Bank and the United Nations system have been seeking to develop the databases of developing states in a systematic manner but several small states are excluded from these databases. The Commonwealth Secretariat has, however, made a deliberate effort to collect data on these small states.

Notwithstanding the data challenges facing small states, several of them have produced progress reports on the MDGs. Within the Commonwealth, assessments have been made of the following countries: a joint report on Barbados and the Organisation of Eastern Caribbean States (OECS), consisting of Antigua and Barbuda, Dominica, Grenada, St Kitts and Nevis, St Lucia and St Vincent and the Grenadines. Single reports exist for Guyana, Jamaica, Mauritius, Fiji, Papua New Guinea (PNG), Swaziland and the Gambia (see for example, UNDP, 2004a and 2004b). This list suggests that the Caribbean and the Pacific countries have been the target of MDGs monitoring since 2000, with regional reviews being produced (see UNDP, 2004c and 2004d; ADB, 2003). These reports use national statistical sources which may lead to problems of comparability for some variables. The World Bank's *World Development Indicators* database is the most comprehensive source of information on the MDGs. This has been the main source of data for determining the progress towards achieving the MDGs in Commonwealth small states.

Goal 1 relates to the eradication of extreme poverty and hunger and aims to halve the proportion of people whose income is less than US$1 per day compared to 1990 by the end of the planning period. Data on poverty are very scarce in small states. While data are available on poverty in the Caribbean for the late 1990s, little is known about the proportion of the population below $1 (at 1993 purchasing power parity) per day. The percentage of the population living below national poverty lines in the Caribbean varied between 13.9 per cent (Barbados in 1997) and 39 per cent (Dominica in 2003). With the exception of Belize, Guyana, Jamaica and Trinidad and Tobago, poverty estimates are available from one-off studies. In countries with more than one estimate of poverty, there has not been any major change in the degree of poverty. Jamaica has witnessed a significant decline in poverty levels, however, from 44.6 per cent in 1991 to 19.7 per cent in 2001. The percentage of the population living in extreme poverty in the Caribbean varies between 0.5 per cent (BVI in 2003) and 29 per cent (Guyana in 1993). In general, the percentage of people living in extreme poverty in the Caribbean has declined over the years. The percentage of people on less than $1 a day tends to be low in the Caribbean region. Naidu (2002) has, however, reported high levels of poverty in some Pacific Island countries. For example, 25 per cent of all households in Fiji existed below the poverty level in 1997, with a further 15 per cent being vulnerable to poverty. In Papua New Guinea (PNG), the Solomon Islands, the Maldives and Vanuatu, it is estimated that as much as 80 per cent of the population lives in poverty. Estimates of poverty for the African countries of Botswana, Lesotho, Namibia and the Gambia ranged from 23.5 per cent of the population to 59.3 per cent during the mid- to late-1990s. Although the lack of data prevents a full assessment of progress towards the eradication of poverty in the small states of the Commonwealth, it is clear that the prevailing high rates of poverty, especially in the African and Pacific states, will make the achievement of this goal particularly difficult without a consistent and determined effort by all parties in small states.

Goal 2 focuses on the achievement of universal primary level education which provides the basic foundation for poverty eradication in small states. This goal is assessed by net primary school enrolment rates and youth literacy rates. Several small states have emphasised the development of their human resources by investing in education and nutrition over the past decades.

Small states in the Commonwealth have performed fairly well with respect to universal primary education as measured by enrolment rates, completion rates and youth literacy rates (that is, of people between 15 and 24 years of age). Net enrolment rates increased over the decade of the 1990s, with rates in the 90s for several small states. The small African countries of Namibia, Lesotho and the Gambia, along with Papua New Guinea (PNG) still have relatively low rates of primary school enrolment. Primary-level completion rates are also relatively high for most small states. These rates are relatively low in the African small states, however.

The achievement of universal primary-level education is therefore highly likely for almost all the Commonwealth small states. There are concerns, however, relating to the quality of the facilities and the education received at the primary level. In many cases literacy surveys have not been undertaken to assess the true level of literacy in these small states. The shortage of well-trained teachers, who usually migrate to more developed countries, has adversely affected the delivery of quality education at the primary level. Along with nurses, teachers are the most significant migrant group from several developing countries in recent years.

While a good quality foundation at the primary school level is critical to the development of the human resource base of a country, the development of universal secondary level education is seen as vital to meeting labour market needs. Small states have a long way to go in this area as few countries have achieved universal secondary level education. Such a development would make universal primary level education very meaningful.

Goal 3 seeks to promote gender equality and empower women by focusing on enrolment in the educational system and membership of national parliaments. The data indicate that there is near parity between boys and girls in terms of enrolment in primary and secondary level education over the period 1990/91 to 2001/2. The ratio of girls to boys enrolled at the primary level tends to be slightly lower than the ratio at the secondary level, especially in the Caribbean. This result suggests that there is some drop out of boys at the secondary level. The small countries in the Pacific, however, exhibit relatively lower rates of female enrolment at the secondary level. At the tertiary level, female enrolment is almost twice that of male enrolment in the Caribbean, with the ratio of female to male enrolment varying between 1.50 (Antigua and Barbuda in 2004) and 3.36 (St Lucia in 2004). Among small states, the Gambia and Papua New Guinea exhibited the lowest ratios of female to male enrolment in the school system.

The relatively high female enrolment rates in the educational system are reflected in the high level of literacy among females relative to males. Indeed, there has been an increase in the human capital of women across the small states accompanied by a rise in their level of participation in the labour force.

Women constitute a significant proportion of the labour force employed in the agricultural sector of small states. Although several states have been engaged in production diversification, especially towards services, the share of women in non-agricultural activities varies between 25 and 50 per cent. Some of the women who work in manufacturing and the services sectors receive relatively low wages, however. Some countries have actively promoted the establishment of export processing zones which specialise in basic repetitive jobs for relatively low pay (e.g., data processing, electronics assembly). Although there has been a relative increase in female employment in non-agricultural work, this does not necessarily reflect an improvement in their socio-economic status.

Women are relatively absent from the political decision-making process, with very low proportions of seats held by them in national parliaments. In the Caribbean, the percentage varies from 0 per cent (Anguilla in 2004) to 31 per cent (Guyana in 2004). The ranges are even narrower for the small Pacific and African states.

In terms of goal achievement, gender equality has been achieved for most small states in the area of education, but there is still slow progress in the labour market and the political arena.

Goal 4 relates to the reduction in child mortality. There has been a general decline in child (under five) mortality rates in the Caribbean and, to some extent, the small Pacific states. Child mortality rates for the Caribbean reached a level of approximately 20 per 1,000 in 2004, with the exception of Guyana and Belize which had rates of 69 and 39 per 1,000 respectively, in 2004. The Caribbean has also had very active immunisation and child health programmes which have resulted in relatively high rates of immunisation against measles (ranging from 78 in Jamaica to 100 per cent in Antigua in 2004). Infant mortality rates per 1,000 live births (under a year) were also under 20 for the Caribbean region. Significant progress has therefore been made in reducing child mortality and improving child health in the Caribbean.

Child mortality rates are generally higher in the small Pacific states than those in the Caribbean. Child mortality and poor health have been particularly problematic in PNG, Tonga, Maldives and Vanuatu, where child mortality rates have been high, though they are declining. In 2002, for example, the under-five mortality rate was reported at 94 per 1,000 in PNG, and 105 in Tonga. Immunisation rates against measles have declined somewhat in the Pacific islands.

The small states of Africa – Botswana, the Gambia, Lesotho and Swaziland – have been experiencing major challenges with respect to a reduction in child mortality and improved child health. Child (under five years) mortality rates ranged from 110 to 149 per 1,000 in 2002, with significant increases being experienced in Swaziland and Botswana. These increases have been partly due to the high incidence of HIV/AIDS in these small states. The rates of immunisation against measles have, however, been fairly high in these countries (generally over 70 per cent).

Achieving the child mortality goal will therefore be difficult for the small African states, while it is highly probable for the Caribbean and, to some extent, the Pacific states. A concerted effort will be needed to improve health care, nutrition, and health education in the Commonwealth small states in order to ensure the achievement of the goal of reducing child mortality by two-thirds by 2015.

Goal 5 focuses on improving maternal health, with a reduction in the maternal mortality rate by three-quarters by 2015. Data on maternal mortality rates per 100,000 live births are sketchy for small states across the Commonwealth. The available data indicate that for the Caribbean small states, the ratios are relatively low (fewer than 100 per 100,000 live births) although there were some increases in Barbados and Trinidad and Tobago between 1995 and 2004. Rates are particularly high in Africa and, to some extent, in the Pacific where access to health care (that is, medical personnel and health facilities) is a long outstanding problem. The challenges posed by diseases such AIDS and malaria and the emigration of medical personnel have further compromised goal achievement in Commonwealth small states. In 2000, for example, the Gambia had a maternal mortality ratio of 540 per 100,000 with 55 per cent of births being attended by skilled health personnel, while in PNG, the figures were 300 per 100,000 and 53 per cent, respectively.

Achieving the maternal health goal will therefore be a challenge, given the current state of healthcare facilities and personnel in the small states of Africa and the Pacific.

Goal 6 relates to combating HIV/AIDS, malaria and other diseases by halting and beginning to reverse their spread by 2015. The main indicators used to track goal achievement are HIV prevalence rate among 15–49 year-olds, children orphaned by HIV/AIDS, the incidence of tuberculosis (TB), tuberculosis cases detected under directly observed treatment short course (DOTS), and contraceptive prevalence rate among women 15–49 years of age. The prevalence of HIV/AIDS is particularly high in the small African states of the Commonwealth such as Botswana, Swaziland, Lesotho and Namibia. The prevalence of HIV/AIDS among females aged 15–24 in these countries was recorded at between 25 to 38 per cent in 2001. Although the prevalence of HIV/

AIDS is relatively high in the Caribbean and some Pacific small states, it is not as high as in the African states. Data on HIV/AIDS are sketchy, however, primarily because of the social stigma attached to the disease. There is a significant degree of under-reporting of HIV/AIDS cases, such that the World Health Organisation (WHO) estimates that for every HIV positive case there are 10 other unreported cases. Some countries have been engaged in educational programmes to reduce the prevalence of the disease. Some success has been achieved in the Caribbean, Botswana and some Pacific countries. Barbados, for example, has established a national campaign and commission to tackle the problem in the workplace and in communities around the country. This effort has involved the social partners – government, labour unions and business associations. One of the fall-outs of the high incidence of HIV/AIDS is the high level of orphaned children (for example, in Botswana, Lesotho and Swaziland). In addition, the human resource base has been severely impaired by the prevalence of HIV/AIDS in these small states that are already challenged by the lack of skilled human resources.

Reported contraceptive prevalence among young females tends to be low and hence compromises efforts to combat the epidemic. Data on condom use by men would also be needed to fully assess the efforts to reverse the spread of HIV/AIDS in small states. Associated with the HIV/AIDS epidemic is the relative high incidence of TB in some small states. There is a positive correlation between the incidence of TB and HIV/AIDS.

Malaria is still a major problem in the small African states and, to a lesser extent, in the Pacific countries (PNG, Vanuatu and the Solomon Islands). There is a very low incidence in Guyana. Except for intermittent outbreaks of dengue fever, the Caribbean regional health authorities have kept a close watch on infectious and vector-borne diseases in the region.

The achievement of Goal 6 will be a major challenge for small states, especially those affected by a relatively high incidence of HIV/AIDS. Lifestyles and attitudes towards sexual behaviour must change in order to halt and begin to reverse the spread of HIV/AIDS in all the small states. There are models among the small states which can be emulated. Improved health and sanitation facilities, better trained health personnel, and public health education programmes can all help control major diseases. Such improvements will, however, stretch the already limited financial and human resources of these small states.

Goal 7 seeks to integrate sustainable development principles into social and economic policies (that is, an integrated development planning and policymaking framework) and to reverse the loss of environmental resources. In the Caribbean, access to improved sanitation facilities is very high. In 2000, over 90 per cent of the population had access to improved sanitation (with the exception of Dominica, 83 per cent, Guyana, 87 per cent, and Belize, 50 per cent). African and Pacific small states still face challenges in providing sanitation facilities for their populations, however. Access rates are relatively low in these states. For example, in 2000, the rates were Fiji (43 per cent), Solomon Islands (34 per cent), Lesotho (49 per cent) and Gambia (37 per cent). PNG,

Samoa and Vanuatu have reported relatively high access rates (that is, over 80 per cent in 2000).

Access to an improved water source rose over the period 1990 to 2000 in most of the small states, with Caribbean countries having population access rates of over 90 per cent during the decade. Some Pacific Islands, however, had low population access rates of less than 50 per cent in 2000. African small states have reported relatively high and improved population access rates for water sources. Several small states have developed systems to manage water resources which are usually scarce in these states.

Forest areas as a percentage of total land area vary across the small states with the geographically larger states having higher rates (Guyana, the Bahamas, Belize, Trinidad and Tobago, PNG, the Seychelles and Fiji). The rates of forestation in these countries have been over 40 per cent, although there is evidence of deforestation over the past decade. With the exception of the African small states of Botswana and Namibia, the degree of nationally protected areas is relatively very small (generally under 1 per cent of total land area) in all the small states.

Probably, the most critical environmental issue facing small states, especially low-lying ones in the Pacific, is climate change and sea-level rise. Although data on GDP unit of energy used is largely unavailable, the degree of carbon dioxide emissions per capita has increased in almost all of the small states of the Commonwealth. Deforestation, coupled with an increase in human economic activities (industrial production, high use of automobiles, etc.) has resulted in a rise in the level of carbon dioxide emissions in small states. Although carbon dioxide emission per capita in terms of metric tonnes was under 10 during the 1990s, small states have contributed in some small measure to climate change. Increases in carbon dioxide emission have been partly related to the type of economic activities and social practices undertaken in these small states. Brunei and Trinidad and Tobago, for example, exhibit relatively high levels of carbon dioxide associated with their petroleum industries.

While there has been some improvement in access to improved sanitation facilities and drinking water, which has had a positive impact on the health of the population of these small states, the degree of deforestation and carbon dioxide emissions can retard the extent to which the environmental goal can be achieved. Furthermore, these problems can result in additional problems for small states (floods, hurricanes, and other natural phenomena) associated with climate change and sea-level rise. The environmental vulnerability of small states, especially islands, would be increased if attention is not paid to the incorporation of sustainable development principles in the development plans and policies of small states.

Goal 8 seeks to develop a global partnership for world development and to identify the financial resources needed to meet the other MDGs. It is a multi-dimensional goal which trys to deal comprehensively with the debt problems facing small states and to make available the benefits of new technologies to these states. In addition, targets are set with respect to:

- an open, rule-based, predictable and non-discriminatory financial and trading system;

- good governance and poverty reduction;

- measures to develop and implement decent and productive work for growth; and

- special needs of least-developed countries, land-locked states and small island developing states (SIDS).

The available data for the Caribbean indicate that there has been a general reduction in overseas development assistance (ODA) as a percentage of gross national income over the past decade (1995–2004), to generally less than 10 per cent. Data are sketchy for African and Pacific states, but it is likely that the pattern is the same as in the Caribbean. Recent efforts have been made by developed countries to assist developing countries to ease their debt problem through the writing off and rescheduling of accumulated debts.

There has been a gradual influx of modern technological devices in small states. The data show a significant increase in telephone lines, cellular subscribers and personal computers as a proportion of the population during the past decade. The cellular phone and wireless technology have made developments in information and communications technologies (ICTs) available to people in remote areas (e.g., African and Pacific small states). Such developments open up opportunities for new or sunrise industries in these states to replace sunset industries which have been subject to intense competition, removal of preferences, and obsolescence in technology. Some countries, however, have not been able to take advantage of these developments as yet – Swaziland, the Gambia, Lesotho, Namibia, Kiribati, PNG and other Pacific countries, for example – due to their low level of penetration by ICTs.

Youth unemployment has been a major socio-economic problem for small states. Although the information is very sketchy, the youth unemployment rate in small states tends to be over 30 per cent (usually twice the national unemployment rate). Several programmes have been developed to resolve this problem over the years but they have not succeeded to the degree that is needed.

While new technologies, usually developed in larger and more developed countries, have been slowly reaching small states, primarily for personal consumption purposes (and limited use for production purposes), the goal of developing a partnership for development still needs to be actively pursued. Small states face major problems and constraints which require the allocation of more technical and financial resources from the developed world.

This review of progress against the MDGs indicates that the small Caribbean states of the Caribbean have made much more progress than those states in the Pacific and Africa. These small states face major challenges to achieve the goals by 2015. The health area will be particularly difficult as HIV/AIDS will affect both human capital formation and domestic production if it is not checked.

4. Overall assessment

The assessment of progress towards achieving the MDGs in the small states of the Commonwealth points to a diverse picture of performance and capability. The Caribbean and some of the Pacific countries have made significant progress. The small African states, however, face major challenges in meeting the goals as progress has been slow for most of them.

In general, small states will face several challenges over the next decade. These include adjusting to the loss of trade preferences; developing new industries and sectors; gaining access to the markets of developed countries for new goods and services; handling the new demands of the international environment with limited financial and human resources (for example, membership in the World Trade Organisation); establishing new forms of governance involving social partners (government, civil society and the private sector); preventing social decay associated with the drug trade and money laundering; financing the adjustment and development process; reallocating resources from consumption to investment; and creating productive and sustainable employment to reduce poverty in these small states.

As indicated earlier, one of the main problems in undertaking an assessment of the MDGs is the lack of data on several of the indicators. The lack of a data-gathering capacity in these small states (and other developing countries) truncates a full assessment of MDGs progress. Some of the goals require data from the year 1990, for example Goals 1, 4 and 5. The assessment of progress against these goals depends on the initial conditions in 1990 and for several of the countries data are simply unavailable or unreliable. In a few cases, the initial values are so high that the final targets may still be unacceptable by international standards. The critical role of data collection in the monitoring and evaluation of the MDGs has been recognised by several international agencies. For example, the World Bank's Data Group has established a Statistical Capacity Building Program (STATCAP) to help upgrade the statistical activities of developing and emerging countries. The programme involves the collaboration of other international agencies and national institutions. The Commonwealth can play a critical role in this project by helping to develop the statistical departments of small states. Such assistance would involve the provision of equipment and the training of staff in several departments of the government since poor physical infrastructure and poor human resource capabilities are viewed as handicaps in the small states of the Commonwealth.

Several small states have not incorporated the MDGs into national planning and budgeting systems. While these states have signed on to the Millennium Declaration and its associated goals, they have not established the machinery to achieve them. It has been suggested that countries should develop poverty strategy papers linked to the MDGs (that is, MDGs Strategy Papers). These papers would incorporate national priorities and concerns and involve consultations among the government, civil society and the private sector. The success of the exercise depends critically on the active participation of all stakeholders. It is expected that the adoption of these papers would strengthen the governance systems in small states. Barbados, for example, recently published its Strategic Plan 2005-25 which is supposed to be *MDGs plus.*

It is clear that the achievement of the MDGs by the end of the planning period would require substantial financial resources. The financial resources of small states are severely restricted and can therefore compromise the achievement of the MDGs. Although Goal 8 focuses on the need for an increase in development assistance, this has not been forthcoming. In 1970, the Pearson Commission recommended that developed countries should increase their overseas development assistance to 0.7 per cent of their gross national product (GNP). The record shows that none of the developed countries within the Commonwealth reached the target by the end of 2004, although the UK recently announced a timetable to achieve it (Commission for Africa, 2005). In 2002, the USA announced that it will increase its core development assistance by 50 per cent over the period 2002-05. These additional funds (US$5 billion) were placed in a Millennium Challenge Account (MCA) which would finance the initiatives associated with the MDGs in developing countries. The funds from the MCA would be distributed to countries that demonstrate a strong commitment to good governance, improved health and education of the population, and sound economic policies that foster private enterprise and entrepreneurship (that is, economic freedom). Several small states in the Commonwealth are eligible for funds from the MCA during the first three years on the basis of per capita GDP: Gambia, Guyana, Kiribati, Lesotho, PNG, Solomon Islands, Vanuatu, Swaziland, Belize, Fiji, Jamaica, Maldives, Namibia, Samoa, St Vincent and the Grenadines and Tonga (Palley, 2003). The Commonwealth group should therefore be more active in pursuing this goal in the context of the MDGs. A needs assessment of the small states would be a first step in this pursuit. The United Nations' Millennium Project has developed a methodology to undertake MDGs needs assessments in these small states (see www.unmillenniumproject.org).

The sequencing of the policies and programmes is critical to the overall achievement of the MDGs. The goals are interrelated and the correct sequencing/timing of the policies and programmes must be specified in order to maximise the benefits of investment expenditure. The administrative machinery of the governments of several small states is weak or overstretched and therefore some degree of institutional and administrative strengthening would be needed. Project management skills would need to be strengthened as a priority in several small states. Some of the educational and training institutions in several states have been developing project management programmes to help in the process, but these programmes need to be deepened and widened. In some cases, regional initiatives would be useful, as we have seen in the Caribbean and the Pacific regions.

It must be recognised that progress towards the achievement of the MDGs is neither a linear nor a smooth process. The dynamics of change and causal effects may mean that in some countries where the foundations are weak, a period of capacity building would be warranted before more rapid progress can be achieved. In other cases, rapid progress may be followed by a slow period. These non-linearities can make the assessment of progress towards the achievement of the goals an uncertain affair unless they are recognised. Monitoring and evaluation will be an on-going exercise in small states, given the vulnerabilities that they face. For example, a major shock such as a hurricane or economic slump can derail progress in the short term. It is important to examine long-term trends bearing in mind the dynamics of the short-term relationships among the MDGs.

An important issue facing the small states of the Commonwealth is the sustainability of the goals beyond the planning period. Although the MDGs represent minimum levels for the developing world, small states need to look beyond the MDGs and 2015. As indicated before, half the 1990 value may still be unacceptable and more work would be needed beyond 2015. The achievement of the targets must not be seen as an end in itself, but a means whereby small states can enhance their capacity to achieve higher and sustainable levels of human development.

A distinction should be made between lag indicators (outcome measures) and lead indicators (performance drivers) amongst the 48 indicators of the MDGs. The indicators for the MDGs are largely lag indicators and focus on the outcomes of policies and programmes. The long-term sustainability of human development depends on the identification of lead indicators or performance drivers that are unique to the country's development strategy. These lead indicators show how the outcomes have been achieved and whether the strategy is being implemented successfully. In effect, a **balanced scorecard** approach to the MDGs is needed as this would make explicit 'the sequence of hypotheses about the cause-and-effect relationships between outcome measures and performance drivers of those outcomes' (Kaplan and Norton, 1996, p.31).

The MDGs focus largely on social, human and environmental development. It is important to recognise that economic expansion is needed to achieve the MDGs. For the small states of the Commonwealth, trade expansion and investment (physical and human) are critical to the goals of economic expansion (see Armstrong and Read, 2003, pp.99–124). There are two basic strategies that have been suggested for achieving the MDGs and hence overall poverty reduction. The UN approach calls for a high level of public investment directed at human development and social infrastructural expansion as a means of attaining economic growth and poverty reduction. The World Bank approach focuses on measures to promote economic growth via institutional reforms and improvements in the investment climate. Economic growth would reduce poverty in the long run. For small states, elements of both approaches are needed, given their basic characteristics. An MDGs-based strategy for small developing states would include improvements in human capital formation and social infrastructure; enhancement of systems to mitigate against natural disasters (for example, early warning systems, better physical planning and siting of human settlements); improved trading conditions with market access to the markets of developed countries; institutional strengthening and capacity building; an improved investment climate to provide opportunities and incentives for business to invest, expand and employ persons; measures to boost productivity and competitiveness; and policies and programmes to minimise intra-country inequalities in the gains from the development process. The members of the Commonwealth would therefore have to collaborate to bring about meaningful and sustainable human and economic development in their small developing member states.

5. Conclusion

The assessment of progress towards the achievement of the MDGs in the small states of the Commonwealth indicates that while several countries are making good progress with many of the goals, some states, especially in Africa and the Pacific, have been confronted by serious challenges. The database for assessing the progress of these small states is not strong and hence monitoring is a difficult and somewhat subjective exercise. Notwithstanding the data problems, the health indicators suggest that the achievement of health-related goals will be problematic. In addition, some areas of gender equality have been progressing very slowly. In the area of international development co-operation, a lot more effort is needed to provide the economic resources to reduce poverty and hunger, which is the primary goal of the MDGs.

The small states of the Commonwealth can be helped to achieve the MDGs through the following forms of assistance from the Commonwealth group of nations: the fulfilment of the ODA target of 0.7 per cent of GNP, which would finance sustainable and critical development projects; the enhancement of human resources development and project management training programmes through the provision of technical assistance; assistance with building statistical capacity in governmental agencies; the establishment of systems to reduce physical vulnerabilities; the fostering of regional integration schemes among geographically configured countries; technical assistance with the design, implementation and evaluation of MDGs-based strategies and plans; the establishment of governance structures involving all the stakeholders in the development process; and the advocacy for better trading arrangements for the small developing states of the Commonwealth in international forums such as the World Trade Organization (WTO) (see, Downes, 2001). The more developed members of the Commonwealth can also use their influence in such financial agencies as the World Bank and the European Development Bank to channel resources to regional agencies such as the Caribbean Development Bank, the Asian Bank, and the African Development Bank to finance MDGs-related programmes and projects. The Commonwealth group of nations can also help with fostering greater economic co-operation and integration among small states. For example, the Caribbean Single Market and Economy (CSME) and the African Union's New Partnership for Africa's Development (NEPAD) provide vehicles for enhancing human and economic development among groups of small states in the Caribbean and Africa. At a wider level, the Commonwealth can provide technical assistance to small states as part of the negotiations between the European Union and the African, Caribbean and Pacific countries. In addition, schemes should be developed whereby people who have migrated from these small states can help their original homelands in the areas of health, education and management. These measures would provide a basis on which small states can introduce internal reforms to achieve long-term human and economic development beyond the attainment of the MDGs.

References

Armstrong H.W. and R. Read (2003) 'The Determinants of Economic Growth in Small States', *Round Table*, 368.

Asian Development Bank (ADB) (2003) *Millennium Development Goals in the Pacific: Relevance and Progress.* ADB, Manila.

Commission for Africa (2005) *Our Common Interest: An Argument.* Penguin Books, London.

Commonwealth Secretariat and World Bank (2000) *Small States Meeting the Challenges in the Global Economy.* Report of the Commonwealth Secretariat/World Bank Joint Task Force on Small States, London and Washington, DC, March.

Demas W.G. (1965) *The Economics of Development in Small Countries with Special Reference to the Caribbean.* McGill University Press, Montreal.

Downes A.S. (2001) 'The Future of the Small Economies of the Commonwealth in a Changing Global Environment' in R. Bourne (ed) *Where Next for the Group of 54? Five Essays on the Future of the Commonwealth of Nations at the start of the 21st Century.* Commonwealth Policy Studies Unit, London, UK, June, pp.39-47.

Downes A.S. (2004) 'The Trade Environment and Small Countries', *World Trade Review*, Vol.3, No.3, November.

Kambon A. and L. Joseph-Brown (2003) *Challenges in Meeting the Monitoring Requirements of the Millennium Development Goals (MDGs): An Examination of Selected Social Statistics for Four Caribbean SIDS.* UNECLAC, Port-of-Spain, Trinidad and Tobago, WP/2003/3, June 30.

Kaplan R.S. and D.P. Norton (1996) *The Balanced Scorecard: Translating Strategy into Action.* Harvard University Press, Boston.

McIntyre, A. (1971) 'Some Issues of Trade Policy in the West Indies', in N. Girvan and O. Jefferson (eds), *Readings in the Political Economy of the Caribbean.* New World Group, Jamaica,.

Naidu, V. (2002) 'The Millennium Development Goals and the South Pacific'. Third International Development Studies Network of Aotearoa/New Zealand Conference, Massey University and University of the South Pacific, Suva, December.

Palley T.I. (2003) 'The Millennium Challenge Accounts: Elevating the Significance of Democracy as a Qualifying Criterion'. Discussion Paper, January 2003, Open Society Institute, New York.

UNDP (2003) *Report on Progress Towards the Achievement of the Millennium Development Goals: Guyana.* UNDP, Georgetown, Guyana.

UNDP (2004a) *Millennium Development Goals: Jamaica.* UNDP, Kingston, Jamaica, April.

UNDP (2004b) *The Millennium Development Goals in Barbados and the Eastern Caribbean: A Progress Report.* UNDP, Barbados.

UNDP (2004c) *Regional Report on the Achievement of the Millennium Development Goals in the Caribbean Community.* UNDP, Jamaica.

UNDP (2004d) *Pacific Islands Regional Millennium Goals Report 2004.* Prepared by UNDP, Secretariat of the Pacific Community and the UN/CROP MDG Working Group, November.

UNDP/UNICEF (2002) *The Millennium Development Goals in Africa: Promises & Progress.* UNDP/UNICEF, New York.

Winters L.A. and P.M.G. Martins (2004) 'When Comparative Advantage is not enough: Business Costs in Small Remote Economies', *World Trade Review*, Vol.3, No.3, November.

Annex I

Status at a glance

Country	Goal 1	Goal 2	Goal 3	Goal 4	Goal 5	Goal 6	Goal 7	Goal 8
Antigua/Barbuda	3	3	3	2	3	3	2	3
Barbados	3	4	2	2	2	2	2	2
Belize	0	3	2	2	3	2	2	2
Botswana	0	2	3	1	2	1	3	2
Brunei Darussalam	0	2	3	3	3	0	0	0
Cyprus	0	3	3	3	3	0	3	3
Dominica	3	3	3	3	3	2	3	3
Fiji	0	3	2	3	3	0	3	2
Grenada	3	2	3	3	3	2	2	3
Guyana	3	2	2	1	1	1	3	2
Jamaica	2	3	2	3	1	2	2	3
Kiribati	0	0	2	3	2	0	1	3
Lesotho	0	0	2	1	1	0	2	2
Maldives	0	0	2	3	2	0	2	2
Malta	0	3	3	3	3	0	3	3
Mauritius	0	3	3	3	2	0	3	3
Namibia	1	2	3	3	1	2	1	0
Nauru	0	0	0	0	0	0	0	0
Papua New Guinea	0	0	0	0	2	0	1	1
Samoa	2	3	2	3	0	2	0	0
Seychelles	0	0	2	3	0	2	0	0
Solomon Islands	0	0	2	1	2	2	1	1
St Kitts/Nevis	3	3	3	2	3	2	2	3
St Lucia	3	3	3	2	3	2	2	3
Saint Vincent	3	3	3	3	3	2	2	3
Swaziland	0	0	3	1	1	1	0	0
The Bahamas	3	3	3	3	3	2	3	3
The Gambia	0	0	1	1	1	1	2	2
Tonga	0	0	0	0	0	0	0	0
Trinidad /Tobago	3	3	3	3	3	0	2	3
Tuvalu	0	0	0	0	0	0	0	0
Vanuatu	0	0	3	2	0	2	2	2

Key:
0 – no data/insufficient data 1 – not likely 2 – Potentially (having underlying capability)
3 – Probably (almost certainly)

About the Contributors

Lino Briguglio is Head of the Economics Department at the University of Malta, Director of the Islands and Small States Institute at the Foundation for International Studies, and Director of the Malta University Centre on the Island of Gozo.

Sarah Jane Danchie is a Research Officer in the Economic Affairs Division of the Commonwealth Secretariat.

Andrew S Downes is a Professor of Economics and University Director of the Sir Arthur Lewis Institute of Social and Economic Studies.

Ueta Fa'asili is the Fisheries Management Adviser at the Secretariat of the Pacific Community.

Semisi Fakahau is a Chief Programme Officer at the Commonwealth Secretariat.

Alexander Gillespie is a Professor of Law at the University of Waikato, New Zealand. He has been awarded fellowships from the Rotary, Fulbright & Rockerfeller Foundations and the New Zealand Law Foundation.

Roman Grynberg was formerly the Deputy Director of Trade and Regional Integration at the Commonwealth Secretariat and is currently Manager of the Economic Governance Programme, Pacific Islands Forum, Fiji Islands.

Virginia Horscroft is a consultant to the Commonwealth Secretariat and a former ODI Fellow, and is based at Queen Elizabeth House – Department of International Development, Oxford.

T K Jayaraman is an Associate Professor in the School of Economics, Faculty of Business and Economics, the University of the South Pacific, Suva, Fiji Islands.

David Joiner is a Senior Economist at Maxwell Stamp PLC and is a former Fellow of the Overseas Development Institute.

Eliawony J Kisanga was a Deputy Director in the Economic Affairs Division of the Commonwealth Secretariat. He holds a PhD in Regional Economic Integration from the London School of Economics. He is the author of *Industrial and Trade Cooperation in Eastern and Southern Africa* and co-editor with David Peretz and Rumman Faruqi of *Small*

States in the Global Economy, published by the Commonwealth Secretariat and the World Bank.

Michael King is a Commonwealth Secretariat fisheries consultant.

Carl L Mitchell is currently an economic consultant in Ottawa. He was formerly a public servant with the Department of Fisheries & Oceans, Canada and was Director of the Economic Affairs Secretariat of the Organisation of Eastern Caribbean States.

Kimberly Ochs is a Research Fellow at the University of Oxford Department of Educational Studies and currently TH Marshall Fellow at the London School of Economics and Political Science.

Claudius Preville is with the Caribbean Regional Negotiating Machinery (RNM) and serves as the machinery's Trade Policy Advisor to the Organisation of Eastern Caribbean States (OECS).

Stephen Redding is a Reader with the Department of Economics, London School of Economics.

Jan Yves Remy was formerly a Research Assistant for the Economic Affairs Division, Commonwealth and is currently a Services Analyst with the Caribbean Regional Negotiating Machinery (CRNM).

Paul Sutton was formerly with the Department of Politics and International Studies, University of Hull. He was the lead consultant on the Commonwealth Secretariat Study on Small States in 1997 and has served as a member of the Caribbean Advisory Group established by the Foreign and Commonwealth Office to advise on policy to improve relations with the Caribbean.

Anthony J Venables is a Professor of Economics at the University of Oxford and Chief Economist at the UK Department for International Development (DFID).

Aliti Vunisea is a Community Fisheries Officer at the Secretariat of the Pacific Community.

Ganeshan Wignaraja is Team Leader (Trade Integration) and Senior Economist at the Office of Regional Economic Integration in the Asian Development Bank in Manila.

Index